SMUTTY LITTLE MOVIES

Smutty Little Movies

The Creation and Regulation of Adult Video

PETER ALILUNAS

UNIVERSITY OF CALIFORNIA PRESS

University of California Press, one of the most distinguished university presses in the United States, enriches lives around the world by advancing scholarship in the humanities, social sciences, and natural sciences. Its activities are supported by the UC Press Foundation and by philanthropic contributions from individuals and institutions. For more information, visit www.ucpress.edu.

University of California Press
Oakland, California

Library of Congress Cataloging-in-Publication Data

Names: Alilunas, Peter, 1974– author.
Title: Smutty little movies : the creation and regulation of adult video / Peter Alilunas.
Description: Oakland, California : University of California Press, [2016] | Includes bibliographical references and index.
Identifiers: LCCN 2016009425 (print) | LCCN 2016011536 (ebook) | ISBN 9780520291706 (book/cloth : alk. paper) | ISBN 9780520291713 (book/paper : alk. paper) | ISBN 9780520965362 (ebook)
Subjects: LCSH: Pornographic films—History and criticism. | Pornography—Social aspects.
Classification: LCC PN1995.9.S45 A44 2016 (print) 2016 | LCC PN1995.9.S45 (ebook) | DDC 791.43/6538—dc23
LC record available at http://lccn.loc.gov/2016009425

25 24 23 22 21 20 19 18 17 16
10 9 8 7 6 5 4 3 2 1

For Beckett—long may you run

Contents

Illustrations

Acknowledgments

As with most academic books, this one was created primarily in isolation. I spent many hours in archives and libraries, on buses and in airports, before dawn and after sunset, alone and lost in thought while struggling to make words that might mean something. But that is not what I remember most; instead, I remember the friendships and associations I made with the many people who contributed in ways both small and large to my thinking, research, and writing. Indeed, this book exists only because of the labor, collaboration, and cooperation of others. Any omissions, oversights, or lapses in memory in what follows are unintentional.

I have tremendous gratitude toward the many colleagues and friends who have been so influential on my life and work. They are scattered far and wide, starting with those who were my classmates on the long journey toward this book: Matt Payne, Kevin Sanson, Kristen Warner, Curran Nault, Kevin Bozelka, Alexis Carreiro, Annie Petersen, Bo Baker, Kristen Lambert, Alyx Vesey, Caitlin Collins, Jacqueline Vickery, Eliot Chayt, Marlene Costa, Alex Cho, Kit Hughes, Evan Elkins, Nathan Koob, Dimitri Pavlounis, Feroz Hassan, Katy Peplin, Ben Strassfeld, Yuki Nakayama, Josh Morrison, and the many others who have shared a seminar or bar table with me over the years. Special thanks to Mike Arnold, a tremendous comrade, sounding board, and co-conspirator. I also want to thank my many students at the universities of Oregon, Michigan, and Texas. For any of them reading this: you get an extra brownie badge to take to the cocktail party.

I've had many important and influential teachers, far too numerous to list here properly. Jonathan Morrow, Nicole Malkin, George Rowe, Kathleen Karlyn, Mary Kearney, and especially Janet Staiger all had profound and direct impact on my academic life. It was at the University of Michigan that the ideas in these pages were hatched. The grants, fellowships, and assistance of various kinds provided to me during my graduate study there made my initial research possible. Special thanks to the staff of the department of Screen Arts & Cultures, who made my work much easier: Carrie Moore, Marga Schuhwerk-Hampel, Mariam Negaran, Phil Hallman, and Mary Lou Chlipala. I was very fortunate to have such supportive mentors and advisors, among them Gaylyn Studlar, Markus Nornes, Johannes von Moltke, Sheila Murphy, Matthew Solomon, Mark Kligerman, Giorgio Bertellini, Colin Gunckel, Caryl Flinn, and especially Richard Abel, who helped me appreciate historiography, so much so that I changed my entire academic trajectory and focus. Dan Herbert was (and continues to be) a superb advisor, ally, and mentor. There's no way I could have taken on—much less finished—this project without him. I will always have tremendous fondness for the years I spent (and the people I spent them with) in Ann Arbor learning how to do a professor's work.

My (very familiar) home at the University of Oregon provided me with even more assistance and support as I finished *Smutty Little Movies*. Various fellowships and grants from the School of Journalism and Communication, the Office of the Vice President for Research and Innovation, and the Oregon Humanities Center made the final stages of this book possible. I'm surrounded and supported by a group of fantastic and encouraging colleagues. Julianne Newton, Leslie Steeves, Janet Wasko, Tom Bivins, Christopher Chávez, Debra Merskin, Gretchen Soderlund, Bish Sen, Gabriela Martínez, Carl Bybee, Carlnita Greene, HyeRyoung Ok, Jennifer Schwartz, Kyu Ho Youm, Troy Elias, Dean Mundy, Todd Milbourn, Lisa Heyamoto, Kathryn Kuttis, Kathryn Thier and many others welcomed me with wholehearted support for this project and for my work in general; I'm more grateful than I can possibly describe. I'm also grateful on a daily (and probably hourly) basis to the remarkable staff, particularly Colleen McKillip, Celina Baguiao, Sally Garner, Melody Olmstead, Joseph Szelesta, and Sue Varani. Michael Aronson, Priscilla Peña Ovalle, Daniel Steinhart, Michael Allan, Sergio Rigoletto, Sangita Gopal, Dong Hoon Kim, Quinn Miller, Masami Kawai, and Andre Sirois have made something really wonderful with the Cinema Studies program; I'm thrilled to be part of it, not to mention an incredibly proud alumnus.

Many colleagues in many fields (especially home video and pornography studies) have helped me in vast and varied ways. I'm indebted to Josh Greenberg, Josh Kitching, Amy Herzog, Frederick Wasser, Eric Hoyt, Joseph Slade, Dries Vermeulen, David Lerner, Kevin Heffernan, Andy Owens, Michael Bowen, Laura Helen Marks, Casey Scott, Joe Rubin, Damon Young,

Ashley West, April Spicer, Mariah Larsson, Elena Gorfinkel, Tom Waugh, Russell Sheaffer, Luke Stadel, Alicia Kozma, Maureen Rogers, and John Stadler. My heartfelt thanks to Lucas Hilderbrand and Whitney Strub for their support and encouragement and for making this book (and my thinking on the subject) much, much better. My apologies to Mary Rizzo for the voluminous footnotes; I can't promise I'll do any better next time. Cynde Moya and Ivan Stormgart at Alta-Glamour, Anissa Malady at the Center for Sex and Culture Library, and the librarians and archivists at the Kinsey Institute at the University of Indiana and at the Leather Archive in Chicago were of tremendous help and very patient in helping me fill in various gaps. John A. Mozzer and Dona McAdams were wonderfully gracious in helping with permissions for their photographs, which ultimately were not used in this book; Art Vernik took the photograph that appears on the cover, and I not only thank him for allowing me to use it, but I also use it as an opportunity to tell everyone to take photographs of adult businesses. Future historians need them.

Highlights of my academic life have included the opportunities to get to know the scholars whose monumental work was the impetus and inspiration for me to take it on myself. I cannot thank Linda Williams, Constance Penley, Gayle Rubin, Chuck Kleinhans, and Eric Schaefer enough. Their influence and impact—direct and indirect—are everywhere in this book and in everything I do in this field.

It was a privilege and pleasure to communicate with Bill Margold, David Jennings, Joel Jacobson, Larry Revene, James Bryant, Carter Stevens, Candida Royalle, Mark Johnson, Steven Morowitz, Paul Fishbein, Mark Kernes, and others from various industries connected with my research. They very graciously and patiently answered my questions about their involvement in the industry. Given the nature of my work, many of those questions involved an area of their lives that, unfortunately, some scholars (not to mention the police, courts, and antipornography activists) have treated disrespectfully over the years, and thus I am extremely grateful for their willingness to trust my motives. It is an unfortunate reality that many people who witnessed the transition of the adult film industry to videotape are advancing in age. Some of the key people in this history have already died, as was the case with Candida Royalle, whose tragic passing gave the project a sad tenor in its last stages—but was also a reminder of the stakes involved.

Many audiences at many conferences heard variations on much of the material in this book and provided invaluable feedback. I am especially grateful to the Society for Cinema & Media Studies, not only for awarding an earlier version of my research the 2014 Dissertation Award of Distinction, but also for long being a warm and welcoming academic home. Gregory Waller and David Church published part of my research in chapter 3 as Peter Alilunas, "*Ginger's Private Party* Flyer," *Film History* 26, no. 3 (2014): 144–55; Joshua Neves and Jeff Scheible published some of my ideas on adult video back rooms as Peter Alilunas, "The Death and Life of the Back Room," *Media Fields* 1 (November 10, 2010), www.mediafieldsjournal.org /the-death-and-life-of-the-back/; Whitney Strub and Carolyn Bronstein included much of my research on *AVN* that appears in chapter 2 in their collection *From Porno Chic to the Sex Wars* (forthcoming, University of Massachusetts Press); and David Church has included some of my thoughts on gonzo and *On the Prowl,* presented in the epilogue, in a forthcoming special issue of *Porn Studies.*

It is impossible to speak highly enough of Mary Francis, my original editor at the University of California Press, whose work I admired long before I had the privilege to work with her. She made this process a pleasure, even during the inevitably complex and difficult parts. Thanks, Mary. I also want to thank Kim Robinson, Raina Polivka, Zuha Khan, Kate Hoffman, Aimee Goggins, Jody Hanson, and the rest of the staff at UC Press and beyond for their assistance and support. Laura Harger's brilliant copyediting and Victoria Baker's masterful indexing were the icing on the cake. Thank you both.

Finally, and most importantly, I thank my family. Carolyn Olive, Kelly Hanna, and Corey Fenster have been incredibly warm and welcoming of me as a member of their clan; I can't imagine life without them. The unconditional love and support of Jack and Gae Alilunas, my parents, have never been in doubt. I never would have been interested in anything that follows had it not been for the intellectually curious home in which I was raised, where knowledge and learning were valued and history was appreciated. Thanks, Mom and Dad. I've tried to create the same environment for my son, who was born as I concocted the idea for this book, said his first words while I was researching it, learned to walk while I was writing it, and amazes me daily with his burgeoning personhood as I put on the finishing touches. Needless to say, he has my unconditional love and support—and the dedication of this book. Finally, my overflowing thanks to Erin Hanna, my colleague, best friend, and partner in good times and bad, who accepts my worst, encourages my best, and fiercely loves me and welcomes my love in return. She is the source of all that light making my world so bright. My life is much better because of her, as is what follows.

Naked Ladies and Ice Cream Bars

> Pornography is the work not of devils but of human beings.
>
> **Robert J. Stoller and I. S. Levine,** *Coming Attractions: The Making of an X-Rated Video* (2003), 11

September 1986. After Sunday church service, a required weekly ritual for my Christian family in Moscow, Idaho, my father unexpectedly made a stop at a convenience store. As my sister and mother waited in the car, I entered the store with him and watched as he bought a handful of ice cream bars and asked to see the manager. I was confused. Nothing had happened, and the ice cream bars looked fine. Their ensuing conversation was quiet and brief: my father politely complained about the presence of *Playboy* magazine behind the counter as the manager nodded and smiled. We returned to the car, eating our ice cream in silence the rest of the way home, my mother and father not speaking about the conversation. I was anxious to debrief in private about the "naked ladies" with my sister, two years older than me and thus much wiser about such things.

Over the years, this incident has occasionally returned to my memory. It is not surprising that my father would complain to the convenience store manager about the magazine; after all, my parents were (and are) staunch religious conservatives and might have even heard a message in church that very day about the scourge of pornography engulfing the nation. That would not have been at all unusual in late 1986, on the heels of the Meese Commission's support of religious communities making just such complaints. Given my mother's subscription to Phyllis Schlafly's aggressively conservative (and antipornography) "Eagle Forum" newsletter, as well as the various books by James Dobson (a member of the Meese Commission) and other Christian conservatives around our house, my father's complaint makes sense. It also does not surprise me that my mother and sister stayed in the car, given my parents' propriety and gendered beliefs about such matters. I may have been taken inside as a prop, to lend my father's complaint an air of sincerity, or the choice may have been instructive, so that I might see the importance of such actions, which were part of a much larger cultural strategy by conservatives to stamp out pornography of all kinds across the United States. *Playboy* may have been the specific object of my parents' scrutiny that Sunday afternoon, but it was also symbolic for them. It could have been anything behind that counter, as long as they believed it to be pornography; the act of protest is what mattered.

Smutty Little Movies is undoubtedly informed by such memories.[1] As a child of the 1970s and '80s, I have vivid (if often unconnected and decontextualized) recollections of pornography during that period.[2] Fleeting glimpses of adult magazines, occasionally passed around on schoolyards or in baseball dugouts. Various family vacations to larger, unfamiliar cities such as New York, where, from a distance, I would see adult movie theaters and arcades, always accompanied by whispered warnings from my mother about the unspoken (but apparently terrifying) dangers lurking inside. The copy of the Meese Commission's *Final Report* at the library that I happened to pick up, quite innocently, before a librarian whisked it away to points unknown, never to be seen on the shelf again. I knew, even before I understood what it was, that pornography was *interesting*. People fought over it. They were scared of it. It was dangerous. I wondered why.

Home video brought significant changes not just to the world, but also to my life. My parents bought a VCR toward the end of the 1980s, a bit later than average Americans but still during the technology's period of explosive growth. Pornography, usually highly controllable in public spaces, could now, conceivably, be right in our home. I (probably like many others in my generation) saw my first adult video at a friend's house during a slumber party while his parents were away; this occurred around the same time as the convenience store incident. I still recall the VCR whirring and clicking as the images appeared on the screen. Unprepared for what happened next, I was, like many after a first exposure to images of human beings having sex, speechless, probably somewhat confused, and no doubt titillated. My friends and I were not sitting in a Times Square theater, at an adult bookstore, or in an arcade. We were at home, in private.

Later, in the 1990s, I worked at video rental stores with thriving, profitable, and carefully sequestered back rooms, where I witnessed steady streams of hurried customers anxious to get back to their cars with whatever adult tapes they had quickly grabbed from the stuffed shelves. My calls to customers to return late tapes—always carefully phrased to downplay the potential embarrassment of hearing that, say, one's husband had failed to return *Butt Bongo Babes* (1993, dir. Jim Enright)—are vivid and historically specific memories of that job. My paychecks were made possible by those back rooms, but they were also endless sources of discomfiture for the store managers, who invariably preferred not to think too much about what they meant for the community and devoted only minimal attention to their contents, even as those rooms kept the stores profitable.

Now, as the study of pornography has become my profession, I'm constantly aware of the social contexts in which I find myself talking to others about my work. At times, I have referred to myself as a "home video historian" (technically accurate), deliberately leaving out the word "adult," depending on where and with whom I'm speaking. Surely every scholar of pornography can relate. This mixture of availability and regulation—really the story of pornography's history—is also part of my story.

The trajectory of my own life is most likely a familiar one to anyone who lived through the technological revolution of home video. In this book, I argue that pornography was not just *part* of the story of home video's early years; it was a *crucial* part. The move of pornography to private spaces, made possible through the gradually more affordable, easy-to-use, and widespread technology of magnetic tape, permanently transformed the cultural landscape. It also stoked regulatory fires that had been burning for decades but now found new sources of fear and outrage in the form of video.

I have no memory of *what* was on the tape I watched at the slumber party, much less its title, but that, in many ways, is irrelevant. What matters is that I—like millions of others who were similarly struck by the availability and capability of the machines hooked to their television sets—watched the tape at all. What was once removed, at a distance, ensconced in public spaces, with all manner of accompanying mechanisms preventing or controlling availability and ease of use, was now much more accessible. This book traces the creations and complaints that accompanied that transition. Yet it is, at its core, a story of naked ladies and ice cream bars.

Smaller Than Life

Adult Video, Pleasure, and Control

> When the full history of porn is finally committed to paper, video will be seen as a truly major event.
>
> **Lawrence O'Toole,** *Pornocopia* (1998), 103

> The question is not *whether* pornography, but the quality of the pornography.
>
> **Paul Goodman,** "Pornography, Art & Censorship," *Commentary* (1961)

If my story begins with my father's complaint to the convenience story manager in 1986, this book starts much earlier, with another public encounter. Deep in an essay from late 1971 outlining and cataloguing his experiences in New York's Times Square adult theaters, historian Joseph Slade buries a curious detail. Outlining the various projection methods in the area venues, Slade describes the screening of shoddy "homemade videotapes" in some theaters.[1] Coming years before videotape technology was widely available to the average consumer, this brief mention raises tantalizing questions. Which theaters were they? What was their films' content? Who were the performers? Who paid for the productions? Were these tapes available for sale to a variety of theaters or made for single locations? Which format were these tapes, and which machines played them? In short: *What was Slade watching?*

What Slade was watching and how, within fifteen years, it would completely transform the adult film industry are the basic questions explored by *Smutty Little Movies.* While pornography had been available on 8mm formats for the home market for some time by Slade's writing, theatrical exhibition of adult films radically changed public perception of the industry.[2] In the mid-1970s, the number of theaters in the United States committed exclusively to playing adult films peaked at around eight hundred.[3] This so-called Golden Age of adult film (defined and described in more detail below) was the zenith of public exhibition of pornography in the United States, yet it was a brief and fleeting era. In 1983, having weathered widespread obscenity prosecutions, changes in national and local laws (and their enforcement), oppressive zoning strategies, and organized protests by anti-pornography feminist, community, and religious groups, the adult film industry still managed to take in roughly $100 million in ticket sales.[4] But enormous changes were already well underway. Only three years later, in 1986, the video industry enjoyed more than 100 million adult video rentals, 1,500 titles released on the format, and more than $425 million in sales revenue.[5] Home video, needless to say, all but decimated the traditional adult theater circuit, permanently changed the industry, and altered the cultural landscape.[6] That Slade watched "homemade videotapes" in spaces that decidedly were *not* homes is not incidental; as I explore in this book, adult video did not start in the home at all.

What Slade saw and wrote about in 1971 in New York City now can be fairly accurately described and—as is the goal throughout this book—given contour and context. He was clearly referring to a small group of theaters that happened to spring up around the time of his visits but disappeared soon afterward (serendipitous timing for a historian, to say the least), and these theaters were hoping to use video technology as a gimmick to draw in small crowds. Five of them were located around Times Square: Channel 69 (called Channel O in advertisements), Channel X, an unnamed storefront theater, the Adonis Cinema Club, and the Tomcat. The first three had the same owner and played straight material, and the latter two featured gay content. All were small operations using television sets and tapes to compete with their celluloid-and-screens neighbors.[7] Channel 69, the first video theater to open in New York, in March 1971, was a second-floor space with a handful of televisions and a $2 entry charge. The owners produced their own content. The other two locations quickly followed, with the same setup. Peter Brennan, writing for *Screw* magazine, is not kind in describing Channel 69's show:

> Not only can't you see the fine details of anatomy but the color
> rendition is terrible. Flesh comes off in various shades of orange and
> green. And the screen is so small that you can't just sit back and get
> engulfed in the sexual activity, you have to keep straining to see.
> Moreover, no attempt is being made to use the creative possibilities of
> video-tape. The program . . . consists mostly of unedited clinical
> closeups of cocks pumping away in cunts and mouths.[8]

The Adonis and Tomcat were slightly different. Both offered televisions in a bar setting along with a stage and featured live shows mixed with loops and video copies from theaters such as the nearby Park-Miller, advertising

Figure 1. The Adonis Cinema Club in New York, a pioneer in the public screening of adult videotapes. *Village Voice*, May 20, 1971, 64.

their offerings as "adult T.V." in an effort to define the new exhibition method (figure 1).[9] They, like the others, did not last long. All were gone by early 1972, just as the celluloid production, distribution, and exhibition of adult films were reaching new heights.[10]

Video would return to Times Square. It would also, eventually, destroy it, as Brennan predicts: "Video tape is little more than a gimmick right now. But the future promises bigger and better things—in fact, it might even put Times Square out of business."[11] But the transition of adult films from celluloid to magnetic tape was not a simple and seamless process; neither did it happen overnight. The history of that process had begun much earlier. Scottish inventor John Logie Baird created the Phonovision video disc system in 1927, using conventional gramophone records; around the same time, Russian Boris Rtcheouloff filed a British patent for a method to record television signals using magnetic material.[12] RCA, under David Sarnoff's urging, developed a videotape playback prototype as early as 1951, and the Ampex Corporation demonstrated a similar machine in April 1956 at the National Association of Radio and Television Broadcasters.[13] Ampex's Quadruplex went on to become standard equipment for the broadcast industry, allowing television programming to overcome time zone differences across the United States while maintaining the appearance of being live, something not previously possible with kinescopes.[14] Following more than a dozen failed efforts by various companies to conquer the home video market, including with its own CV-2000, Sony released the U-Matic in 1971, perhaps the closest precursor to familiar home video players.

By 1974, having gone through various redesigns, the U-Matic increasingly was replacing outdated celluloid equipment in the television news industry, but it never found much foothold in the consumer market.[15] It was with the introductions of the Sony Betamax in 1975, and rival VHS systems (a JVC product, though it would be licensed to a variety of manufacturers) shortly afterward, that true home video finally became possible.[16] As I outline in the first chapter, a handful of early risk-takers in the adult film industry recognized the potential of the new technology, and soon nearly everyone with libraries of celluloid prints began a wholesale transfer to magnetic tape before gradually moving toward video-based production, a process that would take more than a decade to complete. *Smutty Little Movies* examines this transformative period.

The initial impetus for this book was a question posed by Linda Williams in her seminal 1989 book *Hard Core: Power, Pleasure, and the "Frenzy of the Visible"*: "How did [adult] films come to be . . . widely available through over-the-counter purchase or rental to every VCR owner in the country?"[17] Finding the answers in existing literature, as I quickly found out, was complicated. There is no single, comprehensive academic work on the subject—in part because the vast scope and scale of this history lie well outside the bounds of academic research. Small works trace portions of these topics, but these are rare and incomplete. Adult video's history has not been explored beyond a few tentative steps. Cinema histories, home video histories, and even pornography histories rarely mention adult video. Nonacademic research, too, has generally avoided, downplayed, or diminished adult video's history. I believe there are a few, interconnected reasons for this absence, some of which are clearly cultural, and others that are pragmatic and pertain more to the limits of formal scholarship. Unpacking their intertwinements reveals a way forward to a productive future in which more of this history can be unearthed and examined both inside and outside academia.

MISCONCEPTIONS

Cultural reasons to avoid, diminish, and downplay adult video's history stem from what I believe to be a superficially simple, but actually quite complicated, belief: adult video was "bad." This belief contains various misconceptions, all worth parsing in more detail.

Adult Video Ruined the Golden Age

There has been little disagreement that the adult video era was "bad" compared to the Golden Age.[18] That period, however brief, gave hope to the industry and supporters that adult films could gain the type of public reception (and success) that would allow them to find the elusive cultural respectability that would make them "mainstream." Briefly, the period was spurred primarily by the success of *Boys in the Sand* (1971, dir. Wakefield Poole) and *Deep Throat* (1972, dir. Gerard Damiano), both of which crossed over from being simply "dirty movies" into public discourse. Further acceptance came when *The Devil in Miss Jones* (1973, dir. Gerard Damiano), which ranked seventh in total box office gross (not just adult) for its release year, received glowing praise from a variety of film critics, and was even hailed by Addison Verrill of *Variety* as "approaching an art form."[19] Indeed, during this period, critics regularly reviewed adult films, automatically bestowing a patina of respectability; after all, to be reviewed implies the potential for artistry.[20]

The growing popularity and public presence of adult films inspired a Ralph Blumenthal *New York Times* piece in 1973. Coining the oft-repeated term *porno chic*, he described *Deep Throat* as "a premier topic of cocktail-party and dinner-table conversation in Manhattan drawing rooms, Long Island beach cottages, and ski country A-frames."[21] By 1975, director Damiano felt confident enough in the popularity of adult films to run a full-page advertisement in *Variety* seeking Academy Award nominations for his film *Memories within Miss Aggie:* for Best Picture, Best Director, and, for Deborah Ashira, Best Actress (figure 2).[22] While such dreams did not come to fruition, such sentiment and hope represent something profound about the era: filmmakers such as Damiano believed that acceptance and recognition was possible. With spaces such as Vincent Miranda's relatively well-appointed Pussycat Theater chain, red carpet premieres, "crossover" stars such as Linda Lovelace from *Deep Throat* and Marilyn Chambers from *Behind the Green Door* (1972, dir. Jim and Artie Mitchell) moving into the pages of popular magazines and appearing on television talk shows, the mood was, however momentarily, ebullient within the industry. Pornography, more than ever before, was *in the air*. It was a public phenomenon, shown on massive screens, with recognizable and popular stars—just like Hollywood film.

Video was something different. It was private: rented or purchased in small shops and played back in the home on small screens. The glamour of the red carpet premieres faded from view, replaced by "smaller-than-life" images of performers. While many of the Golden Age performers contin-

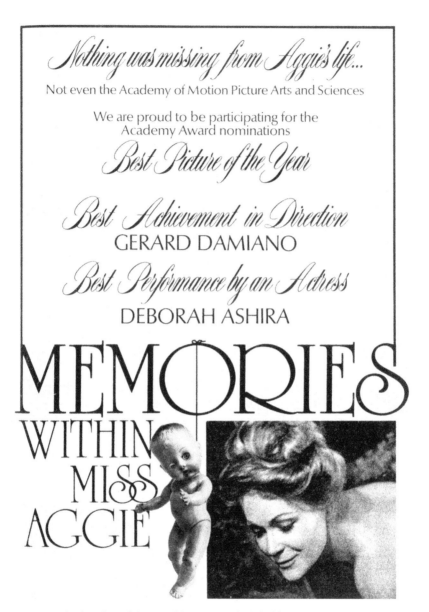

Figure 2. The heights of the "Golden Age" of adult film: Gerard Damiano's Oscar campaign for *Memories within Miss Aggie* in 1975. *Variety*, January 22, 1975, 45.

ued to work in the age of video, they were joined by thousands of new, often forgettable faces, rapidly entering and exiting the business in its unquenchable drive for fresh talent. While the video era gave rise to new stars—such as Ginger Lynn, examined in chapter 3—it did not have the same public presence that the Golden Age, however briefly, carried into popular discourse.[23] Changes brought by video disrupted what would have been a tidy teleological narrative in which pornography ended up somewhere "better" than it did; such discourses have become commonplace, even within somewhat objective narratives of pornography's history. Nicola Simpson, for example, writes: "The success of big screen porn from the mid-1970s to mid-1980s stoked hopes that hard core pornography would attain a status equal or near to other narrative films, only featuring sex. But video undermined that goal."[24]

In the early years of the new technology, adult video producers tried to siphon off some of the "quality" associated with the Golden Age. Since nearly all the earliest adult videos were celluloid features transferred to magnetic tape, such efforts to link video to the Golden Age were made an explicit part of the sales pitch. For example, Cal Vista International, long one of the primary producers of "prestige" adult films, spun off a new division—Cal Vista Video—in the late 1970s but made the association perfectly clear in its video catalogues. "Only our video cassettes are made directly from company owned original negatives on the most expensive equipment, which guarantees the finest quality cassettes modern technology can produce," reads the introductory copy, followed by the company's self-description: "The Rolls Royce of the Motion Picture and Video Industry."[25] The front cover presented a massive image of a Rolls-Royce grill, topped by a nude woman in place of the usual "Spirit of Ecstasy" figure found on the actual car (figure 3). The message was clear: Despite the video format, Cal Vista was selling the same "quality" image associated with celluloid productions.

Adult Video Looked Terrible

Adult video was bad because of how it *looked*. Consider the era: Audiences familiar only with celluloid projection (essentially still photographs projected at twenty-four frames per second onto large screens) were now confronted with electronic signals embedded magnetically on videotape and played back at thirty "frames" per second on cathode ray tube (CRT) television screens. Even if a viewer had never seen or held celluloid, it still held great cultural, even magical power, as Stephen Prince describes: "Tape had virtually nothing in common with celluloid, which contains on its surface

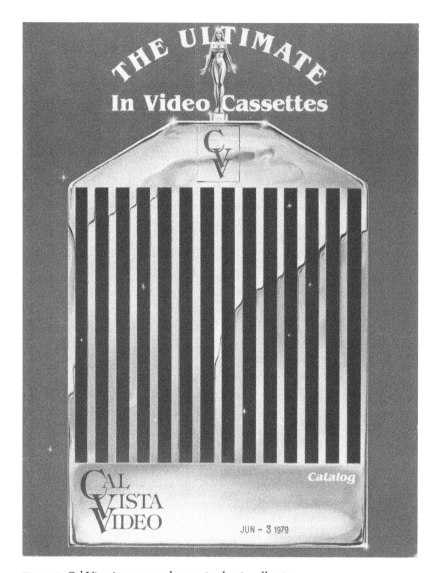

Figure 3. Cal Vista's 1979 catalogue. Author's collection.

the actual still images that come to life in the cinema. These images hold traces of the light that was originally in the scene before the cameras. One can hold a strip of film and see these pictures, can reactivate these traces. By contrast, the videocassette itself, as object, is uninteresting. Lightweight, encased in plastic, it contains no pictures, merely a magnetic signal that requires decoding."[26]

Furthermore, these signals were prone, as Lucas Hilderbrand explains, to all manner of errors, distortions, and "noise," particularly during fast forwarding, rewinding, and returning to play mode, all problems that were amplified after repeated viewings.[27] Tapes looked progressively worse the more they were played.

Eventually, as home video grew to become the dominant means of watching movies, production methods changed to accommodate viewing practices—with more close-ups, closer framing, and limited lighting patterns—what David Bordwell calls "shooting for the box."[28] While the industry may have been thinking pragmatically, others decried the "televisionization" that seemed to be happening to the images themselves.[29] Lest we forget the most decried phenomenon associated with home video, pan-and-scan technology has also been one of the medium's lasting and unfortunate legacies. This process, in which a telecine engineer reframes the original composition during the transfer from celluloid to video ("panning" and "scanning" the image) in order to fill the television frame, has long been widely and roundly criticized for mutilating and destroying original filmic compositions in order to satisfy the stereotype of the consumer who wants every bit of the television screen filled.[30] Video became a bad cultural object, linked to increasing anxieties over the "death" of film, not just within cinephile and critical communities but within academic discourse as well.[31] Given the negative cultural associations already linked with pornography (taken up below), the bad look of video has only amplified these discourses in relation to adult material.[32]

The experience of watching electronic video signals on CRT screens was unquestionably different from watching celluloid, particularly with those productions shot directly on video cameras; this difference, however, has been incessantly coded as bad even by those invested in supporting the industry. As late as 1986, when the technological transition was nearly complete, critic Jim Holliday still referred to adult film produced directly on magnetic tape as "shit-on-video" and suggested such material was "critically and creatively impoverished," including them in his seminal history and guide to adult film only with extreme reluctance.[33] As detailed in chapter 1, some of the pioneers of shooting directly on video tried valiantly to downplay these associations. These creative attempts might be exemplified by Gourmet Video Collection's effort in the early 1980s to tout its techniques as "pure video," which it described as "a product with unsurpassed color clarity and image crispness, which incorporates to the fullest degree the exciting immediacy of closed circuit TV."[34] Despite these attempts to reconfigure video as having "immediacy," the strategy has been historically unsuccessful. Much as video as a whole has long been unfavorably compared aesthetically to celluloid, adult video, too, has been derisively dismissed.

Adult Video Oversaturated the Market

The capability of video to produce, reproduce, and distribute product on a massive, previously unknown economy of scale led to a predictable gold rush of producers looking for quick, easy, and potentially substantial profits. Much as video rental store numbers exploded during this period, supply grew as well. The rising tide of shot-on-video product had a direct effect on the producers still making films primarily for theaters; noted Golden Age director Chuck Vincent claimed in late 1983 that "most people in the X-rated business are going on the theory that the audience wants dirty, smutty little movies."[35] Soon there would be very few shot-on-film productions, and the "smutty little movies"—a descriptor as applicable to the size of the tapes as to their content—would take over the industry. Video stores filled with product, much of it cheaply produced, with most of the investment in box covers, which often deliberately (and deceptively) failed to convey the actual contents.[36]

Epitomizing this glut was undoubtedly Mark Carriere. Uninterested in artistry or narrative and seeking as much financial return on investment as possible, Carriere and his partners at Video Exclusives began cranking out "one-day wonders" in 1983 from a Canoga Park warehouse, flooding stores with their wares, causing a price spiral across the market, and, in the process, growing their operation into a $30 million business. While such rapid shooting practices were not new (despite Carriere's assertions to the contrary), the quick turnover provided by video technology meant that Video Exclusives was able to amass an inventory of finished product that had a profound industrial effect.[37] By the mid-1980s, distributors were selling tapes to retailers for as little as $2.35 each, creating a bargain effect that extended beyond price into the "value" of the content itself.[38] Adult video became disposable, both literally and in the cultural imagination.

The popular perception of the adult video era has become linked to the three assumptions outlined above and has extended into hegemonic territory by way of these three layers. That adult video was bad has become, in fact, its most defining and recognizable historical characteristic. In effect, Carriere and his practices have come to stand in for the entire era, the destroyers of the potential for pornographic "artistry." Even popular culture touchstones that have taken up the topic most often do so from a position of denigration. A noteworthy example of this is surely director Paul Thomas Anderson's 1997 film *Boogie Nights* (1997, dir. Paul Thomas

Anderson), which glorifies the Golden Age by contrasting it with the video era and its "shit-on-video" practices. Anderson crafts a narrative that explicitly blames video for ruining pornography and any chance for it to gain public acceptability. In a crucial scene set on New Year's Eve 1979, Jack Horner (Burt Reynolds), a successful Golden Age director, meets with Floyd Gondolli (Philip Baker Hall), a veteran adult bookstore, nightclub, and peep-show kingpin. Gondolli tries to convince him that home video is the future—even arguing that "videotape tells the truth"—but Horner will have none of it. Accustomed to his small, familiar group of performers, premieres, theatrical screenings, and public presence, video represents an apocalypse to Horner. "I'm a filmmaker," he replies. "That's why I will never make a movie on videotape." Later, he continues: "You know, it if looks like shit and sounds like shit, it probably is shit."

With its symbolic setting at the end of the 1970s, as well as the contrast between the "honorable filmmaker" Horner and the "greedy businessman" Gondolli, Anderson makes the meaning of the scene clear: video was not only a lesser technology, it also represented everything crass and commercial about pornography, the antithesis to the artistic intentions of the Golden Age. A "genuine" filmmaker (and, by extension, "genuine" fans) would never stoop to admitting video could offer the pleasures of celluloid. Tellingly, later in the narrative, Horner's inevitable move to video is coded as tragedy, taking the joy out of the work for him and his stable of performers and crew. The effect, of course, is to hammer home the idea that the Golden Age (and, by definition, celluloid) was ruined by the greed and lack of artistry of the video era.

This example, typical of discourse on the topic, reduces the era and its significance to the stereotype of creative bankruptcy, quick profits, and lack of artistic investment. Adult video has been all but discarded and ignored or positioned as a joke. But what of the people who watched these movies, many of them for the first time, in the privacy of their homes? What of the video store owners who made a living selling and renting the tapes? What of the industry members who created and distributed these tapes—and, in many cases, found themselves at the epicenter of intense legal struggles? For the most part, they have all been collapsed into the perception that the era and its products have no meaning and are just unfortunate, embarrassing markers of the period that followed the Golden Age. A more accurate depiction of the era necessitates examining the industry's interconnected concerns with growth and respectability, marketing its wares and experiences in ways it hoped would not only replicate, but also *surpass* the theatrical experience.

Adult Video Was Not Respectable

There is a fourth factor, too, inflecting the belief that adult video was bad, one with moralistic roots. It extends well beyond adult video and into pornography more generally and the contentiousness with which it is understood and used by culture. Here I am interested in pornography's relationship to *quality* and *respectability*, two terms that have deep significance throughout this book. Historically malleable, definitions of quality and respectability have changed and been adapted over time, but they have always been linked, first and foremost, with notions of "appropriate" gender behavior. Fears over what will happen if boundaries around that behavior are dismantled manifest themselves in a variety of regulatory ways, which nearly always aim to shore up and maintain a hegemonic belief in the disrespectable status of pornography.

Such tensions stretch back well before the advent of moving images. Walter Kendrick traces the history of pornography to the nineteenth century, when (upper-class, white, male) anthropologists unearthed sexually explicit imagery at the ruins of Pompeii and created "secret museums" to keep them away from those less "capable" of understanding them, which is to say the lower classes and especially women. Ultimately, Kendrick argues that pornography is best defined as "not a thing but a concept, a thought structure," and that it "names an imaginary scenario of danger and rescue, a perennial little melodrama in which, though new players have replaced old, the parts remain much as they were first written."[39] This melodrama, he argues, is rooted in the fear that divisional boundaries will be broken and that the result will be open access to anything, for anyone. As Linda Williams explains, Kendrick's summation is that "pornography is simply whatever representations a particular dominant class or group does not want in the hands of another, less dominant class or group. Those in power construct the definition of pornography through their power to censor it."[40] Pornography, in other words, became a visible and definitional category only after the rise of the industrial, "modern" age, when those in power became concerned that anyone could access sexually explicit materials and thus cordoned them off into something available only to those (upper-class white men) with, it was believed, the intellectual acumen to handle the responsibility of viewing them.[41] Once these divisions were in place, pornography began to take on new forms and meanings, frequently political in nature. Often taking the form of satire, pornography frequently targeted government, the law, and organized religion.[42] As this happened, a cultural sea change occurred in which transgression became the objective rather than a side effect. Kendrick is worth quoting at length on this point:

Only in the nineteenth century itself do we begin to find frequent instances of artists deliberately affronting their audiences, treading upon ground they knew to be forbidden. The establishment of a restricted area is itself the boldest invitation to trespass; before the nineteenth century, when no barriers were yet completely manned, there was no strident temptation to leap over them. So long as grossness had a home and stayed there—primarily in satire and comedy—it could be freely displayed to a select audience without inspiring much outrage. But when this sense of propriety was lost, when it began to seem possible that anything at all might be shown to anybody, new barriers had to be erected against a threat that was probably already invincible.[43]

Therein lies the fear: that when "anybody" could see "anything" some sort of threat to the stability and "natural" order of culture was imminent. Pornography, then, does not simply exist; objects *become* pornography, and thus dangerous, through availability and dissemination to the "wrong" people. Laura Kipnis describes pornography as an "oppositional political form," given its capability to illuminate these boundaries.[44]

If the definition of pornography hinges on the wrong people seeing it, respectability serves as an accompanying process of definition ensuring the containment of that which threatens the social order. These concepts have deep roots in the body itself, and particularly the split between the mind and the body—an "upper" and "lower" division. The properties of the lower body, disassociated from the intellectual pursuits of the upper, came to be linked with the disgusting, gross, monstrous, and, given the location of the sexual organs, sex itself.[45] Historically, respectable women have been increasingly associated with "higher" and more protected quality pursuits, while their bodies (and behaviors) have been contained.[46] This is precisely why, as Richard Butsch puts it, "respectability was at its core a gendered concept."[47] Sexuality carries with it the transgressive potential for disruption of all these concepts—most visibly, perhaps, in the form of the prostitute, who violates them all practically at once. The proper role for women (safely inside the home, detached from her own body, limited to higher pursuits, and carefully ensconced in a familial structure as wife and mother) would be *anything* but out in public, commodifying her body sexually with strangers or simply for pleasure rather than procreation. Kendrick's maxim—that pornography names a thought structure, not a thing—comes into even clearer focus when it is placed against this historical backdrop: pornography catalogues and artic-ulates all that violates quality and respectability in its deliberate and unre-pentant overturning of the "normal" social order.

Pornography is, by nature, *not* respectable, which is why it carries such capability for illuminating the social order it labors to transgress.[48] Pornography's inherently transgressive status is also precisely why those seeking to find respectability often attempt to distance themselves from the term itself. The act of renaming is an effort to create and inscribe different meaning and to remove traces of transgression. Andrew Ross connects these divisions with a mind/body split:

> Pornography, it could be argued, is the lowest of the low, because it aims below the belt, and most directly at the psycho-sexual substratum of subjective life, for which it provides an actualizing, arousing body of inventive impressions. That all of pornography's conventions of spectacle and narrative are mobilized toward this greater actualization of bodily impulses runs directly counter to the premises of higher cultural forms, committed to a progressive *sublimation* of these same impulses, whether in the provocative routines of erotica, in the exploratory, transgressive world of avant-garde permissions, in the bourgeois drama of passion and responsibility, or in the aesthete's realm of refined sensibility.[49]

Erotica, a term crucial for this discussion, gained popularity in the 1950s and '60s, indicating a particular level of respectability not granted to pornography, and was used to describe materials that dealt with sex from a perspective of quality.[50] Serving as a boundary guardian, erotica creates a solution for both the public and the industry in that it allows pleasure to slip safely over the mind/body split, from the lower, disreputable body into the higher pleasures of the mind.[51] Put bluntly: It justifies pleasure and makes it safe. As Ross describes it, erotica typically deals in "representational codes of romantic love, with an emphasis on traditionally 'feminine' qualities like tenderness, softness, wholeness, sentiment, sensuality, and passion."[52] This is in contrast to pornography's lower concerns of bodily pleasure, detachment from romance or traditional relationships, and commitment. To summarize the contrast: "art," in order to be art, cannot simply arouse. It must do something more.[53]

Erotica, which often labors to distance itself from pornography through abstract links to "intellectual" pursuits, frequently represents a site of containment rather than liberation. For example, in an effort ostensibly to defend pornography, Susan Sontag ultimately concludes that sexual representations offer a political opportunity to expand one's mind and push conventional limits.[54] As Ross points out, such logic evacuates pleasure for its own sake, keeping the focus "far removed from the semen-stained squalor of the peep show, the strip joint, the video arcade, and other sites of popular pornotopian fantasy."[55] In other words, erotica stays somewhat removed from the body itself and is planted safely in the upper reaches of the mind.

Similarly, Gloria Steinem claims that erotica presents a "sensuality and touch and warmth, an acceptance of bodies and nerve endings," and she defines it as "a mutually pleasurable, sexual expression between people who have enough power to be there by positive choice." She goes on to add, "It is truly sensuous, and may give us a contagion of pleasure."[56] The explicit references to "sensuality" and "warmth" reinforce the essentializing stereotype that women's (and, it should be noted, men's) sexuality should be carefully contained lest it venture out aggressively into territory where it might cause more than a "contagion of pleasure," detached from the mind and located firmly in the body. Annette Kuhn adds explicit links to narrative to this formulation: "In pornographic stories, literary as well as visual, characters are never very strongly developed as psychologically rounded human beings. They perform functions, they take on roles already fixed within the commonplace fantasies that porn constructs."[57] The need for "psychologically rounded" human beings is always present in erotica, for the dismissal of psychology would entail acknowledging the legitimacy of bodily pleasure for its own sake and with no further goal in mind.

Pornography, with its frequent, flagrant, and unabashed dismissal of "before" and "after" the sex act, relishes all kinds of transgressive sexual behavior: stranger sex; group sex; lack of context; lack of familiarity of all kinds; often utter disregard for "tenderness," either before or after the physical act; often very little interest in traditional relationships; and almost none in procreation.[58] Connecting narrative to quality solidifies the link between the upper region of the mind and the pursuit of "something more" than simple bodily pleasure—which, as myriad tensions and anxieties throughout history have shown, is most dangerous when undertaken by women.[59] Frequently embodied and identified by the concept of narrative, that "something more" is a key element that I return to throughout *Smutty Little Movies* as a marker of the strategy that the adult video industry employed in its quest for public acceptance, increased sales, and decreased legal scrutiny.[60] This strategy created a contradictory paradigm in which the industry tried to gain respectability through traditional strategies while simultaneously creating disrespectable content. Most frequently, this effort meant utilizing advertising and marketing discourses designed to emphasize intellectual rather than physical appeals, but these appeals also manifested in literal physical spaces—which would later have deep consequences for video rental stores.

Indeed, the adult film exhibition industry in the 1970s crafted spaces designed to appeal to middle-class audiences and women by invoking respectability discourses. Early attempts at adult film theaters, such as the Sutter Cinema in San Francisco, were marketed to customers as "legitimate" due to the quality of the films playing there, as well as the aesthetics of the spaces themselves. Lowell Pickett, a stag filmmaker and the executive director of the Haight-Ashbury Free Clinic, and Arlene Elster, who had worked as a volunteer at the clinic, opened the Sutter in 1970. Their advertisements boldly claimed the Sutter was "San Francisco's most highly acclaimed erotic art film theater," alongside line drawings of naked women and quotes from James Joyce's *Ulysses*.[61] A *Los Angeles Times* article described the space: "The Sutter exudes élan and the atmosphere of a fashionable art house on the East Side of New York, as opposed to the stale sweat and down-and-out-on-the-bowery sleaziness of similar houses in other cities."[62] A local sexual liberation group, the Psychedelic Venus Church (PVC), put it more bluntly in its newsletter: "Fucking and sucking on screen, plus art."[63] The art was not just on the screen but around it as well, with the goal, as Joseph Lam Duong writes, of filling the seats with "young middle-class couples, instead of the unattached men who currently patronized the industry."[64] Also highly visible in Vincent Miranda's Pussycat Theater chain, such traits represented how the adult theater industry of the era routinely created a chain linking women's bodies to intellectual pursuits to artistic merits to exhibition spaces.[65] This was a literal "something more," even within the walls of the space itself. Such practices, as I show throughout this book, continued into the age of video.

Ultimately, connections between quality and respectability rest on a foundation of rigidly heteronormative, highly classed views of the social order. To detach sex from patriarchal views of the home, privacy, and marriage is to also tacitly suggest that pleasure can exist for its own sake. These strategies—particularly an insistence on narrative—ultimately add layers of *justification* to sex: pleasure, in a narrative context, comes with a *reason*. Tenderness, sensuality, relationships, warmth, sensitivity, love—all these code words, the hallmarks of erotica, imply knowledge, familiarity, something beyond just the sex act itself; that amorphous, protective, and highly desired "something more." The result is a highly proscriptive view of sex that creates boundaries between "normal" and "abnormal." This split reinforces the antipornography feminist view that, as the title of a well-known documentary puts it, pornography is "not a love story," suggesting, with extreme prejudice, that sex should only exist "properly" within a particular, very rigid set of boundaries predicated on relationships and intimacy, and that the mediation of sex should be presented in the same way.[66] "Something more" is something that matters a great deal when examining the history of adult video.

CLARIFICATIONS

The many nuances, subtleties, and contours of this history need to be explored in detail in order to restore some semblance of clarity to the era that moves away from a good/bad dichotomy. Misconceptions and mythologies need to be scrutinized and, when necessary, debunked. As part of that process, five assertions follow, each a key argument in this book.

Video Saved the Adult Film Industry

The adult film industry was in a somewhat dire cultural position at the time the Sony Betamax entered the market. An April 5, 1976, *Time* magazine cover story, vividly titled "The Porno Plague," outlines the landscape, describing the "avalanche of porn" that had seemingly overtaken America (figure 4). The article paints a bleak and desperate portrait of a culture given over to dangerous pornographers, describing in salacious detail the various neighborhoods in major and minor cities where pornography could be found, the apparent helplessness of law enforcement and the courts to stop the flood, and the strategies employed, with little success, by pornography's opponents. The stance taken in the article nearly tips over into moral panic: "Even those who argue that it is not harmful to the user . . . have begun to fear that the porn plague is in fact invading the privacy of those who want no part of it."[67] The tensions around the *publicness* of pornography were taking over the national conversation. Stories such as the one in *Time* were a staple of the 1970s—for example, *Newsweek* ran a remarkably similar piece six years earlier, replete with maps, photographs, and breathless exhortations about the boundaries that the industry was pushing and the harried police forces struggling to contain it. This story's conclusion is a mix of familiar compromise and nervous anxiety: "A little bit of pornography may be stimulating, but an overdose can be numbing to practically anyone."[68]

As *Smutty Little Movies* explores, particularly in its final chapter, many of these allegations carry kernels of truth. Pornography, beginning in the Golden Age, occupied increasing amounts of real estate across the country. Bookstores, arcades, theaters, and related businesses grew rapidly and met heavy resistance in terms of police raids, zoning and obscenity laws, and community protests. The issue of privacy was paramount, creating a paradox for the industry: How would (or could) it deliver its products to willing customers while simultaneously being aggressively targeted as a public nuisance? Even *advertising* pornography was increasingly subject to intense scrutiny; after all, in *Ginzberg v. United States* (1966), the Supreme Court had ruled that mailed advertisements for pornography, if openly

Figure 4. As adult film was making the technological leap to video distribution, the cultural landscape was characterized by increasing moral panic about pornography. From *Time*, April 5, 1976. © 1976 Time Inc. All rights reserved. Used by permission and protected by the Copyright Laws of the United States. The printing, copying, redistribution, or retransmission of this Content without express written permission is prohibited. Courtesy of TIME, Pars. International Corp.

appealing to potential customers' erotic interest, could be considered pandering and obscene under federal statute.[69] Home video was a perfect solution, given its inherent functionality as a *private* medium. While regulatory struggles did not disappear, they did change, and the apocalyptic landscape described by *Time* certainly changed, too, as pornography moved from the theaters and arcades into video rental stores. As Simpson writes, "It is entirely possible that without video, the porn business may not have survived the legal restrictions and poor economy of the late 1970s."[70] While that might be an overstatement, it is clear that the privacy afforded by video technology brought with it a level of security that was unquestionably welcomed by an industry under veritable siege.

Adult Video Altered Debate over the Private Nature of Sexual Pleasure

To move away from a good/bad dichotomy, one task is to examine the role adult video played in altering the debate over privacy and pleasure, which, as the *Time* article illustrates, was already well underway. Tensions over the *public* presence of sexually explicit material had long plagued the industry, with the U.S. Supreme Court weighing in frequently on the rights of citizens to consume pornography. In *Stanley v. Georgia* (1969), the court held that a state could not prohibit the possession of obscene material for private use and thus established the privacy of the home and marked it as a secured, protected space.[71] Four years later, in *United States v. 12 200-ft. Reels of Super 8mm. Film* (1973), the court ruled that this protection did not subsequently provide the right to transport obscenity *outside* the home—further shoring up the sanctity of private spaces while also marking them as potentially suspicious and dangerous.[72] Indeed, the move of adult film to video brought with it tremendous protection for the consumer *and* new anxieties for producers and distributors, anxieties rooted in questions of how to get the product to the protected home space.

In other words, whereas adult movie theaters, arcades, and bookstores were all carefully monitored through various familiar regulatory schemes due to their public nature, video suddenly gave every home in America the capability to become a protected exhibition space. While producers, distributors, and exhibitors had all long been targeted for obscenity prosecution, video brought new waves of attacks that hinged on familiar fears of what people might do with the widespread access to pornography provided by new distribution mechanisms.[73] This proved particularly true in the early period of video rental, when locally owned stores typically carried adult titles without much reservation, opening up the potential for the distribution of pornography on an unprecedented scale. Yet, as the industry solidified, two themes emerged. Traditional regulatory methods (such as obscenity prosecutions and community protests) targeted those stores willing to rent pornography. At the same time, a handful of large corporations with little interest in chipping away at the "normal" social order that it believed held the keys to their profits absorbed the home video rental industry. The latter story ends this book. While companies such as Blockbuster Video offered the potential to supply a tremendous variety of entertainment to the privacy of the home, that variety did not include pornography. In the end, it was not judicial control, police action, or community pressure that most firmly restored familiar and restrictive boundaries around pornography in the wake of the new technology; instead, it was capitalism and corporate policy.

Adult Video Opened New Avenues to Previously Marginalized Audiences

However briefly the Golden Age made a space in which larger audiences found an interest in adult film, the industry nevertheless still restricted the vast majority of those films to public, highly visible spaces in which the film content itself was primarily made up of heteronormative content focused on male pleasures and fantasies and shown in front of predominantly male audiences.[74] To see an adult film meant visiting these spaces—always sites of suspicion, especially for women, given constant fears of prostitution, particularly after the initial allure and novelty of the Golden Age had passed. Video was a watershed moment that allowed the consumption of pornography in private after a trip to the local rental store; while still an interaction requiring public visibility, this interaction carried far less stigma than did a visit to the adult business districts familiar in any large city of the 1970s. Rural and suburban areas in particular, lacking much opportunity for consumers to view the adult films (gay and straight) that filled theaters in cities such as New York, were now prime locations for video stores carrying this new material.[75] Although media of various kinds had been critical for queer identity formation long before home video, the new technology granted a level of privacy to those without access to or interest in existing communities and practices, but who still wanted to explore pornography.

Women and queer audiences now had growing opportunities to obtain adult films within a new distribution and exhibition structure—and the industry (slowly) began creating video content with them in mind. New companies sprang up, such as Candida Royalle's Femme Productions (explored in chapter 3), the first woman-owned and -operated company to take advantage of the new medium, as did lesbian production companies such as Fatale Video, Tigress, and Lavender Blue, all of them practically unthinkable before the reduced technological entry costs provided by video.[76] So-called amateur adult video, featuring nonprofessional performers, also seized video's opportunities for cheaper production and distribution; Homegrown Video, for example, was founded in 1982 by a group of San Diego swingers who began trading their personal videotapes and then, sensing a market for such material, turned it into a business enterprise.[77] These sorts of new practices and approaches were not uncommon in the era.

The outcome for consumers, who had increased access to wide ranges of content, was culturally significant. In late 1986, the editors of *Adult Video News (AVN)* released results from a poll conducted with five hundred retailers across the United States between January and June of that year.[78] The results were (and are) undeniably surprising: while individual men rented 27 percent of all adult tapes, individual women were close behind, at 24 percent. Furthermore, women accompanied by other women rented 8 percent of all adult tapes, and women with men rented 31 percent, meaning that women were involved in 63 percent of all adult video-related transactions (figure 5).[79] Even if these numbers were not entirely accurate (and they were clearly intended to garner publicity), they nevertheless point to the changes brought by home video. Ultimately, the intense regulatory struggles described throughout this book reflect the dramatic new availability of video pornography to previously underserved audiences and the ways in which those audiences took advantage of the opportunity.

Adult Video Permanently Changed Pornography

In addition to massive exhibition and distribution changes, adult video also made profound and lasting changes to the *creation* of pornography. The VCR allowed a greater amount of personal interaction with adult films than had ever been previously available. The potential to schedule when and where consumption would occur, along with the ability to fast forward, rewind, and pause a tape meant that viewers were more directly involved. That involvement meant that viewers could skip or repeat sections of the film that did not appeal to them or, as Hilderbrand so aptly describes, scan "past boring bits."[80] In many cases, and certainly in the popular cultural imagination, that meant skipping through the narrative to get directly to the sexual activity desired by the viewer, letting spectators serve as editors of their own programming.[81] As Caetlin Benson-Allott argues,

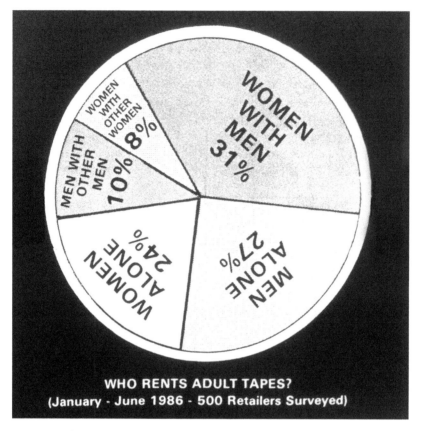

WHO RENTS ADULT TAPES?
(January - June 1986 - 500 Retailers Surveyed)

Figure 5. "Charting the Adult Video Market," *Adult Video News* (August–September 1986): 6–7. Courtesy of AVN Media Network (avn.com).

this perception of control is both somewhat illusory and liberating, offering "no additional subjective coherence or empowerment" for the spectator, but still creating "a new illusion of mastery, a new twist in the fantasy that the image exists just for her." Ultimately, she goes on to argue, "The prerecorded video apparatus changes the object of that fantasy from the power to see anything to the power to see *again*."[82]

The impact on the industry was undeniable: while adult films continued to maintain traditional story structures in the video era, they stepped back from the more narratively and aesthetically complex films of the Golden Age. Eventually, many producers released "compilation" tapes consisting only of sex scenes and entirely devoid of narrative—predicting the online pornography that consists primarily of such material. Increasingly, entire productions containing minimal narrative and instead focusing primarily on various sexual activities became the standard. Given that "loop" films had filled arcades for years, it was a familiar industrial paradigm. New genres, though, such as "gonzo" (examined in more detail in the epilogue), emerged that took full advantage of both portable video camera equipment *and* new spectatorial practices by creating a mode of first-person address aimed squarely at viewers in front of their home television sets rather than in theater auditoriums.[83] Whereas some decried the "televisionization" of cinema by home video, video's characteristics (closer framing, minimal lighting, and increased close-ups) were, perhaps, ideal for adult filmmakers and spectators.

Ultimately, video revealed capabilities that might have been lurking within pornography all along, which is to say that the loop structure familiar from stag films and peep-show booths might have been the ideal form from the beginning. While the Golden Age of adult film might have tipped pornography toward a particular type of cultural legitimacy with its heavy emphasis on narrative and other familiar cinematic paradigms, video exploded in popularity in part because it was an ideal match for consumer desires and technological limitations. As Peter Lehman argues, "Porn may never have been suited fully to the feature format."[84]

Adult Video Was a Crucial Catalyst for Home Video

Situating adult video in the broader history of home video is one of my key goals in this book. As such, it carries on and extends the work done by others in what Benson-Allott has called the rise of "new video studies," a recent surge beginning in the mid-2000s and initiated by scholars asking broad questions about home video from a wide variety of disciplinary perspectives.[85] For the most part, this body of research, while not entirely avoiding or ignoring pornography, has nevertheless decentered the topic while taking on other questions.[86] Nevertheless, these scholars have done valuable work that has contributed much to my research. In his industrial history of home video, Paul McDonald traces some of the earliest distribution history of adult titles on the format, and he notes the serendipitous timing of the new technology, given the regulatory challenges facing the adult industry during this period.[87] Similarly, Frederick Wasser offers an overview of the adult film industry's important contributions to the development of home video, noting, "X-rated material created the infrastructure for video distribution."[88] Dan Herbert's analysis of video store culture includes a deep examination of both the classification process of rental video titles and a look at the "back room," the important space in which pornography was usually cordoned off from the rest of the inventory.[89] Pornography informs much of Hilderbrand's discussion of the materiality and erotics of videotape, and he includes discussions of amateur and celebrity sex tapes.[90] Finally, Josh Greenberg's history of home video includes important links between public-domain films and pornography, as well as analysis of video distribution and store operations that includes adult material.[91] All this work provides valuable entry points for *Smutty Little Movies,* and in many cases it triggered the necessary questions that led to my own conclusions.

The absence of detailed research is a gap in the literature that is ready to be filled. It is important to note that the lack of much sustained attention to pornography within new video studies emphasizes the *already* secondary position that home video history scholarship typically occupies; as Benson-Allott notes, other media studies approaches "seem to consider prerecorded video no more than a convenience, the bastard child of cinema and television studies that must subsist outside the purview of even their highly interdisciplinary studies."[92] As it progresses as a subfield, new video studies should carefully avoid placing pornography into a "back room," away from other subjects and inquiries. It should also avoid what Williams calls "dabbling," in which scholars, not unlike customers at video stores, dash into the pornography section, grab a title or two, and run back out again.[93] The 2014 inauguration of *Porn Studies,* the first peer-reviewed journal dedicated to the topic, might only exacerbate this problem, despite its good intentions; as I have argued elsewhere, the end result might be further cordoning off of pornography studies and an accompanying academic security of knowing that it resides in a "safe" place.[94] Conversely, pornography studies should carefully avoid staying in the back room and should venture out into the rest of home video history.

Perhaps the main reason for the absence of sustained and detailed work in adult video history is that, simply put, it is difficult. Cultural efforts to regulate and contain pornography created a complicated situation for historians, in that the typical problems associated with historical research become amplified in particular and unique ways. Even in its contemporaneous moments, the adult film industry existed on the cultural fringes, often deliberately hiding in the shadows to avoid prosecution and other regulatory pressures. Furthermore, the lack of much established research on the subject means contemporary historians often cannot draw heavily on or extend existing work; given the size and scope of the adult industry, almost any project has the potential to become daunting. The historical footprints of pornography, when they appear at all, often do not lend themselves to "traditional" projects with established research protocols, methods, and sources.

Additionally, while all manner of voices (newspapers, magazines, trade journals, etc.) have long covered mainstream film industries on even the most mundane topics, the adult industry rarely has received such coverage, often appearing only in times of prosecution or panic. It is difficult to locate even the most basic and rudimentary industrial histories of adult film in traditional places. Very few archives (with some notable exceptions) collect adult material, and university libraries generally do not subscribe to or hold collections of adult publications—particularly those that deal in hardcore imagery—or adult films, especially the mountains of forgettable titles from the video era.[95] Aside from *Playboy, Penthouse,* and occasionally *Hustler,* microfilm copies of adult magazines do not exist, and many popular press books on the industry similarly are not housed in libraries or are expensive to acquire. Adult film historians often must construct a personal archive, assembled on the (costly) collector's market.

Scholars interested in adult film often must turn to work outside academia to piece together its history, or pull from a variety of cross-referenced discourses to interrogate the past. As Eric Schaefer notes, "insider" accounts, anecdotal approaches, loose ethnographies, oral histories, and superficial overviews tend to compose much of the work on adult film history.[96] Valuable as these works are (and many are referenced in this book), details often lack citation or supporting evidence and can lead down twisting paths in search of factual confirmation, or, worse, can transmit inaccurate information. Often scholars must rely upon the industry itself for historical research, a situation that can present more verification problems and sometimes a lack of access.[97] Despite these challenges, pockets of evidence do exist, and gathering them is a necessity if adequate historical excavations are to occur. Early viewers' guides to adult video provide invaluable production data and historical snapshots of the industry, and are a must for any adult industry historian.[98] Increasing numbers of industry veterans have been publishing their memoirs, giving scholars a wealth of material from which to initiate research, as well as a means to include these forgotten or ignored voices.[99] A further model in this regard has been the various pornography studies anthologies that have made efforts to include essays written by industry members.[100] Ultimately, for scholars to write the history of adult film, the notion of the archive itself will have to expand, and conventional archives will have to consider why they have not gathered evidence on the topic.[101]

Yet these many challenges do not mean such projects are impossible. They do, however, frequently require an adept, creative approach that shifts focus away from traditional methods and sources, but not necessarily in its core historiographic practices. In this book, I use what I call "trace historiography," a method seeking to locate evidence where it seemingly no longer exists. By searching for traces, often peripheral and, on first examination, unrelated, the echoes and footprints of the past can reveal what might have once been there but has since been lost. To put it another way, the trace historiographer must often examine the smoke rather than the fire to determine how the fire started, what burned, and why. Over the course of this research, it has become clear that much of the remaining evidence of adult video's origins forms a narrative only when assembled from disparate and fragmented sources. It is a puzzle of sorts, one that does not appear to offer answers when seen as individual pieces. While this method is not unique to adult video history, the complex challenges of identifying evidence on an industry often forced into (or deliberately residing in) the shadows make it particularly useful.[102]

The research for this book relied heavily upon Schaefer's notion of a "critical mess": my sprawling personal archive of materials (catalogues, industry magazines, brochures, ad slicks, telephone books, autobiographies, blog posts, industry gossip columns, fan websites, advertisements, etc.), which I used to write this history, does precisely what Schaefer describes—it identifies patterns amid chaos to reach conclusions, rather than using predetermined theses and conclusions.[103] A great deal of the arguments in this book stem from evidence I found while digging through the critical mess and finding what Schaefer calls "fortuitous convergences" with more traditional sources such as newspapers, zoning laws, Supreme Court obscenity rulings, local ordinances, and antipornography publications.

This book is, of course, about sex, its representations, and how those representations changed along with technology; the literal mediation of sex, however, will be the least important and least discussed element in this book. My focus in *Smutty Little Movies* is more about context than content. The years that make up the bulk of this book's investigations—1976 to 1986—were a period bracketed by the widespread transfer of adult film *to* video and the production of material primarily *for* and *on* video, but they also offer a compelling view of accompanying changes within and around the industry.[104] A great deal of further work will need to take on the years following 1986, as the industry settled into new technological production and distribution mechanisms, along with new regulatory changes and challenges.

My emphasis in *Smutty Little Movies* is deliberately on the most visible and financially successful segments of the adult film industry of the period making content featuring primarily heterosexual activities aimed, at least ostensibly, at heterosexual viewers.[105] Despite the immense and unquestionable importance of queer material of all kinds in the history of pornography (including adult video), my decision is an effort to limit the scope and scale of the research to a particular industrial history that has not yet received much scholarly interest while simultaneously occupying a massive historical footprint, rather than being based on some sort of avoidance or political disinterest.[106] Williams notes: "Very few published works have tackled the dominant mainstream of moving image pornography, and I cannot but think that this avoidance of the heterosexual mainstream, especially of its history, has left a large central plot of the garden unattended."[107] *Smutty Little Movies* aims to tend to that part of the garden rather than to think of the topic as a separate greenhouse—which is why I do not qualify my usage of the terms *pornography* and *adult video* with *straight* (or its derivations) throughout this book. This is decidedly not an effort (deliberate or inadvertent) to solidify the cultural binaries surrounding sexuality (indeed, queer histories and theory influence this research in a wide variety of ways) or to collapse the (remarkably heterogeneous) adult film industry into a monolith including only certain types of pornography, but instead to focus on specific industrial segments, products, marketing, and intended audiences that have heretofore gone mostly unexamined. This book does not aim to be comprehensive, nor could it be—much more work needs to be done in this area, from a wide variety of perspectives, on a sprawling number of related topics, and with all sorts of research questions in mind beyond the ones offered here.[108]

In the chapters that follow, I trace two interconnected paths. First, I uncover and outline the history of the industry itself—the people, practices, and decisions that led to the transition of adult film from celluloid to home video—paying close attention to the tensions and anxieties surrounding issues of quality and respectability. Second, I focus on the myriad regulatory efforts across the United States to limit, contain, or eradicate adult video, all culminating in the Meese Commission's 1986 attempt to dictate and institute a national discourse on pornography. Its timing, coming just as home video was exploding into mass popularity, was not coincidental, much as regulatory efforts of earlier eras frequently had occurred in tandem with similar trends of new technology and mass availability. The many opponents of adult film diligently worked (and, indeed, continue to work) to prevent the industry from gaining respectability, credibility, and normalization, because to allow that to happen would tacitly acknowledge that the pleasures and performances depicted in adult film were (and are) also respectable, credible, and normal. In the mid-1980s, the increased availability of home video systems, widespread dissemination of adult tapes, and professionalization of the adult film industry moved this tension to a state of cultural panic around pornography, which I examine throughout this book, particularly in the final chapter.

This panic, while a continuation of the fear-based backlash that had long plagued the industry, nevertheless took on new forms given the availability of pornography in such a widespread manner. In understanding these forms, I draw on three theoretical models: (1) the moral panic; (2) the technopanic; and (3) the sex panic. In his groundbreaking work on moral panics, Stanley Cohen argues, "Societies appear to be subject, every now and then, to periods of moral panic," and he places a great deal of emphasis on the media as an instigator in such crises, suggesting the result is often an escalation and inflation of panic rhetoric.[109] As I illustrate throughout this book, that model was certainly true in the case of adult video, which was frequently the subject of breathless magazine and newspaper reporting that typically favored pornography's opponents. The technopanic model carries particular salience for the period under study, given that home video technology allowed the widespread—and affordable—dissemination of pornography. Alice Marwick argues that technopanics are rooted in fears of modernity combined with a pathologization of young people's use of new technologies.[110] The VCR was hardly the first technology to raise cultural fears of "inappropriate" sexual behavior, bringing to mind Joseph Slade's argument: "Whenever one person invents a technology, another person will invent a sexual use for it."[111] The mid-1980s represents merely one period in the long history of technopanics.

Pornography's connection to technology, as Jonathan Coopersmith argues, might serve as a primary defining feature, and it is worthy of closer examination in order to situate the panic around adult video in a longer historical trajectory.[112] Examples of pornography appear alongside new technologies nearly as soon as the technologies are unveiled and, in fact, predate "technology" itself, stretching back to the realm of cave drawings and folk art.[113] Print technology has long been the source (and target) of various panics—even before the printing press revolutionized the distribution of material to the masses.[114] Development of printing technology, however, changed everything. In what could serve as a prefiguring of adult video, Coopersmith notes, "The immense increase in the circulation of [pornography] and its increasing political content meant easier access because of decreased cost as well as greater availability."[115]

Beginning in the nineteenth century in the United States, Frederick S. Lane argues, the inventions of mass printing and mass distribution were followed by regulatory efforts to contain the spread of "obscene" content; in particular, the appointment of Anthony Comstock to the post of special agent to the U.S. Post Office, to act as de facto national censor, was a turning point in the history of technopanics.[116] The industrial revolution brought other new forms of communication technology that were used for purposes related to pornography and pleasure. In his history of the telegraph, Tom Standage argues, "Spies and criminals are invariably among the first to take advantage of new modes of communication. But lovers are never far behind."[117] Tracing the behavior of telegraph operators, he illustrates how the new technology quickly became coopted for sexual use. While literal records of these behaviors and messages do not exist, Thomas Edison claimed at the time that the some of "the tales passing over the wires [between operators] would find their way into the local newspapers," although many did not because "they were far too smutty or anatomically explicit."[118] The operators, in other words, were quite adeptly sending pornographic messages. The development of the railroad also provided a means to disseminate pornography: George Douglas describes late-nineteenth-century salesmen frequently (and discreetly) selling "faintly naughty literature" at high profits to passengers in train cars.[119]

The telephone, too, became a powerful sexual tool with the development of Dial-a-Porn in the early 1980s. By 1984, the Federal Communications Commission was deluged with public complaints about the services, and in 1985, pornography's opponents, including Donald Wildmon's American Family Association (AFA), pressured the Justice Department into sponsoring a study on Dial-a-Porn's effects. Psychologist Victor Cline, a longstanding antipornography advocate, conducted the research.[120] His conclusion— that "without exception, the children (girls as well as boys) became hooked on this sex by phone and kept going back for more and still more"—illustrates the fears surrounding the use of technology for sexual pleasure and the ways in which pornography's opponents inevitably link the corruption of children to the necessity of regulating the technology.[121]

The development of technologies to reproduce and disseminate images, however, stands out in the history of pornography. As Paolo Cherchi Usai notes, pornographic postcards and magic lantern slides were popular before the turn of the twentieth century.[122] The Mutoscope, a flip-card viewing machine invented in 1894, was more popularly known as the "What the Butler Saw" machine, given its frequent images of women undressing.[123] The creation of photographic technology offered increased realism and ushered in a new era for pornography. Shortly after Louis Daguerre created the daguerreotype photography system, erotic photographs were produced in vast quantities.[124] In his history of pornography, Henry Hyde argues, "The discovery and development of photography led to the manufacture and distribution of erotic and indecent photographs on an enormous scale."[125] Coopersmith cites a particularly useful example for understanding the scope of pornographic photography almost immediately after its creation: the 1874 arrest of photographer Henry Haylor uncovered 130,248 obscene photographs and 5,000 obscene slides in his possession, illustrating the enormous demand for such material by Londoners.[126] In terms of motion picture technology, noted French photographer Eugène Pirou filmed dancer Louise Willy performing her popular striptease "Le coucher de le marié" (the Bridegroom's Dilemma) as early as 1896; Dave Thompson argues that strong evidence exists for a thriving adult film industry in South America by 1900, though none of these films has been found.[127] Janet Staiger notes that kinetoscope parlors from the turn of the century featured the burlesque dances of Dolorita, Carmencita, and Fatima, which neatly fit that technology's time limitations of less than a minute per viewing.[128]

From its inception, intense public scrutiny bordering on panic defines, as much as any other element, the history of film production and exhibition. Staiger describes the early period, from the late 1890s to roughly 1907, as "an initial testing of the waters to determine what types of representations [would] constitute permissible formulaic treatments of nudity, eroticism, sexuality, and so forth."[129] Public response varied among locales, but it inevitably focused on potential effects on children. Staiger offers a particularly important example: in December 1908, New York City Mayor George McClellan Jr. revoked all moving picture licenses in the city to prevent a "public calamity." Citing fire safety and children in theaters without adult supervision as his primary motivators, McClellan immediately stopped all theatrical exhibitions in the city. The real reason, however, was much more complicated. Stemming from a dedicated effort by a group of progressive reformers, McClellan's decision was a victory for those interested in stamping out "obscene" content. Staiger notes: "The reformers who went after the movies had earlier looked at corruption in city government and the social evil because of moral concerns tied to religious beliefs. Furthermore, these individuals would continue to be involved in pressuring the movie business to take a stricter view about what was talked about in the narratives."[130]

The result in New York was obviously not a permanent ban on movies. What the actions did lead to, however, after protracted negotiations and public furor, was the creation of an organized censorship board, the Moving Picture Exhibitors' Association of Greater New York, which later reorganized, first, as the National Board of Censorship and then, in 1915, as the National Board of Review.[131] Working with producers to clear films before distribution, the organization (which incorporated other local censorship boards to create a national system) served as the precursor to later regulatory efforts such as the Legion of Decency and the Motion Picture Producers and Distributors of America (MPPDA). The MPPDA, created by the Hollywood studios in 1922 (and later renamed the Motion Picture Association of America, or MPAA) served as a powerful self-regulatory body that also labored to advance Hollywood's business interests and avoid governmental oversight of content. Accomplished in part by the creation of the Production Code, which later led to the ratings process, such action ensured an internal, rather than external, oversight process to keep "obscene" content out of the industry in order to maintain a respectable (and thus profitable) public image.[132] Indeed, as Jon Lewis notes, "The MPAA supervises the regulation of film content solely to protect studio products in the marketplace."[133] At the core of these histories resides the technopanic created by the invention of motion pictures. Such technology made the moving image available to the public in a widespread manner, and with that availability came the two elements necessary for a panic: the fear of "obscene" content and unregulated exposure to women and children.

Those fears are part and parcel of a sex panic. Following Carol S. Vance and Gayle Rubin, Janice M. Irvine argues that sex panics represent the political "moment" of sex, emerge in particular spaces and times, follow many of the same characteristics of moral panics (such as disproportionality and exaggeration), and eventually recede once the intensity fades.[134] Crucial, too, as Roger N. Lancaster points out, is the importance of harm—which, as was the case with adult video, was frequently undefined and nebulous. As he notes: "Imagined victimization takes precedence over any real victimization"; as I point out in the final chapter of this book, this was a defining characteristic of the panic around adult video.[135] Gilbert Herdt argues that, during a panic, this cultural imagination "becomes obsessed with anxieties about what this evil sexuality will do to warp society and future generations."[136] Fear of the unknown, of the possibly damaging potential pornography carried, crystallized frequently in antipornography discourses, which tended to emphasize imaginary possibilities rather than realities. Herdt's formulation is particularly useful for adult video, opponents of which worried continually about what might become of society if pornography were normalized and thus made respectable. Adult video, with its presence in mainstream video stores, presented that possibility in bold new ways.

Concurrently with (and feeding) the panic, the industry worked to garner the types of respectability and credibility that not only would bolster its bottom lines, but also aid it in becoming recognized as a normal form of business—which, as I point out in the conclusion, is an impossible paradox given pornography's inherently disrespectable status. Ultimately, a portrait of regulation emerges that is not limited to any one area, but rather illustrates the interconnections and overlaps among them, both inside and outside the industry. Following Kendrick, a goal throughout *Smutty Little Movies* is to seek out and understand desire—but rather than the sexual desires commonly associated with adult video, I wish to trace the desire "to regulate the behavior of those who seem to threaten the social order," as well as the many contradictions embedded within efforts to overturn that order.[137] As Michael Newman and Elana Levine have pointed out about television, another media form with similar struggles over respectability and Golden Age yearnings, "Cultural legitimation may seem to be an important step forward for those who value, enjoy, and feel invested in television. But it is premised on a set of hierarchies that ultimately reinforce unjust social and cultural positions."[138] This was certainly the case as adult film made its transition to video. How and where such reinforcements materialized are recurring topics throughout *Smutty Little Movies*.

Chapter 1 examines the early history of adult video from a variety of technological, cultural, and industrial perspectives. I look at technologies and spaces well predating the development of the Sony Betamax in order to trace the tensions of public versus private interactions with pornography. I begin with the Panoram, a device invented in the 1940s and completely unintended for pornography—but ultimately the most important technology in the prehistory of adult video. I also examine the adult motel landscape of Southern California, the crucial role of public-domain films and piracy, and the overlooked pioneers who linked them together to form the roots of a new industry. Much as Donald Crafton points to the fallacy of the "dividing line" with early film technologies, adult video did not have a clear "before and after" moment.[139] Instead, the process was one of slow change, treated suspiciously by many in the industry and taken up as a distribution and production option by only a handful of people willing to take the risk. Finally, I examine how, from the very beginning, the industry itself emphasized quality, in both marketing and production practices, as part of an overall strategy to alleviate anxieties around the new technology and thus build audiences and profits.

Chapter 2 explores the creation in 1983 of *Adult Video News* (*AVN*), a newsletter initially aimed at the public but gradually transformed into an industry trade journal in the vein of *Variety* or *Hollywood Reporter*. In its attempts to provide a more sophisticated, nuanced, and professional set of discourses for adult video, *AVN* represents a major turning point in this history, focusing on the industry *as* an industry rather than merely as content made by unseen, hidden forces. Additionally, *AVN* repeatedly emphasized and encouraged the creation of quality material as a strategy to gain the respectability that would lead to greater acceptability and profits, a stance it also replicated within its own pages and editorial practices. Ultimately, *AVN* crafted something new: a space in which to promote, sell, and celebrate adult video—but it also reified and re-created many of the troubling and controlling frameworks that externally regulated the industry.

Chapter 3 contrasts a pair of case studies involving challenges faced by the women whose performances helped build the adult video industry, and explores particularly the significance of the means of production and control. First, I explore the creation of Vivid Video in 1984, a company that signed performer Ginger Lynn to an exclusive contract. Along with Penny Antine, who wrote all of her Vivid titles, Lynn created a character unabashedly interested in the pursuit of pleasure without the justifications and excuses typically accompanying such behavior. Concomitantly, owners Steven Hirsch and David James turned Vivid into the first shot-on-video company to recognize the potential of the new format, using Lynn as the centerpiece of a new, more aggressive marketing strategy that sought widespread public acceptance. This strategy was, in no small part, based on their efforts to attract women and couples to their titles. Yet Lynn, however popular and important to Vivid's growth, did not hold an ownership stake in Vivid and thus represents the limitations of performance success.

Second, I take up the history and importance of Candida Royalle, both in her literal participation as a performer and producer and in the discourses she crafted on the larger topics of feminist politics within pornography. Royalle, a performer in the Golden Age, founded Femme Productions in 1984 with the goal of creating adult films for women, which she did as writer, director, producer, and owner. While similar to Vivid in terms of her desire for economic success with particular demographics, Royalle's overt politics, feminist strategies, marketing discourses, and narrative and visual content set Femme in radically different territory. Here, I step back and examine in detail Royalle's early career as a performer, an analysis not previously undertaken by historians. I do so in order to connect her own past in the industry with the significant changes she would bring later with Femme, changes that would center on disrupting the preoccupation with male pleasure so central to adult film. Accounting for the ways in which

Royalle and Femme created, implemented, and stridently championed a set of feminist practices, I propose that Femme was, ultimately, not so different (either industrially or ideologically) from other adult film companies of the time—even if the company's goals were necessary and groundbreaking.

Chapter 4 swings the emphasis to more traditional forms of regulation, focusing on local protests, antipornography feminist movements, national efforts by conservative groups, and other attempts to contain the efforts of the adult video industry to find widespread public acceptance and economic success. I argue that a panic, traceable to the move of sexually explicit films from public to private spaces, resulted in a major shift in the cultural understanding of sexuality, pleasure, and pornography. This period of intense change, during which the adult film industry was simultaneously growing its video business and facing significant opposition, can be seen as a critical one in film and technology history. The private user was on the cusp of widespread access to a large variety of sexually explicit material just as a battle was being waged over community standards and pornography. An analysis of the video rental industry's response to the presence of pornography in its stores—and the ultimate crackdown and elimination of that material—illustrates the ways in which this increasing accessibility was finally contained. These regulatory efforts helped define the period (and pornography going forward) in terms of guilt, shame, and fear, rather than liberatory potential or even simple pleasure. "Something more" was further solidified as a baseline for acceptability, not just legally, but also within the cultural imagination.

I conclude Smutty Little Movies by tracking legal efforts of many kinds to limit, contain, and control sexually explicit material in the early 1980s as adult video's popularity began to soar. Exploring court cases, Supreme Court decisions, obscenity prosecutions, zoning laws, federal efforts, and political discourses of the period, I conclude with an examination of the Meese Commission's investigation in 1986—which, not coincidentally, aligns with the period in which the adult film industry completed the transition from celluloid to magnetic tape–based production and distribution. Claiming that the Meese Commission's actions were one of the most critical moments in the history of sexually explicit material, I show that these legal efforts were, in fact, more about attempts to bolster and maintain heteronormative, regressive understandings of respectability and to disassociate pornography from quality. "Something more," in the end, ruled the day. The book ends with an analysis of a force even stronger than the law when it came to containing pornography. Capitalism, in the form of the corporate profits sought by the chain rental store owners who dropped adult titles in the name of "family values," meant the end of this early era of adult video.

This period of transition was about more than technological, industrial, or regulatory change—it was about the intersections of these elements, made visible in larger anxieties and tensions. *Smutty Little Movies* is not a redemption story, much as, at times, I fill out the historical record with the stories of people, companies, events, and strategies that have often been left unexamined. Nor is it a political response to the antipornography discourses that frequently continue to try to dictate how the topic should be studied. Instead, it's simply an effort to examine the immense position that adult video holds in film history and in culture more generally, and to decipher the ways in which adult video both contributed to and participated in essentializing discourses related to quality, respectability, sexuality, and pleasure.[140] Unlike O'Toole, whose epigraph leads off this introduction, I don't believe the "full" history of pornography can ever be committed to paper—but I do agree that adult video must be recognized as deeply historically significant. This is the story of that significance.

1 Panorams, Motels, and Pirates

The Origins of Adult Video

The whole videocassette business was basically founded by pirates and pornographers.

David F. Friedman, quoted in David Chute, "Wages of Sin, II,"
Film Comment (1986)

The point of a porno film is to turn you on, and a theater isn't the best place for that. The ideal context is the home.

Al Goldstein, quoted in Tony Schwartz, "The TV Pornography Boom,"
New York Times (1981)

Historians often point to December 7, 1977, as the moment when the home video rental industry was born.[1] That day, in the *Los Angeles Times,* local entrepreneur George Atkinson placed an advertisement that might have seemed innocuous but would eventually shake the entertainment landscape. "VIDEO CASSETTE RENTALS," the copy read, in bold all-capital letters (figure 6). "Betamax ½" or ¾" formats. Full Length, Color-Sound Features. Low Rental Cost! Call or write for free catalog."[2] Atkinson's action was groundbreaking in that he sensed a significant business opportunity to rent rather than sell videotapes to the home market; before that moment, no one else had made the leap.[3] Atkinson thus invented the home video rental store, and, in less than two years, he grew that simple idea into forty-two affiliated locations, all with the straightforward and simple "Video Cassette Rentals" name on their doors. They rented the handful of then-available tapes for an exorbitant $10 per day (plus either a $50 annual or $100 lifetime membership).[4] In September 1979, he changed the name to Video Station and initiated a full-blown franchising strategy, eventually presiding over an empire of more than six hundred affiliated stores.[5] When he died, on March 3, 2005, his lengthy obituary appeared nationwide, calling him a "pioneer in the movie video rental industry" and crediting him with creating an industry that, by that point, reached well beyond his own affiliates,

Figure 6. George Atkinson's simple—but monumentally important—advertisement for video rentals. *Los Angeles Times,* December 7, 1977, 8.

climbing past twenty-four thousand total video stores, 2.6 billion movie rentals per year, and $8 billion in annual revenue.[6]

The Atkinson mythology paints a tidy teleological portrait emphasizing particular paradigms: a small-business owner with a creative, risky, and groundbreaking idea creates a new venture that explodes into popular and widespread success, eventually resulting in an industry that lives on far beyond the original concept. Atkinson's story, now cemented in a home video history that claims him as the "father" of video rental, reveals something beyond the impulse, however, to implant capitalist mythologies into stories of new technologies; it also reveals the cultural (and historiographic) desire to erase pornography from the origins of home video. No novice, Atkinson was already very familiar with both video and the *Los Angeles Times* advertising department, for it was there, starting in June 1975, that he advertised pornography on cassettes for rent to customers in Los Angeles. Thus he was an active part of an underground and questionably legal economy that laid the foundation for the transition of the adult film industry from celluloid to home video.

While it is historically accurate to say that adult video became available in late 1977 and that shot-on-video titles were produced as early as 1979, such definitions are appropriate only within a capitalist paradigm in which an "official" and, indeed, legal marketplace determines the historical borders of a technology and accompanying economy. Here I shift that definition to confront a group of overlooked historical realities: pornography was available on a variety of cassette formats prior to 1977; adult films were a critical part of the formation of the home video rental industry; and, finally, many of the same people (such as Atkinson) who have been credited with building the mainstream home video industry were also veterans of the pornography trade. Ultimately, the history of home video is the history of adult video.

My focus in this chapter is the pre- and early history of adult video, during which the majority of the industry was still producing content on celluloid. The public space of the adult movie theater still dominated the mid-1970s, and theater owners were still seeing healthy profits at the end of the decade. In 1978, the Adult Film Association of America reported that 780 theaters played adult films to 2.5 million weekly attendees, bringing in $450 million in ticket sales.[7] The adult film business model in the 1970s mirrored that of mainstream Hollywood: production on celluloid and exhibition in large rooms on large screens in front of audiences admitted after buying tickets. Video decimated that model. The industry harnessed the technological capability of home video to alter its production, distribution, and exhibition practices and strategies in order to circumvent various regulatory efforts; ironically, the ways in which it did so reinforced and reproduced many of those same efforts even as it claimed to be upending them. Furthermore, as will become clear, technological steps forward were met with equal regulatory responses, always seeking to contain pleasure. This chapter traces the early history of the industry's change, the slow period in which only a handful of people were willing to gamble (often illegally or on the margins of legality) on the new medium, and the gradual industrial turn toward recognizing video's massive economic potential. Indeed, the move toward privacy was far less cultural than capitalist; while the industry certainly recognized the political power of taking its products away from public spaces, it was primarily interested in the economic boost that move could deliver. As is common in this history, the process started with a machine that initially had nothing to do with pornography.

PRIVACY IN PUBLIC: THE ROOTS OF ADULT VIDEO

On February 21, 1940, the Mills Novelty Company of Chicago, the nation's largest manufacturer of slot machines, signed a deal with the Globe Production Company to form Soundies Distribution Corporation.[8] Globe, founded in 1939 by James Roosevelt (eldest son of President Franklin Roosevelt), would produce three-minute short musical films for a new machine, called the Panoram and manufactured by Mills, which would be leased to bars, cafés, and drugstores.[9] The *New York Times* described the equipment: "The machine resembles a phonograph on a slot-machine principle, but it has in the front a screen on which the pictures will be projected."[10] Eight or nine 16mm films, printed in reverse for rear projection, were fitted onto a large reel and played continuously. Viewers had no choice in their selection, either watching the film the loop happened to be playing or waiting until their desired number came back around. "Soundies" were an overt attempt to supplant the highly profitable jukebox industry by upgrading its technology and including moving images along with music. The Panoram was hardly the only such machine on the market, but it was by far the most capitalized, publicized, and ready for mass production, and it quickly went out across the country, filling up various locales with short musical numbers by artists such as Spike Jones, Jimmy Dorsey, Louis Jordan, and Nat King Cole.[11]

Even before it was officially unveiled on October 20, 1940, a bar owner in Hollywood, California, used a Panoram during an test exhibition to show adult material, proving Joseph Slade's assertion that "whenever one person invents a technology, another person will invent a sexual use for it."[12] A reporter invited to the exhibition, which took place in April 1940, described one film as a "strip tease number" and noted that it would be "unlikely that [it] would be given the Hays propriety seal."[13] Globe, the only producer of Soundies at the time, would not have made the film, so it is clear that the unnamed proprietor understood immediately that locally procured adult material had tremendous revenue potential. The problem was privacy: the Panoram, essentially a large television-like device, was available for anyone and everyone in the venue to see and enjoy rather than for the use of a single customer. The "strip tease number" was more like a public performance, with the screen supplanting the stage. While it was an example of mediated eroticism, it was hardly private.

That started to change by late 1943. George Ponser, a New Jersey–based regional distributor of novelty machines and Soundies, began selling conversion units in November that turned the Panoram into the "Solo-Vue," allowing only the person inserting a coin to see the film (but still letting everyone within range hear the music).[14] An advertisement by Ponser in *Billboard* graphically illustrates the capability of the Solo-Vue modification to bring a modicum of privacy to the otherwise public exhibition of erotic material on the Panoram; additionally, it underlines the gendered politics

Figure 7. George Ponser's Solo-Vue attachment to the Panoram: an early precursor to the privacy afforded later by home video. *Billboard,* November 27, 1943, 122.

surrounding sexual uses of the technology. In a drawing accompanying the copy, one man looks into the peephole now covering the Panoram screen while two other men stand by the machine (figure 7). One says, "Boy, that really must be something!" and the other laments, "Wish that guy would give me a chance."[15] The tease in the ad of "something," coupled with the presence of men only, strongly suggests that the material on the screen must be sexually suggestive.[16] Privacy, in the context of the advertisement, meant privacy for men to pursue sexual pleasure in an otherwise public space.

If Solo-Vue hinted at the Panoram's possibilities, the W.M. Nathanson company pushed the topic right out into the open. In January 1944, the company advertised its "Hollywood Peep Shows" conversion kit in *Billboard,* including a photograph of the finished product that illustrates its purpose.[17] "For Art Students Only" reads the sign above the screen, which is partially blocked on each side by photographs of women posing in lingerie, leaving a small space through which to view the film. Even more important, Nathanson offers an "ample supply of snappy films" to go with the kit, direct from "one of the largest companies in Hollywood." What Ponser and Nathanson were actually selling, however, was neither ground-breaking nor new: the risqué peep-show loop had been a staple of the penny arcade since the 1890s, when enterprising parlor owners realized there was a great deal of money to be made in marketing sexually suggestive content on their Kinetoscopes and Mutoscopes, even when the actual content showed little more than women removing a few clothes and no actual nudity, let alone sex.[18] Just like arcades at the turn of the century, converted Panorams offered films featuring women undressing and performing strip-teases or burlesque routines, certainly with more suggestive movements and less clothing than their predecessors did—but still no actual nudity. These modifications imply two otherwise silent conclusions: local Panoram operators surely had been modifying their own equipment prior to the introduction of mass-marketed conversions (thus suggesting a market), and there was plenty of adult material playing on the machines throughout the country to justify the need for such conversions.

Yet each advance toward making the public exhibition of erotic material more private brought with it a regulatory reaction rooted in the anxiety surrounding pleasure. The phenomenon of independently produced adult material on the Panoram had grown so large by April 1944 that the Soundies Distribution Corporation felt compelled to address it. General manager George Ulcigan, while outlining the company's postwar strategy, noted: "Nothing will help the industry more than top pictures and, inversely, nothing can harm more than films that are bad technically or make use of off-color material."[19] He also claimed that all independent pro-ducers would have to adhere to a contract in which they agreed to abide by two conditions. First, they would have to follow the Motion Picture Production Code, the moral guidelines overseeing Hollywood film produc-tion that the studios had instituted as a form of self-regulation to avoid government interference.[20] Second, the producers would be required to gain approval from the local censorship boards then determining which films were suitable for public consumption. Both were hollow threats, given the independent production and distribution already occurring well outside the reach of official regulatory structures. Indeed, Soundies' anxiety and efforts to control the content proved meaningless. By 1946, the B&B Novelty Company was blatantly advertising burlesque films for the Panoram in the pages of *Billboard*, another sign that the underground economy in such adult material was growing.[21] What wasn't booming, however, was the Soundies Distribution Corporation itself: beset from the beginning by financial difficulties, the production of Soundies ended in late 1946, and the company stopped servicing the Panoram machines in 1947. But the machines had a robust, unplanned afterlife: by the early 1950s, the Panoram had become an adult film exhibition device.[22]

That afterlife wasn't limited to content. In the early 1950s, an entrepreneur in Chicago hung curtains between peep-show machines, thus creating a further measure of privacy (and space for masturbation) that was surely replicated elsewhere.[23] Increased regulatory response to the changes was predictable and swift throughout the country. In 1950, police raided an arcade on Market Street in San Francisco, charging four people with "operating indecent peepshows." The police report stated that the films played on "a rebuilt type of the machine that Jimmy Roosevelt built," labeled "for art students only" and "no minors allowed." Reporters investigated and found 105 Panorams at five locations in San Francisco playing color films for a quarter; black-and-white films were a dime. Descriptions detail women performing various activities, all in a "complete state of undress." In some of these films, women perform stripteases, pose, undress, and brush their hair; in others, they "fish, practice archery, retire, get up, attend boarding school, roll dice, and take long walks."[24] The relatively tame, partially undressed routines of the past had given way to complete nudity, and there would be no going back.[25]

The San Francisco raids were only the beginning. In 1952, Washington, D.C., police busted fourteen arcades; one employee was eventually found guilty of possessing indecent films with the intent to exhibit them.[26] Two years later, Seattle police arrested an operator for exhibiting indecent films on fifteen Panorams in his arcade.[27] In an underground economy not anxious for publicity, these police actions illuminate what was, by the 1950s, clearly a widespread and profitable industry based on a machine that had been completely repurposed. In the late 1950s, for example, Kirdy Stevens, who would later direct the monumentally successful theatrical feature *Taboo* (1980), opened a Panoram arcade on Main Street in Los Angeles and began showing his self-produced color nudie films.[28] Other Southern California producers included William H. Door, Joe Bonica, Vanity Films, and Standard Pictures Corporation, all of whom distributed to both the arcade and home markets. W. Merle Connell's Quality Studios even advertised films for the "peep or panorama."[29] With hardcore sex still relegated strictly to underground stag films, the public exhibition of adult material was, by the late 1950s, still very much about the display of female nudity rather than any type of sexual behavior, which was off-limits in the public space.[30]

Change was happening quickly, however, and most visibly in the theater rather than the arcade. In mainstream public exhibition, the influx of nudist films such as *Garden of Eden* (1954, dir. Max Nosseck) had led to a great deal of public anxiety and tension surrounding the mediation of the female body. In 1957, the Court of Appeals of New York ruled, in *Excelsior v. Regents,* that nudity in and of itself (as shown in *Garden of Eden*) was not obscene.[31] Capitalizing on the ruling, Russ Meyer released *The Immoral Mr. Teas* in 1959, a groundbreaking film that, as Eric Schaefer points out, did not justify the presentation of nudity through narrative, thus ending the classic exploitation era.[32] More important, Meyer shifted the presentation of adult material from the space of the arcade to the space of the theater, which would eventually lead to the Golden Age just over a decade later.[33] But, I would argue, those particular changes in the proliferation, availability, tension, and legal action surrounding the presentation of female nudity onscreen must be regarded differently than the anxieties surrounding the Panorams of the 1940s and the rise of striptease, burlesque, and posing films across the bars, clubs, and pool halls of the United States. Those tensions, centering on the paradox of obtaining a measure of privacy within a public space, follow a different track than the model that would push for exhibition of pornography in a traditional theater setting, despite overlaps in production and distribution of content. It was the Panoram, not the theater, that most directly led to adult video. The modifications to the Panoram signaled the desire for the privacy that video would later bring, albeit with the challenge of enclosing the Panoram's screen within a public space.

The real turning point connecting the Panoram to adult video occurred in 1966, when New York jukebox distributor Martin Hodas stopped at a roadside gaming arcade south of Staten Island and watched a striptease film on a Panoram.[34] Hodas was already familiar with similar equipment, owning a few small machines that played cartoons or old Western movie clips, but he envisioned the combination of the Panoram and adult material on a grand scale throughout New York City. Hodas's idea was not unique; by the mid-1960s, machines playing similar content were already in operation in a group of arcades in Times Square as a minor novelty for tourists. The real challenge was to overcome the city's legal thickets, originally imposed in the 1950s, that prevented such machines and content from playing in the adult bookstores that populated 42nd Street.[35] Key to this expansion would be overcoming the hurdle of anxiety surrounding pleasure in public spaces; for Hodas, that meant constructing an efficient, sanctioned capitalist enterprise.

New York Mayor Robert F. Wagner Jr. and his administration had toler-
ated a limited number of the machines in Times Square but stringently
kept them out of adult bookstores by threatening the few attempts to place
them there with legal notices claiming a city license was required to exhibit
films.[36] After John Lindsay's 1965 election, the limitations continued—and
adult bookstore owners, wary of the costs and long odds, did not take the
city to court after constant rejections of their license applications. Hodas,
well aware of these difficulties, instructed his attorney, Charles Carreras, to
find a way through the legal morass and either obtain licenses or locate
loopholes. In mid-1967, Carreras broke through the bureaucratic wall, getting Hodas a letter from the chief of the Department of Licenses stating
that no city license was required to "install in the New York City area a
coin-operated machine that shows movies."[37] Hodas wasted no time, immediately buying the entire inventory of loop films and twelve Panorams
from the roadside arcade in New Jersey; afterward, however, most of the
city's adult bookstore owners initially rejected Hodas's offer of a fifty-fifty
split on all incoming revenues, with no lease payments, security deposits, or
maintenance fees.[38] Hyman Cohen, of Carpel Books at 254 West 42nd
Street, was the only exception, agreeing to take four of the machines and
try the films.[39] Once again, there would be no turning back after this initial
move forward. That would prove to be true in terms of content as well,
which quickly escalated from simple portrayals of nudity to explicit sex.

By late 1967, Hodas had placed his remaining machines at two more bookstores; ordered thirty similar models from Urban Industries, a manufacturer
in Louisville, Kentucky; opened an office on 42nd Street; and was depositing
$15,000 per day in quarters at a nearby Chemical Bank branch.[40] By summer
1969, there were more than four hundred machines in roughly fifty city locations, and that number surpassed one thousand in 1970—with Hodas in control of 350 of them, making him the single largest owner.[41] By that point, he
was no longer hiding his business interests. While most adult industry members had unlisted phone numbers, innocuous corporate names, and private,
hidden offices, Hodas listed his phone number, put his own name and primary corporate name (East Coast Cinematics) on the directory in the lobby
of his office building, and posted his other thirteen corporate business names
on his door.[42] He was confident enough to give a free-ranging interview to
the *New York Times* that described his entire operation, including the "photo
studio" at his office where customers could take photographs of models—a
brazen front for prostitution.[43] His photograph even accompanied the story.

Hodas eventually bought leases, opened his own bookstores, and went into
production on hardcore film loops such as *Flesh Party* and *Elevator Orgy*.

This decision stemmed from competition: by the early 1970s, approximately ten producer-distributors were in operation, mostly based in California and distributing loops across the country: Kiss, Pretty Girl, Color Climax, Stars of Sex, Collection, Playmate, Kama Sutra, Limited Edition, and Diamond Collection, along with Lasse Braun in Europe.[44] Many of these companies would later be early entrants into adult video, transferring these peep-show loops to videotape. While Hodas placed pornography into the public sphere on an unprecedented scale, others around the United States eventually joined him. Michael Thevis in Atlanta, Reuben Sturman in Ohio, Milton Luros and Robert DiBernardo in New York, and Harry Mohney in Michigan all built vast pornographic empires with similar operations and similar equipment— and also held similar ties to organized crime, with numerous prosecutions and convictions on various obscenity-related charges.[45]

For Hodas and the other pornography entrepreneurs, the problem with the peep show was still one of privacy. The next logical step was to build walls around the machines, enclosing them completely. This idea gave rise to the peep-show "booth," large enough for a person or two to have a small amount of privacy to view the film, played back on an 8mm or Super 8mm projector playing, like the Panoram, continuous loops.[46] Reuben Sturman created the peep-show booth in the late 1960s as part of his Automated Vending pornography empire, sensing correctly that customers wanted more privacy (primarily in order to masturbate) than the Panoram-style machine offered.[47]

There was also the matter of giving the consumer more choice in viewing options, a solution that video finally provided. In January 1981, Richard Basciano, owner of the infamous Show World adult entertainment complex in New York, took the advice of technician Roger Kirschner and installed a bank of VCRs to run video feeds into the booths throughout the building. The system offered the choice of ten videos, controlled by a numbered keypad in each booth. Concerned the new technology would be confusing to customers, Basciano filmed an "instruction video" to run in the booths, featuring well-known performers Desiree Cousteau and Lisa DeLeeuw.[48] As Eric Schlosser notes, the peep show "turned what had been a communal experience into something quite different—a stag film for an audience of one. And before long they were filled with middle-class American men privately seeking a few moments of pleasure."[49] The privacy of those moments, however, was (and continues to be) the source of much cultural and legal consternation.

This consternation hinged on a desire to discourage private pleasure by eliminating the booth's capability for unregulated activities—the very reason for its creation. In other words, even though sexual pleasure is typically considered a private act, its presence within an isolated space in a larger public area meant those pleasures were still, technically, occurring in public. The intense regulatory and policing efforts of the 1960s and 1970s regarding peep shows around the United States focused primarily on behavioral supervision. Lighting, occupancy, aisle width, and doors were all policed in order to monitor (and restrict) activity, and all these regulations point to an effort to discourage pleasure on the part of spectators, even as such pleasures played out on screens inside the booths.[50] As Amy Herzog notes, "Pornography's greatest threat to the social order . . . rests not in its representations, but in its public presence."[51] An increase in suspicion surrounding behavior inside the peep-show booth was accompanied by legal gains in the standing of the home as a protected site of private pleasure, as outlined in the introduction. Given the rulings in cases such as *Stanley v. Georgia* and *United States v. 12 200-ft. Reels of Super 8mm. Film* and the regulatory tensions surrounding peep-show booths, the industry needed to find a way to diminish its public presence, even as it continued to make its products publicly available.

The barrier preventing the move of adult film out of public spaces was technological. Even though many of the same films available in adult bookstore peep-show machines were also available for home use by those who owned their own projectors (often available in the same stores and through mail order), the average person who wanted an occasional private encounter with pornography did not necessarily want to purchase the equipment—let alone the films. That would require going into adult bookstores to purchase them or the magazines in which advertisements for mail order appeared. As adult films became increasingly explicit—and desirable to consumers—the peep-show booth had to become less vulnerable to legal scrutiny. For the industry to take the next step toward modern, efficient capitalist enterprise, the peep show had to be moved away from the adult bookstore, with all its accompanying regulatory oversight. It needed to move into a space more like the home.

A NEW SPACE FOR EXHIBITION: HOTEL VIDEO

Much as the Panoram served as a transitional technology tied to public space, adult video would begin in spaces that were not quite public and not quite private: hotels. Film exhibition in hotels and motels is a crucial link in home video history.[52] Not surprisingly, pornography once again lurked in the corners during the early years of the new practices, always threatening to encroach on "respectable" space. When it did, those involved reinforced rather than resisted the heavily gendered paradigms outlined in the introduction. Pleasure, and particularly female pleasure, represented a threat even within the industrial paradigm that grew to serve it—and, as always, it brought predictable regulatory responses. Eventually, even the adult motels (distinctive from hotels) that unabashedly showed pornography participated in a matrix of regulatory strategies aiming to contain women's pleasure, even as they offered new exhibition spaces. Such regulation was, as I will show, centered on the fear of prostitution; after all, the gender-skewed history of adult film exhibition on the Panoram, at peep shows, and in stag films hardly changed once the films were showed in motels. What was different was the *possibility* of privacy, and of reduced monitoring of what, exactly, was occurring behind the motels' closed doors. It is these motels that serve as the critical link between the peep-show booth and home video, particularly for the ways in which they conceived and sold temporary privacy as a space for sexual pleasure.

Exhibition in hotels began in 1955 when the Sheraton hotel chain agreed to play a number of University of Notre Dame football games in certain locations on closed-circuit television systems, thus bypassing National Collegiate Athletic Association restrictions on televising college football games.[53] In mid-1956, the Hotel TV Broadcasting Corporation announced plans to offer closed-circuit service to two New York hotels featuring in-room programs for tourists, including movie trailers, sports news, dining suggestions, and other entertainment options.[54] Tension between the closed-circuit and television and film industries (always leery of ceding control of their content) prevented a larger move of expanded Hollywood content to hotels over the next decade, and the technology was limited to industrial use.[55]

In June 1971, Computer Cinema, founded by Paul Von Schreiber and Paul Klein (former head of audience research at NBC), quietly began testing a pay-per-view closed-circuit system at the Gateway Downtowner Motor Inn in Newark, New Jersey. Trying out the Ampex 7500 one-inch system, the Sony U-Matic, a Panasonic half-inch player, and the CBS/EVR, the operation employed the machines "at a central point feeding motion pictures to each room through the hotel's master antenna hookup on a midband channel (between 6 and 7) through a converter on top of the individual TV sets."[56] The initial films included *Patton* (1970), *Barbarella* (1968), and *The Dirty Dozen* (1967), at $2.50 per viewing. Other chains, including Holiday Inn, Howard Johnson, and Hilton expressed interest, and Computer Cinema escalated its test project into a pilot operation.[57]

While such activities might have alarmed Hollywood in the past, the results of these tests unveiled something of great importance that the studios had not expected: "A majority of the Computer Cinema viewers had not been to the movies (in a theater) the previous three months, and some reported that they hadn't gone to a film house in as long as five years."[58] It was immediately obvious that pay-per-view movies in hotels were reaching the "lost audience" that traditional exhibition strategies had been failing to capture, a discourse that would be seized upon by the industry.[59] Jack Valenti, president of the Motion Picture Association of America (MPAA), took notice and became a vocal proponent of the technology, noting that the average age of a pay-per-view purchaser was forty-two, while the average theatergoer was just over twenty years old.[60] Valenti was present, in fact, when Trans-World Productions, a subsidiary of Screen Gems (itself a subsidiary of Columbia Pictures), unveiled a rival operation at the Hyatt Regency in Atlanta in October 1971.[61] Trans-World had been in the closed-circuit hotel business since 1968, offering convention broadcasts and tourist information, and, like Computer Cinema, it saw the opportunity to move into distribution.[62] After the successful test at the Hyatt Regency, Trans-World installed the system in four other Atlanta hotels as well as in hotels in Las Vegas, Houston, and Toronto, and it scheduled installations in Honolulu, London, Los Angeles, Montreal, San Francisco, and Chicago, projecting that by the end of 1973 it would have systems in 160,000 rooms in 25 additional cities.[63] Hotel pay-per-view was an incredible success, opening up a vast new market for consumers who wanted to watch movies but not necessarily in the public space of the theater.

The same logic obviously applied on a much more significant scale with pornography. Given that hotel video technology was clearly capable of playing back any kind of content, it wasn't long before signs of anxiety seeped into the discourse. By the time Trans-World was ready to expand into various chains in Waikiki in late 1971, its spokesperson Garry Sherman had addressed the elephant in the room. Trans-World would not play X- or R-rated films, he told *Variety*, because children would be guests in the hotels.[64] By mid-1972, Computer Cinema, too, felt compelled to self-regulate its content. A *Los Angeles Times* article on the phenomenon concludes with a reassuring statement: "Right now, there is nothing to prevent the rawest X-rated films from being shown in thousands of hotel rooms except the 'Hotel's own taste and mine,' according to Computer Cinema's Paul Klein."[65] William Butters of Trans-World was equally adamant at the end of 1972: "Under no circumstances will X-rated movies be offered to subscribers," and the company's contracts with hotels prohibited adult movies.[66] Such vociferous statements reveal, if anything, the inevitability that pornography would eventually make its way onto any new technology. Sherman, Klein, and Butters could not stop the march of adult content into hotel rooms any more than Ulcigan could with the Panoram. It was a matter of when, not if, adult films appeared there.

Given the desire (indeed, the necessity) of the two companies to court the Hollywood studios for content, it made sense for both to avoid adult material, which, in addition to being seen as culturally "unsavory," was also an economic threat to mainstream films in the early 1970s. That threat became very real as early as 1973, when *The Devil in Miss Jones* ranked as the seventh-highest-grossing film of the year, right after the James Bond entry *Live & Let Die. Deep Throat* was the eleventh-highest grosser, just after *Deliverance.* Hollywood's response was to incorporate many of the same adult-oriented elements, push softcore into the mainstream (with films such as *Emmanuelle* in 1974), and use the ratings system to coopt audiences looking for something different, all as a means to regain economic control.[67] Despite these efforts, there was plenty of adult film on the market, and a growing and curious audience for it.

Thus, those in the hotel video industry who were contemplating adding adult material were not without significant options, a reality already well understood by video technology manufacturers. By mid-1970, more than fifteen companies were trying to get a home video system to market, including the CBS EVR, the PlayTape/Avco Cartrivision, the Sony U-Matic, and the RCA SelectaVision.[68] These manufacturers were hunting for content—and didn't exclude adult films. There were ample economic reasons for that inclusion; after all, feature-length adult films were gaining in popularity in theaters and making their producers and distributors considerable profits. Sherpix, for example, headed by Louis Sher, not only distributed groundbreaking adult films, but also played them in its Art Theatre Guild spaces—which totaled more than forty by the early 1970s.[69] Within two years, hardcore films migrated from peep shows and downtown theaters into what *Variety* called the "once-inaccessible class houses" throughout the outer boroughs of New York.[70]

Sherpix's films, distribution methods, and exhibition strategies broke new ground.[71] *Censorship in Denmark* (a.k.a. *Pornography in Denmark: A New Approach*) and *A History of the Blue Movie*, both from 1970 and directed by Alex de Renzy, were among the first nationally exhibited adult films with hardcore footage, and *Mona* (1970, prod. Bill Osco; dirs. Michael Benveniste and Howard Ziehm) was the first hardcore narrative film to play in wide theatrical release. It was also the first hardcore film to enter

Variety's Top 50 box office list.[72] Osco's Graffiti Production Corp. in Los Angeles (which made loops for peep-show booths and features distributed by Sherpix) expected to gross more than $2 million in 1970, a figure that surely caught the attention of early video distributors.[73] Addison Verrill, writing in *Variety* in December 1970, describes the contentious and rapidly changing landscape: "In books of cinema history yet to be written, 1970 is sure to emerge as the year of the hardcore porno explosion, a time when every screen-sex barrier crumbled before the onslaught of technically slick pornography of the type now on view in at least 10 U.S. cities."[74] While Verrill was specifically referring to theatrical distribution, his words were similarly prescient for video.

By early 1971, sexploitation, softcore, and hardcore filmmakers and distributors such as Sherpix, Lee Hessell of Cambist Films, Ava Leighton and Radley Metzger of Audobon Films, and Russ Meyer were deluged with offers to license their material for video.[75] While they all publicly played down the offers, noting that they were for royalties only, Eve Meyer had, in fact, already made an historic deal with Optronics Libraries in December 1970 for video rights to twenty of Russ Meyer's films.[76] Optronics founder Irving Stimmler had been acquiring lesser-known films, public-domain materials, old serials, cartoons, archives of television programs, and other material—ultimately building a library of more than six thousand films and assembling a board of directors that included David Frost, David Wolper, and *New York Times* drama critic Clive Barnes. A *Time* magazine article from August 1970 describes Optronics as also having a catalogue of "sex films."[77] A *Wall Street Journal* reporter noted after the Meyer deal that "much gamier fare than Mr. Meyer's films will be seen on the home screen when—or if—the cartridge TV revolution strikes," clearly foreshadowing the inundation of hardcore material that would flood the market only a few years later.[78]

Sherpix was next, brokering a deal with Cartrivision, the first of the new technologies to go to market. Debuting in June 1972 in Sears locations in Chicago, the ambitious system, a forerunner of the modern VCR, could record and play back television and offered an optional black-and-white camera for making home movies. The machine, however, was integrated with a television set and priced at an exorbitant $1,595. Cartrivision also made an early attempt at home video rental—and the company had no problem including pornography in its rental program. Cartridge Rental Systems, Inc., a joint venture between Cartrivision and Columbia Pictures, included ten adult titles in its initial two hundred rental offerings.[79] Seven of the ten were Sherpix titles, including *Censorship in Denmark, A History of the Blue Movie,* and *Mona.* Cartrivision recognized the potential of adult material on its player, with a company spokesperson calling the market for pornography on home video "gigantic" during an exhibition in late 1972.[80] However, the high price, recurring technological problems, and a mostly disinterested public doomed the company, and it had disappeared from the market by July 1973.[81] Nevertheless, the technological tide had turned. Home video was inevitable—and adult films on video would be, too.

It was during this period of home video's early growth that Sensory Devices, Inc., a subsidiary of Precision Sound Centers of Miami, Florida, finally broke the adult barrier in hotels. On February 29, 1972, the company placed its system into the Hotel Commodore in New York, offering mobile carts holding Zeiss-Ikon Panacolor magazine projectors capable of playing two-hour cartridges inserted into a combination projector-screen.[82] Alongside the twenty-five films on offer, including *Airport* (1970) and *A Man Called Horse* (1970), was the complete Russ Meyer catalogue.[83] By July, the softcore adult titles (which had expanded beyond Meyer's films) were by far the most requested. John R. Garside, the hotel's general manager, offered some slight reassurance to those anxious about the films, saying, "The type of X films that we have are not the porn-house-type movies. In other words, they're not these out-and-out skin flicks. They're more the type that would play in, say, legitimate Broadway theaters."[84] Garside's words were, of course, mostly hollow, and an attempt to separate the hotel from "pornography" by invoking Broadway's respectability and legitimacy. He was also attempting to regulate the potential for pleasure, if moving away incrementally from previous hardline stances that refused even to acknowledge its possibility. Meyer's films were hardly "legitimate" in the sense Garside suggested, even if they were not hardcore, and the other softcore offerings (such as *Fuego,* the 1969 Argentinian melodrama featuring Isabel Sarli and plenty of nudity and simulated sex) were grindhouse and drive-in staples. The Hotel Commodore knew what it had: a product not offered by its competitors, and accompanying privacy, even if Garside seemed reluctant to admit it.

The Hotel Commodore's decision was the beginning of the outrageously lucrative pay-per-view adult film industry in hotels. These early fits and starts led eventually to the creation of Spectradyne in the late 1970s, which blossomed (despite financial problems) in coming decades, along with its later rivals On Command and Lodgenet Enterprises. None of these companies had any problems offering adult material, even if they avoided openly acknowledging it as the core of their business. By 2000, adult films in hotels brought in close to $200 million per year and had a presence in at least

40 percent of the hotel rooms in North America, with significant ownership stakes held (often quietly) by massive corporations such as AT&T, Time Warner, General Motors, EchoStar, Liberty Media, Marriott, Hilton, and News Corporation.[85] In hindsight, the worst possible business decision Trans-World and Computer Cinema could have made was to avoid adult material. For the groundbreaking Hotel Commodore, however, adult films were only a temporary experiment: by February 1973, the hotel switched to the Trans-World system, without adult films, a move that had been planned for some time.[86]

This "official" history illustrates how Hollywood sensed a growing market for its products in a private setting that utilized video technologies, accompanied by growing tensions about content, but it also avoids uncovering the details of a different set of lodging spaces that might be even more historically important. The "respectable" hotel industry took a great deal of time to come to terms with pornography, terms that continue to include silence as a containment strategy. Back in Los Angeles, a group of cheap, inconspicuous adult motels used similar technologies to show hardcore adult films on video. These motels, and the service they provided, were the most important link between celluloid and videotape for the adult film industry.

ADULT MOTELS: HOME AWAY FROM HOME

In early 1971, a steel rooftop railing atop a hotel in Osaka, Japan, accidentally began transmitting the hotel's closed-circuit signal—sending adult content into nearby homes and prompting police to issue a polite warning to innkeepers to make sure such accidents were not repeated. Osaka was home to a phenomenon of an estimated 500 "avec" or "love" hotels, designed for sexual encounters on hourly rates, and as their featured attraction offering "pink films," a softcore genre unique to Japan.[87] *Time* magazine carried a story on the phenomenon in March, including details on how some of the hotels were offering cameras and video recorders for in-room use.[88] Among those who read the article was Don Leon, a lawyer representing a group of motel owners, who quickly seized on the idea as something that might work in Los Angeles.[89] He convinced the group to convert an AutoLodge at 930 West Olympic Boulevard, downtown near the convention center, into an "adult motel," complete with water beds, fur bedspreads, mirrored ceilings, and closed-circuit adult films played on Sony U-Matic machines (figure 8).[90] Much as pornography had moved with technology

Figure 8. The AutoLodge Motel, 930 West Olympic Boulevard, Los Angeles, circa 1970, home to the first closed-circuit adult video system in the United States. Author's collection.

toward privacy via converted Panorams, it now moved with U-Matic machines into motels, an ideal space given their already illicit connotations.

That illicit status was apparent in the initial advertisements for the converted AutoLodge, which appeared in the summer of 1972—and the owners made no effort to hide their intentions. "More than just a COMFORTABLE LODGING—It's a DELIGHTFULLY SENSUAL WAY to UNWIND—MIRRORED LUXURY surrounds you on your own WATER BED as you watch X-RATED FILMS on your own Private CLOSED CIRCUIT TV!" (figure 9).[91] Leon correctly sensed that the Japanese model solved the problems inherent to the tensions of public versus private pleasure by transferring the peep-show booth into a setting more akin to a temporary home. "Our basic concept," he told the *Wall Street Journal,* "was to create an adult-oriented entertainment center where people could find a different kind of atmosphere than anywhere else."[92] The notion of "atmosphere" would play a key role in owners' attempt to distance themselves from the product at the core of their business while simultaneously providing the potential for "something more" that offered at least a modicum of legal cover.

In the spring of 1973, the owners renamed the AutoLodge "the Experience," and by that point it had been joined by others with the same basic business model, including the Hollywoodland, the Charles, and the

Figure 9. An early advertisement for the AutoLodge, emphasizing the privacy provided by video technology. *Los Angeles Times,* August 20, 1972, CAL_44.

El Royale.[93] In fact, some motels had been advertising in earnest in the *Los Angeles Times* alongside adult movie theater listings as early as February 1973, beginning with the Western, in Van Nuys, and the Crest, in West Hollywood. The copy for their joint advertisement read: "Adult Movies in the privacy of your own room! In color on closed-circuit TV."[94] By summer the Starlite, the Aloha, the Kona, and the Encore had joined them, all with similar offerings. *Variety* ran a front-page story on the trend, briefly describing the Experience and noting that its parent company, Leisure Services Inc., had plans for six more locations and was also in the business of "production, distribution, and exhibition of theatrical films."[95] The *Los Angeles Times*, seeing the rapid growth of the market in its own ad pages, carried a lengthy examination in June, the first detailed report on the motels.[96] By that point, the total number of adult motels had reached eleven—and the predictable regulatory response was growing, too. Obscenity busts at the motels became a common event but had essentially no result, and they were certainly not effective in stopping the motels from operating. Leon noted that obscenity charges were typically reduced to "something like a $5 fine."[97]

Of much greater concern to authorities were questions of prostitution and, more generally, by-the-hour trysts. For owners, the obvious solution was to deflect that anxiety at any opportunity, even if only as a gesture. After all, among the primary purposes of the motels was the illicit pleasure of private sex, an often unspoken reality understood by everyone, especially those seeking transgressive pleasures and those seeking to contain them. Furthermore, as Nicola Simpson points out, the space itself was often the setting for what were called motel films just prior to this era: "This ultra-cheap film was usually produced by ordinary people and invariably featured a brief but explicit encounter in a nondescript room, often a small motel that presumably would not ask too many questions of its guests."[98] *Deep Throat*, the best-known (and most-played) adult film in both theaters and motels, was itself produced in part in just such a location.[99]

Leon's strategies hinged primarily on fixing a particular discourse that downplayed these illicit possibilities and associations in favor of something more respectable. He frequently referred to his average customers as "committed couples" and argued that the whole purpose of the enterprise was to provide a safe, discreet, and pleasurable environment for married, middle-class heterosexuals. In a 1975 interview, he went so far as to note that while a marriage certificate was not *required* for booking a room at the Experience, it was nevertheless *preferred*.[100] In nearly every article on the motels, owners and managers stressed repeatedly that they were friendly, clean, and safe environments aimed at middle-aged couples rather than people having affairs or seeking prostitutes.[101] Such discursive strategies, obviously intended to minimize police attention and negative cultural associations, also performed the task of assigning respectability to the motels by emphasizing elements other than pleasure.[102] By constructing a corporate structure with clear goals and desired customers, the motels attempted to shift away from the illicit connotations conveyed by their very reason for existence.

The task was necessary in part to make adult motels appear safe for female patrons: the crucial demographic—just as for theaters—that would ensure success. After all, the privacy afforded by the motel room was in stark contrast to the (often dangerous and unpredictable) public spaces of the peep booth or public theater. Female spectators who might be interested in adult material ran the risk of being mistaken for prostitutes by both other customers and police; there was also, simply put, the potential for unwelcome sexual advances or assaults by the primarily male customers in those spaces. It was crucial for adult motels to solve this problem, even if it meant rigidly regulating women's pleasures and behaviors.

This particular capability—the potential of a private space for women to watch adult films—is perhaps the key to understanding why adult motels historically served as the link between celluloid and home video, even if it is extremely difficult (if not impossible) to find specific evidence for women using adult motels as exhibition (and pleasure) spaces.[103] Nevertheless, that potential and opportunity are critical to understanding the historical trajectory of image pornography's move from theaters to the home. While the eventual complete privacy offered by home video certainly benefited men, that privacy also carried radical potential for a safe and discreet viewing space for women, away from various dangers and cultural judgments. Thus the adult motels were the first real change in the movement of adult material toward privacy, turning the peep booth into something resembling a temporary home and using early versions of the technology that would later revolutionize the adult film industry. Motel owners certainly were aware of the importance of these possibilities. Albert Antiquo, owner of three motels, noted as much in mid-1973: "Some of [our customers], particularly the women, are curious now about adult movies and books. They hear about it all the time, and they'd like to see the real thing, just to satisfy their curiosity—only they're afraid a neighbor or someone else they know would see them if they went to a theater and that would embarrass them. So they come here."[104] Antiquo's comments encapsulate complicated discursive layers: they reveal the economic motivation for the motels; but, however unintentionally, they also illustrate the community's need for just such spaces and protections. They also reveal the constant regulatory impulse to contain and limit pleasure always surging underneath the cultural surface, even by those most invested in the industry's practices.

Once again, the tensions circulating in the interstices between public and private pleasure come to the surface. If, as I have argued, pornography is often successfully contained by utilizing a particular level of public visibility rather than the invisibility of complete privacy, the adult motels existed in an odd, in-between space. Neither out in the open nor completely private, the adult motel was somehow both at once. Rather than thinking of these early adult motels as lodgings that happened to offer adult films, they might be better understood as simply bigger and more private peep-show booths, and thus as transitional spaces. Technology operates as the defining element in this paradigm: the adult motels primarily used Sony U-Matic players in their operations, the primary precursor to the Betamax player that would change the landscape, making them liminal technological spaces. Most important, by repeatedly stressing in interviews that their facilities were intended for middle-class married people, adult motel owners attempted to invoke capitalist and patriarchal ideologies in order to stave off the regulatory cultural impulses that had long sought to limit the sexual pleasures of both the lower classes and women in general—thus reinforcing the "natural order" that I discuss in the introduction. The cultural mythology surrounding such ideologies was simple to understand: if the patrons were middle class, one could assume they would be well educated and thus not susceptible to "inappropriate" sexual pleasures (or, at least in the imagination, arousal at all). Additionally, by being married, the women involved would be safely "respectable," which is to say not prostitutes or, even more important, actively seeking their own sexual pleasure. In addition to stressing that this was their desired clientele, many interviews featured married couples who managed the motel locations, emphasized that single women were not allowed to rent rooms, and, in the case of the Aloha (located in Long Beach), pointed out that the motel even offered a wedding chapel on its premises, with the owner-manager licensed to marry patrons.[105] Circulating underneath all these messages was an intense effort to regulate pleasure within the narrow confines of a respectability marked by patriarchal control. Women's pleasures, even within the "safe" space of the adult motel, were intensely contained and monitored.

The zenith of these respectability strategies came in 1980. Pete and Norma Marino, owners of the Riviera motel in San Clemente, gave an interview to the *Los Angeles Times* tellingly titled, "A Nice Place for a

Family Affair," in which they sell everything *but* sexual arousal and pleasure as components of the business and all but ignore the adult films playing in the rooms. The couple notes, in fact, that their adult daughter (who runs the front desk) gave them the initial idea to convert the operation into an adult motel in order to raise profits. The reporter's description spells out the ways in which such owners labor to disconnect pleasure from the type of capitalist enterprise that would provide the cultural (and legal) security of "something more":

> The Marino family looks about as much like sex motel operators as the Osmond family does. And that's what makes the Riviera so, well, unusual. There are no neon signs touting the X-rated movies shown on closed-circuit TV in the motel's 21 rooms. What little advertising the Riviera does is done discreetly and in small type in family-oriented publications. The typical Riviera patron is an over-40 couple celebrating an anniversary or birthday—not a swinging couple meeting for a secret tryst.[106]

These types of discourses, in which pleasure is downplayed as much as possible, assisted the motels as they reached for respectability. Yet that respectability was possible only if women's behaviors were rigorously monitored and contained, placed into a strict set of cultural ideologies in which the fantasy of the "family" was paramount—a fantasy dependent on patriarchal structures deemphasizing sexual pleasure. Thus, the privacy afforded by adult motels re-created the "home" and all the familial, patriarchal space in which pleasure was a side effect of procreation, and where women had a very specific role. That was what was happening on the surface, at least. In reality, the temporary privacy afforded by the motels' closed doors meant all kinds of pleasures—including those depicted on their closed-circuit television screens—could be had (mostly) without restriction.

The judicial climate surrounding the era in which the adult motels sprouted lends particular resonance to the marketing strategies that positioned such locations as being like "home." After all, despite the advertising campaigns, adult motels were actually *not* like home—they were places for illicit sexual fantasies and pleasures, not least of which was watching the pornography that some might not want to consume at home or in public. The manufacture of this fantasy—this is the home you *wish* you had, and here you can temporarily (and safely) have it—also carried with it the possibility of legal protection. The landmark Supreme Court decision in *Miller v. California* in 1973 rocked the adult entertainment landscape just as adult motels were beginning to thrive. Repeating that obscenity was not protected by the First Amendment and offering a test for its determination, the decision's most important aspect was its basing of that test on community, rather than national, standards.[107] Crucially, *Miller* continued the trend of focusing the judicial lens on *public* regulation of obscenity, rather than expanding regulation into the private spaces of the home. Such emphasis did not escape adult motel owners seeking protection from the types of prosecutions that were facing others in the adult industry. In fact, Leon, drawing on his experience in representing adult film producers and distributors, claimed "there'd be a pretty good legal case for showing films at the motels, since a room legally becomes your home for the duration of your stay."[108] What Leon and other motel owners were arguing for, in effect, was to remove the focus on the content and place it back on the space: as the court had already ruled in 1969's *Stanley v. Georgia*, adults had a right to privacy—even to obscenity—as long as it remained in the home.[109] Temporary or not, the privacy afforded by the motels was the same as the privacy of patrons' actual homes, at least according to Leon.

Privacy for what, exactly, remains a question for historians. What was the content in the adult motels? Who were the suppliers, and who performed in the films? What supply chain brought adult film into the motels? Reassembling this picture reveals an underground economy existing on questionably legal margins. The motels played a combination of stag films and loops, cheaply produced shorts, pirated copies of films then in general release in adult theaters, and, possibly, locally produced material made for the motels—all highly similar to the cheap "homemade videotapes" seen by Joseph Slade in the theaters in Times Square, described in the introduction to this book. A *Los Angeles Times* reporter described the offerings in 1975: "Some are bootlegged versions of today's porn classics such as *Deep Throat* (1972) and *Memories within Miss Aggie* (1974). Some are old, timeworn stag flicks. All are edited, not for taste, but because they must fit on a one-hour video cassette."[110] Offerings at other motels were similarly eclectic. For example, the President Motel in Atlantic City, in late 1973, in addition to *Deep Throat*, offered six films: *Mother, Brother, and I* (1973), *Pledge Sister* (1973), *Diary of a Bed* (1972), *Teenage Love Goddess* (date unknown), *Mona Gets Her Gun* (date unknown), and *Wet, Wild, and Weird* (date unknown). The first three, "one-day wonders" produced quickly and cheaply, were all playing in low-rent theaters in Los Angeles at the same time that the motels showed them, while the latter three were probably quickie productions released first on 8mm or 16mm for the home/stag market and then transferred to videotape for sale to adult motel owners.[111] *Deep Throat*, a cultural phenomenon, was used by many adult motels as a draw.

Given the underground distribution landscape, motel owners were reluctant to talk about their supply chains. Leon, for example, told a reporter: "I don't even know what kind of films they have. We show whatever the market is. I don't know who supplies the market." Yet as a "knowledgeable source" explained to the same reporter, "the films are pirated copies of regular porn movies and are sold on the streets."[112] Leon's supposed ignorance was hardly plausible; after all, he was well versed in the sex film business. As he readily told the press, he had represented adult film industry members in his position as an attorney, but what he did not openly admit was his role as sexploitation film producer and distributor (through his own outfit, Leon Film Enterprises) of such titles as *The Outrageous Mechanical Love Machine* (1971), *Naked under Satin* (1970), and *The Very Friendly Neighbors* (1969).[113] He had also served as chairman and CEO of the International Film Organization along with exploitation film veteran Mike Ripps, the company's president, releasing Albert Zugsmith's late-career sexploitation films *Two Roses and a Golden Rod* (1969, dir. Zugsmith) and *Fanny Hill* (1964, dirs. Zugsmith and Russ Meyer).[114] Furthermore, he had taught a semester-long course at UCLA in 1967 called "Packaging and Legal Aspects of Theatrical and TV Films," probably stemming from his work in that area for veteran exploitation filmmaker Sidney Pink as vice president of Westside International Productions in the mid-1960s.[115] For Leon to claim, as he did to a reporter in 1977, "I have no idea where the films come from," was laughable.[116]

PIRATES AND COPYRIGHTS

Clearly, an underground economy thrived in Los Angeles, circulating the stag films and quickie productions that were a fixture in adult bookstores and the back pages of magazines, and also pirating the films playing in adult theaters.[117] This widespread, organized, and efficient bootlegging system shipped pirated prints (of both mainstream and adult films) around North America and the rest of the world. In February 1975, in just one prominent example, New York police arrested Sol Winkler, who was in possession of more than five hundred master copies of film prints, many of them adult titles, which he was transferring to video for sale to closed-circuit-equipped motels around the United States.[118] Film piracy had plagued the motion picture industry since its inception, but the rise in postwar availability of 16mm projectors to the consumer market had led to a subsequent increase in interest in film collecting that blossomed in the 1960s and '70s.[119] Well before the adult video industry was professionalized, bootleggers and adult motel owners were transferring celluloid to video. With the renewed interest in copyright law in the early 1970s (beginning with the Sound Recording Amendment of 1971 and culminating in the Copyright Act in 1976), film studios and the MPAA, along with the FBI, began vigorously cracking down on pirates, eventually resulting in raids in 1974 and 1975 on collectors and dealers that recovered more than $2 million in films and $150 million in equipment. Additional raids in 1980 in eight U.S. cities led to 150 arrests and 60 convictions.[120] Adult motels represent an outgrowth of such technological capability, essentially creating an alternative exhibition space based on the availability of a commodity that was already on the margins of legality.

The question of whether adult films retained copyright protection in the first place was a legal gray area in the mid-1970s, when the motels began drawing attention. Los Angeles Police vice squad captain Jack Wilson acknowledged as much, saying that tapes in adult motels were "not always obtained legally" but added, "We really don't care if they are pirated or not, since whoever is suffering these thefts is not reporting them."[121] On a practical level, the "suffering" faced by the involved companies could garner no legal relief. As the *Miller* case decided, obscenity had no First Amendment protection—which most assumed also meant no copyright protection. Given that definitions of obscenity were in tremendous flux after *Miller* and were based in local rather than national standards, most adult film producers were wary of seeking legal protection for the continual bootlegging that plagued the industry.[122] For adult motel owners, the situation offered a unique, if hazy, sense of security.[123] They had some protection from copyright infringement even as they were under constant obscenity-related scrutiny.[124] In order to take the next steps toward capitalist legitimacy, the industry had to find ways to resolve the copyright question. After all, commodities must have value to be legitimate; copyright protects that value by acknowledging both its unique nature and its potential for a market. In 1979, the Fifth Circuit Court of Appeals finally recognized that whether an adult film was obscene was a separate issue from whether it had copyright protection, essentially granting that pornography was not only a creative expression, but also had value.[125]

There was another method available to adult motel owners looking to avoid piracy, particularly after the gray areas were cleared up: making their own content. In 1973, the owner of three locations admitted that he had started production on his own line of videotapes after a "well-known pornographer" who stayed at his motel suggested the idea. In partnership with other, unnamed people, the owner produced more than fifty original tapes by mid-1973 and had plans for fifty more. Describing some of the tapes as "sex instruction films," complete with clinical narration, the owner noted of his clientele: "Some of our older guests have a lot of hang-ups about sex. Watching these films, in the privacy of their own room, with a bed right there to practice on, can help them overcome their problems."[126] Such a strategy, however well meaning, was also designed to preempt judicial action by relying on "something more" than simple pleasure: given that laws required material to have "scientific value" in order to be free of obscenity, such clinical approaches were designed to withstand possible legal challenges. These videotapes, long-lost and forgotten, were some of the earliest commercial shot-on-video pornography in North America, and they illustrate the ways in which pleasure frequently must be justified in order to have value.[127]

The mechanics of this underground economy connecting bootleggers to adult motel owners to spectators links this history back to George Atkinson. In order to identify the final pieces of this puzzle, it is crucial to examine what exactly Atkinson was doing in Los Angeles (and who he was doing it with) before the moment at which he became the "father" of modern home video rental in 1977. It is with Atkinson that the concerns of public versus private exhibition coalesced into an industrial solution seized by the adult film industry that eventually converted the private pleasures afforded by videotape into a highly successful commercial enterprise.

GEORGE ATKINSON AND "THE PRIVACY OF YOUR OWN HOME"

Born to a British father and Russian mother in Shanghai in 1935, George Atkinson spent two years in a Japanese prison camp during World War II before moving to Canada and then to Los Angeles.[128] After a decade-long effort to make it as an actor (which progressed as far as bit parts on television shows such as *Mannix* and *Burke's Law*, along with extra work), Atkinson was, by 1975, living in the back of his storefront on Wilshire Boulevard in West Hollywood.[129] There he had been scraping together a living selling and renting various portable movie technologies since the late 1960s.[130] It was in roughly 1968 that he first encountered the Technicolor Instant Movie Projector, an ingenious, affordable device first released in 1962 and designed to play 8mm film on "Magi-Cartridges," which allowed users to simply drop in the film and press a single button rather than tinkering with reels and sprockets.[131] It was another feature that caught Atkinson's attention, however: the projector allowed viewers to play back the 4½-minute, 50-foot cartridges on a continuous loop. That capability, of course, mirrored the peep-show booth and its loop films. Atkinson clearly realized the potential to take the peep-show booth out of the adult bookstore and into more private spaces.

In James Lardner's two historical accounts of the birth of the home video industry, as well as Atkinson's own brief recollection, this discovery of the Technicolor projector led to a much differently phrased realization: older, public-domain films could be rented to the public for "parties."[132] Atkinson, as Lardner describes it, also "sold the idea as a form of free entertainment to Howard Johnson, Holiday Inns, and Shakey's Pizza, among other clients," which typically showed Laurel and Hardy and Charlie Chaplin films on continuous loops.[133] Atkinson also installed the Sony U-Matic in Los Angeles bars after its release in 1971, using closed-circuit channels to play classic boxing matches on video.[134] In Lardner's account, Atkinson was a hard-working, creative salesman, but there was no mention of pornography.

In these various activities, Atkinson participated in the economy of film distribution outside of conventional, mainstream exhibition sites, joining others in that small but thriving public-domain industry. Blackhawk Films, Thunderbird Films, Cinema Concepts, Reel Images, and MalJack Films were just a few of the early distributors of public-domain material, making steady income renting and selling film prints to collectors, school, churches, and museums.[135] MalJack, for example, headed by Waleed and Malik Ali, operated in the Midwest and very successfully cornered the public-domain market before turning to video distribution and production in the 1980s with MPI Home Video. Like Atkinson, MalJack supplied Shakey's Pizza locations with the Laurel and Hardy and Chaplin films that the company relied upon as part of its nostalgic image.[136] Public-domain film distribution was a gray area that frequently blurred into piracy. The most famous example was Tom Dunnahoo, owner of Thunderbird Films, who began his career as a bootlegger; federal marshals raided his operation in 1971 and charged him with selling an illegal print of *Beach Blanket Bingo* (1965). Eleven major Hollywood distributors subsequently sued him for copyright infringement, and he agreed to abide by a court order to stop selling pirated material. He turned instead to selling films that had fallen out of copyright, building a successful operation by the mid-1970s. Nevertheless, Dunnahoo, like other members of the underground film economy in the early 1970s, maintained his own lab to process duplicates from prints.[137] It is not surprising that Atkinson maintained links to such public-domain distributors during this period, given that they were the source of much of the available material his business depended upon—and of facilities that could, potentially, create the valuable copies.

Left out of the histories of Atkinson's activities is that his business was also built on pornography. Well before his December 7, 1977, advertisement in the *Los Angeles Times*, the moment at which he became the "father" of home video rental, Atkinson was renting adult films to consumers in Southern California on cassette and circulating within the same underground economy as the pirates, public-domain operators, bar owners, and adult motel managers who were also intertwined tightly with adult film distribution and exhibition practices. Indeed, trace evidence from this era points squarely to Atkinson as an integral part of the supply chain providing adult films to nontheatrical exhibition spaces in Los Angeles. The Technicolor projector and Magi-Cartridges, the films provided to motels, and the U-Matic machines in bars were the cornerstones of an adult film business. Before 1977, Atkinson called his company Home Theater Systems, and it was located in the same six-hundred-square-foot storefront that would later rent out the first Hollywood films on VHS and Betamax tape in the United States.

Home Theater Systems began advertising in the *Los Angeles Times* on June 8, 1975 (figure 10). The first ad, located on the "adult movies/entertainment" page alongside adult movie theater listings, made the company's product offerings perfectly clear, and also clarified what its choice of the word *party* actually meant:

> Revolutionary film cassettes are here! Now like never before enjoy adult entertainment in the privacy and comfort of your own home! With the simple push of a button, you can now have instant BIG SCREEN ENTERTAINMENT in your own LIVING ROOM. We RENT the entire show— Automatic Technicolor Projector, Large 5x5 ft. Screen, and a large variety of "X" Color Featurettes—all for a low price. Have an exciting Movie Party with your friends.[138]

The advertisement's emphasis on both privacy and a rental system reveals the ingeniousness of Atkinson's business model. By 1975, well before moving on to Hollywood films, he knew there was significant audience interest in watching pornography in the home, rather than in theaters, motels, or peep booths, and in renting, rather than purchasing, the material. Atkinson figured out how to sell temporary privacy directly to the home space. Whereas adult motel owners used their business model (private rooms with closed-circuit television systems available for short-term rental) to expand the peep-show booth, Atkinson went one step further, dropping that booth into the most private (and legally protected) space possible: the home. Like

Figure 10. Before George Atkinson created home video rental, he rented out adult films in Los Angeles. Home Theater Systems advertisement, *Los Angeles Times*, June 8, 1975, CAL_48.

the Panoram, the Technicolor projector could play anything—including pornography, a capability that Atkinson successfully utilized.

With only slight variations in the copy, graphics, and layout, Atkinson ran ads for Home Theater Systems in the *Los Angeles Times* in the adult entertainment section for the next eighteen months. By late summer 1975, Atkinson added a San Diego outlet—and was listing a price of $25 for a twenty-four-hour rental of "hundreds of films" from "Denmark, Hollywood, and France."[139] The San Diego outlet was gone within a month, replaced by a location in Orange County that would eventually be joined by a third in Santa Ana.[140] In June 1977, "Betamax tapes also available" was added to the standard copy, making Atkinson among the first people in the United States to offer adult films on the format.[141] The material on the tapes, while not specified, was probably identical to what Atkinson was offering on the Magi-Cartridges and what was being playing in area adult motels at the same time: loop and stag films and bootlegged versions of adult films then in general release.

The links between adult motel managers, bar owners, bootleggers, public-domain operators, and Atkinson are crucial for historians as they begin to unearth the transition of the adult film industry to videotape, as well as the prehistory of home video more generally. Atkinson was clearly an important figure in the Los Angeles adult economy. While the lines among the groups in that economy remain fuzzy, they nevertheless can be drawn: the adult motel owners obtained their films via a bootlegging underground frequently made up of the same people who were involved in the distribution of public-domain films; at the same moment, Atkinson was supplying public-domain films to area motels and restaurants. Furthermore, bars in Los Angeles—more of Atkinson's customers—were playing pirated adult films over closed-circuit channels during this period.[142] Following these traces reveals him to be at the epicenter of the pre–home video era of semiprivate pornography distribution in Los Angeles.

The most important detail in this history is the *location* where Atkinson took his primary practices. While adult motels extended the privacy of the peep-show booth to the larger space of the rental room, Atkinson took the next logical step into the full privacy of the home, laying out the business model that he would follow to tremendous success only a few years later. What happened to Home Theater Systems, why Atkinson changed the business name to Video Cassette Rentals, and what, exactly, he had access to on videotape triggered the onset of home video rental—and laid the foundation for a modern, efficient, and organized adult video industry.

ADULT FILMS ON VIDEO: THE BEGINNING

On July 1, 1977, *New York Times* publisher Arthur Sulzberger announced that his paper would begin to limit the size and content of adult film advertisements. Pornographic films, Sulzberger claimed, "are as much a blight in print as the displays for pornographic films are a blight on our city streets."[143] While not an outright ban, the guidelines limited content to the name of the film, the name and address of the theater, the hours of performance, and the label "adults only." On August 23, Otis Chandler, publisher of the *Los Angeles Times*, inspired by that decision, *did* institute an outright ban on adult entertainment advertising. Chandler's rigidly moralistic accompanying statement blasted the adult film industry, ignored legal precedent (such as the *Miller* decision), and fed directly into a growing cultural belief that there was something inherently "wrong" with pornography. "The truth is," writes Chandler, "we have been dealing with an indefensible product, one with absolutely no redeeming values, and this phenomenon shows no sign of leaving the contemporary social scene."[144] Marketing Director Vance Stickel, mindful of the $3 million in annual advertising revenue brought in from adult entertainment, disagreed strongly with Chandler's decision—but the publisher held firm. Eventually, a group of adult theater owners sued the newspaper for $44 million, claiming violations of their First Amendment rights and that the newspapers had conspired with Hollywood studios to put adult theaters out of business, but their claims were denied.[145] Chandler had successfully evicted pornography from his corner of the "contemporary social scene," an ideal example of private enterprise regulating pornography and pleasure.

The effect on the adult entertainment industry in Los Angeles should have been significant. After all, the decision immediately shut out adult motels, theaters, and Atkinson's Home Theater Systems from their primary advertising space. The final Home Theater Systems advertisement ran on August 17, 1977, less than a week before Chandler's decision.[146] What Chandler could not have predicted, however, was that the technology that would eventually change the industry was already lurking in the pages of *Los Angeles Times*. Just as Atkinson himself had advertised the availability of adult Betamax tapes in June 1977, others, too, were using the newspaper to market adult video. On January 20, 1977, an audio-video store in Los Angeles named Video Visions had advertised "adult video tapes for your Betamax," and, by May 15, classified advertisements for adult tapes priced at $69 began running regularly in the video section.[147]

However, Chandler's decision left Atkinson scrambling for something new. In the interval between the final Home Theater Systems advertisement on August 17 and the first Video Cassette Rentals advertisement on December 7, Atkinson learned about Andre Blay's Magnetic Video, which had licensed fifty titles from 20th Century Fox, offering them for sale (not rent) to consumers in what was the first step toward a home video industry.[148] While gearing up for mass production of the tapes, to be distributed as part of the Video Club of America, Blay advertised the venture in the pages of *TV Guide* in late November 1977.[149] Among what was estimated to be two hundred thousand U.S. home video player owners, nine thousand people joined the Video Club of America, and many, many more learned about it.[150] One was Atkinson—who had a very different idea in mind than simply becoming a private collector.

With a $3,000 investment from a high school classmate, and working with a local retailer willing to make the purchase (as it was under the $8,000 wholesale minimum), Atkinson purchased two copies of each tape—one on Betamax and one on VHS.[151] He put them on his store shelves, ran the December 7 advertisement in the *Los Angeles Times*, and put into motion what would become the home video rental industry.[152] While no clear evidence exists, I would unhesitatingly argue that there were actually more than one hundred tapes in that first video rental store. Given Atkinson's history as a participant in the underground adult film economy in Los Angeles, his prior marketing of adult films on the Betamax format, and his knowledge of the market for adult material, it is very safe to assume that his early inventory also included pornography.[153] It may be impossible to determine exactly what made up that inventory, but reconstructing a clear picture of the content available on VHS and Betamax does not require speculation.

This early period, between 1976 and 1980, was a wild and somewhat disorganized era, made up initially of distributors searching for available catalogue titles to sell, not rent, on video—an important distinction that defines the early years of home video in general.[154] The process started with Joel Jacobson, an agent with the William Morris Agency who had operated Cinema Concepts with his wife as a side business out of their home in Connecticut since the 1960s. It was a small operation specializing in public-domain art film distribution to churches and schools. As home video began expanding, Jacobson added U-Matic and Betamax tapes to his inventory, and then, in 1976, realized there was a market for legitimately distributed adult material. In July 1976, Jacobson licensed exclusive video rights from Russ Meyer for five of his films: *Vixen!* (1968), *Cherry, Harry, & Racquel!* (1970), *Faster, Pussycat! Kill! Kill!* (1965), *Finders Keepers, Lovers Weepers!* (1968), and *The Immoral Mr. Teas* (1959). Jacobson gave Meyer a $5,000 advance and 50 percent of the revenue for the deal.[155] Jacobson later added two films (with nonexclusive rights) from Radley Metzger, *The Lickerish Quartet* (1970) and *The Libertine* (1968, dir. Pasquale Festa Campanile), along with a French import, *Her and She and Him* (1970, dir. Max Pécas).[156] He started a new company, Home Cinema Service, to sell the films via mail order on U-Matic and Betamax tapes and began advertising in *Videography* magazine in October 1976.[157] Given Jacobson's sole position in the market, he priced the tapes at a staggering $300 (but quickly dropped prices to $229, then $129, then $89.95, and finally settled at $59.95).[158] A graduate school roommate of Jacobson's passed the story to a friend at *Playboy*, which published a short item on the company in December 1976.[159] The first widespread public advertisement for adult video occurred when Cinema Concepts (in a partnership with distributor Valentine Productions) ran an advertisement in *Oui* magazine in July 1977.[160]

Mark Slade, founder of Entertainment Video Releasing (EVR), was another pioneer. In October 1975, the former fashion photographer placed an ad in the *New York Times* seeking capital: "Investors sought for 500 motion pictures to be transferred to video disc for sale to the new upcoming mass consumer market."[161] Though there is very little extant information on Slade, it seems clear that he was another of the public-domain operators, amassing a huge variety of non-Hollywood material for this venture.[162] He was also one of the earliest distributors of adult video: beginning in March 1977, EVR began offering several dozen exclusively licensed hardcore films on U-Matic and Betamax formats, including *Sometime Sweet Susan* (1975, dir. Fred Donaldson) and *Teenage Cowgirls* (1973, dir. Ted Denver).[163] A year later, Slade spun off that portion of EVR into National Video Marketing, as well as the International Video Movie Club, to distribute adult material as part of the "Movies at Midnight" series, which by then included *Memories within Miss Aggie* (1974) and *Portrait* (1974), both directed by Gerard Damiano.[164]

Other companies also entered the market around this time. In March 1977, Magnetic Communications of Oklahoma City sent flyers to three thousand industrial video equipment dealers, advertising twenty adult videos—which it began offering to the general public in June.[165] Astronics Tele-Cine debuted in late 1977, with U-Matic, Betamax, and VHS offerings, eventually including Alex de Renzy titles such as *Babyface* (1977) and *Pretty Peaches* (1978), and advertising in *Penthouse* and *Billboard* magazine.[166] Adult film producer and director Beau Buchanan started the International Home Video Club in spring 1978, aggressively taking out full-page advertisements in *Variety* and *Hustler* magazine to market a collection of adult titles, which included his own 1977 film *Captain Lust* and selections from the Mitchell Brothers such as *Behind the Green Door* (1972). He also offered mainstream material.[167] Buchanan, echoing Atkinson's Home Cinema Services strategy, trumpeted the potential of his products in advertisements: "X-Rated and other exciting movies in the privacy of your own home! Watch what you want when you want to watch it!"[168] The Mitchell Brothers, in addition to licensing their vast (and highly profitable) catalogue to others, formed their Film Group in mid-1978 to distribute their tapes, advertising widely in such places as *Penthouse* and *Home Video* magazines.[169] They even opened a video store at their famed O'Farrell Theater in San Francisco and began taping live sex shows in the Ultra Room, their live-performance space. Resulting titles included *Never a Tender Moment* (1979) and *Beyond De Sade* (1979), both featuring Marilyn Chambers, as well as *Honeysuckle Divine, Live!* (1979), featuring the titular performer and her notorious stage act, in which she inserted objects into and ejected them from her vagina.[170] Freeway Video Enterprises, a spinoff of Freeway Films, founded in the 1960s by Armand Atamian, Lee Frost, and Bob Cresse, began marketing its well-known Golden Age productions, starring John Holmes and directed by Bob Chinn (known as the "Johnny Wadd" series), in early 1979.[171]

Many small distributors entered the scene in the late 1970s, and nearly all disappeared just as quickly as they had arrived. Between 1978 and 1979, for example, *Videography* magazine ran advertisements for Diverse Industries, Erotic Tape Company, Discotronics Films, Inc., Channel X Video, A-1 Video Services, Video Home Entertainment, Video Dimensions, Brentwood, and Hollywood Film Exchange, all of which quickly faded from the landscape.[172] All these companies sold catalogue titles, profiting from the huge archive of adult material that distributors were happy to license. By April 1979, less than three years after Jacobson had tentatively entered the market with softcore films, *Playboy* magazine claimed that "just about every top-quality X-rated movie made in the past several years can be legitimately purchased over the counter" and that adult titles made up two-thirds of all available content on the new format.[173] The promise of Atkinson's business model, which took the pleasures of the peep booth private, had finally come to fruition, albeit in a wild landscape lacking stabilization, long-term strategy, and shot-on-video content.

While these early distributors helped to establish the market, others solidified it and laid the foundation for the staggering success that followed. In the spring of 1977, Robert Sumner's lease on the World Theater in New York, where he had premiered *Deep Throat* in 1972 to record crowds, was set to expire. As president of Mature Pictures in New York, he decided to make his library available on video, as well as licensing the films of the Mitchell Brothers, Alex de Renzy, and Radley Metzger. With a $75,000 initial investment, Sumner began selling an inventory of thirty cassettes for $110 each at the East World Theater, another location he managed.[174] His booth at a video convention in Manhattan in the summer of 1977 was the only one to offer actual films of any kind on cassettes, let alone adult material, and business grew so rapidly that he formed a separate company, Quality X, for the venture.[175] In October 1977, Quality X, the first major adult video distributor to offer hardcore material on video through such methods, began advertising in *Screw* magazine.[176] In the surest possible sign that adult video had value, Sumner also claimed to have developed a proprietary system that would prevent the pirating of his material, which he would duplicate himself rather than outsource.

Others in that group of significant early companies included TVX, founded by legendary exploitation producer Dave Friedman with Phillip Bernstene and former notorious pirate Curt Richter in 1975. The three would rapidly turn the company into one of the largest early distributors, boasting that they were the "first and largest manufacturer," carrying an enormous inventory and supplying more than four hundred stores by 1979.[177] Friedman, like Sumner and others in this early period, recognized the potential of legitimizing the industry and moving it out of the bootlegging shadows. The 1979 TVX catalogue, in fact, stressed the link between legitimacy and quality: "TVX Features: The finest quality adult film video cassettes. Because of their immense popularity, TVX tapes are pirated. Why buy from these bootleggers? Why get ripped off by fly-by-night pirates who sell you 3rd, 4th, and 5th generation copies of TVX tapes?"[178] It was all part of a strategy (much like Sumner's) to garner a larger, more legitimate market—which TVX captured, in part, by also distributing mainstream titles.

Friedman's influence extended beyond Los Angeles. In July 1978, he convinced veteran adult film producer, distributor, and theater owner Arthur Morowitz (who, along with Howard Farber, had founded Distribpix in 1965) to sell TVX tapes in the lobby of one of his adult theaters in New York.[179] Morowitz later described the result: "After one week I sold seven cassettes and I was paid 50% each, so in a short time I made $350 without doing anything. At that point I committed myself totally to video."[180] That commitment turned into two of the earliest video stores in the United States, both called Sweetheart's Home Video Center, located in the lobbies of New York's World Theater and Manhattan Twin theater. By October 1978, Morowitz was advertising the stores in *Videography* magazine as having "the largest stock of adult rated video cassettes in New York," carrying TVX tapes from Friedman, Quality-X tapes from Sumner, and his own line, called Video-X-Pix, which offered the Distribpix catalogue (figure 11). Prices were set at $89.50 for Betamax and $99.50 for VHS.[181]

By January 1979, Sweetheart's was doing well enough that *Screw* publisher Al Goldstein even mentioned the stores in an interview (along with TVX), and Morowitz began making plans to expand the operation.[182] That spring, he opened Video Shack in a small, five-hundred-square foot storefront, which carried all manner of mainstream and adult titles.[183] Shortly afterward, Morowitz moved to what would become his flagship store, a three-thousand-square-foot location on Broadway, eventually growing into a multistore chain and establishing him as a powerful player in the video rental industry, culminating in a decade-long stint as the president of the

Figure 11. Arthur Morowitz, adult theater operator and founder of the Video Shack chain, also opened Sweetheart's Home Video Center, among the first adult video outlets in the United States. Advertisement, *Videography* (October 1978): 97.

Video Software Dealers Association.[184] This move, from theater lobbies to large, video-only stores, symbolizes what happened in the industry itself: the shift in both distribution and exhibition from celluloid to videotape.

Among the many veteran companies that assisted in establishing the adult video distribution marketplace and solidifying its business structures and practices were Arrow Video with Lou Peraino, Cal Vista International with Sidney Niekirk, Select/Essex with Joe and Jeff Steinman, VCX with Norm Arno, Adult Video Corporation (AVC) with Fred Hirsch, General Video with Reuben Sturman, Caballero Home Video and Swedish Erotica with Al and Noel Bloom, Video Taping Services (VTS) with Joe Donato, Video X Home Library with Andre De Anici, and Wonderful World of Video with Harry Mohney.[185] Russ Hampshire and Walter Gernert started Video Company of America (VCA) in 1978, building the company into a powerhouse committed to superior products, enlisting the best talent in front of and behind the camera, and investing in their own duplication facilities and in-house AVID editing systems before even major Hollywood studios had done so.[186] Hank Cartwright founded King of Video in 1979, which distributed the Eros line of adult videos, before creating Major Video, the first "superstore" concept, which was later directly copied by David Cook as the basis of Blockbuster Video, a history described in chapter 4.[187] These companies advertised at video trade shows as well as in their catalogues, which were universally a collection of Golden Age films and contemporary theatrical releases transferred to videotape.[188]

The established adult film producers seemed hesitant to reconsider their products as being primarily *for* the new medium, preferring instead to worry about the gradually diminishing lines at the adult theaters as home video began to increase its market share.[189] Yet there was still plenty of economic incentive to stick with the traditional methods: in 1981, Friedman claimed that an "A-line" adult film would gross, on average, $350,000 in theaters but only $35,000 on video.[190] That was changing, however. Sumner's Mature Pictures, in 1979, broke new ground when it released Gerard Damiano's *People* and *Misbehavin'* simultaneously to theaters and on video, the first time such a strategy had been attempted.[191] In 1981, VCX, which had previously distributed only the work of others, invested heavily in its first production, *High School Memories*, with acclaimed director Sam Weston (who used the pseudonym Anthony Spinelli) and established actors such as Annette Haven, Jamie Gillis, and John Leslie. The marketing campaign included full-page newspaper advertisements, and billboards featured a *videotape* image rather than the cast as background—signaling the industrial changes already well underway. As VCX marketing director Saul Saget noted, "We didn't really produce *High School Memories* for theaters. We're into selling tapes."[192] Theatrical distribution still mattered, but *why* it mattered was changing; as David Chute pointed out in 1981, "The success of an explicit cassette seems still to be linked to the success of a movie in theaters."[193] Such logic points to the shift toward recognizing the economic power of home video—but it also illustrates the cachet celluloid production and exhibition still seemed to have at this point in the transition for producers and audiences, who continued to associate the theater with "quality." Producers, of course, used whatever tactics worked, which increasingly meant treating the theater as a launching pad.

That would prove especially true in 1981, when VCA released *Insatiable* (dir. Stu Segall, credited as Godfrey Daniels), a comeback film for Marilyn Chambers, who had ventured into mainstream films such as David Cronenberg's *Rabid* (1977) after her success in the Mitchell Brothers' *Behind the Green Door* (1972) and *Resurrection of Eve* (1973). *Insatiable* was a box-office success—earning a considerable $2 million in theaters (despite playing only in Los Angeles, San Francisco, and Denver)—but it exploded on video, selling twelve thousand copies at $99.50 each on the first day of release. Eventually it went on to be the top-selling video (not just adult) of the year, and fans waited more than an hour at the Consumer Electronics Show in Las Vegas in January 1981 to see Chambers.[194] These tensions illustrate the industry's position in 1981: still clinging to an older, and gradually failing, exhibition model but acknowledging where that model was headed. Already by that point, two companies were officially shooting directly on the new medium, foreshadowing what would eventually become an industry-wide change, and completing the journey of moving image pornography from the Panoram to the home.

FROM PUBLIC TO PRIVATE: "SHOT LIVE ON VIDEOTAPE"

The first deliberate effort to shoot directly on videotape as part of a corporate strategy occurred—somewhat surreptitiously—in the summer of 1978. David Jennings, a producer, camera operator, and director for Norm Arno at VCX, began his usual preparations for a series of loop productions. This time, however, Jennings planned to shoot simultaneously on Sony U-Matic video and 16mm film after recognizing the affordability of video equipment. The result was *Lights! Camera! Orgy!*, produced in late summer 1978 at Jennings's apartment in Van Nuys. Afterward, Jennings and Joe Loveland, a musician and adult film enthusiast who frequently rented his home in Northern California to Jennings for loop productions, formed Love

LIVE performances by top sex stars. Shot with BROADCAST TV CAMERAS. Gorgeous color. Stunning detail.
BEST POSSIBLE STATE OF THE ART IMAGE QUALITY! In Beta or VHS.
For full program information send $1.00 Refundable with order.

to: **LOVE TV, Dept. VM, 681 Ellis Street, San Francisco, Ca. 94109.**

Figure 12. Love TV, pioneers in shooting directly on video, sought to allay fears about technical quality by emphasizing the "liveness" of the new medium. *Videography* (March 1979): 101.

Television Enterprises (later renamed LTV Enterprises), the first company designed from the ground up to produce and distribute adult videos.[195]

By fall 1978, Jennings had completed three additional shot-on-video features, *The Perfect Gift, Teenage Playmates,* and *Bound,* all one hour long, on a budget of $10,000 each. Advertisements began appearing in March 1979, listing the tapes at $75 each, with news reports describing them as "shot . . . by industry pros who preferred that their names not be mentioned, according to [a] company spokesman who also preferred that his name not be mentioned."[196] Jennings, sensing that video technology might make some viewers nervous, advertised the films as being "shot live on videotape," thus attempting to make the tapes seem more "real" than celluloid productions. The company's first advertisement, in fact, reads: "LIVE performances by top sex stars. Shot with BROADCAST TV CAMERAS. Gorgeous color. Stunning detail. BEST POSSIBLE STATE OF THE ART IMAGE QUALITY!" (figure 12).[197] The first review of the Love TV tapes commends just such elements:

> They've brought the camera in close and held it there so you can see the action. Theatrical films transferred to tape often include many medium and long shots, which will appear satisfactorily on the theater screen but lose all detail when reduced to the size of the tube. Love works mainly with a few close-ups, leaving nothing to the imagination. It's one of the big advantages of shooting specifically for video and Love makes the most of it.[198]

Jennings's contribution to adult film history was significant: if, by summer 1978, video had already shown the industry the future of distribution and exhibition, Jennings demonstrated the medium's potential for production. But he wasn't the only one willing to gamble.

In December 1978, Sal Esposito, who had been distributing adult video out of Reseda, California, since late 1977, approached Maria and Carlos Tobalina, owners of Hollywood International Film Corporation of America, to license their catalogue. Unsure of a price, they asked Bill Margold, their public relations director, who suggested $10,000 per title.[199] Esposito angrily declined, phoning Margold the next morning to complain. Margold suggested Esposito should just go into production directly on video rather than license celluloid for transfer. Much like Jennings, Margold thought the technology could be marketed as shooting "live on video," emphasizing the apparent "realness" that videotape provided. Margold had further suggestions: make the tapes in thirty-minute installments, modeled on television sitcoms, release one per week, and cast rising star Seka as the lead.[200] Esposito agreed and, in late January 1979, along with director Daniel Symms (as David Summers), writer Maxine Hall (as Max Lyon), and performers Seka, Margold, and others, shot *Football Widow* and *Love Story* over a weekend, releasing them under the Scorpio label. They followed these with *High School Report Card* in March with the same crew and *Super-Ware Party* in July with Margold directing. In early 1980, Scorpio produced two more entries with Alan Colberg (as Rene Deneuve) directing: *Inside Hollywood: The Anne Dixon Story* and *Inside Hollywood: The John Barfield Story*, intended to be the first two of a six-part, unfinished "soap opera" series.[201]

The Scorpio group sensed that Margold's narrative ideas might balance out the fear that video would decrease visual quality, and used them to court the respectability that might appeal to female viewers. Colberg (who used a female pseudonym in the films), in an interview on the set of the *Inside Hollywood* series, makes that appeal blatant and even invokes soap operas as a marker of quality rather than a deterrent:

> [The series] is catered toward the demographics of a male and female relaxing in their living room. The story is really rather sophisticated. It's not designed for a male only, it doesn't degrade females in any way, it doesn't call them sluts or prostitutes, or put them in impossible situations that only a woman could be in. It takes a lot of the chauvinism out of it. And the minimum look we expect is equal to any prime time TV soap.[202]

This type of appeal became increasingly common and later formed the basis of Candida Royalle's strategies with Femme Productions, outlined in chapter 3. While Margold's initial idea of modeling adult video on narratives, structures, and strategies familiar to television production carried through with Scorpio, his suggestion to release one per week did not; after the two *Inside Hollywood* productions, Scorpio folded.[203]

Even if they did not reach lasting financial success, Scorpio and Love TV radically altered the landscape of the adult film industry. These companies illustrated the new production and distribution methods that soon everyone would employ—but they also represented the complete alteration of a much bigger paradigm. If the anxiety surrounding pornography had always been rooted in tensions between public and private enactment of pleasure, then home video fully provided an escape for the industry into the safe space of the home. By 1978, *Variety* reported that 50 percent of all material available on videocassette was pornography.[204] The adult industry demonstrated to Hollywood the potential profits in video—a role that some tried to obscure even as it was playing out. In 1979, for example, Bob Brewin, at the annual Consumer Electronics Show, admitted as much: "No one in a leadership position that promises to revolutionize home entertainment really wants to admit that the first stage of that revolution is to bring what used to be called pornography and is now dubbed 'adult entertainment' from the local theatre into the home."[205] On its journey from the Panoram through the peep-show booth and adult motel rooms and finally into the home, pornography transformed technologically, finally becoming a private mechanism for spectators, away from the regulations governing public space.

That transformation, however, came with new challenges. If the industry had long been obsessed with attaining respectability, typically through the mobilization of markers of quality, that attitude did not change with video, even if new technological capabilities ensured rapid production cycles and a glut of new material flooding the market. In the early 1980s, as the industry grew, it retreated somewhat into the shadows, unable to find a way to connect to larger audiences wary of its content and cultural associations. Going private didn't mean the industry wasn't public; there was still the matter of selling the products, after all. The industry struggled to find respectability. In 1981, David Chute noted that "industry spokesmen are nearly unanimous in the belief that only a significant improvement in the quality of the films themselves can ultimately snag a substantial number of new hardcore patrons."[206] The type of quality that industry members meant, of course, was deeply connected to the notion that adult film must do "something more" than simply produce pleasure. Even Atkinson, the man who had, in many ways, initiated the entire enterprise, noted in 1986 that the cultural pressure on mainstream video stores to drop adult tapes might be somewhat justified: "It ain't exactly like defending D.H. Lawrence."[207] This observation illustrates the ongoing tension regarding pleasures of the body versus pleasures of the mind, and ultimately suggests that adult video was somehow "lesser" a work than Lawrence's *Lady Chatterley's Lover* (1928).

Atkinson had some reason to be worried, in the end. It eventually became plainly evident that some producers, most notably Mark Carriere, had abandoned all interest in anything but profit in their quest to feed video stores with product. Called the "Mack Sennett of adult entertainment" by the *Los Angeles Times*, Carriere gleefully ignored any semblance of artistry in favor of supervising multiple crews on single locations shooting as quickly as possible, or stringing together existing scenes in new permutations under new titles.[208] In Carriere's view, quality was irrelevant. What mattered was quantity. In July 1989, for example, Carriere and his brother-in-law John Laolagi rented a YWCA building, the historic Clark Residence, in downtown Los Angeles for what they called a "pornathon." With four crews shooting simultaneously for four straight weeks, the result was forty-seven completed titles, a staggering output characteristic of Carriere's practices—and a snapshot, albeit extreme, of where the industry stood in the years following Jennings's experiments in his apartment.[209]

Well before that point, however, the industry had a ways to go before it could settle into a clear set of industrial practices. In order to build audiences (or at least try), parts of the adult industry labored in the early 1980s to reposition and align adult video with the "something more" that could ease tensions about simple pleasures being enough. Jeff Steinman, president of Essex Video, made such links clear in 1984: "Video has opened new doors and avenues by bringing a quality, adult-oriented product into the living room and the bedroom. It has meant more money and higher quality in X-rated productions. We're no longer selling just shock value. We're now presenting our product on a silver platter. Eroticism is the key to success in this business."[210] Such concerns with quality and respectability, marked by the impulse to create something erotic rather than pornographic, inevitably link back to efforts to contain pleasure—especially women's pleasure—for its own sake. Elliot Abelson, an attorney for various adult film distributors, made that connection perfectly clear in a 1981 interview: "We will see the audience change drastically, and the major influx will be women."[211] For the adult video industry to take its next steps toward modern capitalist efficiency, that influx would need to be navigated carefully.

In the next chapter, I examine a discursive mechanism created to address these and other concerns related to quality: *Adult Video News (AVN)*, a publication designed as a fan newsletter but eventually growing into a trade journal. The quality and respectability strategies it employed forever changed the industry and brought new and lasting meaning to those terms—as well as reproducing and recirculating the same gendered anxieties and tensions surrounding them. Atkinson and others may have initiated the legitimization of the industry, but it would take a publication peripheral to the business to continue that process. If strategies to make pornography private defined, in many ways, the birth of the adult video industry, *AVN* looked for ways to make it public all over again.

2 *Adult Video News*

Selling XXX without the Sex

There are basically two kinds of XXX-rated movies: sophisticated and unsophisticated.

I. L. Slifkin, "Exotic Adventures of Lolita," *Adult Video News* (1983)

Accessibility leads to acceptability.

Steven Hirsch quoted in Clint O'Connor, "Cleveland's X-Rated Connection," *Plain Dealer* (2004)

In May 1983, between an interview with performer Lisa DeLeeuw and a series of short synopses of adult films then in theatrical release, the adult magazine *Video-X* offered a ten-page pictorial, "Video Vixen," featuring model April May.[1] Now a long-forgotten actress who appeared in only a handful of films in the late 1980s, May never achieved a remote measure of stardom. Brief boilerplate "quotes" accompany nine photographs: May lounges on a bed, nude save for a silk robe and high heels, staring directly into the camera, seemingly attempting direct eye contact with the reader. The fact that these ten pages exist in the magazine is hardly a surprise; after all, since *Playboy* first began publication in 1953, countless similar features, all presenting women in various stages of undress directly addressing the camera, have gone to print.[2] Yet the specific reason that May appears in *Video-X*, particularly as that month's "Video Vixen," is somewhat unclear: her first film role was two years later, in *Lust American Style* (1985, dir. Michael Carpenter), performing under the same name. Furthermore, the ten pages reveal no connection whatsoever to adult video, or even film more generally, other than the "Video Vixen" headline, since no particular film is mentioned. On close examination, then, a question arises: Why would *Video-X*, a magazine purportedly devoted to adult video, include this pictorial?

The answer resides in the adult film and magazine industries' limited means to market the representation of sex—their primary product.

Magazines, one of the few spaces in which the industry could reach out directly to potential customers, were the main marketing arm for adult film producers and distributors. Like any industry seeking to retain existing customers and capture new ones, the adult film industry used magazines such as *Video-X* to offer its products in the form of synopses, still images, and interviews, all part of standard marketing and publicity strategies. In the early days of adult video, these magazines did as they had always done: present pictorials of nude women, accompanied by loose "narratives," often in the form of anecdotes, quotes, or simple stories told in pictures. As Rick Altman notes, "In every era, new representational technologies have initially been configured to conform to the codes established by already existing technologies."[3] In keeping with this strategy, very little effort was made to move away from this "sampling" practice or to think of new or creative ways to sell mediated sex. Readers (and the industry) had certain longstanding expectations of, as well as familiarity with, this particular system. It would be naïve to suggest that these expectations did not include, simply put, material for masturbation; nevertheless, sampling did not offer much *beyond* that paradigm to the industry and audiences.

These ten pages in *Video-X* adhere neatly to this pattern. The magazine included the pictures because offering such content was what adult magazines had always done. After all, what else could they sell? Content *was* the product, and magazines served to sell the industry, which generated that content. As Andrew Ross notes, "Increasingly, the porn magazines [were] tailored to function as trailers, previews, fanzines, and supporting literature for the main attraction of the videos and their stars."[4] Yet a fundamental problem percolated under the surface of this model, plaguing the adult industry with issues of legality, cultural associations, and simple economics. As the industry moved its products from theaters to video, it searched for ways to adjust the public marketing of private pleasures, increasingly important once adult video appeared on the shelves of mainstream, locally owned rental stores eager to cash in on the growing demand. This was a significant change from earlier distribution models, in which adult bookstores and theaters were the primary sources of pornography. This new—and rapidly growing—group of video retailers did not necessarily think of themselves in such terms; yet as video's distribution reach expanded, the back rooms of mainstream video stores quickly became primary outlets for precisely such material. Owners may have been indifferent to political aspects surrounding the material, but they were definitely interested in the money flowing into their stores due to its popularity. That necessitated a marketing change.

In tracing the history of this change, I begin with an examination of the early magazines linked to the adult video industry, and the ways in which they partnered with video in their content. This symbiotic marketing relationship used sampling as its primary strategy. While successful for magazine sales and as advertising for adult films, the strategy did not deflect criticism or find new audiences who were not necessarily comfortable with explicit imagery. Starting with an analysis of three magazines from 1980 to provide examples from the early period of adult video, I then move forward to three additional magazines, from 1983, to illustrate how the dramatic escalation of public interest in home video spurred sales and rentals of adult tapes. As I outline in the first chapter, it was in 1983 that adult video began to find explosive success, putting the industry into a unique position: the thousands of new retailers stocking their shelves with adult tapes were not the same audience who were looking solely for samples *from* those tapes. Given that economics were, as usual, the driving force, new communication channels and modes of address among producers, distributors, retailers, and consumers became necessities.

The most important of these channels was *Adult Video News (AVN)*, a newsletter created in 1982 by Paul Fishbein, Irv Slifkin, and Barry Rosenblatt in Drexel Hill, Pennsylvania, as a monthly guide to the adult film industry. *AVN* bridged the gap between the Golden Age of theatrical adult film and the shot-on-video era of the late 1980s by implementing a set of strategies aimed squarely at rethinking the public marketing of private pleasure, especially to retailers who lacked personal interest or investment in pornography but still wanted to capitalize on its economic potential. Currently, the average issue of *AVN* has a circulation of forty thousand, targets primarily retailers and industry members, and features up to five hundred video reviews per issue, which appear alongside copious amounts of advertising. The parent company, known as the AVN Media Network, maintains a large Web presence from its corporate headquarters in Chatsworth, California, a city that is also the epicenter of adult video production.[5] The company is widely regarded as the premier "voice" of the adult industry, a claim it created and frequently self-advertises. Given the powerful (and profitable) contemporary status of the company, it seems, in retrospect, that the success of the original publication was a foregone conclusion. In the early 1980s, however, the idea was risky and groundbreaking in that it gambled on the possibility of a willing (and reachable) audience and an industry amenable to new publishing paradigms. How the advertising and marketing of adult video content developed and changed in the magazine's pages, primarily by avoiding sampling, represents a significant piece of adult video history and is the focus of this chapter.

SELLING XXX WITHOUT THE SEX / **87**

THE EARLY HISTORY OF *AVN*

Starting with its first issue in February 1983, *AVN* built what did not yet exist for adult film: a space to cover and market the industry in the vein of mainstream publications such as *Variety* and the *Hollywood Reporter*. While other adult magazines had offered industry news, gossip about performers, and production updates, they nevertheless maintained a particular status quo: they sampled industry content in the form of traditional photo layouts, centerfolds, and set pictorials. *AVN* implemented a different strategy designed to alter preconceptions about pornography while doing more than just sampling. In short, it launched a process of taste creation aimed squarely at potential consumers and retailers.

Indeed, part of *AVN*'s strategy was to emphasize the normalcy of adult video as a *product*, one to be rented and sold by retailers and acquired by consumers. Yet, even though this strategy emphasized relatively simple economic terms that superficially guided the newsletter's decisions, such tastemaking had deeper ramifications. As Pierre Bourdieu writes, taste "functions as a sort of social orientation, a 'sense of one's place,' guiding the occupants of a given place in social space towards the social positions adjusted to their properties, and towards the practices or goods which befit the occupants of that position."[6] For *AVN*, the goal was to alter that social position, to encourage the adult film industry—and the culture more generally—to elevate pornography into a place of increased respect by shifting the taste discourses around it. A significant and crucial part of achieving that shift was to disavow the sexual content at the core of the industry's content in favor of other elements that could be broadly captured under the umbrella of "quality."

It was that decision—to present the industry's products in a new way that might appeal to consumers and retailers turned off by or disinterested in the traditional marketing of the sexual or pleasurable aspects of pornography—that was *AVN*'s key contribution to adult film history. It also meant the newsletter participated in the same, troubling discourses of "respectability" that have long haunted the adult film industry in various ways. Bourdieu writes:

> The denial of lower, coarse, vulgar, venal, servile—in a word, natural— enjoyment, which constitutes the sacred sphere of culture, implies an affirmation of the superiority of those who can be satisfied with the sublimated, refined, disinterested, gratuitous, distinguished pleasures forever closed to the profane. That is why art and cultural consumption are predisposed, consciously and deliberately or not, to fulfill a social function of legitimating social differences.[7]

Marketing changes and appeals to new retailers during the move of adult video into mainstream rental stores in the 1980s across the United States were a battleground in which Bourdieu's formulation was fervently engaged. Pornography during the video era participated, as it always has, in just such social-difference legitimization—a process illustrated in *AVN*'s pages and critical to an understanding of this period in adult film history.

ADULT VIDEO MAGAZINES AND SAMPLING

By 1980, more than 200 hardcore and 165 softcore magazines offered nudity and sex as their primary content.[8] The best-known among these, *Playboy, Hustler,* and *Penthouse,* offered film reviews to varying degrees but did not cover the adult film industry regularly or in detail. Other, lesser-known magazines such as *Cinema-X, Adam Film World, Video-X,* and *Velvet's Erotic Film Guide* focused on the industry—but did so, as discussed below, squarely within the familiar sampling model. A third group of publications, for video "swappers," was an important antecedent to *AVN* and its efforts to present something different. The *Videophile's Newsletter* was the first of these, founded by Jim Lowe shortly after the 1976 debut of the Sony Betamax. The thirty-six-year-old pop culture collector had placed an ad in *Movie Collector's World* seeking others who might be interested in trading Betamax tapes, and the handful of responses he received led to the creation of a newsletter. His subscriber list grew into the hundreds, then thousands, and Lowe turned the publication into a glossy magazine with full-color, professionally photographed covers. Reaching its peak in 1979 with eight thousand subscribers and newsstand sales, the magazine typically included industry advertising alongside classified ads from collectors looking to trade adult material.[9] It was a groundbreaking publication for home video, connecting users via their specific interests and recognizing the market for video as a valuable, collectible commodity.

Similarly, *Video Swapper,* founded in Fraser, Michigan in early 1981, filled its pages with industry news, ads for equipment, and a classifieds section in which readers offered to trade collections—including adult tapes. Its publishers also took advertisements for adult material. The eleventh issue, for example, from January 1982, features a full-color advertisement on the inside back cover for TVX, one of the earliest and most successful companies (see chapter 1).[10] A similar advertisement for TGA Video fills the back cover.[11] While TGA had nowhere near the success or longevity of TVX, its presence here illustrates the need that early companies had for *any* marketing and advertising outlets. Finding consumers for a new technology required casting a wide net to capture specific audiences wherever they could be found.[12]

The publishers of *Video Swapper* furthered that process when they released *Adult Video Swapper,* a spinoff publication, in September 1983. Printed on cheap newsprint, populated by advertisements from independent producers, and mostly made up of classified postings from collectors seeking to trade material, *Adult Video Swapper* left little historical footprint. Yet it did capture the unique nature of the early adult video industry as it was taking shape. The fourth issue, for example, from December 1983, features an interview with performer Vanessa Del Rio (who also appears on the cover) along with four nude photos from Caballero Home Video releases, demonstrating the magazine's effort to create a professional publication, in part by sampling content from the industry in the traditional style of an adult magazine.[13] The issue also contained an advertisement for Baker Video in Dartmouth, Massachusetts, which was willing to produce custom adult tapes with one of three performers pictured in poorly lit, trimmed photographs. "Have your dreams come to life on your custom made video tape," reads the ad, clearly produced on a typewriter. "Send in your outline and choice of girl. Please keep it within reason."[14] Thus, in a magazine aimed at individual collectors, the two ends of the industry's spectrum come into focus: the professional and established side, with Del Rio and photos from Caballero, and the amateur, with a tiny company hawking its custom products with a handmade advertisement.[15] The publication was, more than anything else, a vivid illustration of the nascent industry building toward a more formal structure. Nevertheless, swapper publications were aimed at a small and specialized market—one that did not include casual consumers or retailers looking for marketing and sales advice.

These magazines' content starkly contrasts with the format of the era's traditional adult magazines. *Adam Film World* was the established veteran, with experience covering the theatrical arm of the industry going back to 1966 under its original name, *Adam Film Quarterly.* The parent publication, *Adam,* had been founded in 1957 to compete with *Playboy,* giving the company vast experience with adult industries, and *Adam Film Quarterly* was renamed *Adam Film World* in 1969. And yet, by July 1980, it was still slightly unsure of how to deal with video. Primarily a collection of stills from various adult films, that month's issue also offers a few pages of what it called "the latest scuttlebutt on the adult film scene."[16] That scuttlebutt includes a report from the annual meeting of the Adult Film Association of America (AFAA), speculation that *The Postman Always Rings Twice* (1981) would "strain its R rating to the limit" due to its sex scenes between Jessica Lange and Jack Nicholson, and features on mainstream Hollywood performers Suzanne Somers and Mamie Van Doren, along with foreign film news and Hollywood gossip.[17]

All this content seems remarkably similar to the type of material found in *Playboy* during the era, which was probably a deliberate strategy designed to appeal to a particular middle-class audience by positioning pornography alongside other, "legitimate" art forms. This tactic did not extend to the advertising, however. Unlike *Playboy*, which gathered revenue from a broad range of companies, including liquor distributors, automobile manufacturers, and home stereo producers, there was very little advertising for anything outside sex-related industries in *Adam Film World*. Toward the back of the July 1980 issue, for example, Mark Richards Movies offers ten 8mm films through direct mail at $24.95 each, describing them as "full length, full color feature super sharp, well lit, [with] breath-taking detail," with ten thumbnail images of topless women. Orders went to a post office box in Los Angeles.[18]

The coverage of home video and adult content available on the new medium in the pages of *Adam Film World* was certainly limited compared to its coverage of theatrical features, but that was to be expected; after all, theatrically released adult films were still a booming business in 1980. Beginning with the cover, however, *Adam Film World* was marking its accommodation to the new format—its headline reads: "Latest X-Raters on Videotape." This coverage does not extend beyond a brief list inside, however. It was still the sampling that sold copies. Featuring stills from eight films then in theatrical release, this issue of *Adam Film World* is primarily a collection of nude photographs, some in color and others in black and white, all carefully chosen to hide erect penises and images of penetration. These editorial policies perhaps most closely match *Hustler's* of that time, which is to say the images of nudity and sex, while boundary-pushing, are not hardcore.

The February 1980 *Cinema-X*, that publication's second issue, runs one hundred pages and makes no pretense to the type of respectability partially employed by *Adam Film World*. Yet it does present its traditional content with a professionalized aesthetic and full-color graphics, as well as a visible effort to guide readers in the adult marketplace. Interviews with director Chuck Vincent and performer Annette Haven, a "letters from readers" feature with performer Leslee Bovee, a piece of erotic fiction, a fan club offer linking readers to their favorite stars, and a gossip column form the content of the issue. A "Rising Stars" section introduces Scarlett Kennedy, Sue

Leighton, and Susanne Nero as having "appeared in numerous films, but [who] are just now being recognized."[19] The magazine, serving as a "guide" for readers, thus acts as a mediator between the industry's offering of new product and a curious public seeking variety. Bovee appears on the cover, in an interview, and as the centerfold; she answers fan mail, acts as an addressee for the fan club, and appears in a two-page advertisement for her films—all of which points to the way *Cinema-X* partnered with the industry as a marketing platform, sampling its products for readers almost as a catalogue might do. Distinction, in other words, was minimal.

In another familiar move, but one given a new twist, this issue of *Cinema-X* includes a three-page "open call" section that promises potential stardom for the average reader. "Each month, *Cinema-X* will provide a free forum for aspiring erotic actors and actresses (18 and older) to present themselves to the adult film industry and the viewing public. The winners will be chosen by popular ballot and will be flown to New York City for a first class, weekend stay at our expense. . . . The winners will be introduced to producers and directors and be given the opportunity to appear in an adult film."[20] The eight featured "readers," all female, in nude poses that mimic amateur photography but nevertheless clearly are images of (presumably) professional models, used by the magazine to concoct a fantasy for consumers.

While the open call feature presents a fantasy of amateur sexuality, more traditional industry sampling strategies are on display throughout the issue. Five lengthy film reviews, accompanied by softcore stills, make up the bulk of the magazine. For example, a six-page review of *Intimate Desires* (1978, dir. Gloria Leonard) encapsulates the magazine's overall approach and tone, with fifteen photographs offering a wide-ranging view of various scenes. The analysis begins with a lengthy plot recap before finishing with a brief critical review that rates the film at "85%":

> The film is long on plot and this interferes with some of the sex scenes, but on the whole it has many things working for it. All the actors are adequate with Marlene Willoughby standing out above the rest. The technical aspects are all top-notch as are the settings and other production values. Unfortunately, the only part of the story that really stands out is the Marlene Willoughby/John Leslie scene and even though it succeeds wildly, it cannot carry the rest of the film.[21]

This tone, balancing praise with criticism, reappears consistently in *Cinema-X* and exemplifies the supportive and encouraging voice that defined the magazine's editorial approach. Gently pushing the industry toward quality and consistency, *Cinema-X* was not afraid to call out technical flaws, subpar acting, or poor direction—all criticisms designed to assist readers in the crowded marketplace.

Much as in *Adam Film World,* the infancy of home video technology meant that *Cinema-X*'s coverage and content of the new medium were at best minimal but not completely absent. The cover of this issue, for example, advertises "Video Tape Tips!" and teases "Adult Home Movie Reviews!" The latter, which could be interpreted as reviews of home video, was actually a series of reviews of 16mm loops from three major distributors: Pleasure Productions, Joys of Erotica, and Diamond Distributors—all very recognizable from the late 1970s and widely available. The accompanying copy illustrates the ways in which adult film magazines of the 1980s still maintained a strong connection to the loop manufacturers of the 1970s: "Each month this section will be devoted to reviewing the finest in adult home movies. These films . . . often feature top stars and quality production values to recommend them."[22] Home video would soon render "home movies" obsolete, but in the early 1980s, the term still referred to celluloid loops. Indeed, the majority of the advertising in this issue is for 16mm loops, aside from a handful of ads for Cinema Tech offering its products on film or videotape—including the "Lesllie Bovee" collection.[23]

The "Video Tape Tips!" story teased on the cover of *Cinema-X* does not even appear in the table of contents. Yet it would become a recurring feature, presenting a snapshot of the medium in its early days. Presenting a "ten best sellers" list (with *Deep Throat* predictably ranked first) and asking readers to write in with questions, the piece also gives a brief history of adult films on tape and the promised "tips" for maintaining video equipment.[24] These last two elements acknowledge the reader curiosity about the mysteries of the new technology: Where did it come from? How do I care for it? Where might it be going? Will it last, or is it a novelty? Are the films the same quality as those playing in theaters? *Cinema-X,* ultimately, in its early days, might have firmly embraced sampling as a strategy, but it also looked ahead (however minimally) to coming technological changes.

Video X magazine, started in March 1980, combines the approaches of both *Adam Film World* and *Cinema-X,* which is to say it uses the "news and information" structure alongside the sampling, expertise, and marketplace paradigms. Black-and-white and color stills run throughout the first issue, much as in the other magazines, but they lack much production value or investment. The real difference—and effort to create distinction—is in the way *Video X* even more blatantly partners with the industry to market its products. In fact, the first issue begins with a checklist of "how to get the most from the world's greatest adult entertainment magazine." First, "Save money by previewing extensive pictorials from no less than 15 major adult video features each month." Second, the magazine helps readers purchase videotapes "directly from our mail-order department, which just happens to boast the world's largest selection of adult video titles at all times." Its catalogue of titles was from Vydio Philms of Surfside, Florida, one of the largest early adult video distributors, which acted as a clearinghouse for larger producers and distributors such as Video Classics, Quality X Video Cassette Company, Cinema-X, Tenaha Timpson Releases, Leisure Time Booking, Gail Palmer's Pleasure Productions, and Wonderful World of Video. Thus the magazine was more than just a marketing platform for adult video producers—it was also a distributor. Readers could find news and information on sex toys, home video industry updates, and equipment trends—and, the logic went, they could conveniently submit orders for tapes, all in one place.[25]

While these early adult magazines had a growing curiosity about video, they still favored loops, Golden Age stars, and celluloid productions. The next three publications I examine—*Velvet's Erotic Film Guide, Adult Cinema Review,* and *Video-X* (a separate magazine from Video X)—all come from 1983, a date deliberately chosen for its alignment with the creation of *AVN.* They offer a compelling explanation of why *AVN*'s creators saw a need for a new kind of publication in the marketplace, one that would discursively differentiate itself in nearly every aspect. Ultimately, what emerges from this snapshot is the clear need for an editorial voice from *outside* the industry, a radical step away from the status quo, one that included discursive expertise that might appeal to readers (and store owners) who might not be interested in sampling but potentially could be informed and educated.

The January 1983 issue of *Velvet's Erotic Film Guide* follows the same general pattern of *Adam Film World,* minus any interest whatsoever in mainstream Hollywood or even culture more generally, but it maintains glossy production values and color photography. Offering standard adult film industry news, interviews, and gossip, the magazine takes a slightly sophisticated approach in terms of its editorial content, including a report from the Sixth Annual Erotic Film Awards and a wide-ranging interview with actor Harry Reems, who had been arrested and convicted on obscenity charges for his participation in *Deep Throat.* Like *Velvet,* its long-running parent publication, *Velvet's Erotic Film Guide* is interested primarily in sampling from adult films then in release. However, apparent too is a clear effort to heighten the tone slightly, to create a trustworthy, "expert" voice, in an attempt to appeal to the growing customer base. In the conclusion to the coverage of the Erotic Film Awards, for example, the editors offer a comparison chart featuring the actual winners and those the magazine would have chosen. Noting that the organizers of the awards named a panel of seven judges from nonadult magazines to pick the winners, the editors offer a completely different set of choices, as well as criticisms of each "wrong" selection.[26] Most important, the editors suggest that the victor in the Best Picture category—*Nothing to Hide* (1982, dir. Anthony Spinelli)— might have been chosen because that film's producer, Sidney Niekerk, also served as AFAA president, the group which sponsored the event.[27] Such a bold editorial move illustrates *Velvet's Erotic Film Guide*'s desire to take on a position as "expert."

Alongside this willingness to offer opinion, analysis, and expertise, the magazine hired performers Lisa DeLeeuw, Candida Royale, and Ron Jeremy, as associate publisher, New York correspondent, and contributing editor, respectively, partnering with the industry and giving readers an "insider" perspective, even if the hiring decisions were based on circulation and required little (or no) actual work from the performers. In the "Video Porn" section, that partnership becomes literal: producer Suze Randall's *Centerfold Collection #6* is covered in a five-page photo feature that includes a direct mailing address and phone number for Newave Productions to order the tape for $49.95.[28] The lines between advertising and content become blurry in these moments, but the intention is clear: *Velvet's Erotic Film Guide* wants the reader to trust its expertise—and, subsequently, to order the industry's products. Despite all these efforts, however, the core problem still remained: the nude photographs and explicit language sampled in the magazine's pages and clearly making up the majority of its content illustrate the ongoing tension surrounding the public marketing of private pleasure.

If *Velvet's Erotic Film Guide* focused on samples alongside industry news and an effort to foreground expertise, *Adult Cinema Review* suffered no such identity confusion. Its October 1983 issue, packed with full-color stills from more than ten films, offers much more than *Adam Film World* in terms of explicit content, although still avoiding images of penetration. There are no efforts to provide news (mainstream or otherwise), no book reports or editorials, and the (clearly fabricated) "letters" from readers serve only to provide even more erotic content.[29] For example, the six-page feature on *Intimate Action* (1983, dir. unknown) concludes with yet another mailing address for readers to send in $79.95 to obtain the cassette directly from Intact Productions: while similar to the structures in place at *Velvet's Erotic Film Guide*, the feature lacks *Adam Film World*'s efforts elsewhere to establish its expertise.[30] If *Velvet's Erotic Film Guide* tried to attract readers who might be looking for guidance as well as samples, *Adult Cinema Review* existed solely to market films to spectators by providing those samples *and* an ordering mechanism without any distractions.

Featuring "reviews, previews, and hot news for the home viewer," *Video-X* followed right along with *Adult Cinema Review* in avoiding the "clutter" seen in publications such as *Velvet's Erotic Film Guide*. The fourth issue of *Video-X's* fourth volume, from May 1983, offers one hundred pages of content dedicated almost completely to sampling. The ubiquitous "letters," a gossip column by Velvet Summers, an interview with DeLeeuw, and a "new stars" feature fill a few pages. Multiple reviews, however, make up the bulk of the content, consisting primarily of hardcore samples from the films (with images of penetration covered with black dots) wrapped with minimal and adulatory copy. The magazine does not make much of an attempt to be critical or offer the guidance that other publications presented, nor is it particularly interested in pushing or encouraging narrative or other markers of "quality." Typical in this regard is its review of *Foreplay* (1982, dir. Vinni Rossi), with seven images from the film bracketed by a synopsis and a conclusion illustrating the magazine's overall tone: "Director Vinni Rossi has succeeded in making a film that leaves redeeming social value to the birds. This is hardcore at its hardest, wham bam, and do it again. *Foreplay* is crammed with tasty hot cooze. And in the world of porn, where quim is queen, the frills don't matter. On that level, *Foreplay* is a winner. For a luscious, lusty look, take a look at *Foreplay.*"[31] This review, like all those in the magazine, uses samples as a springboard to add copy that mimics the film itself. *Foreplay,* an all but forgotten film, was hardly a "winner" according to other critics; it receives barely a mention in other review guides from the period.

The real mission of *Video-X* was to present as much visual content as possible. Two photo features with only tenuous connections to adult film fill more than a quarter of the magazine's pages; in addition to the "April May" piece, a second pictorial offers Ambrosia, who had appeared in six adult films prior to her appearance. Thirteen pages, with eighteen photographs, including a centerfold, highlight Ambrosia as a "succulent newcomer to the world of X-rated film."[32] Ambrosia (André Nelson) would go on to make only six more films and disappeared from the industry by 1985. No copy accompanies these photos (although a brief interview precedes them), and stylistic details, such as lighting and staging, are at a minimum. *Video-X* made little effort to distinguish itself from other publications, and it was hardly a magazine that readers seeking information on the adult video industry could turn to—nor was it, in any way, a useful guide for store owners looking for expertise.

What all these magazines had in common was their position as the de facto marketing arm of the adult film industry, consistently sampling its products and, for the most part, wholeheartedly supporting its content with positive reviews. This work served a particularly useful purpose during the transition from celluloid to video, as the industry undoubtedly benefited from the reliability of its unofficial marketing partners. Later, after the transition was complete, adult film screenwriter Rick Marx criticized these same practices, noting, "The reviews in these magazines have become a direct adjunct of the film companies' publicity departments."[33] If that was indeed the case, it illustrates a larger point: the industry, in order to be legitimized for a larger, more mainstream audience, needed to find new ways to disavow its core content while nevertheless continuing to sell it. Such a delicate balancing act would require new paradigms, a focus on other elements, and, most important, the elevation of mediated sex to something beyond simple bodily pleasures. It would need to find a place to become "something more."

MEDIATING XXX: *AVN* AND THE INVENTION OF ADULT VIDEO

What set *AVN* apart from other publications, and served as a groundbreaking step forward for the marketing of the adult film industry, was that the newsletter was one step removed: it talked *about* the industry and its products rather than sampling them. In other words, *AVN* distinguished itself by radically deemphasizing sexual content and foregrounding expertise and information, selling the *idea* and *context* of the content rather than the content itself. *AVN* added a unique voice that eventually, like no other, signified the transition of the adult film industry to new modes of production and exhibition and, in the end, a modern and efficient example of corporate capitalism, encouraging the industry to move beyond being simple short-term profit seekers dishing out sexually explicit images and to become long-term strategists seeking to redefine the paradigm associated with the product.

From its first issue, *AVN* acted as an important mediator in that it legitimized pornography for retailers, provided a marketing space for producers, and offered information and expertise for viewers. This work raises questions, answers to which may fill in critical gaps in the history of adult video: What brought about the need for a connection among producers, retailers, and consumers of adult film? And how did *AVN* provide that connection so quickly? Much as Josh Greenberg suggests that mainstream home video was "invented" in a relationship that positioned distributors as educators and experts to retailers, I propose that something similar occurred in the realm of adult video that structured *AVN* as both a "voice" for the industry and an "expert" for distributors, retailers, and consumers; in other words, *AVN* invented the discursive realm in which adult video was eventually taken up and understood by retailers and consumers.[34]

A critical part of this change was the recognition by Fishbein and Slifkin that, by 1983, VCR sales had exploded—and that the massive new audience was hungry for content, including the adult material that was steadily finding increased shelf space in the video stores sprouting all over the United States. *AVN* recognized that many in this new audience might be unlikely to visit adult movie theaters or adult bookstores for fear of being associated with "dirty" movies. In other words, *AVN* saw the tremendous economic potential of new types of discourses disavowing the very product that could occupy its pages.

Fishbein and Slifkin certainly recognized the market for such strategies. Beginning in 1980, the two had worked for Movies Unlimited, one of the earliest and largest video stores, while attending Temple University in Philadelphia.[35] That experience offered them a microcosm of the country at large. By 1978, Americans had purchased fewer than 175,000 VCRs, but, after a steep drop in price, that number exploded to 4 million by 1982 and then 26 million by 1985.[36] The steady influx of video retailers seeking to provide consumers with content for their new machines in this period followed a similar pattern, growing from four thousand stores in 1978 to ten thousand in 1983 and twenty-two thousand in 1985, and estimates suggest that single-store operators owned and managed 90 percent of video stores in the early to mid-1980s.[37] Before Blockbuster and Hollywood Video established their massive corporate dominance (and refused to carry adult video, as outlined in chapter 4), the average video store was a single location, a locally owned business with roughly fifteen hundred mainstream titles in stock—along with a very lucrative selection of adult tapes. Profits from adult video, in some accounts, equaled that from children's tapes, illustrating an early rental pattern of "one for the kids, one for the adults."[38]

Indeed, adult film's initial share of the video market was substantial, accounting in some estimates for at least half of all tapes available to consumers.[39] Industry veteran David Friedman noted in 1980 that of the roughly six hundred adult films made between 1975 and 1980, nearly all were available on video, evidence of the industry's quick embrace of the new format even before a substantial customer base existed for the material.[40] In 1984, Keith Justice catalogued more than 2,250 titles in his *Adult*

Video Index; by 1986, Robert Rimmer estimated a total count of more than 5,000 adult titles, far more than he could include in his *Adult Video Tape Guide.*[41] This was a sea change from the average of 120 adult films released to theaters per year in the late 1970s, illustrating the need for mediators to sift through the material on behalf of retailers and consumers.[42] Fishbein notes in 1988 that Caballero Video, Video-X-Pix, Essex Video, Cal Vista, and VCX were already "huge companies" when *AVN* began publication in 1983.[43] Yet those companies lacked marketing and communications platforms with access to retailers and consumers who might be interested in more than just the literal representation of sex common in magazines of the era, or who might be curious to learn more but wanted to do so within the pages of a slightly "safer" publication than *Adam Film World, Cinema-X, Video X,* or the others.

Like speculators sensing an impending gold rush, Fishbein and Slifkin seized the unmapped territory of unfamiliar (but curious) retailers and consumers seeking information about adult video. The two were particularly familiar with such needs from their encounters with customers at Movies Unlimited who had explicitly sought such advice. Fishbein later described these interactions:

> All these new people getting VCRs, the one thing that was common amongst them was, "Hey, can you recommend an adult film?" 'Cause everybody wanted to see an adult film. So, I didn't know. I've maybe seen half a dozen in my life. You know, snuck into theaters when I was 17, that whole deal, like everybody, but I've only seen a few films on video. So we would just go by box cover and what other people rented. So it dawned on us that maybe we could do like a newsletter for all these new consumers who were, you know, renting VCRs but didn't know anything about adult, because for most of these people, they had never gone into a theater to see an adult film, so they were new to adult. They just knew they wanted to see it, but they didn't know why, you know. So, we decided we would do a newsletter for consumers, like a consumer report type thing, and it would be, here's what's coming out on video and this is what you should rent and this is what you shouldn't.[44]

That Fishbein would consider a newsletter the best way to give this advice was, in some ways, very predictable. As a teenager, along with classmate Stuart Franks, he had created *Universal Wrestling,* selling subscriptions for $10 per year and printing the copies at the Franks family's print shop.[45] While at Temple University, Fishbein and Slifkin, both journalism majors, created *In Print,* featuring entertainment and articles aimed at college students. The magazine, described by Fishbein as "cutting edge" in terms of design and content, reached a circulation high of thirty thousand and won a Hearst Foundation journalism award.[46]

The two self-described "film buffs" also wrote a home video column for the *Philadelphia Bulletin,* a now-defunct daily newspaper, and briefly considered national syndication as a possible career path. Reaching readers on the topics of entertainment and home video was very familiar ground, and their experience in mainstream film criticism lent them an outsider's perspective on adult film, as did their Pennsylvania location, far away from the Los Angeles–based adult industry. In 1982, the twenty-four-year-old Fishbein and his partner Slifkin each contributed $300 to the project, and Barry Rosenblatt, a graphic design student, put in another $300 and created the initial design. They assembled a first issue and declared themselves "experts."

While contemporary issues of the newsletter present glossy aesthetics and voluminous industry advertising, the early offerings had a much different aesthetic, tone, and purpose. Released in February 1983, the first issue of *AVN* was a two-color newsletter running eight pages. Mailed to twenty-seven subscribers, it carried a cover price of $2. Fishbein and Slifkin continued to work at Movies Unlimited, running the new business out of a post office box in the same shopping center as the video store.[47] Alongside seven reviews, the issue offered a small section of industry news and an interview with performer Veronica Hart. Later, executive editor Gene Ross described the original idea as a desire to "publish a magazine that would be a classy, intelligent, and informative critique of the goings-on in adult film, and the soon-to-come-on-like gangbusters, shot-on-video industry."[48] Of the first seven films reviewed, only *Valley Vixens* (1983, dir. Bobby Hollander) was shot directly on the new medium; the others were theatrical releases transferred to videotape, a sign that the industry was still making its transition.

Most important, the editors made the deliberate and groundbreaking decision to ensure that the newsletter had no nudity or explicit language, a radical departure from the standard approach at the time, and precisely what Ross meant by "classy" and "intelligent." The initial masthead read, "A Monthly Newsletter for Today's Sophisticated X-Rated Viewer," not only a clear indicator of the credibility, expertise, and sincerity sought by the editors, but also an indicator of the type of audience they were hoping to *avoid.* In other words, the paradigm embodied by a publication such as *X-Rated Cinema,* which had debuted only a month earlier, could not have been more different from what Fishbein and Slifkin envisioned. They hoped readers would trust their proclaimed expertise and approach *to the* industry, rather than samples *from* the industry, a deliberately crafted strategy intended to shift the public marketing of private pleasure. In the process, *AVN* commoditized value in elements other than the literal mediation of sex.

This strategy embodied a staunch commitment to what the editors repeatedly deemed quality, a discourse that came to define *AVN*'s approach to reviewing adult videos and in their self-positioning as experts. In the second issue, Fishbein and Slifkin coauthored "I Want One with a Story!," an essay exemplifying the respectability that they sought for their newsletter, for the industry as a whole, and for the types of readers they thought might be their target. The introduction echoes their experiences as retail clerks:

> The young couple had been married merely a month, and already they needed a spice added to their sex lives. They walked into their local video shop and headed right for the adult films. Leslie, a blonde vixen who really hadn't even seen an X-rated film ("I saw part of *Emmanuelle* once at the drive-in!") looked sheepishly at the salesman, lowered her head, and let herself be dragged into that section of the shop. Max, her husband, had seen some adult films. He knew that there had to be films sexy enough to turn his new wife on. The salesman trotted into the X-rated area and chirped, "May I help you?" Leslie was quick to answer, "I want one with a story." The salesman had heard that request before. He even had a list of the adult films that had plots interesting enough to keep both the novice and the experienced viewer hot and happy.[49]

Here the mediation role sought by *AVN* is clear, particularly with the inclusion of both retailer *and* consumer perspectives within a single narrative. The essay exemplifies the hopeful attitude *AVN* held toward the capabilities of video in overturning many cultural stereotypes surrounding pornography following the Golden Age. It also draws on many of the same themes, images, and mythologies familiar from adult motels (see chapter 1). Crucially, the depiction of a heterosexual married couple seeking adult video advice functions to deflate the longstanding mythology that adult films were the provinces of perverted single men—the "raincoaters" of the theatrical era.

It is not a coincidence that *Emmanuelle* (1974, dir. Just Jaeckin) is mentioned in the piece. Justin Wyatt details how, in 1974, Columbia Pictures marketed the softcore feature to women by, in part, disassociating itself from pornography and highlighting all the elements of "quality": narrative, European origin, intelligence, elegance, and beauty. Columbia president David Begelman notes as much when he recalls his decision to obtain the French film for American release, having seen the audience composition in Paris: "The line outside the theater was made up of about 75 to 80% women. We would have had no interest in the film if its appeal was totally to men. Then it could be taken as pornographic." Later, Columbia's advertising strategy played even more on these elements. The copy on the film's poster read: "X has never been known for its elegance. Or for its beautiful people. Or for its intelligent story line. X has been known for other things. At Columbia Pictures we're proud to bring you a movie that will change the meaning of X. A movie that begins with the sensual and takes it to places X has never been before." Columbia was clearly trying to sell sex without the sex—emphasizing narrative as a means to guarantee quality.[50] By including *Emmanuelle* in this narrative, Fishbein and Slifkin strategically drew upon these discourses to create a particular comfort—and taste—level that would position the ensuing advice as something familiar and "safe."

The advice in Fishbein and Slifkin's essay comes from the clerk, painted as a cheerful and well-trained professional, ready to help customers without judgment. Finally, the encounter occurs at a neighborhood video store rather than an adult bookstore—a clear suggestion of the new market and a reassurance to anxious consumers that such encounters are commonplace, as well as easy to understand in familiar customer-service terms. The takeaway is an economic one: renting adult videos, with the assistance of professional retailers, can be easy, effortless, enjoyable, and done everywhere. Ultimately, the private pleasures inherent to renting the tapes (accessible once consumers return to the safety of their homes) are downplayed here in favor of a clear, reliable, and predictable economic transaction.

The reassurance does not end with the customers: it extends to retailers as well, previewing potential transactions and interactions. Most important, *AVN* subsequently provides the "list" referenced by the clerk, positioning the newsletter as the expert, ready and able to provide customers (and, crucially, store clerks) with recommendations and advice—much as Fishbein and Slifkin had done during their time at Movies Unlimited. Here, then, is the mission statement of *AVN*, spelled out and literalized: whether a viewer is a "novice" or "experienced" (implicit code for female and male), the newsletter is prepared to offer reliable, trustworthy, and expert advice, devoid of judgment, in a safe and reassuring tone—literally modeling what the transaction itself could look like.

This strategy became more important as the industry slowly transformed from celluloid to video production, raising technological anxieties related to *visual* value. Producers, retailers, and consumers initially had little faith in the reproduction quality of shot-on-video productions. A pair of letters to the editor in *AVN*'s March 1985 issue illustrates the discourses around such skepticism and the solutions offered by the newsletter. The first, from a consumer, angrily asks why manufacturers refuse to identify video or celluloid production on the box. "The people where I shop have absolutely no idea what's going on and I'm getting sick and tired of going home and finding these lousy quality videos when I was expecting a movie."[51] If this letter illustrates *why* the industry desperately needs a mediator such as *AVN*, the second offers evidence of *how* such a mediation strategy could work: "I am opening a new store in my town," it reads, "and I must say that my subscription to *Adult Video News* has been very helpful in stocking the store. When it opens next month, I feel it will have the best adult section in the area."[52] This letter, much like "I Want One With a Story!" captures how the newsletter sought to serve consumers as a trusted advisor—in this case answering the disappointment of the first writer with "lousy quality" videos by locating the solution in the well-stocked neighborhood store with knowledgeable and informed management described in the second letter. The newsletter's goal was to reassure consumers that a properly operated store, with the right inventory, would fit the definition of "best," which is to say the types of quality familiar from the Golden Age, albeit with new technology and practices. These characteristics (inevitably praised in the reviews) were remarkably consistent: strong, well-written, and creative scripts; characters engaged in complex situations; and, finally, evidence of technically proficient auteurs presenting sophisticated and thoughtful visual presentation. Sex—that most important distinguishing characteristic of pornography—was frequently an afterthought, disavowed in favor of other quantifiable elements that could provide "something more."

The frustrations regarding visual quality also illustrate a larger tension around new technologies that *AVN* worked to alleviate. Altman describes the way in which audiences draw on prior knowledge to understand new technological forms, but also notes that, in this process, unreasonable expectations and subsequent disappointments become inevitable: "Inheriting from existing media a set of assumptions about the nature—the look and the sound—of reality, new technologies are typically judged to be failures if they prove unable to reproduce reality in the way that contemporary audiences expect. New technologies thus tend initially to be configured not according to their own inherent representational possibilities, but according to current notions, derived from other media, about how reality should be represented."[53]

Thus early tensions around the visual quality of video are highly predictable. Given that celluloid-based film had been the dominant form for the adult industry for decades, it is not surprising that viewers might develop anxieties about the aesthetics of the new medium. Technological change, in other words, always brings as its passenger anxiety for those who want the security of familiarity. *AVN* did much to reassure those viewers, particularly in terms of shifting the discourse about what quality means.

In addition to reviews and industry news and interviews, *AVN* ran numerous, lengthy articles about video as a medium, probing the implications of the transition from adult theaters and the changes brought by new production methods. Veteran Golden Age directors such as Chuck Vincent, Cecil Howard, Anthony Spinelli, and Henri Pachard talked at length about the subject in interviews, and the editors frequently criticized producers who flooded the market with fancy (and often misleading) box covers holding tapes filled with hastily produced and aesthetically impoverished shot-on-video content; *AVN* thus pedagogically trained readers on what to look for (and financially support).[54] *AVN* regularly reviewed theatrical releases and consistently separated shot-on-film (and then transferred to video) from shot-on-video reviews through the 1980s, presumably to the delight of the reader who had written in with the complaint about the need for differentiation. Across both categories, however, *AVN* encouraged consumers to seek out quality, regardless of the medium, which the newsletter invariably defined as the type of narrative and aesthetic sophistication familiar from the Golden Age. Such encouragement had implications far beyond the content itself.

QUALITY, RESPECTABILITY, AND GENDER IN *AVN*

Another, gendered discourse circulates underneath *AVN*'s history. As evidenced by the woman's desire for "one with a story," a particular interest in the promotion of narrative permeates virtually every issue of the newsletter in the first few years and was the cornerstone of its respectability strategy. The editors sought to foreground artistic merits, which meant portraying adult video as sophisticated entertainment. As the introduction to this book outlines, such discourses play into long-standing frameworks built on tensions and anxieties around pleasure—especially women's pleasure. The industry, hungry to increase profits, long sought the female audience for its products. *AVN*, by linking the concept of "one with a story" to potential female viewers, tapped directly into these frameworks, positioning narrative as the key to shifting taste discourses around pornography.

A deep and unintended irony emerges from the continual deployment of this strategy: *AVN*, while actively encouraging the industry to focus on quality as a means of distinction to attract female viewers, fell back on narrative and aesthetics as the markers of that concept. In doing so, it relied on essentialized notions of women, afraid to venture too far into the territory of "simple" bodily pleasures. The active, even incessant, encouragement of "one with story" as an industrial strategy seems, on the surface, designed to motivate the industry toward attention to detail, careful construction of its products, and an investment in the manufacture of sophisticated material—none of which superficially seems like a negative characteristic. After all, what industry (particularly those under a cultural microscope) would *not* want to be associated with such elements? Yet such encouragement also reified notions that women would not want—or should not have—access to pornography or pleasure *without* accompanying attempts to elevate them to pleasures "higher" than simple arousal, pleasures incessantly associated with the "something more" provided, it was most often argued, by narrative.

These sorts of elevation efforts recur frequently in the newsletter's early history. In September 1985, for example, a brief interview with Steffanie Martin of distributor Femme-X makes the strategy clear. "We pre-select tapes geared toward the couple's market," notes Martin. "Our criteria includes that it is a quality production, not offensive to women, good story, good acting, and not shot on a low budget."[55] Much as the newsletter as a whole often did, Martin leaves sex and pleasure out of her criteria, a strange absence in which pornography is described and marketed without its primary generic features.

A longer *AVN* piece in June 1985 that studied the successful marketing of recent adult titles stresses the importance of quality and narrative for store owners, and uses Hal Freeman's 1984 film *X-Factor* as a case study. "A love story . . . the film has appealed to the 'couples' crowd, one of the major reasons for its success. . . . Even customers who do not normally view X-rated films could watch this film without being embarrassed, thereby demonstrating that there is an audience beyond the 'raincoat' crowd."[56] The author goes on to praise *X-Factor* for its sophisticated narrative construction, labeling it as one of the "good ones" that belong in any private collection. "Embarrassment" here might have something to do with arousal—suggesting that "customers who do not normally view X-rated films" (another code, this time for women) require "something more," a justification rooted in intellectual pleasures rather than in the body. Narrative, once again, was the "something more" that provided legitimacy.

Of course, these discourses were not without contradiction as they arose in *AVN*'s pages. Tensions and anxieties circulating around women's pleasure in relation to pornography inevitably erupted, often in places that called out the impossibility of a "one size fits all" essentialist mentality in relation to pleasure. In November 1984, *AVN's* only female columnist, Darla Hewitt, wrote, "Producers of adult films . . . think that less sex and more story will appeal to women. Well, guys, not all women want something like [that]. Some of us—including me—often want to see juicy, up-close, raw sex scenes. . . . I don't always need sensitivity."[57] This is as close as *AVN* came to a piece in which a woman walks into a video store and tells the clerk, "I want one *without* a story." For the most part, adult films of the era sought respectability in their attention to narrative (followed by other elements of mise-en-scène) rather than dismissing its presence. *AVN* certainly encouraged and praised such practices.

Much of the industry, seeking to expand its customer base by adding female viewers, undoubtedly saw *AVN's* efforts as a positive set of strategies. Over time, as the newsletter grew, these strategies, which appealed to much more than a nervous group of new consumers seeking reassurance that adult film could offer "something more" than just bodily pleasures, gradually located a readership in an industry hungry to increase profits. In its early issues, *AVN* connected producers, who made the content, with retailers, who were instructed to maintain a professional, informative demeanor, and finally with consumers, who were encouraged to seek out and support quality. While other adult magazines performed somewhat similar functions, it was the deliberate, calculated decision to eliminate sampling—and the overall avoidance of nudity and explicit language—that distinguished *AVN*. By joining the industry, retailers, and consumers in a web of dedication to the characteristics of the Golden Age, the magazine attempted to foster in all three groups a sense of respectability regarding pornography and to shift taste discourses around it. While *AVN* was conceived as a newsletter for consumers, it did not take long for the industry to realize the publication's potential to assume a much different role. It was the combination of its core functions—mediation of the distribution chain and platform for the industry—that moved *AVN* within a few issues from a small newsletter originally intended for the average consumer to the leading adult film industry trade journal.

AVN'S TRANSITION TO TRADE JOURNAL

In midsummer 1983, Fishbein noticed that *AVN's* subscriber list was filling up with video rental store owners rather than individual collectors. Owners of the era, like the customers who might not have been familiar with adult films but did have the requisite curiosity and equipment, were eager to capitalize on the exploding market but sometimes lacked knowledge of what to stock in their inventory. As Fishbein later explained:

> These stores needed the information. So that's when we said we'd switch deals and said, alright, let's do it as a trade publication instead of saying that this is a hot sexy movie that you should rent, this is a hot sexy movie that you should stock in your store. And so, when we did that, we started giving it away for free to video stores. That's when all of a sudden the business started to grow and then people wanted to really advertise because it was a whole different, you know, a whole different attitude about why they would advertise. They would advertise because of the reaching in and getting wholesale rather than retail.[58]

This was a tonal change from early issues, which targeted individual viewers. *AVN* quickly discovered an unintended but obvious audience. Retailers, not consumers, now found the most use in the newsletter. Rather than the couple in the "I Want One with a Story!" essay, it was the retail clerk who emerged as the most important beneficiary of *AVN*'s new content.

Targeting video store owners and managers rather than consumers (in both content and advertising) marks the point at which the newsletter moved away from an ostensibly fan-oriented discourse to industry mediation. Other structural changes reflecting this shift began to appear. In May 1984, a feature called "Newsline" appeared, offering industry coverage and news aimed at retailers. Much of this information described legal challenges facing adult filmmakers and distributors, a shift offering further evidence that *AVN* desired a closer relationship with the industry. Sales and rental data appeared beginning in June 1984, as did editorials covering a wide range of industrial, political, and economic issues pertaining directly to retailers rather than consumers. Distributors willing to sell complete video collections to retailers started to run full-page ads in September 1984. "Guides to stars" and "essential collections" essays also became fixtures, designed to assist new owners in purchasing initial inventory or revitalizing stale collections: more of the pedagogy aimed at offering knowledge in the form of opinion.

Advertising in *AVN*'s pages also began to seek a different customer base. A brief news item in the March 1983 issue foreshadowed the transformation. Video-X-Pix, a leading adult video distributor, announced via press release that it would sell *The Erotic World of Angel Cash* (1982, dir. Don Walters) for $39.95, well below the typical $60 to $100 prices common at the time. This decision followed the lead of Paramount Pictures, which had similarly decided to lower prices on *Star Trek II* (1982, dir. Nicholas Meyer)

Figure 13. Hollywood's "sell-through" pricing tactics came to adult video in 1983 when Video-X-Pix dropped the retail price of *The Erotic World of Angel Cash* (1982, dir. Don Walters) to $39.95. Advertisement, *Adult Video News* (July 1983): 5. Courtesy of the Kinsey Institute for Research in Sex, Gender, and Reproduction.

to "sell through" directly to customers at affordable rates. Vicki Langer of Video-X-Pix noted: "This will stimulate higher sales while bringing in additional viewers to the industry."[59] Three issues later, Video-X-Pix placed an ad for *Angel Cash* in *AVN*, prominently displaying the reduced price (figure 13).[60] This pair of seemingly innocuous events historically stands out as indicative of *AVN*'s capability to mediate between buyers and sellers of adult film *without samples,* instead covering the day-to-day operations of the industry *and* providing a marketing platform for the results. Similar advertising logically followed, with other companies learning from Video-X-Pix's example. By the fifth issue, distributors had seized the opportunity to market their products with bold (but sample-free) graphics, and by late summer 1983, such ads occupied as much space as the content, setting the trend that has since become standard in the newsletter.

Caballero Video, in the February–March 1984 issue, placed an advertisement addressing video retailers instead of individual viewers, thus initiating a strategy that other distributors were quick to follow.[61] In subsequent issues, Essex Video targeted video store owners by offering various in-store promotions, giveaways, and special rates. These changes are visible in the January 1985 issue: VCA Pictures, arguably the leader in adult video as the industry grew to maturity, claimed in an advertisement that its titles were "guaranteed to bring you explosive profits."[62] Only a few pages later, Starlet Video was still offering a "video club" membership to individual consumers, an outdated model that would soon fade from the landscape, as would Starlet itself, indicating, perhaps, why such models were no longer economically viable.[63] Circulation figures further reflected *AVN*'s emphasis on retailers. Subscriptions increased in its second year to nine thousand, of which four thousand went free to stores—a strong indication of *AVN*'s growing presence in rental locations rather than individuals' mailboxes.[64] Increasingly, retailers had the opportunity to turn to the newsletter for advice, expertise, and information.

This timeline of discursive change parallels the explosive growth of VCR sales beginning in 1984.[65] By 1985, as adult movie theaters across the United States closed, local video stores transformed into primary outlets for sexually explicit material—not just for spectators migrating from the theaters, but also for those new initiates willing to try the material in the privacy of home viewing. When asked in 1984 about video's impact, Al Goldstein, publisher of *Screw* magazine, replied that if he owned an adult theater, he would tear it down and build a parking lot—a prescient idea that theater owners would have been wise to follow.[66] Adult magazines, too, were losing customers to the new technology. In November 1986, *Playboy* cut its advertising rates by 17 percent after a tumble in subscriptions, and *Hustler* lost more than half its readership as home video grew.[67] Ben Pesta all but ceded the market to video in an October 1984 *Hustler* essay: "Cassettes are more involving, more dynamic and more erotic than magazines. They have no pages to turn and no difficult words to read. Their images move and talk. They give buyers of men's publications more of what they're looking for— erotic entertainment—than magazines ever could."[68]

In response, magazine publishers creatively turned to video, with varying degrees of success. Such technological experiments had precedent: *Velvet Talks!* had experimented with audio in the late 1970s by including a vinyl record with the centerfold, with the model talking directly to consumers.[69] The first attempt to do something similar with video was made by *Partner* magazine, which unveiled its first issue in June 1979. In a unique cross-promotion, the magazine offered a companion video via mail order (for an additional $64.98) that it called *The Partner Television Show*, a sixty-minute tape (Betamax or VHS) that presented four softcore "stories" matched with content from the magazine. "Now, for the first time ever," the magazine suggested, "you can watch great erotic episodes spring to life in the privacy of your own home." Its awkward efforts to describe the tape (as a "television show," a "cable TV show with a *60 Minutes*–type format," and "as actual documentary films")[70] speak to the difficulty of describing the product. The first tape consisted of photo shoots with models, interviews with swingers, and a look at a female wrestling league, all detailed in the magazine's pages with photos.[71] The magazine dropped new tapes beginning in June 1981, though it still offered eight previous sets by mail order.[72]

Other magazines, such as *Hustler, Penthouse, Playboy,* and *Screw,* perhaps seeing the popularity of alternative programming, all offered video versions beginning in 1984. In these efforts, they were clearly hoping for the kind of success experienced by *Jane Fonda's Workout* (1982), an exercise tape featuring the actress that revealed a massive market for alternative video programming.[73] *New Look,* created by Andre Blay (founder of Magnetic Video, described in chapter 1), entered the market as a video-only venture in early 1982, featuring interviews with Bob Rafelson and Francis Ford Coppola in its first issue, alongside the "world's first video centerfold," but did not make it to issue two.[74] Adult film producers even attempted to seize the potential of a video "magazine." VCX, among the biggest and most successful producers, introduced *Men's Video Magazine* in 1984 with a dazzling example of marketing hyperbole:

> VCX's Men's Magazine is a glittering showcase of video and artistry and visual fireworks which combines state-of-the-art technology with some of the most gorgeous *femme fatales* ever to grace the television screen. VCX introduces this first installment of MVM to our millions of seasoned video lovers who want to experience high-quality, non-explicit adult programming without sacrificing the power of the erotic image. The format is a lively mixture of single girl video layouts; an interview with adult film superstar Kay Parker; a voluptuous oil-wrestling free-for-all; and an eye-popping abstract dance sequence with a bevy of beautiful bodies.[75]

As with *New Look, Men's Video Magazine* did not make it to issue two. Even Fishbein, seeing the possibility that information *about* video could be disseminated *on* video, released a test issue of *AVN* on videotape in August 1986, calling it *Adult Video News Video Magazine: Volume 1* and including reviews, news, and a "video centerfold" of performer Ginger Lynn (figure 14).[76] There was no second volume, and *AVN* dropped the venture.

Back in the print magazine, *AVN* offered a supportive space for owners seeking reassurance, advice, industry information, and expertise on the flood of customers entering their stores, particularly after the release of the

Figure 14. Among the many efforts to combine old and new technological paradigms was *Adult Video News Video Magazine: Volume 1* (1986, Adult Video News, Betamax). Like the rest, it failed immediately. *Adult Video News Confidential* (July 1986): 17. Courtesy of AVN Media Network (avn.com).

Meese Commission's *Final Report* in 1986, examined in chapter 4. Typical were essays that questioned stereotypes and misconceptions, carefully informing retailers that rape, child pornography, bestiality, and extreme violence were not condoned by the adult film industry, nor were those elements present in the mainstream titles making up a potential inventory. Thus *AVN* offered reassurance to those fearful of the legal problems increasingly associated with adult material.[77] *AVN*'s longstanding role as unofficial legal advisor to mainstream video owners served as an attempt to link the industry together against concentrated government efforts to limit, contain, and eradicate pornography during this period, and, in many cases, *AVN* was one of only a few voices on such topics for independent store owners. The message was consistent, clear, and strategic: If the industry continued to maintain professional practices in its production, distribution, and retail processes, increasing numbers of consumers would follow, along with the cultural legitimacy that would provide legal protection.

As *AVN* grew, more than just its content and audience changed. Slifkin departed, amicably and without compensation, after the first year; Rosenblatt lasted longer but used legal means to negotiate his exit.[78] Fishbein, saddled with debt but more committed than ever to the venture, turned to his former classmate (and wrestling magazine cocreator) Stuart Franks, who came on as a silent partner. Franks, whose Printers Trade business was the printer for *AVN*, deferred the $200,000 owed in back printing costs as part of the arrangement.[79] In February 1985, the magazine switched to a full-color, glossy publication, finally allowing Fishbein to leave his job at Movies Unlimited. The following month, he released a spinoff, *Confidential,* aimed squarely at retailers seeking marketing and legal advice. *Confidential* connected the industry and retailers even more explicitly, patiently reassuring retailers that carrying adult videos was a profitable and legitimate business proposition. The new publication, which described itself as "the Adult Marketing Guide to the Video Industry," offered promotional ideas, coverage of legal issues, consumer feedback, national sales information, and product recommendations—and even more disavowal of pornography itself. A preview of *Adult Video News Confidential* in the February 1985 *AVN* makes that perfectly clear: "Attention: video retailers, distributors, manufacturers . . . this publication features NO nudity and NO foul language. It is very professionally written and produced. Everything is handled in a clean and tasteful manner. It's essential for every video store owner!"[80]

Despite the differentiation efforts, however, nothing in *Adult Video News Confidential* was substantially new or different from *AVN*'s content, though the editors did amplify their direct address to retailers as well as increasing coverage of issues pertaining to video rental. Extending the "I Want One with a Story!" paradigm, the editors of *Adult Video News Confidential* ran an essay titled "How to Make Your Adult Customers Comfortable" in May 1986 that carried on the pedagogical tradition. "If you make the adult patron feel at ease," the editors wrote, "he will become more confident in choosing adult fare and, more than likely, will be one of your steadiest repeat customers."[81] Advice included strategies for organizing the "back room," emphasizing customer service, and, of course, having well-trained staff ready to offer advice and suggestions. *Confidential* allowed video store owners indifferent to pornography to focus on information necessary to stock store shelves, given that it was an increasingly important revenue stream.[82] Nevertheless, it is difficult to identify a substantial difference between the two publications, which may be one reason that *Confidential* eventually folded.

The experimentation continued in March 1987, when Fishbein repackaged *AVN* as a mass-market publication complete with glossy pages and limited color printing. Like *Confidential,* however, *AVN*'s venture in newsstand sales proved brief, ending after four months, probably when particular audiences discovered the "no sampling" strategy. Further experimentation occurred in 1989, when Fishbein released yet another publication related to the industry, this one with maximum disavowal. *Free Speech: The Confidential Bi-Weekly of Obscenity Legislation Defense*, a sixteen-page newsletter focused on the mounting legal problems facing the adult industry, was intended for producers, distributors, store owners, lawyers, and law libraries. The publication, with a circulation of one thousand, cost $129 annually and took no advertising.[83] Despite Fishbein's good intentions, however, the cost was prohibitive and the information was mostly the same (although in greater quantity) as in *AVN*. Publication ceased after a year.[84]

Sexposé, a 1996 partnership with phone sex entrepreneur Ted Liebowitz, was Fishbein's most ambitious magazine project. It reprinted *AVN*'s reviews (in a special "adult entertainment guide" black-and-white newsprint insert) alongside industry gossip, interviews, and advertisements, and it added sampling, the one thing *AVN* had long avoided. The magazine was an effort to create a newsstand publication aimed at the general consumer rather than the industry, and it presented a radically different tone aimed at consumers seeking imagery and titillating content—the two elements *AVN* stood staunchly against from its creation. Gone was the policy of "no foul language," and while the magazine technically offered softcore content, it abounded with the type of pictorials familiar from *AVN*'s early competitors.

Industry gossip, interviews, and advertisements filled the pages, but appeals to producers, distributors, store owners, and other industry members were absent. For example, an eight-page spread on performer Jenna Jameson featuring fifteen photographs makes no effort whatsoever to link her appearance to a video then in release, and it offers only minimal accompanying text.[85] A seven-page article on Vivid Video's *Lethal Affairs* (1996, dir. Toni English) represents a prototypical example of more traditional industry sampling: twenty photographs, most of them taken on-set during production, show performers Chasey Lain and Janine engaged in sexual activity, some of its hardcore images blacked out.[86] *Sexposé* was the inverse of *AVN*, using the industry's products as the content, bringing back the familiar photo spread and centerfold format, and filling its pages with nude pictorials of adult performers and stills from new video releases. It ended publication in May 1998 after failing to make much of a dent in the competitive adult magazine market. Another spinoff, *Fetish*, also proved a quick failure.[87]

These failed publication ventures prove, somewhat ironically, that the original publication had used a successful distinction strategy in bridging the gap among producers, retailers, and consumers. *AVN* set a clear course for the future, designed to garner legitimacy by shifting taste discourses around pornography, in large part by encouraging quality. The company also further integrated itself into the industry it covered; by 1991, Fishbein had moved *AVN* to Chatsworth, California, the suburb of northwest Los Angeles that nearly all of the adult film industry calls home. The outsider was now an insider.

CONCLUSION: LEGITIMIZING THE GUTTER

AVN's success in selling adult film without the sex did not change the publishing industry. Neither did sampling, the primary tool of the adult film industry since its roots, disappear from the magazine landscape. For example, the June 1993 issue of *Video View*, another magazine in the parade of titles that followed *AVN*, overflows with explicit hardcore photographs from dozens of adult videos. Alongside interviews with performers such as K. C. Williams, Jamie Summers, and Savannah are reviews of fourteen films and an article on various titles in the "orgy" genre.[88] The tactics and strategies in *Video View* do not deviate from standard sampling practices, instead drawing potential viewers to material based on the familiar patterns of minimal copy alongside maximum visuals. Ultimately, technological advancements in printing, graphic design, and photography, as well as the individual performers and titles, make up the primary differences between

Video X in 1980 and *Video View* in 1993, as does the latter's return to a direct address to consumers, not retailers.

AVN, while never succumbing fully to the strategy it had so long avoided (except in its *Sexposé* spinoff), nevertheless pushed its own boundaries as time went on. The September 2009 issue, for example, fills 244 pages—but still carries no sampling. Interviews, reviews, industry news, and performer profiles—all the hallmarks of *AVN*'s early days—compose some of the content; hundreds of full-color, professionally designed industry advertisements make up the rest. Filled with graphic images, these ads push as close as possible to sampling within the confines of their space. For example, Red Light District's advertisement for *Hardcore Training 7* (2009, dir. Gil Bendazon) features eight small set photographs surrounding a larger publicity shot of performer Marcellinha Moraes.[89] Six of the eight smaller images contain graphic hardcore sexual acts, with blurred areas over the genitals of the performers, blocking images of penetration and allowing the magazine to stay safely within the softcore/hardcore divide. Thus, while *AVN* stayed true to its strategy of not presenting samples as content, advertisers found ways to incorporate it into their material. Red Light District's advertisement, indicative of the standard pattern found throughout the magazine in the 1990s and 2000s, eliminates narrative, instead stringing together images in hopes that retailers would see enough of the product to ensure customer satisfaction.

Indeed, this is precisely why the eight set photographs in the Red Light District advertisement all show different categories of activity: anal sex, group sex, interracial sex, "lesbian" sex, oral sex, and solo masturbation. Retailers skimming through hundreds of advertisements could quickly ascertain the overall contents. No longer was there any defensive pretense or attempts to justify the contents. The quality of the content was implied by either its variety (as in this advertisement) or its singularity (as in the myriad others throughout for specific genres, such as group scenes, transsexuals, interracial, etc.), which removed narrative entirely. This shift away from narrative calls into question the worrying about sampling in the first place. If respectability was obtained by deemphasizing sex, the result was a gendered outcome that attempted to build on stereotyped notions of what women defined as quality. By unapologetically sampling its products, the adult industry, by the 1990s, had realized that the large numbers of women who were purchasing, renting, and viewing their content were doing so for just that: the content.

In mid-1986, however, as the industry was completing its transition to video, *AVN* was still hopeful that the industry would invest in the traditional notions of quality production that it modeled with its own publishing approach. "The days of overwhelming garbage are vanishing," wrote Mark Kernes. "Competition is fierce and quality will win out."[90] As time went on, that competition enveloped even Fishbein: by the early 2000s, he had parlayed his knowledge and expertise regarding adult video into practice, opening the eight-store Excitement Video adult chain in the Philadelphia area, his home territory.[91] While it is relatively easy to see how *AVN* affected Fishbein, it is much more difficult to ascertain exactly how much influence *AVN* had on individual retailers or consumers. Yet what remains clear is that no other publication tracked the growth, provided expertise, or did more to champion the legitimacy of pornography during this period than *AVN*. Nor, importantly, did any other magazine so successfully create and shape its own status *within* the new industry. In doing so, however, *AVN* did not just attempt to shift taste discourses around pornography; it also reified and solidified heavily problematic gendered stereotypes and practices. Indeed, its effort to discourage sampling also encouraged the notion that women must be "protected" from sexualized imagery and fantasy, an irony that seems in contradiction with its otherwise intense labor toward building the adult film industry into something better. *AVN* eventually became, as it had wanted, the "voice" of the adult industry, even if, as some have argued, the fundamental nature of its purpose as a marketing platform eventually resulted in a reliance on advertising that eliminated objectivity.[92]

Indeed, as the magazine's success grew, it became increasingly difficult to differentiate it from the industry it had long covered. Fishbein sold the company in 2010, slowly easing into a consultant's role and then leaving entirely in March 2012.[93] In spring 2013, he and former AVN CEO Darren Roberts founded X3Sixty Network to provide original television programming related to adult industry news to cable systems in North America and Eastern Europe.[94] The magazine lives on under new ownership, still filling the mediation role it has served for three decades. Looking back in February 1986 at *AVN*'s early growth, Fishbein and Rosenblatt diminished their own economic goals in favor of the political side of their creation: "The adult video industry, constantly under fire and always scorned, needed to be legitimized."[95] Given rising pressure from the Meese Commission, antipornography feminists, and cultural conservatives as the 1980s progressed, that need became increasingly pressing, as explored in the final chapter of this book. *AVN*'s efforts to fill this need, however well intentioned and meaningful, also made the magazine valuable and profitable. While it remains true that the adult film industry was increasingly legitimized in the wake of *AVN*'s efforts, the most visible measure of that legitimacy was economic rather than in terms of cultural awareness and change surrounding pornography, which continued (and continues) to serve as a source of great cultural anxiety, regulation, and debate.

What *AVN* knew from the beginning has been made generally clear in the years since: economic success goes a long way toward creating cultural respectability. Giving financial value to something, in other words, tends to convey its value more generally. In a telling moment at the 2004 AVN Awards, *Hustler* magazine publisher Larry Flynt thanked Fishbein for "lifting this industry out of the gutter," a perfect encapsulation of the way the magazine labored to reconfigure taste discourses around pornography and, in the process, helped to ensure its continued economic survival through the transition to the era of home video.[96] That the comment occurred at an event created by *AVN* also speaks to the legitimizing labor the publication did for the industry. What better moment, after all, than an awards ceremony to make pornography into art?[97]

It was *AVN*'s encouragement of the industry's *other* great transition—from the long-forgotten homemade videotapes Slade watched in the Times Square theaters to modern, efficient corporate enterprise—that might be the magazine's most lasting legacy. In its drive to alter discussions of taste around pornography through its pedagogical practices, *AVN* opted to place value in the commodity rather than in shifting the meaning of pleasure itself. The side effect has been that those discourses, in which pleasure remains suspicious and dangerous, have changed little even as industry bottom lines have dramatically improved.

In the next chapter, I examine two performers and their respective companies—Candida Royalle and Femme Productions, and Ginger Lynn and Vivid Video—that embodied *AVN*'s challenge to improve the quality of adult film by emphasizing its status as a commodity. The stories of these two women, along with their places in the larger history of adult film and its practices *with* and *toward* women, reveal new contours in questions of respectability as the industry continued its transition toward efficient, modern corporate enterprise.

3 The Means of Production

Vivid Video and Femme Productions

My name on a box sells a lot of cassettes.

Ginger Lynn quoted in Paul Fishbein, "Interview: Ginger Lynn,"
Adult Video News (1985): 36

Women didn't discover their power until video came along. Until then
the power belonged to the director.

**Henri Pachard (Ron Sullivan) quoted in Legs McNeil, Jennifer Osborne,
and Peter Pavia,** *The Other Hollywood: The Uncensored Oral History
of the Porn Film Industry* (2005), 366

While the early days of adult video had focused almost entirely on releasing libraries of Golden Age films on videotape alongside experimental shot-
on-video attempts, the new technology created space for many in the
industry to rethink the nature of the content along with its distribution. No
longer was public exhibition the primary strategy, which, combined with
the potential to distribute a wide range of material not limited to theatrical
presentation, meant that adult film producers began to sense the economic
potential of going in new and different directions. Companies entered the
market with products for newly interested and available audiences, which
offered the chance to support wider and more diverse ranges of material,
eventually culminating in the gonzo style (described in the epilogue). New
distribution pipelines appeared, too, and the vast network of video rental
stores around the country sought out product beyond the best sellers or
most widely publicized titles to serve diverse audiences. Just as the Golden
Age had stars, so too would the video era, and the combination of privacy,
availability, and technology created an opportunity to rethink the presentation of sexuality that, in some cases, embraced an unabashed celebration of
women's pleasure.

After all, as I note in the introduction, by midsummer 1986, women
participated in 63 percent of adult video transactions, according to one

estimate by *AVN*.[1] Even if this poll was designed to mitigate antipornography discourses for nervous retailers (and was remarkably homogenous in its conception of women and their transactional encounters), it nevertheless illustrates that the market was more than ready for significant change beyond merely the technological. In a 1982 *American Film* essay, Jean Callahan outlines the growing audience of women seeking out sexually explicit material—but bemoans the lack of attention paid to their pleasures and points of view. After noting the handful of female directors making films with adult content (Gail Palmer, Stephanie Rothman, Svetlana Marsh, and Suze Randall), Callahan points out that their content nevertheless remains somewhat mired in an approach that she describes as "hostile to women's sexuality." She concludes with a question: "When women watch more sexually oriented [material], why shouldn't they find ways to direct the form to their needs as well as find ways to register their disgust with the more misogynistic genres?"[2] Also in 1982, veteran adult film producer and director Roberta Findlay more bluntly noted that "women and also couples would rather see movies that aren't so relentless, that are a little more expressive, that aren't all 'pump' shots."[3] This chapter traces attempts by two companies, Vivid Video and Femme Productions, both created in 1984, to do just that. It is also the story of the two women, Ginger Lynn and Candida Royalle, who were fundamental to those companies in very different ways and with very different outcomes. In many ways, the experiences of Lynn and Royalle symbolize the struggles between the two sides of the camera, and the structures of power that inflect each of those positions.[4]

In 2004, Royalle, founder of Femme, noted in her sex advice book, "People are not going to stop looking at sex, and if women don't take control of the means of production, men will continue to do it for us, continuing to erroneously define female sexuality."[5] Royalle wrote from experience: twenty years earlier, after a relatively short stint as an adult performer, she began creating films geared to what she consistently described as a "women's sensibility." In 1987, *Playboy* magazine called her the "Roger Corman of erotica," recognizing the ways in which she existed outside the industry mainstream and her efforts to help other women take more active production roles.[6] Femme was deliberately political, and its corporate foundation rested on changing the narrative and aesthetic "meaning" of pornography—and in the process challenging hegemonic beliefs fueling the industrial practices of its manufacture. Femme's success led to the "feminist pornography" movement, which in the years since 1984 has grown into a significant market.

If Royalle successfully took control behind the camera to change the depictions and narratives in front of it, Ginger Lynn had a very different kind of power, at least initially—but none of the control. Vivid Video, for which Lynn performed, and whose history is described below, was also invested in changing the pornography landscape, but that investment took on much different and far less political contours than did Femme's. Vivid was interested primarily in altering the marketing practices that had long defined the industry in order to make it as mainstream as possible: it attempted to neuter the stigma attached to sexual pleasure and thus find the largest possible audience. Yet the absence of overt politics is itself political; Vivid, in the end, took adult video into a new realm of modern, efficient, and significantly profitable territory by selling pornography like any other product, often precisely in the ways championed by *AVN*. Lynn's story is radically different from Royalle's: she did not own the means of production, or control it, even as her literal body *was* the means of production for Vivid, given her status as its first performer. Her story exemplifies the struggles and challenges faced by women in the adult video era, whose performances propelled the industry. Lynn did not identify as a feminist during her performance career, has rarely spoken of herself in those terms, and has not been celebrated or reclaimed by feminists, but her career speaks volumes about what defines women's contributions to the industry, particularly when those contributions become popular but are not necessarily financially rewarded.

VIVID VIDEO AND THE DESIRE FOR ACCESSIBILITY

Although Steven Hirsch and Dewi "David" James officially created Vivid in 1984, the company originated in 1972, when Steven's father, Fred, a former stockbroker, took a job as a salesman with Reuben Sturman's Sovereign News Corp., with its vast network of adult bookstores (and peep-show booths), headquartered outside Cleveland in Lyndhurst, Ohio. In 1974, federal prosecutors brought obscenity charges against six Sovereign employees, including Fred.[7] With the trial still in progress, Fred moved his family to the Woodland Hills suburb of Los Angeles in 1975, commuting back and forth on weekends. With financing from Sturman, he started Sunrise Films, which produced and distributed 8mm loops under the "Limited Edition" banner. By 1978, Fred and others in Sovereign News Corp. had been acquitted of all charges; a year later, after moving operations to a small storefront in Northridge, he changed his company name to Adult Video Corporation (AVC) and joined the home video revolution, selling his "Limited Edition" line as well as Golden Age titles licensed from other producers. Eventually, AVC moved into low-budget video productions.[8]

Steven Hirsch, born May 25, 1961, spent three years taking business classes at Cal State Northridge and UCLA before dropping out to work for his father at AVC in sales, marketing, promotion, and accounting. Deep in the adult video distribution business, he directly observed the lack of established marketing and promotional channels available to the industry, which was, for the most part, still mired in an underground economy with limited reach and resources.[9] Undoubtedly, he also observed that his father's company was engaged primarily in marketing films produced by *other* companies, including softcore features such as *Cry Uncle!* (1971, dir. John G. Avildsen) and *The Swingin' Stewardesses* (1971, dir. Erwin C. Deitrich), obvious profit producers for AVC, given consumers unwilling to watch hardcore but still interested in adult material. Mostly, though, AVC released a large selection of double features that were clearly peep-show stag films repurposed on video alongside a smaller group of lesser-known hardcore titles. Indicative of this mixture was *Lovelace Meets Miss Jones* (1975, dir. Felix Delione), a film that featured a repairman (Harry Reems) visiting a lonely housewife (Dolly Sharp) but also included 8mm loops of Linda Lovelace and Georgina Spelvin, filmed before they appeared in *Deep Throat* (1972, dir. Gerard Damiano) and *The Devil in Miss Jones* (1973, dir. Damiano), respectively.[10] *Lovelace Meets Miss Jones* thus attempted to fool unsuspecting viewers into thinking Lovelace and Spelvin had made an original film together; it also illustrates the hustle that many early adult film distributors were performing in an undefined market—and the attitude that very nearly anything would sell on the new format.[11]

What the younger Hirsch witnessed in these strategies was twofold: almost anything would sell, but *owning* the content ensured long-term profits. Despite its primary role as a distributor for others, AVC nevertheless grew highly profitable—tripling its sales between 1983 and 1985 to more than $4 million. With these lessons in mind, Steven left the company in 1981, parlaying his knowledge and experience into a sales position at Cal Vista, a major distributor in the growing industry.[12] There Sidney Niekirk and Jack Gallagher, two veterans of the industry, mentored Hirsch, showing him the nuances and finer points of distributing adult film, which primarily meant maintaining relationships with retailers willing to carry adult titles and establishing connections with possible new outlets.[13]

Traveling the country as part of the national sales team, Hirsch saw firsthand the potential that home video offered audiences waiting to view pornography in the privacy of their homes rather than in the public space of the theater. David James, the head of Cal Vista's mail-order department, was, like Hirsch, eager to start his own company.[14] Taking $25,000 from

James's savings and a $20,000 loan from John Tedeschi, Fred Hirsch's box printer at AVC, Hirsch and James created Vivid Video, with a simple strategy of investing primarily in marketing.[15] They also thought that the privacy of adult video offered something that the theatrical model of the earlier era could not: increased access for female viewers and couples not interested in joining the public "raincoat crowd." This was not a political insight; it was an economic one. As was true of most producers seeking the elusive couples' market, Hirsch and James were looking to boost their sales, which they imagined they could do with a strategic realignment of advertising and marketing discourses that emphasized particular characteristics. The *positioning* of the content, in other words, was a tactic understood very early on by Hirsch, much as it was (in similar fashion) by Fishbein with *AVN*. The couples' market, Hirsch said later, was "something we really felt strongly about, and that we went after."[16]

The primary strategy employed by Hirsch and James in their effort to create a new type of company was to hire a single well-known female performer around whom they could build a marketing and branding campaign. Essential to the idea was an exclusive contract, a strategy borrowed from classic Hollywood business practices but, with a few exceptions, never really utilized by the adult film industry. The strategy had a very practical (and financial) foundation: Hirsch and James did not want other companies to benefit from the visibility that a performer would attain from Vivid's productions and marketing. "If we promoted this girl and made a lot of movies with her," Hirsch argued, "we wanted her not to work for anybody else. It just made sense to me: why should somebody else publicize a movie with her based on my marketing?"[17] In 1984, when Hirsch and James were ready to launch Vivid and produce their first film, there were two obvious choices: Ginger Lynn and Traci Lords. Both performers had enough cachet in the industry to provide the desired boost of preexisting publicity. Vivid decided to pursue Lynn to carry the brand, which, given the catastrophic effects of Lords's 1986 arrest for making adult films while underage, was certainly a fortuitous decision.[18]

Ginger Lynn and "Ginger"

Ginger Lynn Allen, born December 14, 1962, in Rockford, Illinois, began her career in September 1983 after answering an advertisement for "figure models" in the *Los Angeles Free Press*. The ad was for Jim South's World Modeling Agency on Van Nuys Boulevard in Sherman Oaks, the "central casting" office for the adult film industry in the 1980s.[19] After meeting Lynn, South summoned photographers Steven Hicks and Suze Randall.

Hicks, who was about to leave the country, tried to persuade Lynn to wait; but Randall, sensing an opportunity, hired Lynn on the spot for a photo shoot—which ended up in the March 1985 issue of *Penthouse*, in a section titled "Queens of the X-Rated Cinema."[20]

Indeed, between September 1983 and March 1985, Lynn did become a "queen" of adult film, transitioning quickly from magazine model to film performer. Following the shoot with Randall, various photographers hired Lynn for the next seventeen straight days. After initially rejecting offers to appear on film, Lynn quizzed other women in the industry and quickly realized her economic potential. She gave South her audacious demands: script and cast approval, as well as $1,000 per scene. While South laughed at the proposal, producers David L. Frazier and Svetlana Marsh quickly agreed and offered her a contract.[21] Like most performers, Lynn felt she needed experience on camera, and she shot a handful of loops in November 1983.[22] On December 14, 1983, her twenty-first birthday, Lynn flew to Hawaii for the concurrent productions of *Surrender in Paradise* and *A Little Bit of Hanky Panky*, for which she was paid $5,150.[23] Always eager for new talent, producers showered Lynn with offers on her return, and she quickly became one of the most prodigious and sought-after performers in the industry. Within a year, Lynn had appeared in dozens of films. While these were mostly low-budget celluloid productions shown in the remaining (but dwindling) adult theaters and then released on videotape, they were more than enough to justify her inclusion as a "Queen of the X-Rated Cinema" in *Penthouse*.

For Hirsch and James, Lynn was an obvious choice to carry the brand. Lynn's onscreen persona was vibrant, fun-loving, adventurous, and unabashed about pursuing (and enjoying) sexual pleasure. Her squeaky voice, small frame, and blonde hair defined her as the prototypical Southern California "beach bunny" (even though she was actually from the Midwest), making her an ideal representative for the new, Los Angeles–based video industry. Lynn had the "it" factor that made her a star—and, for pornography, part of that "it" was the ability to convey desire for and pleasure in sex, which she did unlike any other performer from the era. Her reputation for willingness to engage in boundary-pushing activities (anal sex, double penetration with two male partners, and energetic scenes with other women) gave a particular aura of insatiability to her early career, but her girl-next-door appearance also made her seem approachable and "real," particularly on the small screen, which favored character over setting and narrative. The "Ginger" persona, to Hirsch and James, had the perfect convergence of elements with which to start a video company.

Toward the end of 1984, Hirsch, his girlfriend Jennifer Lynn Wren, and Lisa Trego (who performed as Loni Sanders and Lisa DeLeeuw, respectively) met Lynn at Gladstone's, the restaurant at the terminus of Sunset Boulevard in Pacific Palisades. The breathtaking view of the Pacific Ocean must have matched Hirsch's pitch, which featured an unprecedented offer: a guaranteed six-figure income; royalties; and script, cast, and director approval, with Hirsch and James selling the films and veterans Wren and DeLeeuw assisting with the productions.[24] Such perks, familiar to established and successful Hollywood stars, were something new in adult film—and, like Hollywood's practices, they were part of a calculated investment designed to entice audiences back to see a reliable, familiar, and successful star. Richard Dyer's arguments about Hollywood star images—that they are manufactured, intertextual commodities that are "made for profit"—are not only applicable to Vivid's strategies, but also fundamental to understanding the mechanics of the role Hirsch sought for Lynn in the company.[25]

Indeed, Hirsch promised to build a creative, massive, groundbreaking, and expensive marketing campaign entirely around "Ginger," drawing upon Lynn's preexisting fame and the persona that had successfully captured audience attention. A large part of that fame would be built on her status as the archetypal "girl next door," a moniker that would stay with her throughout her career. Such imagery stretched back to *Playboy* magazine and Hugh Hefner's deliberate creation of that trope in his centerfolds. As Carrie Pitzulo notes, the image was of "All-American girls who liked sex . . . and who treated sexuality as a fun and joyous pursuit."[26] In fact, Lynn's star persona echoed the first *Playboy* centerfold, Marilyn Monroe, whose sexuality (not just in *Playboy* but throughout her career) was constructed as natural, joyful, spontaneous, enthusiastic—and sophisticated, in order to appeal to middle-class consumers.[27] Just as Hefner had created an image of sexually interested and available young women in order to present a particular fantasy that would built repeat customers, so, too, did Hirsch and James draw upon and amplify Lynn's image in order to build their business. Their plan was to associate Vivid, from the beginning, with precisely the sort of fun-loving and adventurous sexual spirit embodied by Lynn.

In terms of concrete strategy, Vivid planned to release one new title per month rather than saturating the market as quickly as possible, ensuring that viewers who wanted to see Ginger would rent (or buy) the tapes on a regular schedule.[28] Each would feature a comedic plot composed of five to six sex scenes, all shot directly on video at the same remote home, with its exteriors, living spaces, and fireplace serving different functions in each.

Lynn agreed to the deal offered by Hirsch, becoming the first "Vivid Girl," the name later given to Vivid contract performers.[29] This was a radical paradigm shift in the business of pornography, focusing a strategy on long-term profit management through repetition, predictability, and investment. As Nicola Simpson describes, the video era would bring new popularity—in part through strategies such as Vivid's with Lynn—and that would require "the business to become more organized."[30]

Vivid wasted no time after the meeting, quickly going into production at the end of the year, and it released *Ginger* (dir. Scotty Fox) on December 19, 1984. The tape went to number one on the sales charts, selling an initial sixty-five hundred copies and sending a clear message to the industry that Vivid's strategy worked.[31] A key part of that strategy, if not necessarily advertised in the same ways that Lynn's presence was, was the work of screenwriter Penny Antine. Antine, who used the pseudonym "Raven Touchstone," wrote all of Lynn's films with Vivid, as well as her fan newsletter and column for *Club International* magazine, and she was a key component in solidifying the Ginger persona that carried the Vivid brand. A Cleveland native, Antine had moved to Los Angeles in the mid-1960s to pursue an acting career, eventually appearing in small roles on television's *The Beverly Hillbillies* in 1966 and in the films *Caprice* (1967), *Valley of the Dolls* (1967), and *Planet of the Apes* (1968). In 1984, her roommate introduced Antine to director Scotty Fox, who was looking for writers. Antine was hired to write *Intimate Couples* in October 1984 and followed that with *Just Another Pretty Face* in 1985, both for Fox. When Vivid hired Fox to direct *Ginger*, he recommended Antine to write the script. In all, she went on to write more than four hundred adult films, making her one of the most prolific and successful screenwriters in the industry's history.[32]

Antine's signature light-hearted tone and witty plots were a perfect match for Lynn's persona, playing to her performance strengths and emphasizing the pursuit of pleasure rather than its problems in the narrative, a departure from much of Golden Age film. Antine similarly recognized the pleasures of the spectator along with those of her characters, choosing not to pathologize them but instead to recognize the pragmatic nature of such viewing. "A good porno script is a support system for sex without getting in the way of sex," she would later say. "In other words, the plot holds them together and weaves throughout the sex scenes without overpowering them." She also made no real efforts to find narrative justification for the pursuit of pleasure. "I don't take most of my films seriously. [. . .] Most are just light sex stories to get a guy's dick stiff."[33] That might have been Vivid's foundational principle. Nevertheless, *how* Antine went about that process represents a significant feminist moment in adult film history, as do Lynn's performances.

Antine wrote the scripts specifically for the couples' market, and she infused them with a deliberately feminist message that might not have been prescribed by Hirsch and James but nevertheless offered a differing perspective from more typical depictions of women. "I determined very early on that I was never going to show a woman in a subservient position. I was about showing the strength of women."[34] That strength recurs throughout Lynn's films with Vivid, in which Ginger (the character) pursues sex without guilt or shame, controls her own narrative destiny, and always maintains a spirited sense of joy and infectious delight. These traits appear from the very beginning: Fox's original treatment had called for the first Vivid film to be called *Educating Ginger*, which Antine altered. The resulting script, in which Ginger is recruited by a wealthy man to be trained as a potential wife for his son, reverses the "education" in the film's conclusion. Ginger, it turns out, has been carefully manipulating everyone around her for her own gain the whole time. Ginger's level of narrative control came to be a hallmark of Antine's Vivid scripts. *Ginger* set the template for the eleven films that followed: Antine's signature lighthearted tone, emphasizing the joy and humor of sex, along with Lynn's cheerful, quirky, and adventurous personality, always focused on the pursuit of pleasure.

If Antine was subtly nudging Vivid's scripts in feminist directions, the company was not nearly as nuanced in its changes to familiar marketing practices. Foreshadowing the company's future strategies, Hirsch hired a photographer and graphic designer with no experience in the adult film industry to create the box for *Ginger*, a move that seismically changed the landscape by deemphasizing the sexual content in favor of glamour— essentially selling the idea of "Ginger" rather than the sex on the tape, a move made possible, in no small part, by Lynn's preexisting fame before her contract with Vivid.[35] The result was remarkably simple: a medium shot of Lynn in a bikini, exposing nothing, astride a statue of a lion, her blonde hair sweeping out behind her. Naturally backlit on a beach, the image is in soft, shallow focus, emphasizing Lynn as the star, and it offers no sexually explicit imagery. Even the back cover, with Lynn reclining nude next to a pool, is less revealing than early issues of *Playboy*. The choice was bold and calculated, doing more than just disguising the actual content on the tape so that customers would have to buy it to see it. Much like *AVN*, which had entered the market the previous year, Vivid deliberately avoided sampling in favor of emphasizing an aura of quality, indicative of its larger strategy to position itself in the marketplace as respectable and "safe."

Marketing Respectability

It was the third film in the series, *Ginger's Private Party* (1985, dir. Fox), made after *I Dream of Ginger* (1985, also directed by Fox and a parody of the television show *I Dream of Jeannie*), that was a significant turning point for Vivid and the industry in general. Hiring an experienced creative director with no experience in adult film to redesign all of Vivid's promotional material from the ground up, with a new, branded identity in the foreground, Hirsch aggressively pushed for even glossier, stylized aesthetics and a deemphasis on the sex at the core of the products. The creative director, never publicly identified (or publicized) because of his ongoing creative work outside the adult film industry, took on responsibility for every aspect of the company's marketing and promotion. This person would later speak of the changes these new techniques brought to the industry: "Because we didn't know any of the rules, we just created a whole new genre of adult packaging.[. . .] Before Vivid, the packaging was just very seedy and non-mainstream, not conceptual at all. But we made these boxes thematic and beautifully shot, and your wife could pick it up and look at it and not be embarrassed. That never happened before. It was really the beginning of the mainstreaming of adult."[36]

The creative director's statement, while obviously self-serving and promotional, carries kernels of truth. Most adult film marketing materials prior to that point had been cheaply produced and practically disposable, intended to entice store owners into ordering adult tapes based solely on titles, brief descriptions, and artwork that might have little to do with the actual film. When the materials did offer more than just these brief details, they would emphasize samples, using their content as the primary draw. The creative director's use of "mainstream" means the sort of respectability that would draw in large numbers, not just the familiar, reliable base. His link back to the anxiety and "embarrassing" nature of pornography for female viewers illustrates the mechanism for recasting pornography away from its cultural associations with shame. As with *AVN*, that recasting meant investment and attention to details other than sex; after all, pornography (as I describe throughout this book) can never be *fully* respectable—which is why the creative director insists on anonymity even during a discussion of groundbreaking marketing practices that should have made visibility possible.

Indicative of this strategy was the promotional flyer for *Ginger's Private Party*, intended for video rental stores, which radically deemphasizes sexual content to present Ginger's star persona alongside the Vivid brand. The front, which features a large close-up of Ginger's face, cleverly foregrounds a visual depiction of an invitation to a party, while the back makes that invitation literal. The graphics and copy there again downplay the hardcore content in favor of a lighthearted, spirited sense of fun. Only one of the three accompanying photos features nudity and hints of the sexual activity in the film, and even that is remarkably minimal. The final bit of text, "RSVP: Vivid Video," was meant literally, signaling Vivid's intention to construct a chain in which customers (and store owners) would request more titles featuring Lynn. The overall effect is one of sophistication, with the front image depicting a glamorous, well-lit Lynn and emphasizing the exclusivity and specificity of the Vivid brand. The image also reveals Vivid's overt effort to move toward the type of quality associated with erotica more than with the hardcore pornography that made up the content of the film itself—marking an important historical moment in which an adult video company tried to alter the meanings of these discourses. The glossy image presented in the flyer is, of course, at odds with the actual images on the tape, which were cheaply produced and hardly sophisticated in an aesthetic sense.[37]

Following *Ginger's Private Party*, Hirsch solidified Vivid's creative team, initiating eight more titles with highly similar elements. Beginning with *Ginger on the Rocks* (1985), Hirsch brought in veteran director Bruce Seven to direct Antine's scripts.[38] The bulk of the creative labor and financial investment, however, did not go into the technical production of the films, which tend to be stylistically dull and differ little from others of the era. Instead, the investment went into marketing the Vivid brand and cultivating Lynn's star persona. The creative director hired professional photographers (such as B. Skow, who has since gone on to a highly successful career as an adult film director) to shoot Lynn for these covers, while the designs emulated magazines such as *Vanity Fair* and *Cosmopolitan*. The results were strikingly consistent, featuring glamorous portraits of Lynn along with the title and Vivid logo. For *Gentlemen Prefer Ginger* (1985), Vivid made the links to Marilyn Monroe explicit, echoing *Gentlemen Prefer Blondes* (1953, dir. Howard Hawkes) in both the title and cover art, which presented Lynn in a white satin gown and diamonds. The idea behind all this image creation was simple: manufacture a branded image to create viewer (and store owner) expectations for an impossible fantasy that could never fully be satisfied, only revisited.

In early February 1986, Lynn shot her final scenes for Vivid, for the films *Blame It on Ginger* and *Ginger & Spice* (both dir. Henri Pachard), and then ended a career that had included sixty-nine films in twenty-six months. The event that did not go unnoticed by the mainstream press. An *Entertainment Tonight* reporter, for example, was on-set for an interview about her decision to exit the adult industry.[39] Lynn wanted to move into mainstream film acting—and was eager to translate her mammoth celebrity status into crossover stardom. As I describe below, it would not be an easy road.

Prepared and ready for the change, Hirsch signed Jamie Summers to replace her, releasing *The Brat* (1986, dir. Pachard) and keeping the "Vivid Girl" system in place.[40] Eventually more than seventy performers followed Lynn at Vivid, and the company grew into a major producer and distributor of adult material. The company's success continued in other ways as well. In 1998, with the help of Bill Asher, a Playboy television executive with an MBA from the University of Southern California who joined Vivid that year, Hirsch purchased Spice, a softcore satellite television channel with seven million viewers, from Playboy for $25 million. Hirsch and Asher converted the channel into Spice Hot, added Hot Zone and Vivid TV, and began transmitting Vivid's hardcore content on all three. They sold the channels back to Playboy in 2001 for $92 million.[41]

Also in 1998, Hirsch hired Resource Media Group, a publicity firm with no experience working on adult film campaigns, to take Vivid further into mainstream culture, in many ways a logical extension of the strategies undertaken in the mid-1980s.[42] Hirsch noted later: "Up to then, most guys in the adult business were very, very underground, as was the entire industry. We decided to go the opposite route and actually court the media and get them to start writing articles, not only about us, but about the industry: it's legitimate, it's mainstream, you see these movies in your local video store, you see them when you go into a hotel room."[43] In a 2003 profile of Vivid performer Jenna Jameson, a *Vanity Fair* writer notes that "Jameson was recently named the leading female adult star of all time—which pretty much makes her a leading female star, period."[44] This was what Hirsch had hoped for all along: not just mainstream acceptance but a reconfiguring of what *mainstream* itself meant. Hirsch was courting everyone.

The success of these efforts can be seen in the company's bottom line: annual revenues exceeded $100 million by 2003, and by 2005 Vivid was producing a third of all adult videos sold in the United States.[45] In surely the company's biggest "mainstreaming" coup, Showtime aired three reality shows featuring Hirsch and Vivid: *Porno Valley* in 2004, *Deeper Throat* in 2007, and *Debbie Does Dallas Again* in 2009. In 2012, *AVN* awarded Hirsch its first Visionary Award, "created to recognize and honor a leader in adult entertainment who has propelled innovation and taken his company—and the business as a whole—to new territory."[46] In the case of its headquarters, that "new territory" has become literal: Vivid now occupies a sprawling Los Angeles building directly across the 101 freeway from Universal Studios—a deliberate, strategic move placing the company squarely in the public eye, far away from the familiar shadows and right next to "normal" film industry. The move emphasized that not only was pornography increasingly mainstream, it was also big business.

Like *AVN*, Vivid could not completely deemphasize sex: that would have been impossible given the nature of its core content. Instead, the content just needed to be repackaged. The company foregrounded the elements it could market in respectable terms. Hirsch knew that such strategies would lead to greater public awareness, which in turn would open new markets and increase his customer base. Much as the creative director quoted above says, these characteristics would not "embarrass" customers, particularly women, and the gloss and veneer accompanying all the trappings of quality (particularly in the marketing) would lend Vivid's products an unmistakable aura of acceptability. In effect, Hirsch overlaid the characteristics of erotica onto hardcore content, just as the filmmakers of the 1970s Golden Age had done before him. In doing so, Vivid gave the adult film industry its greatest public awareness since that era—its intention from its beginning. Such strategies have also kept Vivid out of legal trouble, a remarkable feat considering the company's size and success. Hirsch and James have faced legal problems only once, in 1991, when they were indicted on obscenity charges in Mississippi for shipping four Vivid tapes to that state. Rather than fight the charges, they quickly and quietly pleaded guilty, paid a $500,000 fine, and served no jail time.[47]

And what of Ginger Lynn, on whose image and performances Vivid Video was built? After her contract with Vivid ended, she continued to appear in adult magazines, released the unsuccessful pop-music single "Fantasy World" in 1986, worked as a radio show host, and maintained a lucrative career as a feature dancer across the country at strip clubs. Her primary objective, however, was to "cross over" to mainstream film performances, something she had been planning for some time before her exit from Vivid. The move proved difficult. "The name Ginger Lynn opens up a lot of doors," she noted in 1987. "Most people will get me into casting because they are curious."[48] But that curiosity, as she acknowledged, did not always transform into actual work. Among other projects, Lynn did appear in Ken Russell's *Whore* (1991) and Daniel B. Appleby's *Bound and Gagged: A Love Story* (1993), both critically acclaimed, but she did not garner the mainstream success she had long desired. Perhaps her most high-profile role was in the 1998 music video for Metallica's "Turn the Page," as a down-and-out exotic dancer who turns to sex work at night to support her young daughter. Tellingly, each of these roles drew upon her existing notoriety as an adult film actress—illustrating the difficulty faced by adult film performers trying to cross over. These depictions flipped her star persona, in many ways acting as reversals of what had secured her original position with Vivid. They also mirrored her reality as she faced legal struggles, including convictions related to tax evasion and drug use.[49]

Lynn returned to adult film in 1999 with *Torn* (dir. Veronica Hart) and followed that in 2000 with *White Lightning* (dir. Hart) and *New Wave Hookers 6* (dir. Antonio Passolini). She has appeared in a handful of adult roles in the years since. In 2003, she finally moved behind the camera, directing *Ginger Lynn's School of Head* and *Ginger Lynn's Girlfriends* for VCX. In the 1990s, she may have tried to disassociate herself from her pornography past (while never condemning it), but since the turn of the millennium, she has undoubtedly embraced her veteran status in the industry and has long hinted at the possibility of an autobiography. She has been included in numerous adult film halls of fame and continues to be included regularly on lists, polls, and surveys of the most popular adult film performers of all time.[50]

While she retained her percentage of the profits from her films with Vivid, the relationship between the company and Lynn has not been friendly in the years since she completed her contract. In fact, the animosity began immediately. In 1987, Lynn told *AVN*, "I didn't sign with Vivid. Vivid and I combined and started together. If there hadn't been me there wouldn't be a Vivid."[51] More recently, during a radio interview in 2004, Lynn told fellow performer Kylie Ireland that "there would be no fucking Vivid Video without Ginger Lynn."[52] Yet, despite her absolutely integral contribution to Vivid—indeed, it was built literally on her body—the company seems reluctant to acknowledge her contribution beyond the most basic level. As Hirsch has become one of the wealthiest members of the industry, and Vivid has become one of the largest and most successful companies, Lynn's contribution seems erased, placed alongside those of all the other performers in the endless content library that Vivid continues to sell.

It is there, in the saleable content, that Lynn's legacy with Vivid resides. Her story speaks volumes about the difficulties facing women in the early years of adult video. In a male-dominated industry built on women's bodies, there were very few extensions of power to performers in front of the camera. As Lynn points out, there would be no Vivid without her; yet Vivid lives on without her. She retains her status as a fan favorite, and her videos and images continue to circulate, yet she does not own them any more than she did when they were produced. Like the countless performers who preceded and followed her, Lynn is frozen in time, on celluloid and magnetic tape (and now in digital files) that can be endlessly resold. The epigraph to this chapter by director Henri Pachard (a pseudonym for Ron Sullivan), who directed Lynn in her final film for Vivid, raises more questions than answers. "Women didn't discover their power until video came along," he notes, adding, "Until then the power belonged to the director." But what was this power? The power of women as spectators to choose videos that appealed to their pleasures, certainly. But what about the power of the women who performed in front of the cameras? In Lynn's case, she absolutely had some fleeting power in terms of the marketplace and audience attention, but when her contract ended, so did that power. Pachard's statement raises still more questions: If, until video came along, power "belonged" to the director, what would happen when women *became* the directors? That question would be answered by Candida Royalle, who, as a performer, never came anywhere near the heights attained by Lynn, but whose legacy on the other side of the camera is crucial to the history of adult video.

"I KNEW I COULD DO IT EVENTUALLY": CANDIDA BEFORE FEMME

San Francisco was the site of Royalle's entry into the world of adult film, as it was for so many other performers prior to and during the Golden Age. The city's economic relationship with sex, however, predates the medium. Since the days of the Gold Rush in the 1850s, the city has maintained a relaxed attitude toward vice in general, and the Barbary Coast neighborhood was lined with bars, brothels, and gambling dens. This attitude became part and parcel of the city's culture, making it an ideal place for the development of the free-love atmosphere of the 1960s. Various sex-related trades thrived in such an atmosphere, constantly pushing boundaries and drawing increasingly larger crowds; on June 16, 1964, in a prominent example, Carol Doda, at the Condor Night Club in the North Beach section of the city, performed topless—typically considered the first time that act had occurred in a public venue in the United States. Within months, dozens of other bars and clubs in the neighborhood followed suit; public nudity, in San Francisco, became big business. In another milestone, in 1967, the Roxie Cinema played the first "beaver films"—short, silent films featuring women showing their genitals—movies that eventually radiated throughout the country and frequently were advertised as "Frisco Beavers." Free-love hippies (many working as dancers) represented a large talent pool for aspiring filmmakers living in the area. In the late 1960s, Jim and Artie Mitchell, Alex de Renzy, and Lowell Pickett, who all also operated theaters in the city, began producing adult films using local performers.[53]

It was in 1971, just as the adult film industry was beginning to produce and distribute feature-length productions, that Royalle, born Candice Vadala on October 15, 1950, in Long Island, made her way to San Francisco.[54] She began singing in jazz clubs and classical choirs and appearing in experimental theater productions, using Candida Royalle as a stage name.[55] She also performed with the avant-garde drag queen troupe the Cockettes and their spinoff Angels of Light, and she played drag queen Divine's daughter onstage in *The Heartbreak of Psoriasis*.[56] The intertwining of political and sexual activities in San Francisco was a major catalyst for her evolving feminist views, as she later recalled:

> I stopped being a member of [the National Organization for Women] a long time ago because I felt they were outdated, they were old-fashioned. You know, I had been a young feminist in college. In those days, the feminist movement really embraced the whole sexual liberation of women. What I saw happening in the early 70s was a shift to "men as enemy" and sex as something you shouldn't share with a man, we should only turn to our sisters now for sex; sleeping with a man was like sleeping with the enemy. And I just didn't like where this was all going. I thought this was very repressive to my sexuality and kind of going back to a very puritanical way of thinking. I didn't think that we were helping anyone by becoming enemies with men; we have to try to work together. I saw NOW as more following, not so much the radical lesbianism or even radical feminism, but just this very conservative place. It smelled to me like the way a sorority is run, like "you'd better think like us or you can't be in our club." I resented this. For me . . . I just couldn't really relate to them.[57]

Needing financial support for her artistic pursuits, Royalle answered an advertisement for nude models in 1974, having worked previously as an artists' model in New York. Upon meeting the agent, however, Royalle was disturbed by his suggestion that she consider performing in adult films—a genre she had never even seen.[58] Two subsequent events changed her mind. Royalle's roommate, Laurie Ann Detgen, entered the business (using the name Laurien Dominique), and Royalle's boyfriend, Danny Isley, a member of the Cockettes and an aspiring actor, landed a leading role in Anthony Spinelli's *Cry for Cindy* (1976).[59] Spinelli, a critically acclaimed Golden Age director, had a large budget for the film, used primarily established performers, and was known for maintaining a professional atmosphere during production. Royalle describes her reaction while visiting the set: "What I discovered was a clean and professional environment, a legitimate industry filled with Hollywood types moonlighting on porn crews for extra cash, and intimidatingly gorgeous young women and men competing for roles."[60] Recognizing the stability and professionalism of the industry, and given her own sexual experimentation at the time and the participation of her friends, Royalle decided to try performing in adult films.

Within Royalle's decision reside the seeds of much of what would later define her industrial approach to producing her own films. Professionalism, legitimacy, conventionally attractive and experienced performers—these became hallmarks of Femme's productions. There was also her evolving politics: "I was an active feminist and reasoned that it was my body to do with what I wanted. After all, the women's movement was about choice: Some women may choose to cast off their aprons and don a suit and join the corporate world. Others may keep their aprons and work at home. I chose to cast off everything and use my looks, my body, my open attitude toward sex, and my healthy sexual appetite to make a living."[61]

Her "casting off" process began in 1974, when Royalle, following common practice, appeared in a few low-budget loops for producer Jerry Abrams as a test to see if she could handle the job. Foreshadowing her future financial acumen, she noted, "I figured if people wanted 'proof,' then I could at least get paid for my 'test.'"[62] It was also her first attempt to prevent herself from being "frozen in time"—she would at least try to maintain some autonomy and control. Following these single-scene, one-day productions, she landed the lead role in Abrams's *The Analyst* (1975, dir. Gerald Graystone, an Abrams pseudonym), putting her career as an adult performer in motion.[63]

The Analyst offers much that helps us to understand how Royalle's ideas about pornography evolved based upon her own experiences as a performer. Playing Anita Gartley, a sexually frustrated wife, Royalle navigates narrative terrain familiar in adult films of the mid-1970s, and is a sharp contrast to the unabashed, joyful pleasures that Ginger Lynn would later present on screen.

In the opening scene, husband Preston (Paul Scharf), having just returned from a business trip, eagerly seeks sex from Anita, but she hesitates, asking if they could start with a drink and talk about his trip. Instead he pushes her down on the bed and pulls off her clothes. "Take it easy," she tells him. "Slow down a little."

Frustrated, he angrily responds, "Honey, your old man has a big strong need going. Now just get into it."

Anita's response prefigures Royalle's mission statement for Femme on women's sexuality: "It's hard to just get into it. I want to, but you gotta be more gentle." From its opening moments, *The Analyst* captures familiar stereotypes: men just want to "get going," while women want to "slow down" and "be more gentle."

As the scene progresses, Preston tries to have anal intercourse with Anita, but she stops him. "It really doesn't feel right," she tells him. "I won't do it like that. I'm not some kind of dog. You're hurting me, now stop it."

He again reacts angrily, roughly pushing his penis into her mouth and informing her, "All your hang-ups about sex make me sick. I'm your husband, remember that? Love, honor, and obey, dammit! You got some pure and holy idea about how disgusting you think good fucking is. I don't want to hear any more of your moral crap."

The rest of the short scene presents, in close-up, rough oral sex until Preston ejaculates on Anita's face (in a so-called money shot, which Royalle would later condemn and avoid in her own films).[64] Her angry response (and indeed the entire sequence) interrogates the myth of women's pleasure as a mere side effect of men's: she spits his semen in his face, telling him, "You are an animal. You are an insensitive son of a bitch. You don't care about what I want. You don't care if you hurt me. You just care about your own pleasure. You're the one with the sick hang-ups."

This sequence (which seems, in the moment, almost like antipornography propaganda) is a prelude to the rest of the narrative, which "educates" women to dismiss any questioning impulse, staunchly reminding viewers that women's pleasure stems from men's pleasure. Anita visits sex therapist Doctor Morley (Tyler Reynolds), who shows her a series of stag films before demonstrating sex techniques with his colleague, Doctor Michaelson (Angele Tufts). In the film's conclusion, Anita returns with her husband to the clinic to watch another set of films featuring "correct" oral and anal intercourse. While Morley makes a minor effort to encourage Preston to think about mutual pleasure, there is no doubt that *Anita* is the one with the problem; nor is there any question that "mutual" pleasure really just means pleasure for Preston and an attitude change for Anita. When the stag films conclude, Morley initiates anal sex with Anita while Preston watches, followed by Preston replacing Morley and finally having "mutually satisfying" anal sex with Anita. Having successfully completed her "training," Anita claims to love the experience, and the film's final moments feature her telling Preston, "I knew I could do it eventually."[65]

Whereas one of Royalle's guiding missions with Femme would be to foster a cultural atmosphere in which couples could safely enjoy adult films together as an aid to mutually pleasurable sex, *The Analyst* presents a repressive and regressive atmosphere. In the film's version of therapeutic mediation, the viewing of such material reifies male fantasies and fosters women's submission to male pleasure as the epicenter of sexual experience, all bolstered by the presence of medical "experts." Much later, medical experts would regularly recommend Royalle's films with Femme to couples seeking adult material, turning the tables on *The Analyst* in ways that could hardly have been predicted when that film was released. Eventually, Royalle became a member of the American Association of Sex Educators, Counselors and Therapists, completing a transition from the "patient" in *The Analyst* to the "expert" with her own films.

Nearly all the films in which Royalle appears as a performer follow templates similar to *The Analyst*'s, with her characters serving as conduits for male pleasure and fantasy—occasionally as literal fantasies, as in the case of another early film, *Love Secrets* (1976, dir. Susan Martin, another Abrams pseudonym). In that film, she plays the (unnamed) secretary to a bored, middle-class office worker (John Seeman) who escapes into his imagination to have anal sex with her on his desk. Extreme close-ups from above and below (what Linda Williams calls "meat shots") make up this portion of the scene.[66] Royalle particularly loathed that framing, as she later described: "I hated the way [scenes like this] were made. The crudeness of them, the fact that you know they would stick these cameras way up your legs and I just couldn't understand why they had to be made so crudely and amateurly."[67] In contrast to her initial experience at her set visit on *Cry for Cindy*, with director Spinelli, whose techniques she praised as professional, films such as *The Analyst* and *Love Secrets* did not have the same level of technical artistry or production structure. The obsession with anal sex in both movies also captures the longstanding industry belief that the core audience (heterosexual male consumers) wanted to see what they could not get in their real-life relationships: oral and anal sex.[68]

Royalle, as noted earlier in the book, appeared in at least fifty-one adult films, covering a wide range of narrative territory and working with directors of all skill and experience levels.[69] She was one of many ensemble players during the Golden Age from 1976 to 1981, never completely breaking through to stardom but appearing frequently as part of the supporting cast. She booked roles in high-profile features, such as *Femmes de Sade* (1976, dir. Alex de Renzy), produced by Jim and Artie Mitchell after their phenomenal success with *Behind the Green Door* (1972).[70] She also appeared in the comedies *Hot & Saucy Pizza Girls*, for which she received an Erotic Film Award nomination for Best Supporting Actress, and *Hard Soap, Hard*

Soap (a takeoff on the television show *Mary Hartman, Mary Hartman*), both made in 1977 for director Bob Chinn. She later described *Hard Soap, Hard Soap* as a turning point in her performance career, saying it was "the first film I enjoyed doing, and I was paid fairly for my time on that one."[71] Eventually comic performances made up the bulk of Royalle's output: films such as *Olympic Fever* (1979, dir. Philip Marshak), *Hot Rackets* (1979, dir. Robert McCallum), and *Pro-Ball Cheerleaders* (1979, dir. Jack Mathew) showcase her dramatic capability by including humor alongside her sexual performances.

It was *Ballgame* (1980), one of her standard comic turns, this time as an imprisoned sex worker who seduces a guard, that provided Royalle with a glimpse into how her own filmmaking process might take shape. Directed by Ann Perry, one of the few female directors in the industry, the sequence illustrates the sort of "sensibility" that appealed to Royalle, an abstract concept accurately captured in author Marianne Macy's description:

> The music is relaxing, and the scene has soft lighting. The cop puts a mat on the floor, and she puts her arms around him and they embrace. The pace is slow and sensual as she lifts her arms above her head to have him gently take off her dress. The camera is behind them, and while they can be seen just as clearly as in other films, it looks flattering. He lowers her to the floor, and slowly kisses his way down her body. The scene conveys a feeling of enjoyment, and watching it is sexy. The camera takes its time moving up and down bodies, stopping calmly to observe. There's a sense of pleasure rather than choppy, goal-oriented graphic couplings. Although this offers just as much detail, the sensibility and style is far different.[72]

Royalle wholeheartedly agreed with such a reading of the sequence, linked its success to Perry's female identity, and added that Perry allowed her to "perform the scene the way I wanted to," foreshadowing the specific narrative and visual style that would come to define her work.[73] It was clear by this point in Royalle's career that her idea of a "women's sensibility" was specific, carried certain narrative and visual characteristics, and could be ascribed to female directors, producers, writers, and performers. These characteristics hinged on issues of quality, justifying the sexual pleasure within a scene through a particular aesthetic approach rather than in physical, material pleasure. The presentation—the "sense of pleasure"—was as responsible for the gratification as the content.

The crystallization of Royalle's feminist ideas also can be seen in a pair of 1980 interviews. "I think there's a future in female-oriented pornography. It's going to take women like myself to get it rolling. It's going to require women actually sitting down and writing scripts themselves," she told *High Society,* illustrating her belief that industrial change would require more than performance.[74] To *Adam Film World,* she made her pedagogical goals specific: "Films are still centered around men," she noted, "men's needs, men's attitudes—and we need more than that. We need to educate our audience. We have a responsibility for what we're showing people."[75] Several of Royalle's core principles come through with remarkable clarity in these interviews: the urgent need to address women's sexual attitudes and pleasures, the pedagogical potential of pornography, and, most critically, the realization that women would need to gain control of the means of production to ensure real change.

By the late 1970s, Royalle sensed her acting career was ending. Giving herself one more year as a performer in films she could be proud of, she moved back to New York and appeared in *Sizzle* (1979, dir. Larry Revene), *Fascination* (1980, dir. Revene), *October Silk* (1980, dir. Henri Pachard), and *Delicious* (1981, dir. Philip Drexler Jr.).[76] Finally, in 1981, Royalle made a much larger move, writing the screenplay for what would be her final film as a performer, *Blue Magic* (dir. Revene) (figure 15). She was at last "sitting down and writing" the script.

The story behind *Blue Magic* is complex and illustrates the difficulty women experienced in simply moving behind the camera without the support and assistance of the men who controlled the industry. In the mid-1970s, Nils Sture Sjöstedt, one of Sweden's preeminent sexploitation and adult film producers, distributors, and adult theater owners, had sent his eldest son, Per, to the United States to learn the adult filmmaking trade and, in the process, invest the family fortune in American adult films as a tax shelter.[77] It was during production in Europe on *That Lucky Stiff* (1979, dir. Chuck Vincent), on which he was working as production assistant, that Per met Royalle, who had been cast in a small role. The film, shot concurrently with *Bon Appétit* (1980, dir. Vincent), found significant success, and Sjöstedt, happy with the arrangement, looked for more investment opportunities. The busy Vincent passed two Sjöstedt-financed projects to cinematographer Revene to direct, with Per as production manager: *Sizzle* (1979) and *Fascination* (1980). It was during the production of *Sizzle* that Royalle and Per began dating, and they married shortly before the conclusion of principal photography on *Fascination;* at the same time, Revene and Per set up a separate corporation, Lunarex, in which to deposit their earnings from the Sjöstedt productions.

It was for Lunarex that *Blue Magic* came together: Royalle scripted, Revene directed, Per produced, and Nils invested. The usual Vincent crew

They were invited to act out their lust.
You're invited to watch.

Starring: Candida Royalle • Samantha Fox • Veronica Hart • Jack Wrangler
Ron Hudd • Josie Jones • Merle Michaels • George Payne
Directed by Larry Revene A Platinum Pictures, Inc. Release

Ⓧ
ADULTS
ONLY

Figure 15. Candida Royalle's first foray into production, as the screenwriter of *Blue Magic* (1981, dir. Larry Revene). Author's collection.

was brought in, and production got underway at a familiar sprawling country estate in Connecticut complete with gardens and multiple interiors—an ideal site for Revene's trademark soft lighting and production designer Eddie Heath's costumes and set decorations, both of which won awards from the Adult Film Critics' Association.[78]

Blue Magic reverses the structures of earlier Royalle films such as *The Analyst* and *Love Secrets*, presenting an alternate scenario in which a woman controls her own pleasure *and* the pleasures of the men (and women) around her. The film subverts and ultimately dismisses typical adult film narratives in which women must "learn" to accept their position in a hierarchy privileging male pleasure and fantasy. It avoids tropes—right down to money shots, particularly on women's faces (so-called facials), which Royalle had long decried—foreshadowing what become Femme's standard practice.[79]

Set in the late Victorian/early Edwardian era, the film opens as the mysterious Natalie Woodhurst (Royalle), who lives in palatial Woodhurst Castle with her butler and chambermaid, invites a group of well-heeled locals for a weekend party. Among the guests is Matthew Getty (Jack Wrangler), a private detective determined to uncover the truth about events at the castle. Woodhurst, a benevolent two-hundred-year-old witch, steals an item from each guest (including a cufflink from Getty), using them to cast spells that drive the guests wild with sexual passion. In the film's conclusion, Woodhurst orchestrates an elaborate orgy, revealing that the pleasures she obtains from such events keep her immortal. Getty, by turns aroused and horrified by the revelation, finally has his answer, but Woodhurst, with another spell, erases his and all the other guests' memories. In the final scene, blissfully unaware of what has occurred, Getty looks down to see his cufflink is missing just as the film fades to black, leaving the viewer with the clear message that it is Woodhurst—a woman—who has all the power, not just over pleasure but its contexts as well.

Blue Magic was both the apex and the conclusion of Royalle's performance career, and a strong indicator of what was to come: a reimagining of how sex could be constructed and presented onscreen in order to redefine women's pleasure. Nevertheless, its production required the investment, expertise, and backing of men within and around the industry who could assist Royalle in creating a women-oriented future.

The Final Steps: From Club 90 to Femme Productions

Following production of *Blue Magic*, Royalle retired from performing in adult films, but her subsequent road to creating Femme was not smooth or swift. She began the process by seeking out ways to understand her career choices. Haunted by her Catholic upbringing, Royalle entered counseling in 1981 with a former sex worker–turned–therapist. "I just wanted to come to terms with the career I had in the sex industry so I that I could understand it and live with it," she said later.[80] Therapy also paved the way for the future. Rather than dismiss the adult film industry out of shame, she resolved to make the changes she had long advocated: "I came to the conclusion that I felt that the concept of adult movies was perfectly valid in some instances, and that there was nothing really wrong with consenting adults performing for other consenting adults to view."[81] She also connected these feelings with her political critiques of pornography: "I saw that there was nothing wrong with I had done, or with the notion of pornography inherently, but rather the underlying societal attitudes toward sex that were revealed in pornography."[82] That combination would be critical for the formation of Femme, but it also illustrates the challenges facing women after their adult film careers had ended and they were coming to terms with the frozen-in-time aspect of such performance.

Continuing to make public appearances that drew on her fame as an adult performer, Royalle returned to the stage with a touring show, modeled on classic burlesque routines. Displaying her trademark political enthusiasm, ambition, and desire to elevate the industry to "something more" than mere pleasure, she noted: "I've come to appreciate strippers as artists. This is a valid profession that deserves more respect than it gets. I think burlesque, with all its fanfare and eroticism, is long overdue for a big comeback, and I hope I'll help lead the way!"[83] She describes the show in two autobiographical essays, outlining the tour stops, the shabby backstage conditions, and the catcalling audiences—all part and parcel of her efforts to illuminate and change the working conditions for women in the industry.[84]

She also stayed on the periphery of the adult film industry, using her experience to land a position as an assistant editor at Drake Publishing in New York. Drake published *High Society, Celebrity Skin* (later called *Expose!*), *Hawk, Cheri, X-Rated Cinema,* and *Playgirl,* along with dozens of other magazines.[85] Many employed adult film performers as writers and editors (as described in chapter 2), typically on gossip and fan columns, as a ploy to increase circulation. Royalle worked on various of the company's magazines, answering fan mail, reviewing films, giving interviews, appearing in magazine pictorials, and writing essays. Indicative of this period of writing (and her growing political interests) is her essay describing how she organized a group of adult performers for a makeshift parade in New York's financial district in 1981 to publicize a burlesque review the following day at the famed Show World Theater.[86] Royalle also worked for Drake in its groundbreaking phone-sex division, calculating the length of the prerecorded messages as well as writing and recording early offerings. A highly profitable industry, phone sex brought a great deal of money to Drake and its employees—much of which Royalle saved and later invested in Femme.[87]

The best example of this period of Royalle's professional writing is "The Royalle Treatment," a regular feature beginning in *Cinema-X* in 1980. All accompanied by nude photo sets of Royalle on a beach, the essays follow a similar theme: first-person narratives in which she travels somewhere and has romantic, passionate, and no-strings-attached sexual encounters. Well-crafted erotic stories, the pieces demonstrate Royalle's flair for narrative and hint at the kinds of storylines she would later develop with Femme. "I'll take you along with me on all the wildest adventures I can manage to find myself in," she writes in the first installment, "and give you only the spiciest details."[88]

After three months of working in-house, Royalle realized she was overqualified for the position and could make more money as a freelance writer for Drake and other publishers.[89] Her essay in the July 1982 *High Times*, a typical mixture of titillating prose and historical background commissioned by then-editor Larry "Ratso" Sloman, presents an overview of her past. Detailing her personal background, adult film career, and a handful of her standard feminist critiques, the piece also mixes in anecdotes about her sexual escapades (on- and off-camera) with well-known performers such as John Holmes and Jamie Gillis.[90] The piece represents the height of her post-performance writing career, capturing the delicate balance she typically struck among critique, history, and sensationalism, keeping one foot planted in sex as entertainment and the other on the ground of political commentary. These would be key, defining characteristics for Femme.

Writing these pieces, however, was clearly a temporary measure for Royalle, who was still debating how to make changes in the adult film industry. In an interview in *High Society* in October 1982, she demonstrates an increasingly proscriptive tone in her usual critique: "I don't like it when [adult films are] exploitive, when the producers choose the easy way out and fail to show the people what they should really see. I guess I'd like to say that I'm going to be around for a while, but I'm going to do it my way and I think they'll have a lot to learn if they hear what I have to say. I'm all for men and women having sex, but let's just do it the right way and have fun!"[91]

The suggestion that there was a right way to have sex would be a Royalle hallmark later with Femme; here, in its nascence, the comment stands out for its direct attack on the adult film producers who were, apparently, doing it "wrong." Royalle hints most strongly at her future in September 1983, when, in an essay for *Blue Move Expose!*, she makes clear what would bring her back to adult film: "A common question is whether I'd consider a major role in another erotic film. As I always answer . . . the movie would have to be something different, something really new under the erotic sun. Perhaps a feature film aimed at women, with erotic fantasies tailored just for us."[92]

It was a baby shower for performer Veronica Hart in the spring of 1983 that pushed Royalle back into filmmaking—this time fully behind the camera. Hart, Royalle, and the other veteran performers at the party shared their experiences, commiserated over the challenges of appearing in adult films, and offered one another encouragement. That summer, the burgeoning support group, called Club 90 (in a reference to host Annie Sprinkle's address in New York City), began to meet monthly. The original participants were Veronica Vera, Gloria Leonard, Sharon Mitchell, Sue Nero, Kelly Nichols, Sprinkle, Hart, and Royalle—though Mitchell, Nero, and Nichols left shortly after the group's creation.[93] Their shared political stance on the industry and its need for female perspectives and voices had a profound impact on Royalle's thinking, giving her a sense of community and support for her ideas.

During this same period, feminist artists from the New York–based collective Carnival Knowledge, organized in 1981 to explore issues related to women's sexuality, met Royalle, Vera, and Sprinkle at a pornography trade show.[94] Intrigued by their feminist rhetoric, Carnival Knowledge began a long series of meetings with the Club 90 women to transform the informal gatherings into a stage performance at what would become the art show *The Second Coming*.[95] Opening in January 1984 at Martha Wilson's Franklin Furnace performance-art space in New York City, the groundbreaking show was based on the following questions, painted in red on the space's walls: "Could there be a feminist pornography? A porn that doesn't denigrate women or children?" Given her long-term move in precisely these directions, it is not surprising Royalle welcomed the invitation, telling the other members: "This is our opportunity. No one can take this away from us now. Let's tell the world who we really are and what we're really about."[96] The show—a collection of books, videos, artwork, live mud wrestling, monologues, and "domestic" pieces on topics ranging from masturbation to eating—was a startling array of material exploring the connections between feminists and pornography.[97] The event culminated with *Deep inside Porn Stars*, a stage show re-creating one of Club 90's meetings, complete with a set depicting Sprinkle's living room.[98] Intended to remind the audience that these women were individuals, mothers, sisters, and daughters, the show began with the members in evening gowns, moved to personal narratives from each, and concluded with them all having replaced the "sexy" clothes to wear sweatpants, sweatshirts, and flannel nightgowns—thus revealing the "true" women underneath.[99]

During Royalle's moment in the spotlight, she pulled a sweatshirt over her gown and offered her birth name to the audience. She presented an autobiographical slideshow with pictures from her childhood, from various stage shows, and from the San Francisco jazz clubs where she had performed.[100] She ended the monologue with what amounted to a sneak preview: "I see myself as a revolutionary of sorts, maybe one day making women's films to replace the tired old men's films that still exploit women and promote archaic sexuality. After all, I'm still young and I have a lot of dreams."[101] It was the most public pronouncement yet of her ideas and goals, and it gestured toward the "something more" she wanted adult films to include.

In the performance's liner notes, Leonard and Sprinkle write that the event was "a unique opportunity to be aligned with other feminist artists, usually considered arch-adversaries of the adult entertainment movement," while the organizers add, "We welcome this moment when women, regardless of calling, can respectfully stand together."[102] The performance was a success—even inspiring Broadway producer Joe Cates to offer the group a deal to make the show bigger and better, and, of course, profitable. The group declined, citing their desire to keep creative control of their ideas.[103] Ultimately, *Deep inside Porn Stars* represents an important historical moment in that it foregrounded the female voices of performers, exploding the mythology that women were merely silent and subservient vessels in the male fantasies typically presented onscreen and illuminating the potential for pornography created by and for women.[104] It was also important for the connection it made between adult film performers and feminists; as I detail in the final chapter, the mid-1980s continually boiled with feminist tensions over pornography. Thus, the invitation of the Club 90 members by a feminist group was a moment of rare public unity. Perhaps most important, the event explicitly acknowledged that adult film performers could *claim* feminism; as Hart would later say of the event, "It's the first time we've ever been invited to work with feminists—which I think most of us consider ourselves to be—in a thing about pornography. All of the contact I've had with feminists was always anti-porn. They wouldn't even discuss porn."[105] For Royalle, it furthered and validated her evolving political identity.

By late January 1984, the stage was set for Royalle to move back into adult film production. She also had an economic interest: the explosion of Golden Age films on video meant that new audiences were seeing her performances for the first time—but she was seeing none of the profits. It was probably a moment in which she understood the lack of control she had over her own image, something many performers eventually face. "All of a sudden my name was becoming sort of reborn and I was not reaping any of the rewards," she would later say. "I decided if they are going to exploit my name and make money, I'm going to exploit my name and make money off of it too but I'm going to do it with something I believe in, that I feel has integrity."[106] Following *Deep inside Porn Stars,* Royalle, who had been contemplating precisely such strategies for years, made her move.

"Finally, There's Femme"

In the early 1980s, as Royalle began solidifying her ideas for her own production company, R. Lauren Niemi, a Midwestern photographer, moved to New York with a desire to create erotic music videos for women.[107] During preparation for *Deep inside Porn Stars,* a friend arranged for Royalle to meet Niemi. The two shared their very similar ideas about film production, concluding that they could form a partnership, with Niemi directing and Royalle writing and producing.[108] The two agreed that the growing market for adult video lacked a "woman's perspective" and that getting women behind the camera was necessary to change that problem. While the idea of couples' films was not unknown, Royalle and Niemi agreed that feminist politics should be an explicit part of adult film production rather than an afterthought or a tacked-on marketing strategy. "We had an agenda," Royalle said later. "I thought that there was a real opportunity to explore and see whether I could create adult material that was sex-positive, and gave people some information, that gave them something back when they watched.[...] I think that most pornography out there has absolutely no agenda, other than to make money."[109] While Niemi and Royalle agreed on the political goals of the company, and on Niemi's music video concept, the two nevertheless were stuck in the same place where Royalle had long been mired: all ideas and no capital.

Throughout her career, Royalle went to great lengths to describe the necessity of women taking control of the means of production to create lasting change. Years after Femme's success was solidified, for example, Royalle argued that "until women grow up and claim our power and realize that success comes only with strength, courage, and hard work, they will sit and wait forever for that knight in shining armor or Prince Charming, whether they call a distributor, a husband, or . . ."[110] She trailed off before getting to the role that enabled her own career behind the camera: her father-in-law. Ironically, for all her passion against such a strategy, it was a familiar man firmly entrenched in a paternal role with deep existing ties in the industry who initially provided Femme's capital. Royalle's father-in-law, Sjöstedt, overheard Niemi and Royalle talking about their ideas, and upon his return to Sweden he agreed to finance Femme Productions if they could find distribution. In part, this clearly was another of his attempts to find offshore homes for his Swedish profits as a way to avoid taxes, much as he had done earlier with *Blue Magic.*[111] While Royalle would go on to tremendous success with Femme on her own, it was this seed investment that provided the startup costs for the company—surely illustrating the extreme difficulty faced by women seeking to enter the ranks of adult film producers, particularly during video's infancy, and also perhaps explaining why Royalle insisted on making startup funding a crucial part of her advice to other women seeking to take up positions of power behind the camera.

By February 1984, with Sjöstedt's financing contingent on distribution, Femme was in business with Royalle as president and Per as vice president. Royalle arranged meetings with various distributors, only to be consistently rejected. She later described the difficulty: "When I approached the big distributors, they said, 'Oh, Candida, that's a nice idea, but women aren't interested, and there's no such thing as a couples' market.'"[112] Since the industry had been obsessed for years with expanding their base by drawing in female viewers and couples, this response speaks volumes about how the "good old boy" network reacted to a woman starting her own production company without their involvement. Taking women's money was one thing, but encouraging or assisting them to get behind the camera (and into the profits) was clearly another. Royalle finally met with Russ Hampshire, founder of VCA. Initially skeptical, Hampshire eventually agreed to distribute Femme's videos under a royalty system whereby Royalle would continue to own the films—a structure that paid off handsomely later.

Femme's first project put into practice all the many ideas and strategies Royalle had been pondering for so long. Simply titled *Femme* and released in 1984, the film contains six music video vignettes that play out a series of fantasies, with lines blurred between the "reality" of the participants and their erotic daydreams. Endless long takes, slow zooms, soft lighting, more foreplay than intercourse—*Femme* features everything Royalle had discussed for years, right down to the absence of money or meat shots. The film enacted visually and narratively all the ideological elements she had long claimed were the "right way" to depict sexual pleasure onscreen. Even the box cover captures this (figure 16). Faces, not bodies, fill the box, with a telling tagline: "Created by women for people who love." *Loving*, not just fucking, was the "something more."

Royalle and Niemi quickly followed *Femme* with *Urban Heat* (1984), another series of music video vignettes, and then *Christine's Secret* (1986), which was Femme's first foray into more traditional dramatic fare, following the title character as she checks into a country inn and fantasizes about the staff. The critics were not kind. In a typical review of these early offerings, *Video-X* critic Lenny Wide suggests that *Urban Heat* is about as exciting as watching a "bowl of fish" and claims it was not even necessary to finish watching the film before writing the review.[113] *Gent* magazine is more polite about *Three Daughters* (1986), Femme's fourth film, acknowledging the aesthetic and narrative differences Royalle was after, even as the review concludes by noting that "despite all those redeeming characteristics, some of the scenes in Candida's films are occasionally too long and boring."[114] Such a mixed response was probably to be expected; after all, Royalle's criticisms of the industry over the years, combined with her very different narrative and visual strategies, were deliberately provocative and no doubt threatening to those accustomed to a certain type of adult film. In any case, Royalle was not necessarily interested in pleasing the critics or the industry. She was after a much larger, mainstream audience who would appreciate what she was trying to achieve. Royalle, like so many others before (and after) her, sought respectability, that characteristic that would bridge the gap between smut and art in order to legitimize widespread commerce.

Her primary impediment was the ongoing difficulty of selling Femme's approach to wholesalers and retailers and thus getting the products to the customers she most desired: middle-class women who probably had no experience or interest in going to adult bookstores or even mainstream video store back rooms to browse through the typical offerings.[115] Femme's fortunes began to change in 1985 when a friend sent Royalle a notice from *Glamour* magazine seeking women to talk about their curiosity in erotic movies. For Royalle, it was precisely the opportunity for which she had been waiting. She assembled a media kit that included samples, a detailed cover letter, and other material. It was enormously important, since Femme was having trouble convincing mainstream publications even to carry its mail-order advertisements.[116] The effort was successful: *Glamour* made Femme the centerpiece of its article, titled "How Women Are Changing Porn Films." It even led with copy from the voiceover in the promotional

Figure 16. *Femme,* Candida Royalle and R. Lauren Niemi's inaugural 1984 production, was also the name of their groundbreaking production company. Author's collection.

trailer for *Femme:* "Finally, there's *Femme* . . . the fantasies that women have been dreaming about all these years. *Femme,* conceived and produced by women, explores human desires from the exhilarating perspective of a woman who knows. . . ."[117] The rest of the piece was just as complimentary, drawing heavily on Royalle's marketing, particularly in its definition of the burgeoning field of material: "The new films . . . go for more plot (meaning more motivation for sex); more happily married couples (providing an emotional context for sex); better-looking men for women to look at; older women in sex scenes; more kissing, more foreplay and more attention paid to the woman's sexual pleasure and climax; more humor; and more women on top—literally and figuratively."[118] The article could not have been a bigger success. Employing virtually all of Royalle's rhetoric, positioning Femme as the vanguard in the growing field, and highlighting the three Femme films then available to the public, *Glamour* finally opened the door to mainstream female viewers by using keywords—*motivation* and *context* chief among them—that provided a cover of safety.

Virtually every major U.S. news outlet picked up the article, and Royalle made numerous subsequent media appearances, even debating antipornography feminist Catharine MacKinnon on the *Phil Donahue Show.*[119] Impressed by the media coverage, Hampshire and VCA began aggressively marketing the Femme line.[120] *Time* magazine was the next major coup for Femme, in early 1987. "Romantic Porn in the Boudoir" is the article's title, and, alongside a photograph of Royalle, it notes: "Royalle's four films are considered the best examples of porn in the feminist style. The sex scenes flow from female passion and needs, not male lechery, and women tend to initiate the sex."[121] Royalle's public appearances became Femme's primary marketing strategy, leading to a constant stream of magazine profiles, newspaper articles, television show appearances, and public speaking engagements. Femme was no longer seeking out the mainstream; it was firmly ensconced in it. Despite the growing public acceptance, however, not everyone appreciated her "women's sensibility" ethos. For example, Norma Ramos, the general counsel for Women against Pornography, found no difference whatsoever in Femme's practices. "That it is a woman . . . behind the camera doesn't matter to us. Her films do exactly what other pornographers do, which is reduce women to body parts. Pornography eroticizes women's inequality. It's prostitution on paper or celluloid."[122]

After *Christine's Secret,* Niemi left the company, perhaps unhappy with Royalle's desire to make narrative films. In 1986, Hampshire and VCA ended the royalties arrangement with Femme, offering instead to buy out the (then) three existing films for $35,000 each, which Royalle rejected, choosing instead to form Femme Distribution with her husband, Per.[123] Within this new model, Femme released another fourteen films, including a "star directors" series for which Royalle brought in her Club 90 colleagues Gloria Leonard, Veronica Vera, Annie Sprinkle, and Veronica Hart to direct short vignettes. The most ambitious Femme project, *Revelations* (1992), directed by Royalle and shot on celluloid, offered a science fiction narrative in which a future totalitarian state forbids sexual activity for anything other than procreation. By 2005, Royalle had returned to producing, bringing in other directors for new Femme projects, which included efforts to branch out to more diverse groups, such as Latina and African American women and couples, with offerings such as *Caribbean Heat* (2005, dir. Manuela Sabrosa) and *Afrodite Superstar* (2007, dir. Venus Hottentot).

Eventually, Royalle tired of the stress involved with distributing her own films, and in 1995 she made a deal with Phil Harvey of Adam & Eve, among the largest distributors of adult-related products, to finance and distribute new Femme productions.[124] In 1996, she branched out again, this time teaming with Dutch designer Jandirk Groet to create Natural Contours, a line of "intimate personal massagers." The company marketed the sex toys with discourses familiar from Femme, using *tasteful, elegant, discreet,* and *classy,* among other descriptors.[125] By the 2000s, Royalle had firmly cemented her status as a visionary, entrepreneur, director, producer, feminist, activist, author, and expert—everything she had clearly been hoping for during her early years as a performer. The mythology created by her marketing positioned her as "a woman who knows," and that powerful knowledge was based around the "right way" to have sex, as well as the secrets of what women really wanted in terms of pornography. Hailed by sex educators, academics, and journalists as exemplars of a positive and feminist approach to mediated sexualities, Royalle's films were elevated beyond the crass commercialism of mainstream pornography, which had the added effect of protecting them from legal suspicion. Such critical acceptance was the ultimate "something more."

Indeed, Femme never faced serious threat of obscenity prosecution. Over the years, Royalle argued that Femme's approach might represent a larger threat to antiporn opponents than more "traditional" adult films, an argument she based on her notion that she was freeing women from sexual guilt and shame. "If porn movies are banned, the people who are going to be shut down first are people like me," she said in 1986. "Porn will be pushed underground and the sleazeballs will control it."[126] As much as such statements served Femme's marketing needs, however, they could not have been farther from the historical truth. Unlike many of her contemporaries,

Royalle received remarkably little legal attention and cultural criticism. Only once, following the release of *Urban Heat* in 1984, did the government consider prosecution, after the tape had been confiscated by the customs office in New York and declared obscene. The case, however, never made it past that stage, as Royalle's future partner, Adam & Eve founder Phil Harvey, decided to fight the case to establish precedent, which prompted the government to abandon the effort.[127] This startling absence of legal pressure, in the face of a concentrated, rigorous, and destructive assault by federal and local authorities on the adult film industry in the 1980s, illustrates clearly just how "safe" Femme had become in the end. If adult movies were banned, in other words, Femme's might be the only ones left.

CONCLUSION: THE CHALLENGES OF "GOOD" PORNOGRAPHY

Femme's industrial impact was swift. Royalle had long suggested that the major distributors and producers hesitated even to acknowledge the existence of a female market, but that had changed, and significantly. Other companies began releasing tapes intended for couples, that genre always coded by the industry as "for" women, and publications such as *AVN* added that classification in their sales charts. While Royalle did not invent the idea, her success with Femme led to an industrial shift resulting in more attention, acknowledgment, and money targeted on female viewers (and many male ones) who might want something different. Seeking that market was one thing, but finding the nuanced tone that Royalle had mastered was an entirely different matter. As Royalle had long said, the industry for the most part just repackaged old content with new, "for-women" marketing practices. Regardless of motive, however, women working behind the cameras in the adult industry garnered attention.

A trio of early examples stands out. The first is an article, from May 1986, that appeared in *AVN*. Offering an overview of the handful of women (including Royalle) then working behind the scenes, the piece stands out historically for recognizing their important contributions. Author Lee Irving links Royalle to the legacy of the women who had come before her and those she worked alongside: Marga Aulbach, Suze Randall, Gail Palmer, Anne Randall, Drea, Joyce Snyder, Joanna Williams, Svetlana, Veronika Rocket, Summer Brown, Helene Terrie, Ann Perry, and Roberta Findlay. Yet there was also a tone to the piece that further essentialized female spectators even as it acknowledged their growing interest in the marketplace: "More than 60% of adult rental transactions in video stores involve women, whether they are by themselves or with their husband, boyfriend, or girlfriend. Couples that have never watched XXX-rated entertainment are now popping them into their VCRs. This shift in demographics of watching adult films—from primarily men to, now, couples—has dictated a need for films with more sensitive stories that appeal to both sexes."[128] This notion of sensitive stories, as noted in the introduction, differentiates male and female pleasures, limits possibilities for women (and men), and once again requires justifications and contexts for sexual pleasure.

The second example comes from the November 1986 "Porn Films for Couples" issue of *Adam Film World and Adult Video Guide*. Editor Carl Esser's introduction reveals the stereotypes embedded within the industry's perception of women:

> As the VCR boom brings in more women to porn, the "Couples Movie" is fast becoming a staple of the industry. Within that category there is still a variety of choice, as a couple movie need not be all sugar and spice. The DRAMA section of this issue reviews pictures strong on plot and intrigue; ROMANCE is for sweethearts who look for affection and foreplay in porn; try a COMEDY—you might be able to "laugh her into it"; or how about CLASSICS, not new, but unforgettable; FOR WOMEN deals with movies made about women or with a female audience in mind; women who like porn can handle a WALL-TO-WALL movie, if the ladies in the picture are not mistreated; and occasionally women have a taste for EXOTICA, so we've included a few pictures for special interest audiences.[129]

These comments reveal the ongoing tendency to foreground male audiences even when marketing to women: the (somewhat disturbing) "laugh her into it" suggestion and the use of the pronoun *you* give away the game. Industry practices, even as they moved toward new, more inclusive paradigms, still held tightly to particularly regressive beliefs about women's spectatorship.

The final example comes from an essay, "Does It Take a Woman to Make a Good Couples Film?" in the same issue of *Adam Film World and Adult Video Guide*. Author Desiree Valentine briefly examines that question (with somewhat ambiguous answers) before cataloguing the women then working behind the camera. On the question of what defines pornography for women, Valentine answers: "What that means, stated simply, is pictures that won't send women fleeing from the room. So the female characters in many of the new pornos are treated better and have more depth than the bimbos of the old stag movies, and often it is they who choose their sex partners and determine the nature and style of the engagement."[130] A low bar, to be sure, when porn for women mostly came down to the existence of a degree of sexual autonomy and intelligence, further highlighting the industry's difficulty in deciding what pornography for women actually meant in pragmatic terms.

The piece's final section is virtually a copy of *AVN*'s similar effort to highlight women in the adult film industry. Valentine briefly examines Femme and Royalle, along with other notable women, adding Patti Rhodes to Irving's earlier list. Valentine's description of Femme follows the standard template: "There are very few external come shots . . . [and the] sex is more sensuous than raunchy, accented by better music than one usually hears in a video. Candida allows her actors to pick their own partners, and usually lets the cast perform the sex in their own way."[131] Once again, that most vague of adjectives—*sensuous*—is employed to stand in for a host of narrative and visual elements separating Royalle's work from "raunchy" mainstream pornography. Such efforts, much like the issue as a whole, point out the industry's struggle to pin down precisely what pornography for women would, could, and should look like.

While industry publications increasingly covered the female market and began acknowledging women behind the camera, not all efforts to copy Femme found economic success—or even made it to market. In May 1986, to describe just one such example, Dreamland Home Video announced plans to produce a line of tapes called "Danielle Romances," aimed at women and couples and "similar to paperback romance novels." Brent Pope, sales manager for Dreamland, echoes Royalle in the company's press release: "There will be a lot of build up to the sex scenes with more tenderness and foreplay. And there'll be only two or three sex scenes in each feature." President John Arnone is in just as much of a hurry to distance the tapes from "conventional" pornography, adding: "And no gynecological shots." The final, most essential ingredient was the addition of ex–Club 90 member Sharon Mitchell as series director, giving the line, as Arnone claims, a "distinctly woman's point of view."[132] Despite these grand plans, however, and obvious effort to capture some of Royalle's market share, Dreamland's plan never came to fruition, and it never produced the tapes.

Others, however, did find success. Adam & Eve, Royalle's future distribution partner, produced two films in 1984 featuring veteran performer Nina Hartley that added an explicitly pedagogical aspect to adult film. *Nina Hartley's Guide to Better Cunnilingus* and *Nina Hartley's Guide to Better Fellatio* were the first entries in what would become a groundbreaking series of instructional videos.[133] Hartley, a popular performer, has successfully mixed feminist politics with sexual performance throughout her (ongoing) career in a way that few others have been able to accomplish.[134] In a 1993 essay, Hartley scathingly criticizes antipornography feminist activists, defends her career choice, and echoes much of Royalle's politics. "I reject the notion that there is some secret feminist orthodoxy, some single standard of measuring who is a 'real' feminist," she says, claiming, much as the Club 90 performers did, a feminism that does not preclude an autonomous and pleasure-seeking sexuality.[135] Adam & Eve's line of Hartley videos speaks volumes about the changes in the industry in the mid-1980s in terms of recognizing the expanding marketplace, the potential for sex education via adult film, and the desire for alternative perspectives and content that comes *from* women rather than through typical narratives obsessed with controlling them in the name of male pleasure or gendered containment. Nevertheless, the videos rely on the idea that "something more" than just pleasure is a required presence.

Royalle's approach with Femme and her willingness to seize control of the means of production has also influenced a new generation of adult film-makers. Tristan Taormino, Anna Span, Petra Joy, Maria Beatty, Shine Louise Houston, Anna Brownfield, Erika Lust, and Courtney Trouble are among the many women who have followed Royalle's lead, and they frequently cite her as a guiding force and pioneer for their own work, which is overtly political and explicitly feminist.[136] Similarly to Royalle, they often invoke quality, basing it on particular narrative justifications and visual approaches, to give a deeper meaning to the sex they portray, and re-creating Royalle's political stance that there are "right ways" to depict sexual pleasure.

Anne G. Sabo, in her book examining the rise of pornography for women, cites Royalle's influence on the industry and presents a checklist, based directly on Femme's films, for "good" pornography. She argues that "design and content" are the items that determine whether the sex is being portrayed in the "right way," and these elements justify the potential pleasures embedded in pornography through a variety of narrative and visual techniques. In one notable section, Sabo writes that "good" pornography includes "high cinematic production value," a script that "build[s] the sex into a realistic context," realistic settings and costumes, and, in a case of hyperspecific detail, "truthful sighing."[137] Under a subsequent broad heading, "Progressive Sexual-Political Commitment," Sabo calls for a "new [cinematic] language for gender democratic heterosexuality" and "a gender democratic gaze of devoted mutuality." She concludes by suggesting that progressive adult films will confront "political censorship and the historical baggage of guilt and shame around sex."[138] The list—a tall order, to be sure, for any adult film—ironically claims that more freedom can be achieved by limiting and containing narrative and visual approaches to pornography to a very specific set of highly egalitarian fantasies. Pleasure, it seems, should be found as much in the overt, deliberate *absences* as it is in what is onscreen.

While these guidelines directly confront the typical "formula" common to most heterosexual pornography, they also inscribe a new set in its place. Left out are those viewers who desire something else entirely, or who find pleasure in transgression or subversion. Furthermore, by linking "good" pornography to all manner of intellectual tactics, both visual and narrative, Sabo, Royalle, and others fail to see their reinscription of the deeply regressive "higher/lower" divide, which pushes women into explaining and justifying their sexual behavior beyond a simple desire for pleasure. There must be "meaning," in the end, for pleasure to exist beyond itself as an end, and for that pleasure to be achieved in the "right" way.

In a 2012 interview, Royalle takes this logic to its extreme, accusing some female directors of falsely claiming feminism simply by dint of being women. She makes the money shot the litmus test of her argument, much as she had always done, denying any possibility of its pleasure for women. She argues that a truly feminist adult film "should be something women really relate to, that speaks to them. It's not enough to say, 'Well, hey, you know what? I'm a girl, and I like having cum in my face.'"[139] Later, in her last major essay on the topic, such concerns clearly remain at the forefront of her thinking:

> It's as if it took an entire generation before women felt brave enough to step behind the blue camera, whether for commercial sale or to post on the Internet. But is it "feminist" simply because it's made by a woman? When I watch porn directed by a woman I'm hoping to see something different, innovative, something that speaks to me as a woman. All too often I find myself disappointed by what turns out to be the same lineup of sex scenes containing the usual sex acts, sometimes more extreme, following the same old formula and ending in the almighty money shot. Rather than creating a new vision, it seems many of today's young female directors, often working under the tutelage of the big porn distributors, seek only to prove that they can be even nastier than their male predecessors. And it's not so much the type of sex that offends me, it's the crude in-your-face depiction that seems more interested in shock value than anything female viewers might enjoy.[140]

Ultimately, Royalle's "for women, by a woman" approach, while representing a critical and historically important break from the formulaic industrial obsession with male pleasure, also represents an ironic moment in which an effort to avoid and eliminate essentialism inadvertently led directly back to that very mode. "True" feminism, in other words, has no room for certain depictions of pleasure. Perhaps this is an inescapable problem for adult film producers: the moment any type of sexuality or gendered approach is privileged, after all, it defines all others as wrong or misguided. In a 1994 interview, well after Femme had turned into a successful corporate machine, Royalle describes her products as "tastefully explicit" and tries to encapsulate her philosophy: "A lot of it is about permission-giving to women to have full sexual lives. Hiding certain elements only perpetuates shame."[141] Yet whether it was by "hiding," avoiding, or eliminating "certain elements," Royalle had been doing just that for years, albeit with political motivations intended to eliminate rather than create shame or embarrassment. Nevertheless, Femme created a paradox for viewers by avoiding money and meat shots, emphasizing narrative, and foregrounding a vague (and narrowly defined) sensuality, which raises a perhaps unavoidable question: Does that make fantasies that do not adhere to such paradigms wrong, harmful, or shameful?

Among Royalle's most important historical legacies was her masterful ability to market herself and Femme's products as the "solution" to a "problem" endlessly circulated as part of cultural obsessions with both pornography and women's sexuality. Indeed, every few years, a new cycle begins: cultural anxiety over women's interest in pornography (and sex more generally) is answered by pointing toward the availability of pornography for women, ultimately suggesting that such products offer positive potential—but also implying that there is a defined, "safe" area for women to explore pleasure. Royalle's presence in such reports is a constant, as it has always been since her appearance in the 1985 *Glamour* article. Familiar adjectives such as *tasteful, sensual, erotic, subtle, romantic, narratives,* and *motivation* populate these discourses, as if taken straight from Femme's marketing materials, and further shore up the longstanding myth that a very particular "sensitivity" is needed in regard to women's sexuality.[142] More recently, the cycle has turned to the question of whether or not pornography can be "empowering" for women—yet another way in which pleasure for pleasure's sake alone has become unthinkable.[143] Royalle did not create or initiate these discourses, but she did corner the early market on asserting that her position was the sole solution.

In some ways, Royalle ended up where she started: positioned in a binary in which one kind of sexuality and gendered behavior is foregrounded at the expense of others—albeit from a politically progressive stance that calls out the supposed hegemony of conventional power structures. Royalle's history illustrates the difficulty of the idea that a "progressive" pornography can exist at all, as well as bluntly calling attention to the complex question of whether women in a variety of industrial, performative, and spectatorial positions can truly achieve control. If Royalle reconfigured what "the sex is all about" in pornography, as Linda Williams argues, she also, in the process, tried to define what it should *not* be about—an inevitable side effect of any strong position on the topic.[144] In 1999, as part of a "directors of the decade" roundtable, Royalle herself captured this paradox: "My motivation was to create movies that have a woman's voice, that were more tender, that women could be comfortable watching, and that broke all the formula rules. I really wanted to break that formulaic approach to filming sex. I really feel that everyone—you know, until then—was sticking to the formula: these are the sex acts you should show, and this is how the camera output should be; this is what the camerawork should look like."[145] Yet well before that point, Royalle had already created her own formula, much as it was layered with politically progressive intentions to foreground high production values and narrative justifications in order to elevate its depictions of sexual pleasure.

Her formula has been harnessed in complicated ways. In 1992, Sandra S. Cole, professor and director of the Sexuality Training Center at the University of Michigan, described Royalle's films with Femme as being "not made for prurient exploitation but for self-satisfaction."[146] While acknowledging Royalle's important historical contribution and groundbreaking changes in the industry, this stance raises questions: What about those viewers who might find pleasure in prurience? Can "self-satisfaction" also be prurient? Were Ginger Lynn's unabashed sexual explorations any less politically progressive than those produced under the Femme banner simply because they lacked the same ideological and aesthetic containers? As Gayle Rubin argues, "One of the most tenacious ideas about sex is [that] there is one best way to do it, and that everyone should do it that way."[147] When it comes to the depiction of—and advocacy for—sexual pleasure, even the most "positive" presentations and accompanying ideologies inadvertently bracket off pleasures and behaviors into various values. Such was the case with Femme, which broke apart the conventional approach to depicting sexual pleasure with the intention to more accurately capture women's sexualities, but which also created new limitations and boundaries as to how those sexualities could be defined.

Yet it is crucial to recognize the significance of power in this history. Royalle, whose own experiences, both in the culture at large and in front of the camera, created a desire to foster change, was all but alone in the early years of video as a woman building her own production company in a deeply unwelcoming industry. Bracketing off and limiting the definitions of "correct" fantasies, when seen through this contextual lens, might be considered less as a regressive step and more as an overdue and necessary political reaction to the overwhelmingly male-dominated practices (sexual, industrial, narrative, performative, and so on) that defined the industry and its reception. It was precisely Royalle's move behind the camera and into an ownership role that made such a difference—however problematic— possible. Lynn, whose performances were created and shaped in large part by Antine's creativity, also altered how women could experience, define, and pursue pleasure onscreen. Nevertheless, Lynn remained squarely in the camera's eye rather than choosing where and how the camera looked. In this, she was not unlike the "girls next door" in *Playboy*, who similarly did not control the camera's gaze or the company behind it. Owning and controlling the means of production, in the end, still define the long-term stories of these two women, as well as the industry at large.

In the following, and final, chapter, I explore the contours and depths of the cultural backlash against many of Royalle's predecessors and competitors in the burgeoning field of adult video. As Royalle's adult films for women made some pornography safe by internally regulating its fantasies and constructs, and as Vivid Video sought (and found) a modicum of respectability— alongside tremendous economic success—through the radical overhaul of its marketing practices, other producers, directors, performers, distributors, retail store owners, and viewers faced much different outcomes. While the pornography industry, with the rise of the video era, made significant progress in transforming itself into an efficient, modern, and streamlined capitalist enterprise, it did not do so without unrelenting resistance from those who wanted to keep it in the shadows. The story of the *external* regulation of adult video, which concludes this book, might be the most important one of all.

4 Saving the Family

Video Rental Stores and the Toxicity of Pornography

> To deny the need for control is literally to deny one's senses, unless such denial is based upon a conclusion that there is nothing evil or dangerous about pornographic material.
>
> **"Statement of Charles H. Keating, Jr.,"** in *The Report of the Commission on Obscenity and Pornography* (1970), 622

> If pornography incites to anything, it is the solitary act of masturbation.
>
> **Gore Vidal, quoted in Robert J. Stoller and I. S. Levine,** *Coming Attractions: The Making of an X-Rated Video* (2003), 10

In 1981, the citizens of Maricopa County, Arizona, elected Tom Collins, a Vietnam veteran and former police officer, as county attorney.[1] Maricopa County, among the nation's largest by population, has its seat in Phoenix, serves other cities such as Tempe and Scottsdale, and then had 1.5 million residents within its boundaries.[2] Collins, with the encouragement of Citizens for Decency through Law (CDL), a Phoenix-based grassroots group, dedicated himself to prosecuting adult video and bookstores throughout the county on obscenity charges.[3] In October 1983, Collins hired Randy Wakefield as a trial prosecutor, tasking him with making the cases a top priority.[4] Collins's efforts to that point had failed primarily because adult video and bookstore owners had successfully argued that county officials had targeted them unfairly, given that mainstream video rental stores in "better" neighborhoods offered the same titles.[5] Collins and Wakefield, in response, broadened their scope. On March 13, 1985, Wakefield announced to reporters that mainstream video rental store owners had a few days to clear their inventories of "sexually explicit movies" before the county would take legal action against them for trafficking in obscenity.[6]

   The events in Maricopa County were a struggle over "community standards" and community space, and they reflect what was increasingly happening across the United States. Home video technology had made it possible for pornography to enter the home on an unprecedented scale—but, more importantly, it also had allowed it to move into "safe" retail extensions rather than remaining in the quarantined areas typically associated historically with adult material. The reaction to these developments, as I explore in this chapter, was moral, technological, and sexual panic (see the introduction). This panic, which gained momentum into the mid-1980s, came on the heels of what Natasha Zaretsky calls the "transformation" of the family in the 1970s, a period in which a confluence of discourses (feminism, war, economic anxieties, cultural shifts, and so forth) led to "a heightened level of fear about the future of the American family."[7] But, as she argues, the fear during that period wasn't just about the family—it was about the security and longevity of the nation itself, which had to be idealized and kept safe via images of the traditional family unit. The threat that pornography had long represented to such images was intensified in unpredictable, chaotic, and profound ways the moment it found a new, more visible entry point into the home.

Throughout the 1980s, response to adult videos followed a predictable pattern that emphasized fear of their encroachment. Jane Miller, of Minneapolis's Pornography Research Center, offered an archetypal response in 1985: "Pornography is creeping into the mainstream. What would have been off-limits even in a red-light district a few years ago is now available for people to see in their living room."[8] Charles Ruttenberg, attorney for the Video Software Dealers' Association (VSDA), recognized a year later that the video rental industry was also becoming a key component of the adult film distribution chain. "We are the leading means of communicating pornographic material to the American public," he noted, and not very happily.[9] A 1985 VSDA survey estimated that 75 percent of the nation's twenty thousand video stores carried adult titles, accounting for roughly 13 percent of total sales and rentals; a year later, estimates put total VCR sales at 25 million, and the annual sale and rental total for home video cassettes at $2.3 billion.[10] At least fifty companies specialized in the production and/or distribution of adult video by the mid-1980s, releasing more than two hundred new titles every month.[11]

No longer was adult video something played only on adult motel closed-circuit systems, rented in the underground economy of Los Angeles by pioneers such as George Atkinson, or shot as an experiment by filmmakers such as David Jennings. Instead it was nearly everywhere, available for rent in the video stores popping up on street corners and in strip malls. Yet that growth met serious, continual, and consequential resistance that sought to reclaim the community standards that should define how and where pornography could exist. The use of local, rather than national, standards to determine pornography's legality was a relatively recent phenomenon stemming from the 1973 U.S. Supreme Court decision in *Miller v. California*. That decision built upon and extended an earlier case, *Roth v. United States* (1957), which had established the use of community standards in the process of determining obscenity. *Roth* defined *obscenity* as something "that to the average person, applying contemporary standards, the predominant appeal of the matter, taken as a whole, is to prurient interest, i.e., a shameful or morbid interest in nudity, sex, or excretion, which goes substantially beyond customary limits of candor in description or representation of such matters. . . ." Furthermore, *Roth* required that defining a given work as obscene necessitated considering it as a whole and finding it, as Justice William Brennan Jr. wrote, "utterly without redeeming social importance."[12] As a result, constraints on pornography were somewhat loosened, and the industry expanded in the 1960s and '70s as producers and distributors found ways to justify their products by including elements other than explicit content or by ensuring that the whole work was not pornographic.[13] The concept of "something more" could also be used as legal cover.

The court's 1973 decision in *Miller v. California* strengthened the community-standards portion of *Roth*, requiring that obscenity standards be based on applicable state laws, and it eliminated Brennan's "utterly without redeeming social importance" proscription in favor of new language: "whether the work, taken as a whole, lacks serious literary, artistic, political, or scientific value."[14] Pleasure was utterly disregarded by the court as a viable "value" and instead was regarded with suspicion as the basis of the "prurient interest" that could threaten the social order.[15]

For Collins and Wakefield, all that mattered was their suspicion that the adult videos rented in Maricopa County violated their perception of community standards and thus met the *Miller* requirement for prosecution. Their warning to storeowners in 1985 was, ultimately, merely a formality. David Gibson, the owner of Arizona Home Video in the Phoenix suburb of Glendale, heeded the warning and stopped selling and renting adult tapes the day of the announcement. Despite this, on March 25, 1985, a Maricopa County grand jury, at Collins's and Wakefield's urging, returned indictments against Gibson and two of his employees on seven felony counts of violating Arizona's obscenity laws, stemming from transactions prior to the warning involving five adult videotapes.[16] Potential penalties were severe: five years in prison and up to $1,370,000 in fines.[17] Other Arizona video store owners rallied around Gibson, forming a coalition for his defense, with more than 120 stores eventually contributing to a legal aid fund.[18] Foreseeing dire consequences for the industry if video stores continued to be prosecuted, adult video distributors Vidco and General Video of America (GVA) contributed additional financial support.[19]

Gibson's trial began in mid-October 1985, and he presented as his defense a variation on the argument that had previously plagued Collins: Arizona Home Video could not be violating community standards because other video stores all over Maricopa County offered the same adult material and were not facing prosecution.[20] The trial ended in a hung jury in November, and Judge Alan Kamin subsequently dismissed a second trial, ruling that Collins and Wakefield had violated their agreement not to prosecute storeowners who removed the tapes after the warning.[21] Despite these victories, however, Gibson faced legal fees of more than $140,000, as well as the cultural stigma of being branded a purveyor of obscenity by Maricopa County.[22] The case illustrates how the battle lines around pornography permanently shifted with the widespread movement of home video in the mid-1980s away from the easily identifiable locations and spaces of the past and into the "better" neighborhoods, where average citizens (rather than only "perverts") could easily find it.

As I argue in chapter 1, the legitimization of the adult video industry began when people such as Joel Jacobson, Robert Sumner, George Atkinson, and Arthur Morowitz decided to operate their companies like any other mainstream business, and in response similarly aggressive efforts by pornography's opponents to counter its growing normalization immediately sprang up. Collins's decision to prosecute Gibson was a critical moment for the opposition and is representative of other such efforts in the country at large. By prosecuting a mainstream video storeowner, Collins sent a message that pornography was not just illegitimate; it also had the potential to *contaminate* the legitimate. In mid-1985, Anna Capek, leader of an antipornography group in Lincoln, Nebraska, echoed such anxieties in her comments to reporters about adult video's increasing presence in mainstream video stores: "It subverts healthy sexuality. This is not aimed at the sleazy raincoat crowd. They rent to decent middle-class people."[23] Capek's fears were deeply indicative of the era—and bolstered prosecutors such as Collins in their belief that "sleaze" would contaminate "decent" people. In the end, the imperiled status of the home itself was transposed onto the retail spaces that provided pornography.

In this chapter, I explore these tensions by documenting how efforts by the adult video industry to become an efficient capitalist enterprise were met with a vigorous and strident opposition that formed at the nexus of grassroots outrage and juridical regulation. The industry had made the public encouragement of private pleasure its business, but it found itself in an increasingly paradoxical situation: selling private pleasure still required public marketing and distribution, meaning the encouragement still had to occur in the open, even if the behavior could move behind the closed doors of the home. Mainstream video stores, which gave adult video vast amounts of visibility, were still public spaces—and not wholly cordoned off for pornography. The result was moments such as Gibson's trial, in which "better" neighborhoods began to stand in for a larger discussion of pleasure and its relationship to space and economics. In 1986, William Swindell, vice president of CDL, outlined the stakes surrounding the issue: "You can't take an objectionable tape . . . and make it all right by selling it at ABC video store in the good part of town."[24] The palpable fear in Swindell's statement—that merely relocating something "objectionable" would render it "all right"— in many ways defines the struggles around the adult video industry in the 1980s. The *New York Times*, in 1981, ran a story detailing precisely such gains: "The erotic landscape is expanding to include clean, well-lighted suburban stores . . . and everyday people. Thanks to new technologies such as video-cassette recorders . . . sexually explicit entertainment has found a pipeline into the bedrooms of couples across America."[25] This was a struggle over the meaning of pleasure—"the bedroom," in the discourse of the time—played out in the space of the video rental store.

Much as Capek believed that pornography "subverts healthy sexuality" without presenting any evidence, antipornography discourses of the era repeatedly demonized an imaginary enemy rooted in fears of cultural contamination—and increasingly took on the contours of a panic. In 1985, for example, Swindell described adult video in hyperbolic terms: "We're talking about ultimate sexual acts, some would say perverted acts. A lot of these cassettes contain depictions of rape, bestiality, sadomasochism."[26] The fear of contamination was so profound for Swindell and others that what pornography *could* be was magnified well beyond what it actually *was* in the service of a greater political goal: to solidify a desired mythology of community standards and thus eradicate adult video.

I argue below that this panic was rooted in three intertwined elements: (1) the proliferation of a machine designed for private use and capable of playing sexually explicit content; (2) widespread access to that content via the growth of mainstream rental stores willing to carry it; and (3) the professionalization of the adult film industry, which allowed it to meet growing customer demand. I trace this panic through moments of both cultural and legal regulation. Cultural regulation included grassroots protests by various conservative (and often religious) organizations; the discourse of antipornography feminist groups; and corporate decisions by video chains to avoid or eliminate adult material. Legal regulation took familiar forms: investigations and arrests, obscenity trials, court decisions, municipal decisions, and zoning regulations. This all culminated in the Attorney General's Commission on Pornography, more commonly known as the Meese Commission, which completed its *Final Report* in 1986. While the *Report* itself all but ignored adult video in the literal sense, the fears surrounding its proliferation and availability underscored the commission's recommendations and comments.

I undertake this examination in part by focusing on previously unexamined or overlooked examples indicative of the wider cultural context, paying particular attention to the lengths pornography's opponents went to restore "decency" by targeting video store owners. The panic discourses eventually created a paradoxical environment that continues to define the cultural landscape: the adult film industry faced increasing scrutiny, difficult legal challenges, and vociferous condemnation from a vocal and active opposition even as its widespread public presence suggested that its struggle for accessibility and respectability was over. Ultimately, it was video rental stores that quietly became the most important and contested ground in this period, a liminal space in which all the fears about pornography, pleasure, and behavior were enacted. Capitalism eventually won this battle: large corporate chains simply decided not to offer adult video. As Gayle Rubin argues, "There are ... historical periods in which sexuality is more sharply contested and overtly politicized. In such periods, the domain of erotic life is, in effect, renegotiated."[27] The battleground of adult video—particularly the relationship among activists, law enforcement, and legislators—in the mid-1980s was a site of just such renegotiation.

COMMUNITY STANDARDS: LEGAL REGULATION OF ADULT VIDEO

In the 1980s, mainstream video store owners increasingly found themselves in the crosshairs of a vocal public minority pressuring prosecutors to stop the encroachment of pornography into "decent" neighborhoods. That minority, however, started its efforts by protesting more traditional outlets for pornography, and its successes in that realm emboldened later opposition. For example, in 1980, in the Detroit suburb of Clinton Township, a group calling itself Clinton Citizens for Progress started to picket an adult

Figure 17. Protestors celebrating outside an adult bookstore in Clinton Township, Michigan, in 1980. © Mary Schroeder, *Detroit Free Press* via ZUMA Wire.

book and video store immediately after it opened. "It's a breeding ground of filth and we don't want it here," member Beverly Huntley told reporters.[28] The relentless members (who eventually numbered in the hundreds) were a constant presence outside the store, gathering signatures to give to township officials, until, fifty days later, owner Nick Placido shut the store.[29] The members celebrated by burning their now-unnecessary signs (figure 17).

As opposition to adult video grew throughout the country, tensions began boiling over about the apparent creep of pornography out of traditional adults-only outlets and into retail environments that otherwise catered to "normal" patrons and families. In the Cincinnati suburb of Fairfield, a 1984 case became a national example for anxious video store owners concerned about grassroots pressure.[30] Members of Concerned Citizens for Community Values (CCCV), a local conservative group, confronted Jack Messer, owner of the eight-outlet Video Store chain, wanting him to get rid of his adult videotapes.[31] Messer, incensed, decided to fight back—even if it meant, as he suspected, that he would be arrested and charged with obscenity. "Once the community sets a standard," he said later, "I'll have no trouble abiding by it. But when they haven't set a standard, you can't give a small group of people the right to censor what you have in your store."[32] CCCV, as Messer predicted, took its fight to Fairfield authorities.

In June 1984, undercover police purchased five adult videos in one of Messer's outlets and promptly arrested him, along with an employee, on charges of pandering obscenity.[33] Members of CCCV and the local Assembly of God church picketed in front of the store, and Fairfield city law director John Clemmons subpoenaed Messer's business records—including the membership list and all rental transaction records for the store's twenty thousand customers.[34] The strategy was a deliberate attempt to disprove what prosecutors knew would be Messer's response: that the widespread demand for adult material in the city meant it was well within the community standards permissible under *Miller v. California.* The list and transaction records, Clemmons believed, would show that the majority of the store's customers were coming from outside the community, and therefore violating its internal decency standards.

This tactic further illustrates the growing fear of contamination. CCCV and Fairfield authorities believed the "decent" people of Fairfield could not possibly be renting the material and that outsiders were responsible—an attitude that meshed well with their belief that pornography was outside the normal bounds of healthy sexuality. A judge quashed Clemmons's subpoena, but the case still went to trial. Ironically, Messer used the very same records to show, as he later put it, "that the adult tape customers were no different from other customers, and the community had accepted this stuff for years."[35] His employee was exonerated, but the jury was unable to reach a verdict on Messer's guilt or innocence. Undeterred and still under community pressure, prosecutors arrested Messer again on similar charges, but the case was thrown out for improper jury selection—yet prosecutors still would not quit, and they arrested Messer again. A third trial commenced in 1986. This time, the city brought in CDL vice president and attorney Bruce Taylor to prosecute the case, ironically revealing that Fairfield deemed it perfectly acceptable to bring in an outsider to define and defend values and standards that the city believed were being tainted by other, less respectable outsiders.[36] In response, Roy Whitman, chief of psychiatry at the University of Cincinnati, testified for Messer that the adult videos in question were normal sexual outlets for healthy people and that the "range of sexual normality" was wide among the people of Fairfield.[37] On March 26, 1986, the jury acquitted Messer 6–2, but the cost, as it had been for David Gibson in Arizona, was steep: Messer had some $80,000 in legal bills and suffered the constant presence of picketers and the stigma of being a "pornographer."[38]

Such regulatory efforts predated Messer and Gibson, and in fact some had started as soon as pornography appeared on video. In late 1979, the Los Angeles Police Department began taking an interest in the city's adult video distributors, and by January 1980 an undercover operation was underway to pin obscenity charges on anyone and everyone involved in the dissemination of video pornography. Detective Jack Rabinowitz opened Unique Video Specialties, a phony distribution business, and solicited material from wholesalers. A trip to the Consumer Electronics Show in Las Vegas in mid-January brought him even more contacts, and by March the operation had yielded tapes from all the major companies then operating in Los Angeles.[39] On March 13, 1980, police simultaneously raided fourteen locations involving nine adult video producers, seizing business records and inventory. They also requested arrest warrants from the courts for twenty individuals on obscenity charges. Seized records showed that, in the previous four weeks, the nine companies had produced 185,000 tapes, making up 80 percent of the total sold in the United States during that time.[40] While the busts certainly publicized police interest in the growing enterprise and further demonized pornography, they ultimately made little difference: the warrants remained unfilled, and no arrests were ever made.[41]

Just two months later, however, another case with national scope dominated headlines. The ambitious operation later known as MIPORN (for Miami Porn) had begun in November 1975 in Dade County, Florida, only a few weeks after Sony released the Betamax to the consumer market. Detective Al Bonanni, operating a phony distribution front called Amore Productions, ostensibly intending to ship pornography to South America, ingratiated himself into the underground adult film economy. Authorities quickly realized the network of producers and distributors reached far beyond Florida and sought help from the FBI.[42] Already in motion on its own undercover operation, the FBI folded the two into a single large-scale investigation and, in October 1977, initiated MIPORN. The intricate project utilized two agents, Pat Livingston and Bruce Ellavsky, who, under the pseudonyms Patrick Salamone and Bruce Wakerly, established Golde Coaste Specialties, yet another phony distribution business. On Valentine's Day 1980, four hundred FBI agents in ten states conducted raids on thirty businesses and indicted forty-five people on obscenity charges and thirteen others for film piracy.[43] It was the most sweeping, organized, and direct attack on the adult film industry in American history—and it captured, as one FBI official told reporters, "every major [adult film] producer and distributor in the country."[44] Even more important than the arrests and subsequent convictions, however, was the larger message sent to both the industry and the public: pornography was dangerous, in need of constant regulation, and posed a threat to society. The investigation set a tone for the coming decade.[45]

All these efforts to eradicate pornography, however, failed to address the problem on a national level. Pornography's opponents sought something more systematic, organized, and coordinated to punish those responsible for contaminating "decent" neighborhoods through legal means. To counter the worrisome legitimization that pornography was gradually afforded with the inclusion of adult titles in video rental stores, the vocal and active minority wanted to reinforce a hegemonic response requiring guilt and shame as the only viable reactions to "protect" the family. In 1984, President Ronald Reagan gave that minority precisely what it wanted: an officially sanctioned effort to reposition pornography as something harmful. It was nothing less than an attempt to cement the discourse about community standards into a homogenous, hegemonic set of indisputable national beliefs.

THE MEESE COMMISSION: FIXING THE DISCOURSE

On May 21, 1984, during the signing of the Child Protection Act, legislation amplifying penalties related to child pornography, Reagan announced the creation of a national commission to study the effects of pornography on society. "Pornography is ugly and dangerous," he said. "If we do not move against it and protect our children, then we as a society ain't worth much."[46] Reagan's decision, and his comments, fed directly into the growing panic over pornography, particularly his invocation of the need to "protect our children." Indeed, Reagan had been elected on a "pro-family" platform in 1980, during which he called repeatedly for a return to "traditional" moral values.[47] He had been aided by various conservative and Christian groups in that regard—all of which were ready and waiting for precisely this moment to restore the "moral order" of society.[48]

In fact, such groups had already pressured Reagan on this very issue: on March 28, 1983, members of Morality in Media, a federation of antipornography groups claiming to represent 100 million Americans, met with Reagan in an effort to push him into naming a "smut czar."[49] James B. Hill, president of the group, outlined a plan for a coordinated attack by the Justice Department, Postal Service, Customs Service, and FBI that, if pressed vigorously, would mean "the back of the pornography industry would be broken within 18 months."[50] In May 1983, one hundred Roman Catholic bishops and a dozen Eastern Orthodox bishops followed up with a letter pressuring Reagan to take action.[51] Reagan eventually acquiesced to these growing demands, assigning responsibility for establishing a pornography commission to then–Attorney General William French Smith in early 1985, but it was Edwin Meese III, Smith's successor, who took charge in May of that year. Meese, a longtime advisor to Reagan, was the White House's unofficial liaison to the evangelical Christian community, had a strict constitutionalist perspective on the Supreme Court, and maintained a rigid, unrelenting stance on law and order.[52] There was no doubt that the commission would reflect his approach.

The creation of the Meese Commission was not an isolated act; it was born as a response to the findings of an earlier commission. President Lyndon Johnson had set up the President's Commission on Obscenity and Pornography in 1969, and it continued its work under Richard Nixon and released its *Report of the Commission on Obscenity and Pornography* on September 30, 1970. Yet the 1970 *Report* reached an unanticipated (and unprecedented) conclusion. After consulting a wide variety of experts and examining broad sets of data, the eighteen-member commission, chaired by University of Minnesota Law School Dean William B. Lockhart, issued a dramatic recommendation: "Federal, state, and local legislation prohibiting the sale, exhibition, or distribution of sexual materials to consenting adults should be repealed."[53] The commission decried the complete lack of evidence for the belief—propagated by conservative groups—that pornography caused violence, juvenile delinquency, and immoral character. They also advocated for increased sex education, concluding: "In general, persons who are older, less educated, religiously active, less experienced with erotic materials, or feel sexually guilty are most likely to judge a given erotic stimulus 'obscene.'"[54] Nixon had expected the commission's findings to support traditional conservative perspectives seeking to condemn and heavily regulate pornography, and the actual findings caused widespread anger and disbelief.

Nixon, who had long been rhetorically engaged in panics about the dissemination of pornography throughout the country, saw the findings as a dangerous attack on the foundations of "decent" culture. After taking office in 1969, in fact, he had seized on mail-order pornography as a threat, saying American families were being "bombarded" through their mailboxes. As Whitney Strub argues, "Nixon's language repeatedly emphasized the home, presenting it as a fragile place of private family refuge under lurid assault from salacious smut peddlers."[55] Such language was part of a much larger set of political discourses positioning the home (and the family—

always white and middle-class—inside it) as both threatened and threatening, at risk of being contaminated and thus contaminating the rest of the neighborhood. Suburbia, for its "safety" far away from the dangerous city, was constantly on the edge of moral collapse. Pornography's presence not only highlighted those anxieties; it made them visible in ways conservatives would have preferred remain uncovered.[56]

As expected, Nixon immediately and categorically rejected the commission's findings: "So long as I am in the White House, there will be no relaxation of the national effort to control and eliminate smut from our national life."[57] The Senate, on October 13, 1970, voted 60–5 to denounce the *Report* and reject its major findings. Senator John J. McLellan, Democrat of Arkansas and sponsor of the measure, summed up the collective reaction: "The Congress might just as well have asked the pornographers to write this report."[58] Not everyone on the commission held a differing opinion. Charles H. Keating Jr., the lone Nixon appointee (who was given the post when Kenneth B. Keating—no relation—resigned in June 1969), had been a vocal and persistent critic during the entire process, disagreeing with nearly everything at every turn. He wrote a dissenting statement to the *Report* that emphasized the urgent need for more regulation. "Pornography," he argued, "has reached epidemic proportions."[59] Keating's presence on the commission sent a clear message that Nixon was not interested in seeking impartial conclusions; after all, as the founder of CDL in the mid-1950s, Keating was the preeminent antiobscenity crusader in the United States. CDL's strategies and ideologies not only made their way into his dissenting opinion in the *Report*, but also had a dramatic impact on later events during the video era.

Keating also behaved as a general nuisance during and after the proceedings, criticizing the makeup of the commission, accusing its members of bias, and suggesting that hearings had violated public access laws. Upon its completion, he filed for and received a temporary restraining order that briefly delayed publication of the findings, a disagreement eventually settled out of court.[60] Keating's angry response hijacked the media's coverage of the findings, moving the discourse away from its progressive conclusions and trying to replace them with the same hegemonic beliefs that CDL had long been feeding the public, based around three premises: (1) pornography and obscenity were the same; (2) pornography was obviously dangerous; and (3) eradicating pornography required vigorous and continual prosecution. Debate and discussion were unnecessary, and any disagreement was the work of pornographers or suspicious sympathizers—most of whom were academics, a group Keating held in strong contempt.[61] Keating also took his condemnation to the pages of *Reader's Digest,* where his trade-mark panic discourses reached a broad and substantial audience.[62]

Panic was a familiar strategy for Keating, who built CDL on its tactics: position pornography as a threat to the family and the nation; create a one-sided debate demonizing the opposition; and utilize legal strategies based around obscenity laws rather than a language of "censorship," all with the goal to eliminate, not contain, pornography.[63] Furthermore, CDL advocated community politics over federal action and strenuously encouraged local authorities to enforce obscenity laws and grassroots organizations to protest both lack of prosecution and the very presence of pornography in their communities. The strategy was remarkably effective: rather than stirring up hysteria or engaging in moralizing discourses susceptible to charges of censorship, Keating and CDL instead crafted an atmosphere in which "the law" was positioned as the important element rather than religious or political judgment, giving the strategy a legal legitimacy and circumventing criticism. Thus, by appointing Keating to the commission, Nixon sent a clear message that any outcome other than strict dismissal of the legitimacy of pornography, along with urgent calls for increased prosecution under existing laws, would be unacceptable.[64] New legislation, pornography's opponents thought, would stall in the court system, be rejected by the public, or simply take too long to pass.

Reagan's formation of the second commission was clearly a deliberate effort to sweep away the findings of the earlier commission and restore "harm to the family" as the primary charge against pornography. In his initial 1984 announcement, he directly addressed the matter: "I think the evidence that has come out since that time, plus the tendency of pornography to become increasingly more extreme, shows that it is time to take a new look at this conclusion, and it's time to stop pretending that extreme pornography is a victimless crime."[65] Meese agreed and explicitly blamed video, noting that the technology was "bringing too much pornography into the home," making it dangerous, suspicious, and in need of control.[66] Such beliefs were signaled in the mandate given to the new group: "[To] determine the nature, extent, and impact on society of pornography in the United States, and to make specific recommendations to the Attorney General concerning more effective ways in which the spread of pornography could be contained, consistent with constitutional guarantees."[67] The language could not be more telling: it presupposes a pornography problem and an institutional failure to solve it; additionally, it ignores the previous commission's effort to move away from just such an approach.

On May 20, 1985, a year after Reagan's decision, Meese announced the commission's members, selecting prosecutor Henry Hudson from Arlington

County, Virginia, to head the group.[68] Hudson had all but wiped out pornography in Arlington County through vigorous law enforcement efforts, garnering the praise of Reagan in meetings with leaders of the Morality in Media activist group in March 1983.[69] "Arlington County basically is a residential community," Hudson claimed, "and citizens have very little tolerance for adult bookstores and publications."[70] Hudson, like Meese and Reagan, believed firmly in the "decent neighborhoods" paradigm, in which pornography had the dire potential to contaminate hegemonic family structures.[71] Despite Hudson's assurance that "this is not going to be a commission that that is trying to disgorge dirty thoughts from people's minds," he made no distinction between pornography and obscenity, claiming that "pornography is not covered or protected by the First Amendment," the standard strategy taken by pornography's opponents to get around constitutional protections.[72] Alan Sears, an antipornography prosecutor from the U.S. Attorney's Office in Louisville, Kentucky, with experience in more than twenty state and federal obscenity cases, was named executive director. Another key participant in the panic discourses, Sears said, after the commission's conclusion, that "the largest consumers of pornography in this country are children."[73] Sensing the bias from the beginning in the commission's makeup, Barry Lynn, legislative counsel to the American Civil Liberties Union, noted that he feared the commission would "dream up new ways to curtail speech about human sexuality" and that "a train marked 'censorship' . . . has just left the station."[74]

Ten others made up the rest of the commission, which Meese and Hudson both called a balanced group, even though nearly all were conservative opponents of pornography. Harold "Tex" Lezar had worked for William F. Buckley Jr., was a former Nixon speechwriter, and served as the assistant attorney general for legal policy.[75] Edward J. Garcia was a Reagan-appointed U.S. district judge in California.[76] Diane D. Cusack, a city councilor from Scottsdale, Arizona, advocated rigorous obscenity prosecutions, and, while she acknowledged that not all pornography was obscene under the *Miller v. California* test, she also said it was nevertheless objectionable to "the strongest unit of society—the family" and claimed that it "challenges one of those understandings held by society for thousands of years— that sex is private, to be cherished within the context of love, commitment, and fidelity."[77] Later, after the commission had concluded its work, she claimed that prosecution was the only way to "put the pornographers out of business."[78] Frederick Schauer, law professor at the University of Michigan and an authority on obscenity laws, had argued in various articles that pornography was not constitutionally protected.[79] Park Elliot Dietz, professor of law, medicine, and behavioral psychiatry at the University of Virginia, believed that pornography was a threat to society's moral stability.[80] James Dobson, who in 1977 had founded Focus on the Family to advocate for religiously based social conservatism, and Reverend Bruce Ritter, a Catholic priest and the founder of Covenant House, a charity for homeless teenagers, were particularly noteworthy additions, as each had no compunction whatsoever about expressing their longstanding, religiously driven views on the evils of pornography throughout the proceedings.[81] The other three members of the commission were the least aligned with conservative politics. Deanne Tilton-Durfee was a former social worker and president of the California Consortium of Child Abuse Councils; Judith Veronica Becker taught clinical psychology at Columbia University and had vast experience in working with sex offenders and victims of sexual abuse; and, finally, Ellen Levine edited *Women's Day* magazine and was vice president of CBS Magazines.[82] Levine was the only member of the media invited to join the commission. No one from any adult industry was part of the commission, though some did testify at the hearings.

Whereas the 1970 commission had two years and a $2 million budget for its work, the second attempt was given twelve months and less than $500,000. It funded no original research, instead relying on its "Workshop on Pornography and Public Health," hastily organized (at the request of Hudson) by Surgeon General C. Everett Koop.[83] Unlike the first report, undergirded by an array of social scientists' observations and collections of data, the second relied on a parade of witness anecdotes about of the dangers of pornography in their lives as its primary "evidence." Twelve hearings in six cities were held between June 19, 1985, and January 22, 1986, with 208 witnesses appearing—among them 68 policemen, 30 self-described victims of pornography, and 14 representatives of antipornography groups.[84] The few scientists who did participate later accused the commission of misrepresenting their research and strongly criticized its results.[85] Levine and Becker offered particularly strong criticism, saying that the efforts to "tease the current data into proof of a causal link between [pornography and violence] cannot be accepted."[86]

Meese took delivery of the *Report* on July 9, 1986, at the Justice Department.[87] During his press conference, Meese stood under a partially topless female statue, *The Spirit of Justice*, sending photographers scrambling to capture the indelible, deeply ironic image (figure 18).[88] Concluding that pornography was indeed harmful to society, the *Report* offered ninety-two specific recommendations, all of which were designed to stifle pornography or prevent it from reaching the marketplace, and which essentially condemned

Figure 18. The indelible image of Attorney General Edwin Meese III receiving the *Attorney General's Commission on Pornography: Final Report* on July 9, 1986. Copyright Bettmann/Corbis/AP Images.

anyone who derived pleasure from it as dangerous and perverted.[89] Central to the commission's efforts, and taken directly from the CDL playbook, was the overt strategy of broadening the definition of obscenity as much as possible. In keeping with the tactics of panic, it also tried to exaggerate the "crisis"— and connected it to the need for the new commission, suggesting the previous one had clearly failed to address an "obvious" problem, writing: "Since 1973, the nature and extent of pornography in the United States has changed dramatically. The materials that are available today are more sexually explicit and portray more violence than those available before 1970."[90]

"Available today" is the key phrase: while the *Report* only occasionally mentions video specifically, that technology and its capabilities influenced nearly the entire document, which highlights the growth and reach of pornography—both obvious references to video's contributions. This emphasis on the spread of adult material was tied directly to the commission's focus on what it argued was the increasing "extremity" of adult material. Such phrasing occurs throughout the *Report,* which adopted a three-part strategy: disavow the prior commission's efforts; focus on *violent* pornography in order to claim that *all* pornography harms viewers; and characterize pornography as an epidemic requiring vigorous and immediate prosecution. As William E. Brigman writes, the recommendations were "designed to reorient, or repackage the war on pornography. Although the new laws appeared to be aimed at child pornography, they were designed to regulate the producers of all sexually explicit materials out of existence."[91] Ultimately, the commission made its desire to dismiss the conclusion of the 1970 report abundantly clear: "We reject the argument that all distribution of legally obscene pornography should be decriminalized."[92]

Specifically, the 1986 *Report* differed from the prior commission's findings in several distinct ways, all designed as a response to the professionalization of the adult industry. If adult film producers and distributors were striving to make more efficient capitalist enterprises, the legal reaction also had to become more efficient and professionalized. First, the commission vigorously pushed to encourage application of the Racketeering Influence and Corrupt Organizations (RICO) Act in obscenity cases, not only to serve as a deterrent, but also to bankrupt those engaged in pornography.[93] "In addition to the penalties already prescribed by statute," the commission wrote, "a defendant would be subject to forfeiture of any profits derived from or property used in committing the offense."[94] RICO, as I explore below, changed the landscape of pornography prosecutions by introducing a devastating new legal weapon. Second, the commission encouraged prosecutions under pimping, pandering, and prostitution laws—which, as they pointed out, had the benefit of circumventing the issue of obscenity entirely.[95] Paying people to have sex was the basis of the adult film industry, the commission reasoned, and thus fell squarely under such regulatory laws.[96] Third, they supported the creation of a national obscenity task force in order to organize, coordinate, and assist with prosecutions around the country.[97] Fourth, the commission actively, stridently, and urgently encouraged opponents of pornography to engage in activist grassroots protests—a right accorded to them under the First Amendment—an encouragement they did not extend to the adult industry, despite identical constitutional protections. This was an overt suggestion designed to utilize the power of the marketplace to shut down the industry.[98] Grassroots groups frequently had been highly successful (as the examples in this chapter have shown), and they were part of a larger movement at the time across the country toward direct political activism.[99] It was this blatant encouragement of grassroots protest—which had already proven to be effective in shaming community leaders and business owners—that most worried adult video retailers. "I'd like to keep [adult tapes] in stock," said a Chicago store owner to a reporter following the *Report*'s release, "but it's not worth the hassle."[100] That was precisely the point of picketing and protesting, which now had a stamp of very official approval: pester, annoy, blame, and shame business owners into dropping their adult inventories or push local legislators into more direct and forceful action.

The last recommendations of the *Final Report* that I spotlight focused on regulation of peep-show booths. The commission argued that peep-show facilities should "not be equipped with doors" and that "the occupant of the booth should be clearly visible to eliminate a haven for sexual activity," adding, "Any form of indecent behavior by or among 'Adults Only' pornographic outlet patrons should be unlawful."[101] These recommendations, among the least controversial (and shortest) in the *Report*, nevertheless bluntly illustrate the commission's stance on space and pleasure—as well as its overt attempts to control queer sexual practices, given that the "indecent behavior" inside peep-show booths almost always occurred between men. Pleasure—something to be avoided, contained, regulated, eliminated, or made unlawful—is treated in the recommendations as something indecent, dangerous, unacceptable for public discussion, and in need of discouragement, especially when it could occur between people of the same sex. The finding also illustrates the careful tiptoeing the commission did around the very purpose of pornography, which the *Report* treats in a clinical, removed fashion, and certainly does not acknowledge as a source of potentially healthy pleasure. Carole Vance, who attended the hearings, reaches a similar conclusion: "Pornographic images were symbols of what moral conservatives wanted to control: sex for pleasure, sex outside the regulated boundaries of marriage and procreation. Sexually explicit images are dangerous, conservatives believe, because they have the power to spark fantasy, incite lust, and provoke action."[102] Discourses of shame ultimately define the commission's legacy, and its refusal to invite anyone to testify about the possibility of pleasure—or even to acknowledge that such people existed—illustrates most directly the ideological agenda at its core.[103] This set of recommendations also points to the importance of space: because the commission couldn't regulate the home (and the pleasures that could be explored there), it relocated that regulatory desire to space that *could* be controlled without much resistance. That adult bookstores—and especially peep-show areas—were often queer spaces simply made for even less resistance, given the hegemonic, and frequently silent, propensity in culture to tolerate (and encourage) the regulation of queer spaces and behaviors, especially when they "stray" into visible territory.[104]

Such discourses around pleasure might be most evident in the individual statements by the commissioners, which are nearly entirely a collection of moralizing judgments. Park Elliot Dietz's statement, for example, encapsulates not just his own views, but also much of the panic then gripping culture more broadly about the potential for pleasure from pornography, and is worth quoting at length:

> I, for one, have no hesitation in condemning nearly every specimen of pornography that we have examined in the course of our deliberations as tasteless, offensive, lewd, and indecent. According to my values, these materials are themselves immoral, and to the extent that they encourage immoral behavior they exert a corrupting influence on the family and on the moral fabric of society. Pornography is both causal and symptomatic of immorality and corruption. A world in which pornography were neither desired nor produced would be a better world.[. . .] A great deal of contemporary pornography constitutes an offense against human dignity and decency that should be shunned by the citizens, not because the evils of the world will be eliminated, but because conscience demands it.[105]

James Dobson is no less vitriolic in his statement, arguing that "pornography is a source of significant harm to the institution of the family and to society at large" and claiming that "what is at stake here is the future of the family itself." Echoing Morality in Media's belief (and picking up the language James B. Hill had used in 1983 to address President Reagan), he also states that "America could rid itself of hard-core pornography in 18 months" if the commission's recommendations were followed.[106] Bruce

Ritter is equally severe, positing that "all sexually explicit material solely designed to arouse in and of itself degrades the very nature of human sexuality and as such represents a grave harm to society and ultimately to the individuals that comprise society."[107]

The possibility of women's pleasure in particular is distorted so completely in the *Report* that one could conclude from reading it that such pleasure did not even exist, and that any "inappropriate" sexual behavior could destroy society's moral foundation through its apparent attack on the family. The burden of responsibility placed on women in the *Report* ultimately makes female sexual pleasure—derived not just from pornography but from any source—seem like grotesque perversion. In one of the few moments in the *Report* where its relentless containment of women's sexuality is called into question, Becker, Levine, and Tilton-Durfee defend a right to consensual behavior: "We respect ... the rights of all citizens to participate in legal activities if their participation is truly voluntary," they write. "We reject any judgmental and condescending efforts to speak on women's behalf as though they were helpless, mindless children."[108] Yet the *Report* primarily addresses women's sexuality in terms of victimization.

Women's sexuality is addressed most directly in the *Report* through the voices and ideological frameworks of various antipornography feminists. Courted strategically by the commission for their perspectives on pornography, the result was a paradoxical alignment between two unlikely groups. As Vance argues, "The commission's staff and the Justice Department correctly perceived that an unabashedly conservative position would not be persuasive outside the right wing. For the commission's agenda to succeed, the attack on sexually explicit material had to be modernized by couching it in more contemporary arguments, arguments drawn chiefly from antipornography feminism and social science."[109] In one of the more perplexing alliances of the 1980s pornography panic, the decidedly antifeminist conservatives bent on destroying pornography found themselves not only warmly welcoming feminist activists to their hearings, but also invoking and praising their rhetoric and strategies—with substantial and calculated alterations—in the *Final Report*.

HARM, DEGRADATION, AND SHAME: ANTIPORNOGRAPHY FEMINISM

As Nan Hunter points out, the "core of the feminist debate about pornography occurred during a ten-year bell curve" between 1976 and 1986, but its roots stretch back much further, through the second wave of the larger feminist movement, which had long been concerned with issues of power, representation, sexuality, and violence.[110] The antipornography specifics of the movement coalesced with the formation of three groups in the mid-1970s: Women against Violence against Women (WAVAW) in Los Angeles, Women against Violence in Pornography in Media (WAVPM) in San Francisco, and Women against Pornography (WAP) in New York. Each group was concerned with what it perceived to be the links between pornography and violence against women, specifically rape, which became the focal point.[111] The movement grew quickly, leading to rallies, marches, and conferences on both coasts, where activists began to solidify their message: free speech concerns had overshadowed the harm pornography caused to women by inciting men to violence and rape, and it was a visualization of that same violence. These sentiments were summarized by activist, WAP member, and author Andrea Dworkin at a pornography conference at New York University in December 1978: "All over this country, a new campaign of terrorism and vilification is being waged against us. Fascist propaganda celebrating sexual violence against women is sweeping this land. Fascist propaganda celebrating the sexual degradation of women is inundating cities, college campuses, small towns. Pornography is the propaganda of sexual terrorism."[112] Such rhetoric, which filled Dworkin's 1979 book *Pornography: Men Possessing Women,* aligned with the panic then sweeping through conservative groups, which similarly argued that pornography was not only toxic but caused harm to women and the family—even if the two groups' views on women's place in society could not have been more diametrically opposed.[113]

The antipornography feminist movement, particularly in New York, escalated its tactics to involve more direct confrontations, creating slide shows (featuring extreme and violent examples, hardly representative of the vast majority of pornography) and leading guided tours of Times Square adult bookstores and theaters.[114] Resistance and disagreement from other feminists came in late 1979 when Samois, a lesbian S/M group founded in 1978 in San Francisco, began to publicly confront WAVPM about its insistence that all forms of violence in pornography were equally in need of eradication—even those that were consensual.[115] Samois published *Coming to Power: Writings and Graphics on Lesbian S/M* in 1981, and members of WAVPM countered with the anthology *Against Sadomasochism* in 1982.[116] The pitched battles that ensued become commonly known as the "feminist sex wars," in which "pro-sex" feminists argued vociferously against what they perceived to be censorship and the repression of normal, healthy sexuality.[117] Gayle Rubin, one of the founders of Samois and a frequent target of antipornography feminists, sums up the period and the ways in which antipornography feminists mistakenly chose their target: "Pornography has become an easy, convenient, pliant, and overdetermined scapegoat for problems for which it is not responsible," she argues, adding, "Gender inequality and contemptuous attitudes toward women are endemic to this society and are consequently reflected in virtually all our media, including advertising and pornography. They do not originate in pornography and migrate from there into the rest of popular culture."[118]

The legacy of the antipornography feminist movement most clearly resides in a series of civil rights ordinances written by Dworkin and lawyer Catharine MacKinnon in 1983. First attempted in Minneapolis, the legislation made pornography (which it defined as the "graphic sexually explicit subordination of women through pictures and/or words") a civil rights violation and a form of sex discrimination, allowing women who had been "harmed" by its effects to sue producers and distributors in civil court and collect damages.[119] The Minneapolis city council passed the ordinance in December 1983, but Mayor Donald Fraser vetoed it immediately. It passed again in July 1984 but was vetoed again by Fraser. Simultaneously, another version of the ordinance, focused specifically on pornography containing violence, was passed by the Indianapolis city council and signed into law in May 1984 by Mayor William Hudnut.[120] It was struck down as unconstitutional by the Seventh Circuit Court of Appeals in *American Booksellers Association v. Hudnut* (1986), a decision upheld by the Supreme Court, which affirmed that pornography that was not obscene was constitutionally protected, even from a civil rights perspective.[121] Further attempts were made in Cambridge, Massachusetts, and Los Angeles in 1985, as well as in Bellingham, Washington, in 1988, but all failed for similarly violating the constitutional protections held by nonobscene pornography.[122]

None of this stopped the Meese Commission from aligning with the antipornography feminists. MacKinnon and Dworkin testified in the hearings, and Dworkin's full testimony was included in the *Report*.[123] The commission, while acknowledging that the Supreme Court had rejected Minneapolis-style ordinances, agreed with the intentions of the approach—even suggesting that traditional obscenity laws could be strengthened with the addition of civil damages, clearly ignoring the fact that antipornography feminists had long been opposed to obscenity laws as moralistic and antisexual.[124] In the end, the commission essentially hijacked antipornography feminism for its own political gain, distorting and manipulating its discourses in a twisted effort to eliminate pornography rather than challenge underlying social structures and power disparities. Vance outlines the specifics of this process, particularly in terms of differences over the meaning of *degradation*, a term used frequently by both groups: "For anti-pornography feminists, pornography degrades women when it depicts or glorifies sexist sex: images that put men's pleasure first or suggest that women's lot in life is to serve men. For fundamentalists, 'degrading' was freely applied to all images of sexual behavior that might be considered immoral, since in the conservative worldview immorality degraded the individual and society."[125] Issues of power, inequality, male dominance, and patriarchy were disregarded by the commission because, as Vance concludes, there was never any real doubt that the desired goal for the *Report* was to shift the discourse away from those very issues and to reinstate a paradigm in which "the only reliable protection for women was to be found in returning to the family and patriarchal protection."[126] Pleasure for pleasure's sake—a recurring theme in pornography—disrupted that paradigm.

Upon the *Report*'s release, antipornography feminists, unlike the social scientists who felt their work had been misinterpreted and misused in pursuit of a political agenda, did not protest or criticize the findings. Rather, Dworkin and MacKinnon *praised* the commission's conclusions, arguing that the *Report* recommended the types of civil rights legislation that had already been rejected by the Supreme Court, and WAP founder Dorchen Leidholdt claimed she was not "embarrassed at being in agreement with Ed Meese."[127] Ultimately the paradoxical alignment of the two groups, which could not have been more stridently opposed in terms of the ideologies governing their stances, is a deeply illustrative example of the ways in which the panic surrounding pornography often created, as it were, strange bedfellows. It also reveals the patriarchal power of the commission itself, which systematically and successfully shifted the discourse surrounding pornography back to a hegemonic, assumed state of danger. On that level, it succeeded wildly in erasing any lingering traces of the earlier commission's efforts to rethink the cultural climate, particularly in terms of pleasure, which it defined and described (with a great deal of ironic pleasure) as a threat.

AFTER MEESE: THE ASSAULT ON ADULT VIDEO

The commission's power had been demonstrated even before the *Report* was released. While the initial test of its power did not involve video, it nevertheless prefigured what was to come. In February 1986, following testimony by Donald Wildmon, founder of the National Federation of

Decency (which later became the American Family Association [AFA]), and with the direction and approval of the commission, executive director Alan Sears sent a letter to twenty-three drugstore and convenience store chains that carried adult magazines. The letter notified them that the commission had "received testimony alleging that your company is involved in the sale or distribution of pornography" and that "this commission has determined that it would be appropriate to allow your company an opportunity to respond to the allegations prior to drafting its final report section on identified distributors." He closed the letter with an ominous warning: "Failure to respond will necessarily be accepted as an indication of no objection."[128] Obviously fearful of what appeared to be a threat of impending obscenity prosecution, Southland Corporation, owner of 4,500 7-Eleven stores (and franchisers of an additional 3,600), bowed to the pressure and pulled *Playboy, Penthouse,* and *Forum* magazines from its shelves in mid-April.[129] Southland president Jere Thompson issued a public statement that might as well have come from the commission: "The testimony indicates a growing public awareness of a possible connection between adult magazines and crime, violence and child abuse."[130]

By late April 1986, Peoples Drug, Dart Drug, and Rite Aid joined Southland in pulling the magazines, and on May 1, Thrifty Drug capitulated as well, removing *Playboy, Penthouse,* and *Playgirl* from its 582 stores and issuing a brief statement saying that the empty magazine racks would be used to "improve displays and give more space to 'family-type' magazines."[131] Conservative groups, predictably, applauded the decisions. Wildmon, denying that his testimony or the letter had had anything to do with it, said: "These decisions have been made by some socially conscious businessmen who are thinking about how they can better serve the interests of family values."[132] His own notion of how to serve those interests was certainly specific, consisting primarily of spooning religiously motivated panic to an anxious public looking for scapegoats. Both his books from this period fed the mythology of the besieged family needing protection from the "filth" invading "decent" neighborhoods. The first, *The Home Invaders* (1985), offers this breathless cover tagline alongside a photo of two children watching a television: "A shocking analysis of TV and the media, and how you can help stem the mind-polluting tide seeking to submerge us all!" The second, *The Case against Pornography* (1986), describes the "more than 14,000 'mom-and-pop' video stores" (as well as an unnamed "drugstore chain") that could potentially be carrying video pornography across the country and concludes with a chapter called "How to Start a Local Antipornography Group" and a Model Obscenity Statute provided by CDL.[133] Wildmon was at the forefront of the charge to eradicate pornography through any means necessary; the magazines on convenience store shelves, ultimately, were just a single salvo in a much bigger campaign that he and his followers waged through grassroots action.

Magazine publishers were outraged by the events. *Playboy's* lawyer Bruce Ennis decried the decisions, asserting the original letter was a deliberate intimidation effort with no basis in law, and Maxine J. Lillienstein, general counsel to the American Booksellers Association (ABA), condemned the actions: "This is the kind of conduct one might expect from organized crime or from a totalitarian dictatorship, not from an official agency of the United States Government."[134] In May 1986, *Playboy,* the Association of American Publishers, and the ABA filed suit against Meese and the commission, alleging that they had created a "blacklist" amounting to prior restraint of free speech, and *Penthouse* filed a similar suit alleging "intimidation and coercion" by the commission. Specifically, *Playboy's* suit demanded that the commission omit a list of retailers from the *Final Report,* withdraw its letter to retailers, and advise them that the *Report's* conclusions did not find *Playboy* to be obscene or in violation of the law.[135] On July 3, Judge John Garret Penn granted the requests, noting, "It can be argued that the only purpose served by that letter was to discourage distributors from selling the publications, a form of pressure amounting to an administrative restraint of the plaintiff's First Amendment rights."[136] The *Final Report,* as ordered, did not include the list. Yet Sears never backed down from sending the letter, saying later that its intention all along had been "fairness" and that it ultimately made no difference because the circulation of adult magazines had been precipitously dropping anyway, a clear sign that "the American people have been voting with their pocketbook for a long time."[137]

Sears was correct about adult magazine circulation numbers. By 1986, *Playboy* had fallen from a high of 7 million in 1972 to 3.4 million; *Penthouse* from a high of 4.5 million in 1978 to 2.7 million in 1986; and *Hustler* from a high of 1.9 million in 1976 to 800,000 in 1986.[138] It would be disingenuous, however, to suggest that people were simply turning away from pornography. Adult video's entry into the market and rapid growth during this same period was undoubtedly responsible to a large degree for these losses. *Hustler* magazine conceded as much in late 1984, writing, "Will X-rated videotapes make men's magazines obsolete? You can bet on it."[139] Adult magazines were simply the victims of new technology, not a decrease in public interest in sexually explicit content.

Nevertheless, "voting with the pocketbook" might have been the message the commission wanted to send all along, particularly in its encouragement of grassroots opposition. Although the verdict in the *Playboy* case might appear to be a victory for the adult industry, it was, in the end, remarkably useless. The stores did not restock the magazines, and conservative groups, emboldened by their growing power, fed the panic by demanding further action. It was an overwhelmingly successful test by the commission of its power to reconfigure discourses around space and standards. As Vance notes, "The true genius of the Meese Commission lay in its ability to appropriate terms and rhetoric, to deploy visual images and create a compelling interpretive frame, and to intensify a climate of sexual shame that made dissent from the commission's viewpoint almost impossible."[140] The next step was to make the *Report*'s recommendations a reality. On October 23, 1986, Meese announced the formation of a team of prosecutors to handle pornography cases, the creation of a national center for obscenity prosecution that would serve as an information clearinghouse and training facility, and a mandate requiring each of the ninety-three U.S. Attorney's offices around the country to have at least one lawyer trained in pornography prosecution. It was, he said, the beginning of an "all-out campaign against the distribution of obscene material."[141] The primary target would not be magazines but adult video.

To illustrate the new empowerment and determination felt by members of law enforcement, prosecutors, and the judiciary following the release of the *Report*, one need look only a few miles away from where it was written. On August 14, 1987, Dennis Pryba, his wife, Barbara, and her sister Jennifer Williams were indicted in Fairfax County, Virginia, for distribution of obscene materials through a chain of video and bookstores. Furthermore, the indictments were made under federal RICO laws, the first time in the United States such tactics were used in relation to pornography and a direct application of the Meese Commission's recommendation.[142] While David Gibson and Jack Messer had been relentlessly targeted and prosecuted multiple times by zealous officials, the Pryba case had an entirely new and different significance: if convicted, the three faced forfeiture of all their assets—not just their businesses but their homes, vehicles, and *anything* potentially related to the income garnered from the sale of the pornography in question. Authorities charged that the Prybas had systematically linked multiple pornography-related businesses since 1973, had distributed obscene materials through those businesses, and, due to prior obscenity convictions, had committed predicate acts, the crucial requirement to invoke RICO prosecution.

The Pryba investigation had begun in September 1985 when Fairfax police and FBI agents from Alexandria, Virginia, began to work together in a joint probe of Washington, DC's adult businesses, but the case more accurately serves as the legacy of the Meese Commission's direct recommendation to use RICO laws to eradicate adult video.[143] In fact, Henry Hudson, as a reward for his work heading the commission, was nominated by Reagan to serve as U.S. Attorney for the Eastern District of Virginia—and it was his office that spearheaded the Pryba case, thus bringing the recommendations full circle.[144] Pryba and his wife operated the nine-location Video Rental Centers chain in the DC area, as well as the Educational Books chain of adult bookstores, which had three outlets. Prosecutors, electing to use the RICO Act, charged the Prybas with three counts of racketeering, four counts of interstate transportation and distribution of obscene videocassettes, three counts of interstate transportation and distribution of obscene magazines, and two counts of tax evasion. Williams, the bookkeeper for Educational Books, was charged with two counts of racketeering and seven counts of interstate transportation of obscene materials. If convicted, the Prybas faced 101 years in prison and fines up to $25,000 on each racketeering count, up to $5,000 on each obscenity count, and up to $100,000 on each tax evasion count, as well as complete forfeiture of all of their assets.[145] At issue were four adult videos and nine adult magazines seized in raids on the Prybas' businesses in October 1986 that, prosecutors admitted, had generated a grand total of $105.30 in sales and rentals.[146] This was a symbolic effort to regulate space and establish community standards.

The prosecution by Hudson's office was not designed to punish Pryba or regulate his business activities. The indictments were intended to stop him, permanently, from selling pornography. DC-area officials had long been aware of Pryba, a protégé since the late 1960s of Herman Womack, an infamous former George Washington University philosophy professor turned adult bookstore owner, publisher, and gay rights pioneer, who had been convicted of obscenity in 1961 and 1971.[147] The latter conviction permanently barred Womack from engaging in commerce related to pornography. Pryba was also convicted, in May 1971, on six counts of selling and exhibiting obscene films.[148] That conviction did not deter him from engaging in the pornography trade; by 1981, he had left behind the highly restrictive zoning policies of metropolitan DC for the more open suburbs of Silver Spring and Takoma Park, Maryland, and the *Washington Post* identified him as a "former pornography kingpin" of DC.[149] Takoma Park residents were not pleased, forming the Concerned Citizens' Effort to stop what they saw as the encroachment of pornography into their "decent" neighborhood. "People have to pass [Pryba's bookstore] to go to work and to church and to school," noted organizer Brian Weatherly, once again illustrating the fear that pornography would contaminate "normal" society.[150]

Prosecutors agreed. Between 1981 and the racketeering indictments in August 1987, juries convicted Educational Books fifteen times on obscenity charges, and in 1985 convicted one of the Video Rental Center outlets for renting obscene material (a verdict thrown out by the Virginia Supreme Court for improper jury selection).[151] Still, an undeterred Pryba continued to exercise his constitutional right to rent and sell pornographic material—until, emboldened by the Meese Commission's recommendations, authorities turned to RICO. Following the seizures and indictments, the trial commenced in Alexandria in October 1987, and on November 10, a federal jury, after three days of deliberation, found the Prybas guilty on all the obscenity and racketeering counts and acquitted them on the tax evasion charges; they also convicted Williams on two counts of racketeering and seven counts of interstate transportation of obscene materials.[152] On November 16, the jury ordered the Prybas to surrender all their business assets—including their warehouses, the entire inventories of the nine video stores and three bookstores, and five company vehicles. Hudson put the value of the assets at well over $1 million but expressed disappointment that the jury did not also seize the couple's home and personal car, illustrating the degree to which he had gleefully inherited Comstock's mantle (see the introduction).[153] RICO laws permitted such action, arguing that the fruits of illegal ventures could not be used for further profit, even if the materials were otherwise constitutionally protected and never brought to trial to determine obscenity.[154]

On December 18, 1987, Dennis Pryba was sentenced to fifty-eight years' imprisonment (with all but three of them suspended), five years' probation, and five hundred hours of community service and was fined $75,000. Barbara Pryba was sentenced to thirty-seven years' imprisonment (all suspended), three years' probation, and five hundred hours of community service and was fined $200,000 dollars.[155] Educational Books was fined a total of $200,000, and Williams received three years' probation.[156] During the sentencing, District Judge T. S. Ellis III urged Barbara Pryba to "find employment in some wholesome area" and suspended her sentence because he did not want to separate her from the Prybas' thirteen-year-old son— a concern he did not extend to the boy's father.[157] The court immediately dispatched marshals to padlock the doors of all the Prybas' businesses. On April 9, 1990, the Fourth Circuit Court of Appeals upheld the conviction, and on October 14, 1990, the U.S. Supreme Court declined to hear the case, thereby upholding the lower court's ruling.[158] In denying the Prybas' claim that the seized goods were constitutionally protected, the appellate court wrote, "The First Amendment may be used as a shield, but it is not a shield against criminal activity."[159] The circuit was complete: the "criminal activity" referenced by the court was the history of obscenity charges, meaning the entire case was built around the distribution of pornography. The Prybas' career as purveyors of adult material was over, and RICO laws were embraced as a successful prosecutorial strategy.[160]

For the Justice Department, however, the Pryba case was only a prelude. In 1986, prior to the release of the *Report*, prosecutors indicted only ten people on obscenity-related charges in the United States; that number rose to seventy-one in 1987 and showed no signs of slowing down.[161] The Pryba case, however high-profile and complex, was just one among many. Six owners of five video stores were arrested in December 1986 in St. Louis after a three-month undercover investigation led to the seizure of more than three hundred adult videotapes.[162] In September 1985, owner Donald Wiener, his son Steven, and three employees of Lemon Grove Video Exchange outside San Diego were arrested and charged with distributing obscene matter in relation to six adult videotapes.[163] In keeping with the legacy of MIPORN, authorities often created elaborate undercover operations and phony businesses. In January 1985, for example, two Los Angeles police officers, posing as the owners of "Blue Moon Video," attended an adult video convention in Las Vegas and feigned interest in various distributors' catalogues. The resulting investigation led to the indictments of more than twenty people in February 1986.[164] Panic rhetoric was a key part of the case, with authorities exaggerating and distorting the seized materials in order to justify the "protection" of the public. In a prototypical example, Los Angeles city attorney James Hahn told reporters, "Videotapes seized by the police during this operation go far beyond the average public perception of pornography."[165]

Various communities opted for methods other than prosecution, frequently bordering on prior restraint of free speech without trial. In mid-1986, prosecutors in Michigan's Livingston and Oakland counties sent letters to video stores warning them that eight titles had been deemed obscene, giving them the opportunity to pull them to avoid prosecution.[166] Often containment efforts crossed beyond pornography. In 1986, a North Carolina sheriff ordered a rental store owner to remove copies of Paramount Home Video's *Strong Kids, Safe Kids,* an educational film starring Henry Winkler that is designed to teach children about the dangers of child abuse, because it uses correct anatomical terms such as *penis, anus,* and *vulva.* Ironically, the film suggests that children "shouldn't be punished for using obscene or sexual words" and advocates for early sexual education.[167] North

Carolina authorities obviously disagreed. Obscenity, it seemed, often extended even to *descriptions* of the human body, not merely its representations. Such action was in line with the panic, particularly in its fear of the corruption of children.

Even those companies only peripherally related to the industry felt the wrath of community and legal pressure. In spring 1986, Noel Bloom (the founder of Caballero Video, which was sold that year to other members of the company) and the owner of Creative Video Services (CVS), moved his new company to the quiet Los Angeles suburb of Thousand Oaks. CVS specialized in duplication of videotapes—including adult videos. A small group of incensed local citizens banded together to form Citizens against Pornography (CAP), aligned it with CDL, and declared war on Bloom, who had earlier been targeted in the MIPORN investigations.[168] Marilyn Wade, vice president of CAP, spoke at a public forum that included Mayor Alec Fiore, saying: "We won't permit the onslaught of garbage into our town."[169] Frustrated city officials, however, could do nothing, since forbidding the company from doing business would violate CVS's constitutional rights. Instead, Fiore vowed to monitor the facility's activities, promising prosecution at the first sign of obscenity. The fear of an "onslaught of garbage" (even if said garbage was behind closed factory doors) was really the fear that the imagined wall of respectability around Thousand Oaks might come crashing down through the mere presence of pornography in its boundaries.

Preoccupying activists such as those in CAP were municipal zoning issues, another key element in adult video's regulatory history. Cities, struggling to accept that pornography was, barring obscenity, constitutionally protected, had long sought ways to restore "decency" within their borders. Zoning provided an ideal solution, allowing municipalities to ignore more traditional legal means in favor of geographic efforts to regulate, contain, or eradicate adult industries.[170] It was an ingenious set of ideas that continues to act as the primary regulatory framework for pornography-related businesses in the United States. Most notorious among these efforts was undoubtedly the city of Boston, which, in 1974, designated a downtown area known as Liberty Tree Park as the only space where adult-oriented businesses were allowed to operate. More commonly known as the Combat Zone, the area drew intense scrutiny due to what was perceived to be its centralization of crime and violence.[171] By 1977, the city had used the Boston Redevelopment Authority (originally created in the 1950s) to close down the adult businesses and create a more "respectable" neighborhood.[172] Cities across the United States, desperate to get rid of the "porno plague," increasingly turned to similar zoning strategies.[173]

Two specific Supreme Court decisions stand out historically as illustrations of how cities inserted community-standards ideas into municipal zoning strategies that were designed, ultimately, to eliminate rather than protect pornography. In the first, *Mayor of Detroit Young, et al. v. American Mini Theatres, Inc., et al.* (1976), the court upheld a Detroit ordinance forbidding adult businesses from congregating together within a thousand feet of churches or schools or within five hundred feet of a residential zone. It was, in effect, the opposite of Boston's strategy for clearing out the Combat Zone, as it was intended to concentrate pornography and keep the "decent" parts of town from being infiltrated. The court argued that such a strategy was a routine part of land use regulation and was designed to keep the city safe from the crime and violence associated with areas such as the Combat Zone.[174] For adult businesses, however, it was a reminder that they were different, "diseased," and highly suspicious—and were subject to municipal regulations not faced by other types of commerce.

In 1986, the court decided a second case, *City of Renton, Inc. et al. v. Playtime Theatres, et al.*, in which it upheld a Renton, Washington, ordinance that had amplified the Detroit model. In addition to the distance regulations, Renton created "zones," similar to Boston's, where adult businesses could operate, but dispersed them in small areas where no congregation could occur, thus dramatically limiting land parcel availability. The court upheld the ordinance, arguing that Renton had merely created a "time, place, and manner" regulation rather than restrictions on content. Thus the city had concerned itself with "secondary effects" rather than restricting speech, a crucial distinction that allowed cities everywhere to contain the locations of adult businesses with extreme prejudice—as long as an area was available somewhere within the city.[175] For the adult industry, *Young* and *Renton* meant that cities could regulate it through either dispersal or containment zoning strategies—and, all the while, position it discursively as threatening the "respectability" of the communities in which store owners resided.[176] The possibility of pleasure, once again, was left out entirely of the community-standards debate.[177]

Mainstream video store owners—with their inventories of adult material—reacted to the escalation of censorship efforts in a wide variety of ways, with some forming coalitions to hold firm against prosecutorial and zoning efforts and others welcoming the chance to "clean up" the rental industry. The spectrum of reactions at the 1986 VSDA convention typified the lack of unity. With the *Meese Report* looming, tensions were high going into the annual dealers' gathering. Given the theme "Freedom of Choice" by organizers in a effort to recognize the censorship struggles faced by retailers, the event nevertheless did not offer a single official discussion, panel, or workshop on topics related to adult video (a standard offering at previous gatherings), instead preferring to address it indirectly—perhaps out of concern that cultural censorship efforts might escalate to include R-rated films as an extension of pornography's spreadable "toxicity."[178] Christine Hefner, president of *Playboy*, gave the keynote speech, in which she attacked the Meese Commission and its supporters. She encouraged store owners to resist cultural censorship efforts, noting that they were the most important line of defense in a larger battle. "If retailers interpret the report as a legitimization of extreme pressure groups' right to dictate their merchandising mix," she noted in a related interview, "then it won't matter what the majority of consumers want in terms of choice. We will have self-censorship." She also warned retailers that pornography's opponents would return again and again with increasing demands if not met with firm, organized resistance.[179] Despite these admissions of support, not every VSDA member felt encouraged by the organization. Reuben Sturman, for example, the veteran adult film industry member and owner of GVA and the Visual Adventures chain in Cleveland, argued, "If the adult video marketplace were to disappear tomorrow morning, the powers in the VSDA would be thrilled and delighted."[180] While the adult video marketplace would not disappear, it was set to radically change.

"WHAT A DIFFERENCE!": CORPORATE POLICY, THE FAMILY, AND TOXIC PROFITS

While tensions around adult video swirled in the courts, on the streets, in the VSDA convention hall, and in the Meese Commission's *Final Report*, the major battle against the encroachment of pornography into "decent" neighborhoods ended quietly and without opposition in a handful of corporate boardrooms. The effort waged by the opponents of pornography found no better ally, ultimately, than capitalism. While the overwhelming majority of early video store owners carried (and profited from) adult titles, they were mostly independent, single-store operators or members of small regional chains. Stores had a few methods for stocking adult tapes. Many kept them in a back room, typically located near the rear of the store, cordoned off with a curtain or swinging door of some kind, marking them as semiprivate but still somewhat open—a strategy that gained popularity after the Meese Commission's encouragement of grassroots protests.[181] If a separate room was not available, some stores placed the boxes on a shelf that was, at the very least, isolated in some way from other content within

Figure 19. The shame associated with renting adult video—along with the ubiquitous "back room"—eventually became so recognizable as to be a joke. From *Roseanne*, aired January 14, 1997.

the store and visible from the service counter. Finally, some stores kept books of lists or box covers at the counter for customers to flip through to make their selections.[182] To various degrees, all three strategies (with the separate room being the most private) marked the customers as doing something "different" or potentially embarrassing or shameful.[183]

The 1997 episode "Hit the Road, Jack" of the sitcom *Roseanne*, despite airing more than a decade after the period examined in this book, perfectly captures the mechanics of such rooms and the shame surrounding them in a brief punchline moment. A man browses adult videos in a back room. After being spotted by another patron, he quickly pulls the curtain shut, giving him the semiprivacy characterizing such spaces (figure 19). The scene is played for laughs—most obviously because the man wears a full motorcycle helmet the entire time, covering his face and further hiding him from the other customers. The humor here stems from the potential shame such spaces held for patrons even as they opened up pornography to new, vast audiences who might never have stepped foot in an adult bookstore or theater but who now had only to go to a different section of their usual video rental stores to find pornography. The motorcycle helmet prevents those around the man from recognizing him—but not from knowing that he is looking for pornography, despite the veneer of anonymity.

Indeed, as the rental industry matured, pornography represented an obstacle to those store owners seeking sanctioned forms of respectability and fearing the impact such shame might have on their bottom lines. Jonathan Coopersmith argues that "one tendency across technologies and businesses is that, as they mature and reach wider audiences, some participants have tried to improve their status by repositioning themselves and their products. They may accept some market loss for a gain of prestige and legitimacy."[184] This proved especially true for the home video rental industry, which, in its quest to avoid the panic spreading across the country, increasingly positioned itself as "family-oriented" in order to keep pace with the family-values rhetoric so discursively prevalent during the 1980s. In simple terms, that meant one thing: jettisoning adult video as quickly and permanently as possible from mainstream rental stores and returning the economic landscape to a state of demarcation, where pornography could be found only in "appropriate" spaces.

George Atkinson's Video Station chain, examined in chapter 1, steadfastly carried adult video until it failed in the mid-1980s, but it was virtually alone in that decision as mom-and-pop rental stores grew into an increasingly formal, corporatized network of franchises. The only other major video rental operation in the 1980s to offer adult video was Movie Gallery, founded in Dothan, Alabama, in 1985 by Joseph T. Malugen and H. Harrison Parrish. While only a small chain in the late 1980s, with a total of fifty outlets by 1987, the company's aggressive mergers and stock offerings in the late 1990s and early 2000s eventually gave it more than two thousand stores by 2003.[185] In many of its stores, the company carried adult video, recognizing that, despite making up only 5 percent of revenues, the material had a long shelf life and a base of interested customers.[186]

Beyond Movie Gallery, however, large-scale video rental corporations developed without adult tapes. Turkish immigrant Erol Onaran started his career repairing television sets in the 1960s, began selling movies on video in 1980, and eventually built his video rental business into more than two hundred Erol's Video stores—all without adult titles.[187] "It's a matter of our being a family-oriented company," said Onaran in 1984. "People can come in and take anything off the shelf and not be offended."[188] Onaran never wavered from the policy, and the stores, a fixture in the Mid-Atlantic states, permanently refused to offer adult video to its customers.

Sounds Easy, founded in 1980 in Salt Lake City, Utah, eventually grew to more than 130 stores, with founder David Meine firmly refusing to carry adult tapes from the beginning. When the panic erupted in the mid-1980s and owners began banding together to defend their constitutional rights to stock, rent, and sell pornography, Meine blasted them: "What percentage of our customers already perceive the video store as a porn outlet and are no longer renting adult movies? I cannot understand how stocking X-rated movies allows a video store to be a respectable, family-oriented business."[189] Meine's belief was indicative of a larger discourse in which a store could be only adult- *or* family-oriented but not both: pornography could not economically coexist with respectability.

The depth of his belief, as well as the illusory idea that only "outsiders" would rent adult video, can be seen in an incident involving Meine in the mid-1980s. Learning that a franchisee in Minnesota was in violation of the corporate pornography policy, Meine went to confront him and restore order. Before doing so, however, he silently observed the customers and their adult video selections. What he saw shocked him: "It was all these business-men and housewives," he noted. "I had been picturing all these biker types, but heck no."[190] Meine's comments illuminate the power of cultural beliefs in the toxicity of pornography, its capability to contaminate "decent" neighborhoods, and the way it must always be assigned to an outsider rather than to the "normal" people making up the community in order to demonize its threatening potential. Yet his comments also reveal the power of the highly gendered, familial structures at work: Meine's specific identification of "businessmen" and "housewives" was not incidental. Those two descriptors, making up what he (and others) clearly perceived to be the normal social order, had to be protected, even if that meant paternalistically protecting them from themselves. Despite the evidence confronting him, Meine was undeterred. Sounds Easy did not change its corporate policy.[191]

Adventureland Video, founded by Martin Ehman in Pleasant Grove, Utah, in 1981, grew to more than six hundred locations by 1986, most of them in rural areas and all with a strict policy forbidding adult video. The company went even further in November 1985, with all locations asking customers to sign a petition asking the Hollywood studios to release edited versions of R-rated films. "Many excellent movies cannot be brought into the home because of scenes they contain," the petition read. "Therefore, we, the undersigned, support Adventureland Video in their effort to have motion picture studios produce and distribute, for family viewing, edited versions of existing R-rated movies." More than ten thousand customers had signed the document by late 1986.[192]

National Video, founded in 1981 in Portland, Oregon, by Ron Berger, grew by 1986 to become the largest video chain in North America at the time, with more than eleven hundred locations—many of which were obtained through mergers and acquisitions. On April 1, 1986, a three-member store-owner committee voted unanimously to force new and existing franchisees to abide by a policy forbidding adult video. Proving Coopersmith's argument about exchanging temporary profit loss for perceived long-term gain, Berger noted, "We're likely to be taking a step backward in terms of market share" but added that the move was designed to be part of "the image we're trying to cultivate," which was, as committee chairman Michael Katz said, to be "synonymous with family entertainment."[193] In its quest to position itself and gain legitimacy, National Video further linked the "family" to the gendered mythology about the consequences of encouraging women's sexual pleasure: "We depend on the support of the family—the mother, the children—and have always had that message," claimed Sherri Canel, its public relations spokesperson.[194] Women, here reduced to the most simplistic maternal ideal, could not possibly be interested in adult video and, indeed, would undoubtedly threaten the company's profit potential if it carried the contaminated product. Commtron Corp., the largest video distributor in North America, took similar action in February 1986, dropping adult titles from its inventory. "We'd like to be a family oriented company," said national sales manager Vern Ross, "and felt like this was not an area we wanted to be associated with."[195] Profit was one thing, but the perception of perversion was another.

The decisions of the largest video rental chain and largest distributor to ban adult video illustrates the ways in which the perceived toxicity of pornography can lead to corporate (re)action. These companies, always pointing to the mythology of the family as the basis of their fears, instituted policies that distanced themselves from the business of "inappropriate" pleasure. Katz, in a moment of candor that exemplifies the lengths video store chains went to claim they weren't involved in censorship, noted that the company still believed in "freedom of choice" for its customers—as long as that choice did not include adult video. "There are always going to be places to satisfy that demand. We're not saying, 'Ban it outright from the individual.' We're just saying that we won't be a part of it."[196] The editors of *Adult Video News Confidential* condemned the decision, pointing out that families were precisely who was renting adult video, part of the "one for the adults, one for the kids" trend the magazine had long observed.[197] "One for the family" became the guiding corporate principle instead, with the belief that "one for the adults" would be handled by adults-only businesses, safely demarcated geographically and heavily regulated.

Finally, there was Blockbuster Video. The corporate juggernaut that redefined the video rental landscape had its roots in the economic imagination of Hank Cartwright, a former adult video distributor. Cartwright, an early Pizza Hut franchisee, violated SEC regulations in 1983 by selling stock in his King of Video distribution business early to a group of investors. Forced to leave the company, Cartwright, looking for other business opportunities, purchased five Captain Video stores in Nevada. In March 1985, sensing that the small video stores then dominating the market could be improved with wider selections, he opened a 4,500-square-foot store in Las Vegas, which included adult tapes. That location quickly became the basis of a franchise operation under the name Major Video, part of Cartwright's National Entertainment company.[198]

In 1985, David Cook, who had found success selling computer software to oil companies beginning in the late 1970s, visited Cartwright and inquired about opening a Major Video franchise. The two did not close the deal (even after Cook offered to buy Cartwright out)—but Cook, with his partner Kenneth Anderson, decided to open his own store using Cartwright's model.[199] On October 19, 1985, the first Blockbuster Video store opened at a busy intersection in Dallas, complete with the blue and yellow colors, computerized inventory systems, and nearly ten thousand titles that would later define all the company's stores. Another trademark present that first day was a policy to not carry adult video. Cook, echoing National Video's stance, later claimed the decision was not related to any moral principles: "While we don't care if people watch pornography, we just don't want to sell it to you. A lot of families come to our store . . . because they didn't mind their kids running around the store because they wouldn't see any garbage."[200] Cook's comments illustrate the growing false belief within the video rental industry that there was nothing moralizing about refusing to stock adult titles; such decisions, ultimately, erased any chance that pornography could leave the demarcated spaces where it would permanently be associated with the need for regulation and containment.

Among the initial customers at the first Blockbuster store was Scott Beck, who, along with his father, Larry, bought 9 percent of Blockbuster's stock; they also convinced two of their former business colleagues, Peer Pederson and John Melk, to invest.[201] By early 1987, the fledgling company had eight corporately owned stores and eleven franchises, with plans to create one thousand more. On February 3, 1987, Melk invited his former boss Wayne Huizenga to tour the suburban Chicago location, and the two, along with another colleague, Donald Flynn, put together a deal to buy 35 percent of the company for $18.5 million ten days later.[202] In the 1970s and early

1980s, Huizenga had built the nation's largest garbage-hauling service, Waste Management, Inc., and all six men had made fortunes together at that company, acquiring and consolidating hundreds of independent mom-and-pop outfits into a $6 billion business. When Huizenga left Waste Management in 1984, he utilized the same consolidation practices to acquire more than a hundred service-related companies in auto-parts cleaning, dry cleaning, lawn care, bottled water, and portable toilet rental, generating $100 million annually as a result.[203] When Melk approached him in early 1987, Huizenga was ready for the next challenge, and video rental seemed to fit what the *New York Times Magazine* would later describe as his tried-and-true criteria: "A pedestrian service business, with a steady cash flow, in an industry of under-capitalized mom-and-pop companies ripe for consolidation."[204] The observation that Charles Ruttenberg, VSDA attorney, had made only a year earlier—that the mainstream home video rental industry was the "leading means of communicating pornographic material to the American public"—was rendered moot.

Blockbuster's subsequent meteoric rise permanently altered home video rental in the United States. By the end of 1987, the company expanded to 133 stores; two years later there were 1,079, and by 1994, when Blockbuster merged with Viacom in an $8.4 billion deal, there were 3,600.[205] By 1991, the company controlled 10 percent of the video rental market and had revenues larger than its ninety-nine closest competitors combined.[206] In part, this was due to a decision Huizenga had made early on when he hired two McDonald's marketing veterans, Tom Gruber and Luigi Salvaneschi, who initiated a relentless strategy of saturating the country with Blockbuster outlets and establishing a corporate image based on unquestionable decency. Gruber created marketing slogans for the company, such as "Wow! What a Difference!" and "America's Family Video Store," all of which subtly promised there would, under no circumstances, be any pornography in its inventory.[207] Gruber noted the change: "When the industry started, all that was available were 200 or 300 legitimate movies and a lot of pornography."[208] Blockbuster's strategy hinged on changing both categories.

Huizenga, who did not own a VCR, rarely watched movies, and thought video stores were, in the words of a 1991 *New York Times Magazine* profile, "dingy little retailers that purveyed porno from behind windows splattered with peeling movie posters," never even considered carrying adult titles, and he banned them from all the chains that Blockbuster swallowed up.[209] At its peak, the company may have controlled only 20 percent of the video rental market—but that 20 percent was spread far and wide, dominating virtually every locale in the country. Blockbuster's decision to avoid adult video, made originally by Cook and carried forward by Huizenga and his management team, effectively did what all the years of protests and prosecutions could not: it blocked adult video from finding space in the "decent" neighborhoods across the United States that were free from intense zoning regulations.

The chains' decisions raise a deeper question: what happens to pornography when its largest potential distributors refuse to carry it? As with Southland Corporation's decision to bow to cultural pressure and stop carrying adult magazines in its 7-Eleven stores, these policies prohibiting adult video meant that the vocal minority's rhetoric, which sought to defend "decent" people from pornography, had successfully influenced corporate practice. The courts might have guaranteed various rights to citizens regarding pornography, but that did not mean private companies had to sell or rent it. Their willingness to forgo potential income—15 percent of total receipts, on average—speaks to the ways that the "toxicity" of pornography in the mid-1980s superseded even the capitalist impulse to maximize profit. Furthermore, the widespread belief that "there are always going to be places" for pornography reveals the cultural impulse to keep pornography under intense scrutiny and regulation. The "appropriate" place, apparently, would be adults-only businesses, cordoned off from "decent" people and subject to intense zoning controls. While many tried to pin the censorship efforts on conservative groups with religious agendas, the reality was much more complicated. The slow pushing of pornography back into the shadows following the rise of adult video came from a wide variety of sources, including the executives of video store chains determined to draw upon family-values mythology for their own bottom lines—while ignoring adults with families who had shown interest in renting the material.

Indeed, overlooked by everyone was the dramatic loss to those consumers who most benefited from the move of adult video into mainstream stores: women. While mainstream video stores (particularly chain stores) could have offered safe, discreet, and widely available spaces for women to obtain pornography, the actions by the corporate chains illustrate the fear that such availability might simultaneously be tacit support for women's sexual pleasure. Chuck Kleinhans and Julia Lesage argue that the importance of public space cannot be separated from discussions of gender and pornography—and that the problematic gendered ideologies *within* pornography often get reproduced *around* pornography. "Men's access to sexually explicit material for arousal indicates a social structure that limits and oppresses women," they write. "Commercial pornography is men's turf. It not only obsessively repeats male sexual fantasies, often misogynist, it also reinforces more generalized male heterosexual privilege to express and define sexuality."[210] For Blockbuster and other companies, corporate profits, ultimately, were less important than ensuring that pornography remained men's turf, whether or not they articulated it in such terms.

CONCLUSION: ADULT VIDEO AND THE CULTURE OF SHAME

The regulation of adult video continued long after the corporate chains had made their crucial decisions to exclude it from their inventories; after all, it was still a thriving industry, even as its distribution was reconfigured away from chain rental stores. That was still not enough for those seeking to wipe out pornography altogether. Meese's national team of advisors turned into the National Obscenity Enforcement Unit (NOEU) in 1987 and escalated nationwide efforts to eradicate pornography. Eventually, nearly every major adult video producer and distributor was ensnared in the unit's prosecutorial net.[211] Grassroots protests, too, dramatically amplified their efforts, aggressively targeting anyone who dared disagree with them. On September 30, 1987, Jerry Kirk's National Coalition against Pornography announced a nationwide push to demand the vigorous enforcement of obscenity laws. Kirk, mobilizing the language of panic, suggested that all pornography eventually leads to child molestation, so it all needed to be eliminated.[212] Authorities tended to listen to the vocal minority, lending credence to their position: in early 1988, William F. Weld, head of the Justice Department's Criminal Division, said: "This will be a big year for prosecutions. It will involve cases across the country."[213] That was because of "Project: Postporn," initiated in 1987 and reminiscent of the earlier MIPORN investigation. Led by agents trained by Alan Sears, who had graduated from executive director of the Meese Commission to working for CDL, it targeted dealers advertising through the mail.[214] The core of the NOEU strategy was to drive pornographers out of business through the use of multiple prosecutions. NOEU attorneys simultaneously indicted adult industry members in various jurisdictions around the country on the same charges—a strategy discouraged by the Justice Department but endorsed by Weld *only* for obscenity cases, a particularly brutal concept that left no doubt as to prosecutorial intentions. The pornography prosecutions of earlier eras had conformed to common legal tactics and strategies, but this was something new and potentially cataclysmic to the industry. Yet there was even more: any company or individual that managed to survive the multiple-prosecutions framework would then be indicted in their own district on RICO charges.[215]

Weld's predictions about the scale of the prosecution proved to be accurate. On July 1, 1988, twenty people and fourteen companies were indicted on obscenity charges, leading to nearly all being forced out of business entirely. The same day, Brent Ward, U.S. Attorney for Utah and chairman of the Attorney General's Subcommittee on Obscenity, told reporters: "I think it's an accepted fact that the depiction of explicit sex acts . . . has the effect of conditioning individuals to committing those acts and conditioning society so that that is accepted as the norm."[216] In other words, the pressure by conservative groups on law enforcement was so effective that, by the time of Ward's press conference, sex itself (the definition of "those acts") was something to be treated as suspicious and perverted.[217] That attitude became even more pronounced—and generalized—at the end of the 1980s, as the so-called culture wars reached new heights and arguments erupted over the very definition of *obscenity,* with conservatives such as Donald Wildmon and his army of AFA supporters, Senator Jesse Helms, and many others seizing on creative output (including photographer Robert Mapplethorpe's photography, documentarian Marlon Riggs's PBS television programs, and rap group 2 Live Crew's music) as dangerous sites in need of control.[218] That these sites frequently involved queer sexualities of color was not an accident; the battles over pornography had primed the conservative movement to expand both its reach and its rhetoric. While this book has taken up the most mainstream, financially successful, and publicly visible segments of the adult video industry during its nascent period (which means it has dealt primarily with heterosexual content ostensibly aimed at heterosexual viewers), further work on the history of adult video (in all its periods) will need to take up both queer sexualities and the way that race has operated textually, industrially, and spectatorially in the industry.[219]

Despite the continual blitzkrieg against its very existence, the adult video industry kept moving forward, selling "those acts" much as it had always done. Output continued to rise, signaling that whatever the *public* disagreements over pornography, consumers still wanted their *private* pleasures, and they wanted them in increasing amounts. Community standards, in other words, meant different things in terms of public and private consumption. In 1984, adult industry attorney John H. Weston estimated that there were 54 million individual adult video rentals in the United States—a number that jumped to 104 million by 1986.[220] As much as pornography's opponents wanted to portray people interested in sexual pleasure as perverts, outsiders, sinners, or threats to "decency," the truth was, they were simply ordinary people, everywhere, in vast and increasing numbers.[221] Bill Margold, an industry veteran who testified before the

Meese Commission, put it another way, describing the United States as a "nation of hypocrites . . . that [masturbate] to us with their left hand and condemn us with their right."[222]

The industry, too, was complicit in much of this regulation, albeit working from a different perspective. I have argued throughout this book that the adult film industry's quest to gain respectability by invoking discourses of quality simultaneously conveyed deeply gendered ideologies that contained and limited women's sexuality. Ultimately, such strategies, which superficially seemed to support women's sexuality in ways absent elsewhere in the culture, ironically aligned with those of pornography's opponents—who fought vigorously against any effort by the industry to achieve that respectability. Though diametrically opposed, these two positions inadvertently shared one critical feature: both refused to admit that women might obtain sexual pleasure from something other than highly justified behavior. The industry sought to increase market share by foregrounding narrative, style, and other markers of quality, while its opponents refused to cede that women's pleasure could be justified outside of contained, limited, and frequently religiously based structures. In other words, both sides agreed pornography lacked the "something more" needed to make it respectable; what that something more really meant, however, was centered squarely on women's pleasures and played out in culture at large. If women had long held the position of cultural gatekeepers, then the fears of contamination so widely held by those terrified of pornography's encroachment into the mainstream in the 1980s were in actuality articulating a familiar narrative in which women's behavior was in danger of being radically corrupted—thus putting all of society at risk. As Kleinhans and Lesage note, "The whole social discourse around sexuality functions to constrain women in the public sphere."[223]

The long journey of pornography—from stag film to Panoram to peep show to adult motel to VCR—was accompanied, at every turn, by intense regulatory reaction, but the industry never disappeared, however much its opponents desperately wanted. Arthur Morowitz, among the first to seize on the potential of the video medium, identified that crucial dichotomy in September 1986 when he argued for pornography's staying power: "Meese and his followers will be gone some day," he said, "and [adult] video will still be here. And people out there will still be happily having orgasms."[224] Morowitz was wrong in the first part of his statement, however—Meese's followers have never left. They have remained, waiting to assert control over pleasure. Indeed, the two sides of the pornography debate have always coexisted, often serving each other's ideological needs. For the moralists, adult video has represented the perfect threat, one invoked regularly to protect a slippery and illusory notion of the "family." Yet those same moralists have also served, as has always been the case, as the best possible marketing tool for an industry forever served by its illicit and "dangerous" status. Neither could, or will, simply disappear.

Thus, while it might be tempting to endorse Morowitz's comment as an easy answer to the complicated questions raised by these histories and in this book—and to believe that somehow, eventually, pornography will become respectable because people have always and will always consume it—a deeper layer must be considered. Al Goldstein, publisher of *Screw* magazine and another veteran with a similarly long view of the industry, recognized that the regulatory debate itself defined pornography perhaps better than anything else and, in fact, kept it alive. Despite all the efforts by the many people within and surrounding the industry to seek respectability by invoking quality, Goldstein intrinsically knew that pornography could never achieve that mythical status as long as it presented explicit sex. In a *New York Times* editorial following the release of the *Meese Report*, Goldstein eloquently captures that dilemma: "Puritan proscriptions and the cult of the taboo is the raison d'être of the whole adult entertainment industry, and the Commission's report is eminently satisfying to it in both regards."[225]

This push and pull, in which the adult video industry attempted to escape regulatory constraints even as it knew its outlaw status was key to its success, succinctly describes the climate under investigation in this book. Michel Foucault famously observed that this ad infinitum discussion was itself a perpetual machine of pleasure and regulation.[226] As he notes, "Pleasure and power do not cancel or turn back against one another; they seek out, overlap, and reinforce one another. They are linked together by complex mechanisms and devices of excitation and incitement."[227] Such tensions maintained the cultural belief during this period that shame and guilt were the only appropriate responses to pornography. In 1984, adult industry lawyer Allen Brown struggled with the necessity of separate, discrete spaces for adult titles within mainstream video stores, which would later become the ubiquitous back rooms familiar to patrons. "There's a catch-22 there," he noted. "Mixing adult titles with the rest of the films is delinquent in terms of fairness and courtesy to the public. But to segregate them, you open yourself up to saying, 'See, you knew they were dirty.'"[228] That liminal position, in which adult video existed somewhere between being "dirty" and part of the "rest" of the video store, defines the industry in its early period and points to the ways in which it could never really escape either position. Respectability, when it comes to pornography, is always just out of reach.

Limousines and Legacies

> We don't even know if this is gonna be a film. We're just fucking around tonight.
>
> **Jamie Gillis,** *On the Prowl* (1989)

> Videotape tells the truth.
>
> **Floyd Gondolli (Philip Baker Hall),** *Boogie Nights* (1997)

Toward the end of *Boogie Nights,* Paul Thomas Anderson's 1997 paean to the Golden Age of adult film, veteran director Jack Horner (Burt Reynolds) has finally succumbed to pressure to shoot on video rather than celluloid. Clad in a tuxedo and riding in the back of a limousine, Horner is flanked by Rollergirl (Heather Graham) and camcorder-wielding Kurt Longjohn (Ricky Jay). His idea is simple, if novel: drive down Ventura Boulevard in Los Angeles and pick up strangers to have sex with Rollergirl. "We are on the lookout," Horner says. "That's what we'll call this—*On the Lookout.*" Wearily, he feigns enthusiasm alongside the glassy-eyed Rollergirl (figure 20). Rather than offering some sort of electric spark, the "authenticity" of the shoot is coded as depressing and wholly unerotic. The unnamed young man they pick up (Kai Lennox) recognizes both Horner and Rollergirl, a former high school classmate whom he calls by her birth name, Brandy. The ensuing encounter turns rough, with the young man ignoring Horner's request to "take it slow." Eventually Rollergirl pushes him off, and Horner throws him out of the limousine. "Your fuckin' films suck now anyway," the young man hollers back at Horner. An incensed Horner responds, "You have some fucking respect," and then beats the young man on the sidewalk. Rollergirl joins Horner, kicking the young man in the face with a skate. In the scene's closing moment, she screams, "You don't ever disrespect me."

The scene plays as Anderson's personal diatribe against the invasion of home video into his beloved Golden Age of adult film, pummeling the young man as a stand-in for the audience that turned its back on narratives

Sunday, December 11th, 1983

Figure 20. Burt Reynolds (Jack Horner) and Heather Graham (Rollergirl), *Boogie Nights* (1997, dir. Paul Thomas Anderson).

that "took it slow." It is an argument about legacy. "Video is the enemy to me," Anderson later said. "The moment there was a chance for [the industry] to breathe and sort of open up and develop a new genre . . . it was sort of taken away by videotape."[1] He was wrong only in the sense that the industry didn't continue along his preferred path. In fact, there is a deep level of irony to both his comments and the *On the Lookout* sequence, given that it recalls what might have been adult video's most creative moment.

That moment occurred in 1989, when veteran Golden Age performer Jamie Gillis produced and directed *On the Prowl*, the first in a series. The obvious inspiration for *On the Lookout*, though it was made six years later than the fictional film version, the project features Gillis, alongside performer Renee Morgan, in a limousine on the streets of San Francisco, looking for strangers willing to have sex. Fellow adult film director and Gillis confidante Duck Dumont bankrolled the project and held the camera. Like *On the Lookout*, the film presents a series of unscripted sexual adventures; unlike that film, it does not end with a vicious beating or tragic commentary about the state of pornography.[2] *On the Prowl* was inventive and deliberately risky. "The idea is, we're going to go around town tonight and pick strangers off the street . . . and see what we get," Gillis says in its opening moments.

Figure 21. Jamie Gillis's credit, *On the Prowl* (1989, dir. Jamie Gillis).

What they got was a shift to a new form that has since become all but ubiquitous in the industry. Indeed, *On the Prowl* foreshadowed what was to come not only on home video, but also online in terms of both distribution and spectatorship. Unscripted and focused on (and fetishizing) "reality" and "authenticity," this new style privileged raw depiction of sexual pleasure without traditional narrative, aesthetic, or performative considerations.[3] It was an effort to capture some sort of "truth" about sex—and it was very much in line with the relentless, longtime obsession within pornography so accurately described by Linda Williams.[4] Unlike adult films from the Golden Age, *On the Prowl* moved closer (or so Gillis wanted to believe) to truth by eliminating layers of narrative distance. Gillis even eschewed the traditional "directed by" credit before the film, replacing it with "video concept by" (figure 21), clearly trying to suggest that a new form was emerging, one that even he (and Dumont) couldn't fully define or describe. Gillis's desire for difference stemmed from the deep dissatisfaction he felt with the mechanical tedium of the industry by the late 1980s. He later described his flagging enthusiasm: "There was no real sex going on—just a group of people wondering who they had to fuck so they could get paid and

Figure 22. *Left to right:* "Juan" signing release sheet; Jamie Gillis; and Renee Morgan, *On the Prowl* (1989, dir. Jamie Gillis).

go home. I wanted to liven things up."[5] Adult films had long played on viewers' fantasy and imagination—the spectator imagining her- or himself in the onscreen action—but *On the Prowl* took the trope a step further, with literal "spectators" suddenly thrust into action meant for the screen after they signed simple release forms (figure 22). "The guys wouldn't be paid, they would be there for the sex," as Gillis described it. "Wow! A revolutionary idea! A sex film with real sex!"[6]

That this livening up of pornography—and desire for "real" sex—would come from Gillis is not historically insignificant; among his hundreds of other performances was as sexologist Dr. Seymour Love in *The Opening of Misty Beethoven* (1976, dir. Radley Metzger). In part because of its deliberate sophistication and source material (George Bernard Shaw's *Pygmalion*), the film has represented to many the apex of the Golden Age.[7] *On the Prowl* is anything but sophisticated in the conventional sense, and light-years away from *Misty Beethoven* in nearly every regard. Most of *On the Prowl* is made up of awkward, unscripted conversations, failed searches for participants, and men who can't maintain erections. Those who can are poorly lit and fumble to "perform" adequately with the seasoned and professional (not to mention patient) Morgan. This fantasy is less about the mechanics of bodies and sex than it is about the titillating unpredictability of a random encounter—exactly what Gillis wanted.[8]

The film immediately spawned imitators. In 1989, shortly after *On the Prowl* was made, Ed Powers and John Stagliano released *Bus Stop Tales* and *The Adventures of Buttman*, respectively, both featuring a similarly raw, unpredictable, and "real" style. Then the floodgates opened, and many, many thousands of similar titles have been produced in the years since. Seeking some way to describe the new films, Gene Ross, then editor of *AVN*, suggested *gonzo*. It was a deliberate reference to author Hunter S. Thompson's exaggerated combination of first-person journalism and fiction—in effect, a heightened "documentary" style seeking some inner truth rather than mere reality, which Thompson most famously exhibited in *Fear and Loathing in Las Vegas* (1971).[9] Enrico Biasin and Federico Zecca outline the specifics of gonzo pornography:

> [It] bases its style on giving up narration: its aim is not to be found in the production of a tale relating sex scenes to the unfolding of a plot, but rather in the simple reporting of actions that are captured in their "natural" deployment.[. . .] A Gonzo "film" neglects the presentation of a linear narrative plot, one that relies on the logical succession of a number of actions within a consistent diegetic universe, in favor of a set of separated episodes that are kept together by the simple sharing of the textual surface.[10]

In addition to significant narrative alterations, gonzo also radically disrupts the aesthetic model of the Golden Age. These films often use a single hand-held camera (frequently held by the performers) and tend toward longer takes, a general deemphasis on editing, and either natural or minimal artificial lighting. The cumulative effect is an aesthetic that emphasizes "raw" action, presented without interruption or editorial control. Technology is seemingly deprioritized—even as it is highly privileged—thus implying that the artifices of previous eras (narrative, cinematography, editing, performance, etc.) created unnecessary distance from the "real" action, recalling the "shot live on video" discourses of the late 1970s, described in chapter 1. The VCR had moved the action closer to the spectator, and this new form tried to increase this proximity via presentation. In its abandonment of traditional narrative justifications to skip right to the action, as it were (thus mimicking and even anticipating the spectator, remote control in hand), gonzo foregrounds the *what* rather than the *why* when it comes to pleasure.[11]

This strategy typically appears in what Jay Kent Lorenz calls "an adult video that *appears* documentary in nature, that features a male narrator-cum-host who usually doubles as the videographer and is often involved in the video's sexual activity."[12] Gonzo films creatively incorporate the economic and technological characteristics of video production and reception to turn them into an aesthetic practice, illustrating what David James has called the "internalization" of the conditions of production.[13] Often they present "amateur" performers in "behind-the-scenes" environments, taking viewers into the meta-level of filmmaking and offering no traditional storylines or fictional narratives in a recognizable sense—even as they reinvent (and not necessarily very originally) narrative by making it appear real. This is itself, of course, a fiction. Ed Powers, for example, is a character created by Mark Krinsky, and his "documentary" style was carefully developed and repeated throughout his films, just as it was through all those that followed. Nevertheless, gonzo's presentation and emphasis on "reality"—not to mention the enthusiastic and overwhelming reception it received—throw traditional conceptions of narrative into question.

The video technology of the 1980s was the perfect production and exhibition system for gonzo, making it both possible and successful. As Peter Lehman writes, the disruptive and radical potential of the form goes well beyond simple aesthetics: by foregrounding "real" dialogue between performers, as well featuring average body types (both male and female) and lacking traditional narratives, these films and their directors "innovated new forms" and displayed creativity on par with any of the auteurs of the Golden Age of theatrical adult film.[14] They also support my contention throughout this book that "quality" is a shifting, malleable concept rather than being tied to any one period or set of characteristics. Gonzo unapologetically put the sex back into the foreground in adult films and made pleasure the primary onscreen purpose of adult film rather than generating layers of justification to disguise that pleasure as "something more" that could be hidden, obscured, or made safe through other means.[15]

Gonzo, in fact, might even best be described as the deliberate employment of "disrespectability" strategies, which shift *away* from seeking superficial widespread acceptance in favor of wallowing in the taboo of pleasure without narrative justification. This was really not much of a step from where adult video production was already residing, with the loosest of narrative structures that were often completely ridiculous. Producers such as Mark Carriere often seemed creatively bored with narrative, using the flimsiest of pretexts and a title to wrap some sex scenes into eighty or so minutes.[16] Gonzo, as Gillis put it, was an attempt to "liven things up" beyond what was undeniably getting repetitive. Given such dismissal of conventional narratives and the rise of interest in exploring "reality," it is hardly surprising that the form has come to be associated with "extreme" pornography of the very sort that has long troubled critics and opponents and led to the kinds of regulatory pressure outlined in the preceding chapter of this book. *On the Prowl* led to myriad titles and series that push the limits and boundaries of what pornography "means." As Biasin and Zecca note, this has led to the "proliferation of new sexual practices (reverse DP, gang bang, deep throat, swallow, multiple facial, ass-to-mouth, cum swapping, anal gaping, etc.) frequently of fetishist origin, and their subsequent institutionalization into new iconographic conventions which have come to figuratively constitute characterizing elements of Gonzo style."[17] These conventions are often difficult to equate with "obvious" pleasures, and they push feminist limits, particularly in the sense that they capture graphic depictions of S/M practices that rely on consent to give and receive pleasures that are often far from normative. I have argued throughout *Smutty Little Movies* that the pleasures presented within pornography often hinge on the *absence*, rather than the inclusion, of particular content, and gonzo similarly engages in such metadiscourses in its construction. What is frequently absent in gonzo pornography, though, is justification, not behavior. This is not a small difference.

Additionally, as Eugenie Brinkema points out, gonzo often blurs the line between representation and action.[18] This frequently involves pushing physical limits. Biasin and Zecca describe the presentation in this genre of "undeniably *athletic* skills allowing the performers' body to reach 'peaks' of performance that are unequalled in the history of pornography."[19] While purporting to get closer to reality, such films are often quite the opposite: they labor mightily to create a narrative that appears to have no narrative at all. Nevertheless, the absence of overt narrative justification is precisely what lends the form such power, given that it disrupts the sorts of normative paradigms described throughout this book. It is also what tends to make pornography's opponents the most nervous. For example, Gail Dines, perhaps the best-known contemporary antipornography feminist, writes, "By far the biggest moneymaker for the industry, this type of pornography makes no attempt at a story line, but is just scene after scene of violent penetration, in which women's body is literally stretched to its limit."[20] Like those who came long before her, Dines cannot separate performance and representation from reality; that, of course, was precisely Gillis's original goal. The desire to blur those lines, to find and capture the "real" moments of pleasure, to eliminate performance—such impulses circulate under pornography all the time, even as it cloaks itself in various ways and at various times in respectability strategies to find safety and economic success, and to hide its own gleeful disrespectability.

Those impulses, and all their accompanying tensions, define not only gonzo's legacy, but adult video's as well, and they represent an ideal endpoint for analysis of this early period. If, as I argue in the preceding chapter, pornography's history is inextricably tied to its regulation, then gonzo captures that ouroboros-like pattern—it flaunts "transgressive" and boundary-pushing desires rather than trying to outrun or escape them. Yet, as much as Gillis and others have sold gonzo as something closer to reality, there is nothing real about it. After all, like all pornography, gonzo is made up of performances, and the mediation itself is what defines it. Gillis's efforts to escape that mediation could not succeed in *On the Prowl*; neither could the thousands of others who followed with their own attempts to capture some ephemeral and nebulous "truth." Changing camera placements, operators, editing patterns, lighting setups, locations, narratives, and technologies does not really matter—nor should it. The endless debate over "something more"—or, in the case of gonzo, "something less"—is *itself* a form of something more, a way to cycle discursively over the meanings of sexual pleasure onscreen.

This is an argument about legacy. Even the limousine in *On the Prowl*, it turns out, was as artificial as everything else. Dumont insisted that Gillis use it to add some sophistication to the film. "I wasn't happy about the limo," Gillis said later. "I dreamed of raunchy, sleazy sex without any Hollywood gloss."[21] The legacy of adult video is that limousine, which stands in for another kind of dream, the one that wanted sophistication even as it sought sleazy sex without justification. *On the Prowl* captures that dichotomy; it is constructed artifice even when all artifice is seemingly abandoned, and it reveals an industry desperate for respectability but always falling short. The obsession with justification, with boundaries and limits, with ensuring that pleasure does not tip over into prurience: all point to a particular anxiety over normalcy. As Michael Warner argues, "Sooner or later, happily or unhappily, almost everyone fails to control his or her sex life. Perhaps as compensation, almost everyone sooner or later also succumbs to the temptation to control *someone else's* sex life."[22] The period under investigation in this book is unique in the specifics of those compensations; the broader struggles and tensions, however, have been played out before and will play out again, albeit with their contours occasionally reshaped and relocated, and with new technologies—such as the Internet—substituted for old.[23] Video was merely one player on a much larger and wider stage, and gonzo simply the most recent addition to the cast. The show itself will go on, equipped with new limousines and still desperately searching for its fleeting legacy.

Notes

PROLOGUE. NAKED LADIES AND ICE CREAM BARS

1. I am not the first (nor will I be the last) home video scholar to foreground my own memory and, at times, nostalgia. See Lucas Hilderbrand, *Inherent Vice: Bootleg Histories of Videotape and Copyright* (Durham, NC: Duke University Press, 2009), xiii–xvi; Caetlin Benson-Allott, *Killer Tapes and Shattered Screens: Video Spectatorship from VHS to File Sharing* (Berkeley: University of California Press, 2013), 23–24; and Daniel Herbert, *Videoland: Movie Culture at the American Video Store* (Berkeley: University of California Press, 2014), 9–10.

2. A brief note on terminology: I use the word *pornography* in this book rather than its derivations (particularly *porn*) in agreement with Linda Williams, who writes:

> I believe there is a risk in aligning our own work of scholarship too closely with the work of the pornography industry—even when what that industry produces seems more diverse, transgressive, or experimental than the usual fare. When scholars of pornography adopt the slang of an industry for the name of their object of study, it is a little like film or cinema studies calling itself 'movie studies' or "flick studies." . . . Pornography Studies needs to work even harder to adopt a critical stance independent from its major industry. ("Pornography, Porno, Porn: Thoughts on a Weedy Field," *Porn Studies* 1, nos. 1–2 [March 2014]: 34)

Similarly, I do not refer to adult film performers as *porn stars*, a term that I believe removes the realities of labor (as well as the reality that not all performers are "stars") from the landscape and marks those performers only by the sexual acts in their performances.

INTRODUCTION. SMALLER THAN LIFE

1. Joseph W. Slade, "Pornographic Theaters off Times Square," *Transaction* (November–December 1971): 37.

2. Eric Schaefer, "Plain Brown Wrapper: Adult Films for the Home Market," in *Looking Past the Screen,* eds. Jon Lewis and Eric Smoodin (Durham, NC: Duke University Press, 2007), 201–26.

3. Chuck Kleinhans, "The Change from Film to Video Pornography: Implications for Analysis," in *Pornography: Film and Culture,* ed. Peter Lehman (New Brunswick, NJ: Rutgers University Press, 2006), 156–57.

4. Ibid., 157.

5. Ibid., 157; Al Stewart, "Smut out of Rut, Defying Its Foes," *Variety,* January 17, 1990, 36.

6. Adult movie theaters did linger on well past the advent of home video, albeit on a much smaller scale, and they continue to survive. David Church, "'This Thing of Ours': Heterosexuality, Recreational Sex, and the Survival of Adult Movie Theaters," *Media Fields Journal* 8 (May 9, 2014), www.mediafields-journal.org/this-thing-of-ours/ (accessed February 7, 2015).

7. Peter Brennan, "The Lick, Lick Show," *Screw,* May 24, 1971, 23.

8. Ibid.

9. Ibid.; Adonis Cinema Club advertisement, *Village Voice,* May 13, 1971, 70; Tomcat Theater advertisement, *New York Times,* October 12, 1971, 50.

10. The original Adonis, which appears to have closed in late 1971, reopened (as a celluloid exhibition space) in the massive former Tivoli Theater space on 8th Avenue in Manhattan in March 1975. For two decades, it was one of the most important and well-known gay community sites and adult movie theaters. It also served as the setting for *A Night at the Adonis* (1978, dir. Jack Deveau). Rich Cante and Angelo Restivo, "The Cultural-Aesthetic Specificities of All-Male Moving-Image Pornography," in *Porn Studies,* ed. Linda Williams (Durham, NC: Duke University Press, 2004), 142–66.

11. Brennan, "The Lick, Lick Show," 23.

12. Ben Keen, "'Play It Again, Sony': The Double Life of Home Video Technology," *Science as Culture* 1, no. 1 (1987): 13–14.

13. James Lardner, *Fast Forward: Hollywood, the Japanese, and the Onslaught of the VCR* (New York: Norton, 1987), 57–60.

14. Keen, "'Play It Again, Sony,'" 18–19.

15. Lardner, *Fast Forward,* 73.

16. Ibid., 148–49. For a more complete examination of this early history, see Lucas Hilderbrand, *Inherent Vice: Bootleg Histories of Videotape and Copyright* (Durham, NC: Duke University Press, 2009), 37–49.

17. Linda Williams, *Hard Core: Power, Pleasure, and the "Frenzy of the Visible"* (Berkeley: University of California Press, 1989), 95.

18. For example, a Facebook fan group dedicated to the adult video era calls the video period the "Silver Age." Despite the members' unabashed adoration of video as a technology, as well as of performers and filmmakers who never worked on celluloid, they still share a tacit agreement on the universal superi-

ority of the celluloid era. I have encountered this attitude so many times and in so many places that I consider it to be hegemonic discourse.

19. Addison Verrill, *"The Devil in Miss Jones," Variety*, February 21, 1973, 18, 24.

20. For more on the role of critics during the Golden Age of adult film, see Raymond J. Harberski Jr., "Critics and the Sex Scene," in *Sex Scene: Media and the Sexual Revolution,* ed. Eric Schaefer (Durham, NC: Duke University Press, 2014), 383–406.

21. Ralph Blumenthal, "Porno Chic: 'Hard-Core' Grows Fashionable—and Very Profitable," *New York Times Magazine,* January 21, 1973, 272.

22. *Memories within Miss Aggie* advertisement, *Variety,* January 22, 1975, 45.

23. For more detailed examinations of the tensions surrounding adult film and Hollywood during the Golden Age, see Jon Lewis, *Hollywood v. Hard Core: How the Struggle over Censorship Created the Modern Film Industry* (New York: New York University Press, 2002); and Kevin S. Sandler, *The Naked Truth: Why Hollywood Doesn't Make X-Rated Movies* (Newark, NJ: Rutgers University Press, 2007).

24. Nicola Simpson, "Coming Attractions: A Comparative History of the Hollywood Studio System and the Porn Business," *Historical Journal of Film, Radio, and Television* 24, no. 4 (2004): 649.

25. Cal Vista Video catalogue, 1979 (author's collection).

26. Stephen Prince, *A New Pot of Gold: Hollywood under the Electronic Rainbow, 1980–1989* (New York: Charles Scribner's Sons, 2000), 124.

27. Hilderbrand, *Inherent Vice,* 11–15.

28. David Bordwell, *The Way Hollywood Tells It: Story and Style in Modern Movies* (Berkeley: University of California Press, 2006), 148–51.

29. Vincent Canby, "A Revolution Reshapes Movies," *New York Times,* January 7, 1990, 15. Also see Janet Wasko, *Hollywood in the Information Age* (Cambridge: Polity Press, 1994), 166–67.

30. Prince, *A New Pot of Gold,* 126–30.

31. Michael Z. Newman, *Video Revolutions: On the History of a Medium* (New York: Columbia University Press, 2014), 50–61.

32. As Max Dawson has pointed out, however, television critics labored mightily (and ultimately unsuccessfully) in the 1960s and '70s to craft "quality" discourses around home video's potential meanings and uses, while manufacturers cultivated complex relationships with consumers to create a mass market. "Home Video and the 'TV Problem': Cultural Critics and Technological Change," *Technology and Culture* 48, no. 3 (July 2007): 524–49.

33. Jim Holliday, *Only the Best* (Van Nuys, CA: Cal Vista Direct, Ltd., 1986), 187.

34. Gourmet Video Collection catalogue, circa 1984 (author's collection).

35. L. R. Goldman, "Interview: Chuck Vincent," *Adult Video News* (October 1983): 1. (Hereafter *AVN.*)

36. For more on adult video box covers, see Joseph Slade, "Inventing a Sexual Discourse: A Rhetorical Analysis of Adult Video Box Covers," in *Sexual*

Rhetoric: Media Perspectives on Sexuality, Gender, and Identity, eds. Meta G. Carstarphen and Susan C. Zavoina (Westport, CT: Greenwood Press, 1999), 239–54.

37. John Johnson, "Demand Is Strong, but Police Crackdowns and a Saturated Market Spell Trouble for One of L.A.'s Biggest Businesses," *Los Angeles Times,* February 17, 1991, 8.

38. Stewart, "Smut out of Rut, Defying Its Foes," 35.

39. Walter Kendrick, *The Secret Museum: Pornography in Modern Culture* (Berkeley: University of California Press, 1987), xiii.

40. Williams, *Hard Core,* 12.

41. Kendrick, *The Secret Museum,* 1–32.

42. Lynn Hunt, "Introduction: Obscenity and the Origins of Modernity, 1500–1800," in *The Invention of Pornography: Obscenity and the Origins of Modernity, 1500–1800,* ed. Lynn Hunt (New York: Zone Books, 1993), 9–45.

43. Kendrick, *The Secret Museum,* 57.

44. Laura Kipnis, *Bound and Gagged: Pornography and the Politics of Fantasy in America* (Durham, NC: Duke University Press, 1996), 123.

45. Mikhail Bahktin, *Rabelais and His World* (Bloomington: University of Indiana Press, 1984); Norbert Elias, *A History of Manners* (New York: Pantheon, 1978).

46. Barbara Walter, "The Cult of True Womanhood: 1820–1860," *American Quarterly* 18, no. 2 (Summer 1966): 151–74; Harvey Green, *The Light of the Home: An Intimate View of the Lives of Women in Victorian America* (New York: Pantheon Books, 1983).

47. Richard Butsch, "Bowery B'hoys and Matinee Ladies: The Re-Gendering of Nineteenth-Century America," *American Quarterly* 46, no. 3 (September 1994): 375.

48. For an example of these types of capabilities, see Laura Kipnis, "(Male) Desire, (Female) Disgust: Reading *Hustler,*" in *Cultural Studies,* eds. Lawrence Grossberg, Cary Nelson, and Paula A. Treicher (New York: Routledge, 1992), 373–92.

49. Andrew Ross, *No Respect: Intellectuals & Popular Culture* (New York: Routledge, 1989), 200–01. Emphasis original.

50. Kendrick, *The Secret Museum,* 244.

51. Ross elaborates on this formulation, drawing from Roland Barthes: "The limited and mundane libidinal economy of *plaisir* is contrasted with the higher, transgressive experience of *jouissance* . . . itself based on the Freudian distinction between the 'economic' pleasure principle and the destructively 'spendthrift' death drive" (*No Respect,* 184). Erotica, in other words, appeals to the mind, while pornography can appeal only to the body.

52. Ibid., 185.

53. This critical distinction forms the basis of American obscenity law. The difference between simple arousal and "something more" can also be taken to imply the concept of "value." *Miller v. California* (1973), the landmark Supreme Court decision that still operates as the legal guideline on obscenity in the United States, uses this concept as its core principle. "Art," according to *Miller,*

cannot simply arouse, for simple arousal would lack the "value" elevating it beyond "prurient interest." Pleasures of the body for their own sake, in other words, do not equal the pleasures of the mind—where value apparently resides. For more, see Whitney Strub, *Obscenity Rules: Roth v. United States and the Long Struggle over Sexual Expression* (Lawrence: University of Kansas Press, 2013); Thomas C. Mackey, *Pornography on Trial: A Handbook with Cases, Laws, and Documents* (Santa Barbara, CA: ABC-CLIO, 2002), 211–17; *Miller v. California*, 413 U.S. 15, Supreme Court of the United States, June 21, 1973, LexisNexis (accessed February 10, 2012).

54. Susan Sontag, "The Pornographic Imagination," *Partisan Review* 34 (Spring 1967): 184.

55. Ross, *No Respect*, 185.

56. Gloria Steinem, "Erotica and Pornography: A Clear and Present Difference," *Ms.* (November 1978): 53. Other feminists would later criticize Steinem's utopian view. Ellen Willis, for example, decries it as a "goody-goody concept" associated with femininity, not feminism, in her "Feminism, Morality, and Pornography," in *Powers of Desire: The Politics of Sexuality*, eds. Ann Snitow, Christine Stansell, and Sharon Thompson (New York: Monthly Review, 1983), 460–67.

57. Annette Kuhn, "Lawless Seeing," in Kuhn, *The Power of the Image: Essays on Representation and Sexuality* (Boston: Routledge & Kegan Paul, 1985), 44.

58. Gayle Rubin theorizes this "good/bad" dichotomy and outlines the notion of what she terms the "charmed circle" of sexual behaviors within culture. She writes, "Sexuality that is 'good,' 'normal,' and 'natural' should ideally be heterosexual, marital, monogamous, reproductive, and non-commercial. It should be coupled, relational, within the same generation, and occur at home. It should not involve pornography, fetish objects, sex toys of any sort, or roles other than male or female. Any sex that violates these rules is 'bad,' 'abnormal,' or 'unnatural.'" Pornography, in its depictions and on-set performances, flagrantly and deliberately violates these rules, marking it as an extreme example of what she calls the "outer limits" of sexuality. "Thinking Sex: Notes for a Radical Theory of the Politics of Sexuality," in *Pleasure and Danger: Exploring Female Sexuality*, ed. Carol S. Vance (London: Pandora Press, 1992), 280–81.

59. Jane Juffer expertly identifies how much of the process, as I have described it, has been sidestepped by women who find sexual pleasure in myriad forms removed from "traditional" pornography, such as adult video. As much as women have been relentlessly subjected to discourses of domestication, Juffer points out that various types of resistance can also be found within those discourses that also provide pleasure. From that perspective, women frequently avoid many of the regulatory mechanisms I outline in this book in the pursuit of pleasure, successfully negotiating and resisting the very types of domestication that seek to limit their access to and pleasure from pornography. *At Home with Pornography: Women, Sex, and Everyday Life* (New York: New York University Press, 1998).

60. Very little has changed in recent years, particularly with the influx of "feminist" pornography, as I examine in more detail in chapter 3. For many,

pornography still requires narrative or other markers of "something more" to attain quality status. For example, adult film producer Erika Lust, in her 2010 book otherwise loaded with defenses of pornography for women and replete with dismissals of "erotica" and the tired mythology that women are not "visually oriented," still argues that adult films for women are all about "intimacy and relationships." *Good Porn: A Woman's Guide* (Berkeley, CA: Seal Press, 2010), 16.

61. Kenneth Turan, "Sex Films in San Francisco Reach Plateau of Legitimacy," *Los Angeles Times,* October 30, 1970, I20; Joseph Lam Duong, "San Francisco and the Politics of Hardcore," in *Sex Scene,* ed. Schaefer, 307.

62. Turan, "Sex Films in San Francisco Reach Plateau of Legitimacy," I20.

63. Quoted in Lam Duong, "San Francisco and the Politics of Hardcore," 302.

64. Ibid., 306.

65. Arthur Knight, "Adult Film Group in Quest to Gain Respect," *Los Angeles Times,* February 1, 1974, 14, 17; Nancy Skelton, "Pinocchio to Porn with Vince Miranda," *Los Angeles Times,* April 15, 1974, SD–A1.

66. That film, *Not a Love Story: A Film about Pornography* (1982, dir. Bonnie Sherr Klein), was used by Women against Pornography (WAP) during informational antipornography meetings and provoked intense debate among feminists. See Lisa DiCaprio, "*Not a Love Story:* The Film and the Debate," *Jump Cut* 30 (March 1985): 39–42.

My intention here is not to ignore the practical, lived realities of women in a culture that, as this history shows, has labored mightily to contain their desires, behaviors, and beliefs. Women are always already caught up in cultural formations seeking to contain their pleasures, and any struggle against that containment is immediately marked as transgressive and suspect. Pornography, an epicenter of these struggles and debates, has long been a partner to many of these containment strategies, as I show throughout this book. As Linda Williams argues, "Pornography [has] long been a myth of sexual pleasure told from the point of view of men with the power to exploit and objectify the sexuality of women" (*Hard Core,* 22). As such, pornography has frequently participated in, rather than prevented, the construction of binaries and boundaries around gender and sexual behavior—one of the guiding assertions of this book.

67. "The Porno Plague," *Time,* April 5, 1976, 58.

68. "Pornography Goes Public," *Newsweek,* December 21, 1970, 32.

69. *Ginzberg v. United States,* 383 U.S. 463, Supreme Court of the United States, March 21, 1966, LexisNexis (accessed September 1, 2015).

70. Simpson, "Coming Attractions," 647.

71. *Stanley v. Georgia,* 394 U.S. 557, Supreme Court of the United States, April 7, 1969, LexisNexis (accessed January 29, 2013).

72. *United States v. 12 200-ft. Reels of Super 8mm. Film,* 413 U.S. 123, Supreme Court of the United States, June 21, 1973, LexisNexis (accessed January 29, 2013).

73. This anxiety might have been amplified by familiar nuanced regulatory controls over gender and sexual behavior in the privacy of the home already in place in discourses surrounding the television set, discourses that had been carefully articulated and internalized since the early 1950s. Adult video side-stepped much of this "privacy in public" paradigm, preferring to reclaim actual privacy instead of simply relocating public behavior to the home. See Lynn Spigel, "Installing the Television Set: Popular Discourses on Television and the Domestic Space, 1948–1955," in *Private Screenings: Television and the Female Consumer,* eds. Lynn Spigel and Denise Mann (Minneapolis: University of Minnesota Press, 1992), 3–40.

74. Whether or not those male audiences were interested in—or even paid attention to—the content on the screen is an entirely different matter; as Samuel Delany has shown, demarcating public spaces for straight pornography consumption (theaters, adult bookstores, etc.) means remarkably little when it comes to the sexual behavior of patrons in that space. Nevertheless, in some ways, such realities might have made these spaces even less inviting or welcoming to women. *Times Square Red, Times Square Blue* (New York: New York University Press, 1999).

75. Daniel Herbert's research into the practices of surviving small-town and rural video rental stores is invaluable in this regard. *Videoland: Movie Culture at the American Video Store* (Berkeley: University of California Press, 2014), 135–41.

76. For an analysis of the aesthetic practices of these companies, see Eithne Johnson, "Excess and Ecstasy: Constructing Female Pleasure in Porn Movies," *Velvet Light Trap* 32 (Fall 1993): 30–49.

77. Rodger Jacobs, "Homegrown Video," *Xbiz*, January 3, 2006, www.xbiz.com/articles/80042 (accessed May 13, 2014).

78. "Charting the Adult Video Market," *AVN* (August–September 1986): 6–7. Given that *AVN* was distributed to both mainstream shops that included adult tapes and to stores carrying exclusively adult material, it seems safe to conclude that the five hundred retailers included both types.

79. Ibid.

80. Hilderbrand, *Inherent Vice*, 8.

81. This process took on even greater capability with DVD. In the early 2000s, Digital Playground released a series of "interactive" titles, such as *Virtual Sex with Taylor Hayes* (2000), that gave the viewer real-time control over the camera placement, sexual positions, demeanor of the female performer, and style of action, all by way of the remote control and a series of menu choices. There were even efforts to make such control voice-activated (presumably to free up the viewer's hands for other activities). Randy Dotinga, "You Gotta Hand It to the Porn Coders," *Wired,* June 25, 2002, http://archive.wired.com/science/discoveries/news/2002/06/53300 (accessed June 5, 2014).

82. Caetlin Benson-Allott, *Killer Tapes and Shattered Screens: Video Spectatorship from VHS to File Sharing* (Berkeley: University of California Press, 2013), 205. Emphasis mine.

83. These types of changes in production practices echo arguments made by Benson-Allott, who identifies similar formal alterations in nonadult media practices in an in-depth case study of the trajectory of zombie movies made by director George Romero. Ibid., 25–69.

84. Peter Lehman, "Revelations about Pornography," in *Pornography*, ed. Lehman, 92.

85. Benson-Allott, *Killer Tapes and Shattered Screens*, 12.

86. For primary works on home video history, see ibid.; Sean Cubitt, *Timeshift: On Video Culture* (New York: Routledge, 1991); Julia Dobrow, ed., *Social and Cultural Aspects of VCR Use* (Hillsdale, NJ: Lawrence Erlbaum, 1990); Gladys Ganley and Oswald Ganley, *Global Political Fallout: The First Decade of the VCR, 1976–1985* (Cambridge, MA: Harvard University Press, 1987); Mark Levy, ed., *The VCR Age: Home Video and Mass Communication* (London: Sage, 1989); Paul McDonald, *Video and DVD Industries* (London: British Film Institute, 2008); Wasko, *Hollywood in the Information Age;* Ann Gray, *Video Playtime: The Gendering of a Leisure Technology* (London: Routledge, 1992); Hilderbrand, *Inherent Vice;* Barbara Klinger, *Beyond the Multiplex: Cinema, New Technologies, and the Home* (Berkeley: University of California Press, 2006); Newman, *Video Revolutions;* Herbert, *Videoland;* James Moran, *There's No Place Like Home Video* (Minneapolis: University of Minnesota Press, 2002); Yvonne Spielmann, *Video: The Reflexive Medium* (Cambridge, MA: MIT Press, 2008); Frederick Wasser, *Veni, Vidi, Video: The Hollywood Empire and the VCR* (Austin: University of Texas Press, 2001); Manuel Alvarado, *Video World-Wide* (Paris: UNESCO, 1988); Roy Armes, *On Video* (New York: Routledge, 1988); and Joshua M. Greenberg, *From Betamax to Blockbuster: Video Stores and the Invention of Movies on Video* (Cambridge, MA: MIT Press, 2008).

87. McDonald, *Video and DVD Industries*, 111–113.

88. Wasser, *Veni, Vidi, Video*, 95.

89. Herbert, *Videoland*, 62–64.

90. Hilderbrand, *Inherent Vice*, 66–72.

91. Greenberg, *From Betamax to Blockbuster*, 50–52.

92. Benson-Allott, *Killer Tapes and Shattered Screens*, 11.

93. Linda Williams, "Pornography, Porno, Porn: Thoughts on a Weedy Field," *Porn Studies* 1, nos. 1–2 (March 2014): 32.

94. Peter Alilunas, "The Necessary Future of Adult Media Industry Studies," *Creative Industries Journal* 7, no. 1 (2014): 393–403.

95. Valuable archives of adult material do exist, most notably at the Kinsey Institute for Research in Sex, Gender, and Reproduction at Indiana University, Bloomington; the Institute for Advanced Study of Human Sexuality in San Francisco; and the Leather Archives & Museum in Chicago. Williams provides a list of archives and research sites in *Porn Studies*, 491–94.

Caitlin Shanley offers a similarly thorough list of archives and libraries in "Clandestine Catalogs: A Bibliography of Porn Research Collections," in *Porn Archives*, eds. Tim Dean, Steven Ruszczycky, and David Squires (Durham, NC: Duke University Press, 2014), 441–55.

96. Eric Schaefer, "Dirty Little Secrets: Scholars, Archivists, and Dirty Movies," *Moving Image* 5, no. 2 (Fall 2005): 86.

This collection of literature is too large to list here, but there are a few note-worthy examples: William Rostler, *Contemporary Erotic Cinema* (New York: Penthouse/Ballantine, 1973); Kenneth Turan and Stephen F. Zito, *Sinema* (New York: Praeger, 1974); Luke Ford, *A History of X: 100 Years of Sex in Film* (Amherst, NY: Prometheus Books, 1999); Legs McNeil, Jennifer Osborne, and Peter Pavia, *The Other Hollywood: The Uncensored Oral History of the Porn Film Industry* (New York: Regan Books, 2005); Carolyn See, *Blue Money: Pornography and the Pornographers* (New York: David McKay, 1974); Jill C. Nelson, *Golden Goddesses: 25 Legendary Women of Classic Erotic Cinema, 1968–1985* (Duncan, OK: BearManor Media, 2012); Andrew J. Rausch and Chris Watson, *Dirty Talk: Converations with Pornstars* (Duncan, OK: BearManor Media, 2012); Robert J. Stoller and I. S. Levine, *Coming Attractions: The Making of an X-Rated Video* (New Haven, CT: Yale University Press, 2003); and Steven Ziplow, *The Film Maker's Guide to Pornography* (New York: Drake, 1977).

97. The adult film industry, no less than its nonadult counterpart, requires that scholars be mindful of what John Caldwell has called the "inverse credibility law," whereby "the higher one travels up the industrial food chain for insights, the more suspect and spin-driven the personal disclosures tend to become." *Production Culture: Industrial Reflexivity and Critical Practice in Film and Television* (Durham, NC: Duke University Press, 2008), 3.

98. Two important early examples are Robert H. Rimmer, *The X-Rated Videotape Guide* (New York: Arlington House, 1984); and Keith L. Justice, *Adult Video Index '84* (Jefferson, NC: McFarland & Company, 1984). The Internet Adult Film Database (iafd.com) and the Adult Loop Database (adult-loopdb.nl) have become essential online resources that fill similar contemporary research gaps, collecting and cataloguing vast amounts of historical production data.

99. For several examples pertinent to the era under study in this book, see Christy Canyon, *Lights, Camera, Sex!* (Canyon Publishing, 2003); Ron Jeremy, *The Hardest Working Man in Showbiz* (New York: It Books, 2008); Traci Lords, *Underneath It All* (New York: It Books, 2004); Georgina Spelvin, *The Devil Made Me Do It* (Georgina's World, Inc., 2008); Howie Gordon, *Hindsight: True Love and Mischief in the Golden Age of Porn* (Albany, GA: BearManor Media, 2013); Seka, *Inside Seka: The Platinum Princess of Porn* (Albany, GA: BearManor Media, 2013); Jerry Butler, *Raw Talent* (Amherst, NY: Prometheus Books, 1990); Hyapatia Lee, *The Secret Lives of Hyapatia Lee* (1st Book Library, 2000); Marc Stevens, *Mr. 10½* (New York: Kensington Publishing, 1975); Marilyn Chambers, *My Story* (New York: Warner Books, 1975); Robert Rosen, *Beaver Street: A History of Modern Pornography* (London: Headpress, 2010); David Jennings, *Skinflicks: The Inside Story of the X-Rated Video Industry* (Bloomington, IN: 1st Books, 2000); Larry Revene, *Wham Bam $$ Ba Da Boom! Mob Wars, Porn Battles, and a View from the Trenches* (New York: Hudson Delta Books, 2012); and Wakefield Poole, *Dirty Poole: A Sensual Memoir* (Maple Shade, NJ: Lethe Press, 2011).

Of particular and timely importance in regard to adult industry voices speaking for themselves is *The Rialto Report* (therialtoreport.com), an ongoing series of invaluable interviews conducted by Ashley West with Golden Age industry members.

100. Two recent examples: Nina Hartley, "Porn: An Effective Vehicle for Sexual Role Modeling and Education," in *The Feminist Porn Book: The Politics of Producing Pleasure,* eds. Tristan Taormino et al. (New York: Feminist Press at the City University of New York, 2012), 228–36; and Candida Royalle, "'What's a Nice Girl Like You . . . ,'" in *The Feminist Porn Book,* eds. Taormino et al., 58–70.

101. Exceptions to these attitudes do exist in the archival community. Dwight Sanson writes: "It is time, then, for film archivists to embrace, rather than shun, the pornography in our collections, as there is much to be learned from these films in terms of film history." "Home Viewing: Pornography and Amateur Film Collections, a Case Study," *Moving Image* 5, no. 2 (Fall 2005): 140. Dan Erdman has made similar arguments in an effort to openly recognize and include adult material in archival collections. "Let's Go Stag! How to Study and Preserve Dirty Films with a Clean Conscience," presentation, "Sex, Media, Reception: New Approaches Conference," Ann Arbor, MI, February 15, 2014.

In 2014, Eric Schaefer successfully formed the Society for Cinema and Media Studies Scholarly Interest Group for Adult Film History, part of an effort to build community among scholars and historians in order to share research information. Eric Schaefer, "Pornography Is Geography: Porn, Place, and the Historiography of Early Theatrical Hardcore," presentation, "Society for Cinema and Media Studies Annual Conference," Seattle, WA, March 20, 2014. In the absence of more formal archives and centralized collections, this is a significant, fruitful, and necessary step. As part of its mission, Erdman and I are creating the Adult Film History Project, an online archival space for adult film history researchers, a long-term project intended to alleviate many of the problems outlined in this book. Its expected launch date is early 2017.

102. Lynn Spigel uses similar strategies in her work on postwar suburban life, in which she draws on Carlo Ginzburg's conjectural model. Arguing that the process of historiography is akin to hunters or detectives searching for clues to reconstruct past events through conjecture and symptomatic analysis, Spigel outlines an ideal process for adult film historians. *Welcome to the Dreamhouse: Popular Media and Postwar Suburbs* (Durham, NC: Duke University Press, 2001), 12–13; Carlo Ginzburg, "Morelli, Freud and Sherlock Holmes: Clues and Scientific Method," *History Workshop Journal* 9, no. 1 (1980): 5–36.

103. Eric Schaefer, "The Problem with Sexploitation Movies," *Iluminace* 3 (2012): 151. Schaefer was inspired by the idea of "critical-mess collecting" after reading a portrait of obsessive bibliophile Michael Zinman. See also Mark Singer, "The Book Eater," *New Yorker,* February 5, 2001, 62–71.

104. The two largest production houses at the time, VCA Pictures and Caballero, began shooting primarily on videotape rather than celluloid in 1986. Lawrence Cohn, "Pornmakers Surface in the Mainstream," *Variety,* March 9, 1988, 3, 26.

105. This content includes so-called girl–girl scenes featuring two women engaged in sexual activities together, which traditionally have been understood as intended for straight male viewers, a staple of the era under investigation.

106. A few prominent examples of scholarly work on gay pornography: Jeffrey Escoffier, *Bigger Than Life: The History of Gay Porn Cinema from Beefcake to Hardcore* (Philadelphia: Running Press, 2009); Richard Fung, "Looking for My Penis: The Eroticized Asian in Gay Video Porn," in *How Do I Look? Queer Film and Video*, ed. Bad Object-Choices (Seattle: Bay Press, 1991), 145–68; Thomas Waugh, "Homosociality in the Classical American Stag Film," in *Porn Studies*, ed. Linda Williams (Durham, NC: Duke University Press, 2004), 127–41; Thomas Waugh, *Hard to Imagine: Gay Male Eroticism in Photography and Film from Their Beginnings to Stonewall* (New York: Columbia University Press, 1996); Richard Dyer, "Gay Male Pornography: Coming to Terms," *Jump Cut* 30 (March 1985): 27–29; Thomas Waugh, "Men's Pornography: Gay vs. Straight," *Jump Cut* 30 (March 1985): 30–35; John Champagne, "'Stop Reading Films!' Film Studies, Close Analysis, and Gay Pornography," *Cinema Journal* 36, no. 4 (Summer 1997): 76–97; John Robert Burger, *One-Handed Histories: The Eroto-Politics of Gay Male Video Pornography* (Philadelphia: Haworth Press, 1995); Cante and Restivo, "The Cultural-Aesthetic Specificities of All-Male Moving-Image Pornography," in *Porn Studies*, ed. Williams, 142–66; Heather Butler, "What Do You Call a Lesbian with Long Fingers? The Development of Lesbian and Dyke Pornography," in *Porn Studies*, ed. Williams, 167–97.

107. Williams, "Pornography, Porno, Porn," 26.

108. That work includes the overlooked history of pornography in the underground video movement, which began in earnest with Sony's release of the PortaPak half-inch video camera in 1965. Deirdre Boyle notes, "Hundreds of hours of documentary tapes were shot by underground groups, tapes on New Left polemics and the drama of political confrontation as well as video erotica." "From PortaPak to Camcorder: A Brief History of Guerrilla Television," *Journal of Film and Video* 44, nos. 1–2 (Spring–Summer 1992): 68. The first notable example was in September 1969, when Global Village played two shows every Friday and Saturday night to packed houses after opening its New York screening space. Nine monitors played simultaneous content—including cofounder John Reilly's video *John and Samantha Making Love*, which Global Village also distributed. Moments such as these, which overlap with more conventional industry histories, are in deep need of scholarly recovery. For more, see Boyle, "From PortaPak to Camcorder," 67–79; Davidson Gigliotti, "Interview with John Reilly," December 14, 1999, http://davidsonsfiles.org/johnreillyinterview.html (accessed September 8, 2015); Chloe Aaron, "The Alternate Media Guerrillas," *New York*, October 19, 1970, 51; *John and Samantha Making Love Compositions* advertisement, *Radical Software* 1, no. 2 (Autumn 1970): 19; and Michael Shamberg and Raindance Corporation, *Guerrilla Television* (New York: Henry Holt, 1971).

Similarly overlooked is the history of pornography on cable television, with Luke Stadel's research representing an important start: "Cable, Pornography, and the Reinvention of Television," *Cinema Journal* 53, no. 2 (Spring 2014): 52–75.

109. Stanley Cohen, *Folk Devils and Moral Panics: The Creation of the Mods and Rockers* (London: MacGibbon and Kee, 1972), 9. Cohen's emphasis on the media—while useful for my research on adult video's history—stands in contrast to other scholars' work. Stuart Hall, Chas Critcher, Tony Jefferson, John Clarke, and Brian Roberts argue instead that moral panics stem from political motivations, particularly through the actions of the judiciary and the police. Erich Goode and Nachman Ben-Yehuda offer their own criteria for identifying a moral panic that examine a variety of cultural forces and groups rather than simply assigning direct agency to either the media or government bodies. Hall et al., *Policing the Crisis: Mugging, the State, and Law and Order* (New York: Holmes & Meier, 1978); Goode and Ben-Yehuda, *Moral Panics: The Social Construction of Deviance* (Oxford: Blackwell, 1994).

110. Alice E. Marwick, "To Catch a Predator? The Myspace Moral Panic," *First Monday*, June 2, 2008, http://firstmonday.org/article/view/2152/1966 (accessed December 1, 2009).

111. Joseph W. Slade, *Pornography in America: A Reference Handbook* (Santa Barbara, CA: ABC-CLIO, 2000), 9.

112. Jonathan Coopersmith, "Pornography, Technology and Progress," *Icon* 4 (1998): 96.

113. Kendrick, *The Secret Museum*, 6–10; Bernard Arcand, *The Jaguar and the Anteater: Pornography Degree Zero*, trans. Wayne Grady (London: Verso Books, 1993), 197–210.

114. For more on the history of pre–printing press pornography, see Henry L. Marchand, *The French Pornographers, Including a History of French Erotic Literature* (1933; New York: Book Awards, 1965); and Elizabeth L. Eisenstein, *The Printing Revolution in Early Modern Europe* (Cambridge: Cambridge University Press, 1983), 93.

115. Coopersmith, "Pornography, Technology and Progress, 97.

116. Frederick S. Lane III, *Obscene Profits: The Entrepreneurs of Pornography in the Cyber Age* (New York: Routledge, 2001), 15.

117. Tom Standage, *The Victorian Internet: The Remarkable Story of the Telegraph and the Nineteenth Century's On-Line Pioneers* (New York: Walker and Co., 1998), 127.

118. Ibid., 132.

119. George H. Douglas, *All Aboard! The Railroad in American Life* (New York: Paragon House, 1992), 63.

120. "Many Demanding Curb on Phone Pornography," *New York Times*, February 19, 1984, 80.

121. Victor Cline, *Pornography's Effects on Adults and Children* (2002), stop.org.za (accessed January 6, 2015). After numerous judicial and Congressional efforts to eradicate Dial-a-Porn (including outright bans, time restrictions, access codes, and other regulatory strategies), the Supreme Court ruled in 1989 that "indecent" speech was protected by the First Amendment, while obscene speech was not. Immediately after the decision, Senator Jesse

Helms of North Carolina enacted Pub. L. No. 101–166, more commonly known as the Helms Amendment, to section 223(b) of the Communications Act of 1934. It banned "indecent" Dial-a-Porn use by minors, as well as adding section 223(c), which required users to request access to Dial-a-Porn services in writing from their telephone service provider. It also required all Dial-a-Porn providers to notify telephone companies in writing of their (legally permitted) indecent communications services to potential adult subscribers. A Federal Appeals Court upheld the constitutionality of the new laws, claiming they did not constitute prior restraint, and the Supreme Court declined to hear the case. See *Sable Communications of California v. Federal Communications Commission,* 492 U.S. 115, Supreme Court of the United States, June 23, 1989, LexisNexis (accessed April 5, 2013); "47 U.S.C. § 223 : US Code—Section 223: Obscene or Harassing Telephone Calls in the District of Columbia or in Interstate or Foreign Communications," (1989), FindLaw, codes.lp.findlaw.com (accessed April 5, 2013); Carlos Briceno, "Law; 'Dial-a-Porn' Industry Battles U.S. Restrictions," *New York Times,* April 13, 1990, B5; David G. Savage, "'Dial-a-Porn Dealt High Court Setback," *Los Angeles Times,* January 28, 1992, VCA 13.

122. Paolo Cherchi Usai, "Pornography," in *The Encyclopedia of Early Cinema,* ed. Richard Abel (New York: Routledge, 2005), 525.

123. Paul Clee, *Before Hollywood: From Shadow Play to the Silver Screen* (New York: Clarion Books, 2005), 133.

124. Lane, *Obscene Profits,* 41–44.

125. H. Montgomery Hyde, *A History of Pornography* (New York: Dell, 1964), 110–11.

126. Coopersmith, "Pornography, Technology and Progress," 99; Hyde, *A History of Pornography,* 121.

127. "Who's Who of Victorian Cinema: Léar (Albert Kirchner)," British Film Institute, n.d., www.victorian-cinema.net/lear.php (accessed November 10 , 2009); Dave Thompson, *Black and White and Blue: Adult Cinema from the Victorian Age to the VCR* (Toronto: ECW Press, 2007), 29–35.

128. Janet Staiger, *Bad Women: Regulating Sexuality in Early American Cinema* (Minneapolis: University of Minnesota Press, 1995), 56.

129. Ibid., 60.

130. Ibid., 92.

131. For the histories of early organized censorship efforts and boards of review, see Lee Grieveson, *Policing Cinema: Movies and Censorship in Early-Twentieth-Century America* (Berkeley: University of California Press, 2004).

132. Tino Balio, *The American Film Industry* (Madison: University of Wisconsin Press, 1985); Richard Maltby, "The Production Code and the Hays Office," in *Grand Design: Hollywood as a Modern Business Enterprise,* ed. Tino Balio, History of the American Cinema (Berkeley: University of California Press, 1993), 37–72; Thomas Doherty, *Pre-Code Hollywood: Sex, Immorality, and Insurrection in American Cinema, 1930–1934* (New York: Columbia University Press, 1999).

133. Lewis's work on how the MPAA and the Hollywood studios reacted to the economic threat that the adult film industry, just prior to the advent of home

video, posed to the mainstream film industry illustrates how the tensions surrounding sexuality, pleasure, and pornography can simultaneously open and close cultural dialogue on these topics, as well as how hegemonic cultural beliefs about "inappropriate" gender behavior inevitably leads to capitalist reactions bolstering dominant (and regressive) ideologies. Lewis, *Hollywood v. Hard Core*, 3.

134. Janice M. Irvine, "Transient Feelings: Sex Panics and the Politics of Emotion," *GLQ* 14, no. 1 (2008): 1–40.

135. Roger N. Lancaster, *Sex Panic and the Punitive State* (Berkeley: University of California Press, 2011), 20–21.

136. Gilbert Herdt, "Introduction: Moral Panics, Sexual Rights, and Cultural Anger," in *Moral Panics, Sex Panics: Fear the Fight over Sexual Rights,* ed. Gilbert Herdt (New York: New York University Press, 2009), 5.

137. Kendrick, *The Secret Museum*, 235.

138. Michael Z. Newman and Elana Levine, *Legitimating Television: Media Convergence and Cultural Status* (New York: Routledge, 2012), 3.

139. Donald Crafton, *The Talkies: American Cinema's Transition to Sound, 1926–1931* (Berkeley: University of California Press, 1994), 4.

140. Constance Penley puts this question another way in a pedagogical context: "What happens when a class of student researchers asks the same kinds of questions about porn that they have already addressed in their other classes on film and media history and theory?" "A Feminist Teaching Pornography? That's Like Scopes Teaching Evolution!" in *The Feminist Porn Book,* eds. Taormino et al., 184.

1. PANORAMS, MOTELS, AND PIRATES

1. See, for example, Eugene Marlow and Eugene Secunda, who write: "George Atkinson . . . is now generally regarded as the first retailer to promote the rental, rather than the sale, of prerecorded videocassettes." *Shifting Time and Space: The Story of Videotape* (New York: Praeger, 1991), 130.

2. Video Cassette Rentals advertisement, *Los Angeles Times,* December 7, 1977, 8. In his two seminal works on the history of home video, James Lardner writes that Atkinson had run an earlier, smaller advertisement in the *Los Angeles Times* reading "Video for Rent," as well as a coupon to mail in for more information, as part of an effort to gauge public interest. Lardner quotes Atkinson as saying: "In less than a week, I had a thousand coupons," leading to the December 7, 1977, advertisement. This story has been repeated throughout subsequent home video histories. Lardner offers no date or additional explanation for this story, and after a thorough search of the *Los Angeles Times,* I can find no evidence of the earlier advertisement. James Lardner, "How Hollywood Learned to Stop Worrying and Love the VCR: Home Video Has Diminished the Power of the Studios—but Not Their Profits," *Los Angeles Times,* April 19, 1987, N13; James Lardner, *Fast Forward: Hollywood, the Japanese, and the Onslaught of the VCR* (New York: W.W. Norton, 1987).

3. There was one other precedent for renting movies on videotape. As early as July 1974, the Video Center in San Francisco began operating a video

"lending library." For a $30 initial fee, plus $10 for subsequent loans, members (of which the store claimed roughly a hundred) could check out U-Matic, EIAJ cartridges, or open-reel videotapes along with Panasonic or JVC video players. "Entertainment releases of films and concerts, and . . . videotapes of local groups and some key rock acts" were available. Paul Jaulus and Stephen Traiman, "In-Store Videocassette Labels Tie in Promo," *Billboard,* July 6, 1974, 1, 33.

4. Jennifer Bayot, "George Atkinson Dies at 69; Pioneer in Renting of Videos," *New York Times,* March 9, 2005, A23.

5. "Industry History," Entertainment Merchant's Association, n.d., ent-merch.org, (accessed January 11, 2013). Video Station went public in 1982 but subsequently plunged into financial problems. In early 1983, the State of California opened an investigation on tax discrepancies in Video Station's accounting procedures, and Atkinson left the company in September 1983. In December 1984, Video Station filed for Chapter 11 bankruptcy protection and began operating under court-approved reorganization in August 1985. In 1987, Atkinson, his brother, and a former employee were indicted by a federal grand jury for securities fraud and perjury. In mid-1988, George, who had earlier pled guilty before a trial to filing false financial statements, was sentenced to three months in a community treatment center, five years' probation, and two thou-sand hours of community service. Michael A. Hiltzik, "Video Station: State Tax Dispute Led to Discrepancy," *Los Angeles Times,* April 15, 1983, E2; Jube Shiver, "Video Rental Firm Files for Chapter 11 Protection," *Los Angeles Times,* December 13, 1984, J1; Al Delugach, "3 Ex-Officers of Video Chain Face Fraud Suit," *Los Angeles Times,* September 25, 1987, E3; Al Delugach, "2 Former Top Executives of Video Station Indicted," *Los Angeles Times,* November 19, 1987, E3; "Briefly," *Los Angeles Times,* March 29, 1988, F2; "Briefly," *Los Angeles Times,* May 11, 1988, E2.

6. Bayot, "George Atkinson Dies at 69," A23; Dennis McLellan, "George Atkinson; Pioneer in the Movie Video Industry," *Los Angeles Times,* March 12, 2005, B17.

7. Lee Grant, "It's Strictly Business for Porn Makers," *Los Angeles Times,* February 20, 1979, E1.

8. "Plan Film Slot Machines," *New York Times,* February 22, 1940, 30.

9. Roosevelt writes very briefly about this period, and about Soundies, in *My Parents: A Differing View* (Chicago: Playboy Press, 1976), 252–55.

10. "Plan Film Slot Machines," 30.

11. Other "visual jukebox" companies included Metermovies, Inc., the Phonofilm Company, Phonovision Corporation of America, Tonovision Corporation of America, and Talkavision, Inc. None made it to market. "Music Machines," *Billboard,* January 18, 1941, 80.

For more on Panoram history, see Andrea Kelley, " 'A Revolution in the Atmosphere': The Dynamics of Site and Screen in 1940s Soundies," *Cinema Journal* 54, no. 2 (Winter 2015): 72–93; Amy Herzog, "Illustrating Music: The Impossible Embodiments of the Jukebox Film," in *Medium Cool: Music Videos from Soundies to Cellphones,* eds. Roger Beebe and Jason Middleton (Durham, NC: Duke University Press, 2007), 30–58; Amy Herzog, "Fetish Machines: Peep

Shows, Co-Optation, and Technological Adaptation," in *Adaptation Theories,* ed. Jillian St. Jacques (Maastricht, Netherlands: Jan Van Eyck Academie Press, 2011), 47–89; Amy Herzog, "In the Flesh: Space and Embodiment in the Pornographic Peep Show Arcade," *Velvet Light Trap* 62 (Fall 2008): 29–43; Gregory Lukow, "The Antecedents of MTV: Soundies, Scopitones and Snaders, and the History of an Ahistorical Form," in *Art of Music Video: Ten Years After* (Long Beach, CA: Long Beach Museum of Art, 1991), 6–9; Gregory Lukow, "The Archaeology of Music Video: Soundies, Snader Telescriptions, and Scopitones," in *1986 National Video Festival Program* (Los Angeles: American Film Institute, 1986), 36–39; Maurice Terenzio, Scott MacGillivray, and Ted Okuda, *The Soundies Distributing Corporation of America: A History and Filmography of Their "Jukebox" Musical Films of the 1940s* (New York: McFarland, 1991); Wally Hose, *Soundies* (St. Louis: Wally's Multimedia, 2007); and Scott MacGillivray and Ted Okuda, *The Soundies Book: A Revised and Expanded Guide* (New York: IUniverse, 2007).

12. Joseph W. Slade, *Pornography in America: A Reference Handbook* (Santa Barbara, CA: ABC-CLIO, 2000), 9. The Panoram was officially unveiled during a gala three-day ceremony at the Waldorf-Astoria hotel in New York that grandly publicized Roosevelt's presence and his status as a captain in the Marine Corps Reserve. He abruptly resigned as president of Soundies only a few days later, after being called to active duty, but retained his unsalaried position as Globe's vice president and member of the board of directors. Globe, which he still owned, continued to produce short films. "James Roosevelt Quits," *New York Times,* October 31, 1940, 10.

13. D.W.C., "Return of the Peep Show," *New York Times,* April 21, 1940, 122.

14. "Ponser Purchases Conversion Units," *Billboard,* November 27, 1943, 117.

15. George Ponser Company advertisement, *Billboard,* November 27, 1943, 122.

16. There is something undeniably homoerotic about this scene, just as there is in the peep-show booth and pornography in general. The men in this advertisement could be drawing pleasure from watching one another, and there is no way to know the fantasy playing out on the screen (or, more important, in their minds). While early adult films playing on Panorams did not depict hardcore sexual practices or show male performers, the men in this advertisement (just like the men standing in front of actual Panorams) might have drawn a great deal of pleasure from watching other men experience pleasure. As Stephen Strager points out, male spectatorship of pornography often involves men watching other men perform sexually, which pointedly illustrates the fluidity of sexual desire and identification. Female spectators, too, can experience this sort of identification with female performers onscreen—and the spectrum between these two viewing positions is nearly limitless and highly malleable. Ultimately, pornography (perhaps more than any other genre) radically calls attention to the complicated ways in which identification works. Strager, "What

Men Watch When They Watch Pornography," *Sexuality and Culture* 7, no. 1 (Winter 2003): 50–61.

17. W.M. Nathanson advertisement, *Billboard*, January 1, 1944, 70.

18. Anthony Bianco, *Ghosts of 42nd Street: A History of America's Most Infamous Block* (New York: HarperCollins, 2004), 161. Striptease numbers were already playing in the late 1930s in peep-show arcades, as evidenced by a 1938 review of content available on "automatic 'peephole' machines" on Chicago's South State Street. "Strip Tease Films Showing in Chicago under City License," *Motion Picture Herald*, September 24, 1938, 56.

19. "Vet's Plan, Better Pix, Service School and Revenue from Ads Spotlight Soundies Post-War Plans," *Billboard*, April 15, 1944, 64.

20. The Production Code system was used to regulate Hollywood film production between 1930 and 1968 and was subsequently followed by the modern ratings system and its postproduction evaluative criteria. For more on the Production Code and its immense and important history, see Richard Maltby, "The Genesis of the Production Code," *Quarterly Review of Film and Video* 15, no. 4 (March 1995): 5–32; and Richard Maltby, "The Production Code and the Hays Office," in *Grand Design: Hollywood as a Modern Business Enterprise, 1930–1939*, ed. Tino Balio, *The History of the American Cinema*, vol. 5 (New York: Charles Scribner's Sons, 1993), 37–72.

21. B&B Novelty Company advertisement, *Billboard*, April 13, 1946, 108.

22. Herzog, "Fetish Machines," 62; Terenzio, MacGillivray, and Okuda, *The Soundies Distributing Corporation of America*, 10–16.

23. Al Di Lauro and Gerald Rabkin, *Dirty Movies: An Illustrated History of the Stag Film: 1915–1970* (New York: Chelsea House, 1988), 117.

24. Westbrook Pegler, "Frisco Peepshows," *Chester Times*, October 16, 1950, 6. Such films recall Linda Williams's analysis of Eadweard Muybridge's early zoopraxiscope human body films, particularly the ways in which nude female bodies were differentiated in his films by the addition of narrative justification. While male bodies engage in physical activities such as throwing, running, jumping, kicking, boxing, and wrestling, the female bodies engage in "picking up and putting down," along with primary passive postures such as sitting, standing, and kneeling. Even in those similar movements, as Williams points out, when women walk, run, and jump, Muybridge adds superfluous details such as a hand over a mouth. Props, too, convey this narrative justification, and frequently lend an air of eroticism to the women's bodies. Williams argues that this justification leads to "the unmistakable structure of the fetish," in which women's bodies are simultaneously eroticized and disavowed, and that "by denying the women any existence apart from the marks of difference, Muybridge exerts a form of mastery over that difference." "Film Body: An Implantation of Perversions," in *Narrative, Apparatus, Ideology*, ed. Philip Rosen (New York: Columbia University Press, 1986), 507–34.

25. For an overview of burlesque history, see Robert C. Allen, *Horrible Prettiness: Burlesque and American Culture* (Chapel Hill: University of North Carolina Press, 1992).

26. "Peep Show Change Man Found Guilty in Film Case," *Washington Post,* October 4, 1952, 15.

27. Herzog, "In the Flesh," 29–43.

28. Stevens and two partners built their own film-developing laboratory in 1957 to process their adult films; before that point, most sexually explicit content was imported from Europe. Stevens, along with his wife, Helene Terrie, who wrote nearly all his scripts, went on to a very long and distinguished career in the adult film industry before his death in 2012. Mark Kernes, "Legendary Director Kirdy Stevens, of 'Taboo' Fame, Passes at 92," *AVN,* November 3, 2012, http://business.avn.com/articles/video/Legendary-Director-Kirdy-Stevens-of-Taboo-Fame-Passes-at-92–493023.html (accessed November 6, 2012).

29. Eric Schaefer traces the theatrical exhibition of burlesque films during this era, noting that between 1949 and 1959 at least fifty feature-length burlesque features were produced, along with dozens of short films—many of which were cut and repurposed for peep shows and arcades, as well as the home market. However, as he notes, "the incessant cutting and recutting resulted in multiple permutations . . . so we will probably never know exactly how many actual features and shorts were produced during this period." "The Obscene Seen: Spectacle and Transgression in Postwar Burlesque Films," *Cinema Journal* 36, no. 2 (Winter 1997): 44–50.

30. For more on the general history of stag films, see Di Lauro and Rabkin, *Dirty Movies;* Dave Thompson, *Black and White and Blue: Adult Cinema from the Victorian Age to the VCR* (Toronto: ECW Press, 2007); Arthur Knight and Hollis Alpert, "The History of Sex in Cinema: Part Seventeen: The Stag Film," *Playboy* (November 1967): 154–58; and Thomas Waugh, *Hard to Imagine: Gay Male Eroticism in Photography and Film from Their Beginnings to Stonewall* (New York: Columbia University Press, 1996), 309–22.

31. *Excelsior Pictures Corp. v. Regents of the University of the State of New York,* 3 N.Y.2d 237, Court of Appeals of New York, July 3, 1957, LexisNexis (accessed February 14, 2013); Slade, *Pornography in America,* 150.

32. Eric Schaefer, *Bold! Daring! Shocking! True!: A History of Exploitation Films, 1919–1959* (Durham, NC: Duke University Press, 1999), 8.

33. For more on Meyer, see David K. Frasier, *Russ Meyer: The Life and Films* (New York: McFarland, 1997); Adolph A. Schwartz and Russ Meyer, *A Clean Breast: The Life and Loves of Russ Meyer,* 3 vols. (Los Angeles: Hauck Publishing, 2000); and Jimmy McDonough, *Big Bosoms and Square Jaws: The Biography of Russ Meyer, King of the Sex Film* (New York: Random House, 2005).

34. Bianco, *Ghosts of 42nd Street,* 157–80.

35. Hodas offers a slightly different account in interviews with William Sherman, telling him that it was a vending machine repairman on 42nd Street who suggested that old nickelodeon-type machines could be repurposed to show adult films on a wide scale. Sherman, *Times Square* (New York: Bantam Books, 1980), 22. For Hodas's own account in an interview with Ashley West, see "Martin Hodas, King of the Peeps," *Rialto Report,* June 29, 2014, www

.therialtoreport.com/2014/06/29/marty-hodas-king-of-the-peeps-podcast-38/
(accessed June 29, 2014).

36. Bianco, *Ghosts of 42nd Street*, 162.

37. Ibid.

38. In another account, Hodas claimed he bought his initial inventory of fifteen Panoram machines from veteran arcade game distributor Mike Munves, who was storing them in a basement, for $2,500. "Martin Hodas, King of the Peeps."

39. Bianco, *Ghosts of 42nd Street*, 162.

40. Ibid.

41. Ibid., 188.

42. Sherman, *Times Square*, 21.

43. Richard W. Shepard, "Peep Shows Have New Nude Look," *New York Times,* June 9, 1969, 58. The *Times* article, and Hodas's accompanying confidence, put him even more squarely in the crosshairs of police and prosecutors. The city tried repeatedly (and unsuccessfully) to institute licensing requirements and held frequent organized-crime inquiries and hearings, trying to link Hodas to the Mafia, as well as frequently investigating him for obscenity. In 1972, Hodas and two associates were indicted for firebombing two massage parlors; the two acquaintances were convicted, but Hodas was acquitted. In 1975, he was convicted of tax evasion and sentenced to a year in prison. Chemical Bank, in 1981, severed its ties with Hodas, claiming "disapproval" of his business interests, a decision upheld by a federal judge after Hodas filed suit. Hodas also pled guilty to two counts of violating U.S. interstate commerce laws for transporting twelve hundred hardcore videotapes from New York to Buffalo in July 1983 that were intended for shipment into Canada, for which he served another year in prison. As late as 1985, he still controlled more than 90 percent of the peep shows in New York City, and in the mid-1990s, he acquired additional theaters and bookstores.

For the most detailed accounts of Hodas's early interactions and struggles with New York's law enforcement and regulatory communities, see Sherman, *Times Square;* "Peep-Show Producer Is Called Evader of Federal Income Tax," *New York Times,* October 22, 1970, 69; Eleanor Blau, "Investigation Chief Proposes Licensing of 'Peep Show' Outlets," *New York Times,* October 27, 1970, 51; Paul L. Montgomery, "Dirty-Book Store Run by Police Gains Indictment of 18 Here on Pornography," *New York Times,* April 21, 1972, 20; "Peep-Show Merchant Denies Crime Role," *New York Times,* July 27, 1977, 13; Martha M. Hamilton and John Kennedy, "Judge Says Bank Can End Its Service to Porno Seller," *Washington Post,* February 21, 1981, D8; Zuhair Kashmeri, "Mountie Helps Jail New York City 'Porn King,'" *Globe and Mail,* February 12, 1985, M3; "Indict Martin Hodas," *Variety,* July 18, 1973, 20; Bruce Lambert, "Back in Business: Once (and Future?) King of Times Sq. Porn," *New York Times,* September 25, 1994, CY6; Dave Saltonstall, "Peep Show King Eyes New Times," *New York Daily News,* November 12, 1995, www.nydailynews.com/archives/news/peep-show-king-eyes-new-times-article-1.709719 (accessed January 25, 2013); "Martin Hodas, King of the Peeps."

44. Josh Alan Friedman, *Tales of Times Square* (New York: Delacorte, 1986), 77.

45. Herzog, "In the Flesh," 32; Legs McNeil, Jennifer Osborne, and Peter Pavia, *The Other Hollywood: The Uncensored Oral History of the Porn Film Industry* (New York: Regan Books, 2005), 104–10; Eric Schlosser, *Reefer Madness and Other Tales from the American Underground* (New York: Penguin Books, 2003), 109–210; U.S. Attorney General's Commission on Pornography, *Attorney General's Commission on Pornography: Final Report* (Washington, DC: U.S. Government Printing Office, 1986), 1037–1212; Jay Allen Sandford, "Battle of the Peeps: An Insider History of San Diego Porn Shops," *San Diego Reader*, October 23, 2008, www.sandiegoreader.com /weblogs/bands/2008/oct/23/battle-of-the-peeps---an-insider-history-of-san-di/ (accessed January 23, 2013); Michael Satchell, "The Big Business of Selling Smut," *Parade*, August 19, 1979, 4–5.

46. Reporter David Gelman claimed in 1971 that, by 1969, "there were 1,000 cassette operated peep shows in New York, and a $5 million industry where two years earlier there had been nothing." It is unclear what Gelman meant by "cassette operated," since all research points to New York peep booths operating with standard projection equipment at that time. "Pornography in New York," *Washington Post*, June 7, 1971, B10.

47. Schlosser, *Reefer Madness*, 129. By 1973, Sturman had fifteen full-time employees constructing the cheap booths, shipped prefabricated all over North America. See McNeil, Osborne and Pavia, *The Other Hollywood*, 106.

FBI agent Bill Kelly called Sturman "by far the most important pornographer in the history of the world." Sturman created a mainstream magazine and comic book distribution business in the 1950s, added adult magazines, and within two decades was the largest distributor of pornography in the United States. He was also linked to organized crime throughout his career. Using dozens of different aliases, hundreds of shell companies, and elaborate accounting strategies, he managed to successfully avoid obscenity and other prosecutions throughout his career. But he was convicted in 1989 on tax evasion charges, forced to pay $2.5 million in fines, and sentenced to ten years in jail. A charge of interstate transportation of obscene material resulted in a plea bargain for Sturman, but he was caught trying to bribe a juror and sentenced to nineteen additional years for extortion. Captured after briefly escaping from prison in California, he died in federal prison in Lexington, Kentucky, in 1997. McNeil, Osborne, and Pavia, *The Other Hollywood*, 104–207, Kelly quote 104.

48. Friedman, *Tales of Times Square*, 68–74.

49. Schlosser, *Reefer Madness*, 129.

50. Of particular interest to law enforcement were the "glory holes" cut into the walls, facilitating sexual pleasure between adjoining occupants. Such behavior was and is commonplace at peep-show arcades, adult movie theaters, and other spaces designed with ostensibly heterosexual sexual practices in mind. For a useful examination of these apparent contradictions and their importance in adult film history, see Samuel R. Delany, *Times Square Red, Times Square Blue* (New York: New York University Press, 1999); John

Champagne, "'Stop Reading Films!' Film Studies, Close Analysis, and Gay Pornography," *Cinema Journal* 36, no. 4 (Summer 1997): 76–97; Lauren Berlant and Michael Warner, "Sex in Public," *Critical Inquiry* 24, no. 2 (Winter 1998): 547–66; José Capino, "Homologies of Space: Text and Spectatorship in All-Male Adult Theaters," *Cinema Journal* 45, no. 1 (Autumn 2005): 50–65; and Timothy J. Gilfoyle, "From Soubrette Row to Show World: The Contested Sexualities of Times Square, 1880–1995," in *Policing Public Sex: Queer Politics and the Future of AIDS Activism*, eds. Ephen Glenn Colter et al. (Boston: South End Press, 1996), 263–93.

51. Herzog, "In the Flesh," 37.

52. Kerry Segrave, *Movies at Home: How Hollywood Came to Television* (New York: McFarland, 2009), 116–17.

53. "Hotel-Theatre Network Set on Notre Dame Grid," *Variety*, July 20, 1955, 27; Hy Hollinger, "Closed-Circuit TV's Potential Brightens: Eye Tint Horizons," *Variety*, December 12, 1956, 26; Hy Hollinger, "Closed-TV: A New Industry," *Variety*, February 29, 1956, 29.

54. "Now You Can Stay in Your Hotel All Day and Gander What's Going on in N.Y.," *Variety*, July 11, 1956, 2.

55. Nathan L. Halpern, "Closed-Circuit TV Invited $30,000,000 in Billings," *Variety*, January 7, 1959, 95.

56. Les Brown, "Computer Cinema: How Feevee Fared in Newark Hotel against Free-TV," *Variety*, September 29, 1971, 30.

57. Ibid.; "Hotel Shows Films on TVs," *Los Angeles Times*, October 8, 1971, G12. For detailed technical information on the operation of closed-circuit hotel systems of the era, see Morton Dubin, "A Study on the Business of In-Room Movies at Hotel/Motel Rooms," *Backstage*, April 7, 1972, 34, 38; and Morton Dubin, "Further Discussion Relating to the Systems That Bring Movies to Hotel Rooms," *Backstage*, July 21, 1972, 5, 12, 13.

58. Brown, "Computer Cinema," 30; John J. O'Connor, "To the Critics: How Would You Improve Things?" *New York Times*, October 10, 1971, D17. Hollywood's reluctance to embrace new technologies, stemming from a fear of potential threats, was not limited to hotel exhibition. Later the studios would initially labor to block the Sony Betamax due to its "time shifting" recording capabilities. Such actions culminated in a landmark 1984 decision by the Supreme Court, which ruled that making home video recorders for purposes of time shifting does not constitute copyright infringement but is instead fair use, as well as holding that manufacturers of such equipment cannot be held liable for copyright infringement. The decision not only opened up the modern VCR market for home recording, but also significantly benefited the studios and the market for prerecorded content. See *Sony Corp. of America v. Universal City Studios, Inc.*, 464 U.S. 417, Supreme Court of the United States, January 17, 1984, LexisNexis (accessed February 19, 2013); Peter Decherney, *Hollywood's Copyright Wars: From Edison to the Internet* (New York: Columbia University Press, 2012), 169–81; and Stephen Prince, *A New Pot of Gold: Hollywood under the Electronic Rainbow, 1980–1989* (New York: Charles Scribner's Sons, 2000), 99–107.

59. Leonard Sloane, "Pay-as-You-View Movies for Hotels," *Variety,* November 14, 1971, F5; Douglas Gomery, "The Coming of Television and the 'Lost' Motion Picture Audience," *Journal of Film and Video* 37, no. 3 (Summer 1985): 5–11; "Pix Must Broaden Market," *Variety,* March 20, 1968, 1; Robert Sklar, *Movie-Made America* (New York: Random House, 1975), 269–304.

60. Jack Gould, "Pay-TV for Apartments Is Proposed," *New York Times,* October 8, 1971, 86.

61. Columbia Pictures was not the only studio to participate in hotel exhibition: MGM held a stake in Metrovision, and Paramount Pictures was a partner in Athena Communications, Inc., two smaller companies that tested closed-circuit equipment in hotels in Toronto and Little Rock, Arkansas, respectively. Neither company survived the rapid changes in the industry. Albin Krebs, "'Hotelevision' Introduces Uncut Movies as Part of Room Service," *New York Times,* October 25, 1972, 94.

62. "Hotel Pix-for-Pay from Trans-World in Atlanta Preem," *Variety,* October 6, 1971, 31.

63. Bob Knight, "Older, Well-Heeled Fans Big Potential via Hotels' Closed-Circuit Movies," *Variety,* October 13, 1971, 1, 54; Trans-World advertisement, *New York Times,* June 22, 1972, 55.

64. "Columbia's Hotel Films Setup to Invade Hawaii Sometime During 1972," *Variety,* October 27, 1971, 38.

65. Norman Mark, "Saturday Night at the Hotel?" *Los Angeles Times,* July 25, 1972, G10.

66. Jerry Beigel, "Pay-TV System Offering Four Channels Introduced," *Los Angeles Times,* December 18, 1972, E24; "Pay TV Includes X-Rated Fare," *Chicago Tribune,* August 31, 1972, N8.

67. Justin Wyatt, "The Stigma of X: Adult Cinema and the Institution of the MPAA Ratings System," in *Controlling Hollywood: Censorship and Regulation in the Studio Era,* ed. Matthew Bernstein (Piscataway, NJ: Rutgers University Press, 1999), 238–63; Jon Lewis, *Hollywood v. Hard Core: How the Struggle over Censorship Created the Modern Film Industry* (New York: New York University, 2000).

68. "Video Cartridges: A Promise of Future Shock," *Time,* August 10, 1970, http://content.time.com/time/magazine/article/0,9171,876748,00.html (accessed October 5, 2009); Barbara Isenberg, "Video Cassettes Offer Potential for Future but Problems for Now," *Wall Street Journal,* December 16, 1970, 19.

69. "Sherpix: The Unusual Company with an Unusual Future," *Independent Film Journal,* April 27, 1972, 20–21.

70. Addison Verrill, "Porno on 'Family' Showcase," *Variety,* February 23, 1972, 1, 69.

71. Schaefer traces the transition of adult film from loops and stags to features in detail in "Gauging a Revolution: 16mm Film and the Rise of the Pornographic Feature," *Cinema Journal* 41, no. 3 (Spring 2002): 3–26.

72. "'Mona' 1st Film of Hardcore to Make Top-50 List," *Variety,* February 10, 1971, 3.

73. Ibid., 5.

74. Addison Verrill, "Bill Osco, Boy King of L.A. Porno, Grossing Over $2,000,000 Presently; 10-City Nucleus' 'Actors' A-Plenty," *Variety*, December 30, 1970, 5.

75. Addison Verrill, "TV Cassettes Bid for Sex Pix," *Variety*, January 27, 1971, 1, 54.

76. "Eve Meyer Sells Films to Optronics Libraries," *Boxoffice*, December 7, 1970, 7.

77. "Video Cartridges." Despite this ambitious start, Optronics failed to take off, mostly due to the incompatibility of the players then on the market and the general chaos within the industry. By September 1971, Optronics was focused primarily on installing EVR machines in record stores (utilizing Stimmler's connections as a former vice president with MGM's record division) as part of a deal with eight major record companies to advertise their bands in taped performances—essentially early music videos. In February 1972, Optronics merged with Trans America Films in order to pursue record store deals full-time. Stimmler noted at the time of the merger that "the [home video] industry just has not developed as quickly as we anticipated." Radcliffe Joe, "Disks Pushed in Stores Via CTV," *Billboard*, September 4, 1971, 1, 19; Radcliffe Joe, "Optronics Libraries Merges with Trans America Films," *Billboard*, February 19, 1972, 49; Isenberg, "Video Cassettes Offer Potential for Future but Problems for Now," 19.

78. Isenberg, "Video Cassettes Offer Potential for Future but Problems for Now," 19.

79. Cartridge Rental Systems, Inc., *Rental Program Library* (Raleigh, NC: Cartridge Rental Systems, Inc., 1972), 7. Anthony Reveaux also briefly mentions adult titles available in the Cartrivision catalogue (as well as offering an excellent overview of that technology) in "New Technologies for the Demystification of Cinema," *Film Quarterly* 27, no. 1 (Autumn 1973): 50.

80. Quoted in C.P. McCarthy, "A TV Star—and Only $1595?" *S.F. Examiner*, September 7, 1972, 4.

81. For more on Cartrivision, see "First Home V'cassettes on View," *Variety*, June 14, 1972, 42; Dwight Newton, "A Cartridge Miracle Set," *San Francisco Examiner*, September 8, 1972, n.p.; Anne Douglas, "Age of TV Cassette Recorder and Player," *Chicago Tribune*, June 17, 1972, 21; Leonard Wiener, "Video Tape Promises TV of Your Choice—Someday," *Chicago Tribune*, April 15, 1974, C9; Paul McDonald, *Video and DVD Industries* (London: British Film Institute, 2008), 31; Marlow and Secunda, *Shifting Time and Space*, 113; and Frederick Wasser, *Veni, Vidi, Video: The Hollywood Empire and the VCR* (Austin: University of Texas Press, 2001), 62–63.

82. Everett H. Ortner, "12-Channel Sound-Movie Cassette Plays for Two Hours," *Popular Science* (August 1968): 83.

83. "Films in Cassettes Tee Off in N.Y.'s Hotel Commodore at $4.50 per Room," *Variety*, March 1, 1972, 2, 70.

84. Quoted in Andy Grundberg, "I Lost It at the Commodore," *New York Magazine*, July 3, 1972, 56.

85. James Sterngold, "A Room with a Cyberview," *New York Times*, December 23, 1996, D1, D9; Timothy Egan, "Erotic Inc: Technology Sent Wall

Street into Market for Pornography," *New York Times,* October 23, 2000, www
.nytimes.com/2000/10/23/us/erotica-special-report-technology-sent-wall-
street-into-market-for-pornography.html (accessed February 16, 2013).

86. "Pay TV Includes X-Rated Fare," N8.

87. The first of these establishments, appropriately named Love Hotel (or
Hotel Love, as its swiveling sign was two-sided) opened in Osaka in 1968 and
was quickly followed by others. Following the Osaka Expo in 1970, love hotels
spread throughout Japan. Erik Slavin, "My Months in a Love Hotel," *Stripes,*
March 25, 2007, www.stripes.com/military-life/my-months-in-a-love-hotel
-1.63008 (accessed February 17, 2013).

For more on the history of Japan's love hotels, see Sarah Chaplin, *Japanese
Love Hotels: A Cultural History* (New York: Routledge, 2007). For more on
pink films, see Jasper Sharp, *Behind the Pink Curtain: The Complete History of
Japanese Sex Cinema* (London: FAB Press, 2008); and Abé Markus Nornes, ed.,
The Pink Book: The Japanese Eroduction and Its Contexts (Ann Arbor, MI:
Kinema Klub, 2014).

88. "Modern Living: Sinema in Osaka," *Time,* March 22, 1971, 62.

89. Owen J. Kilbane, in December 1972, opened the Hillcrest Motel in
Cleveland, Ohio, with closed-circuit adult films, a limousine with adult videos,
and the option to rent a video camera to make personal tapes. Countering Leon,
Kilbane would later claim to *Playboy* magazine that his was the first such motel
in the United States. "As Ohio Goes . . . ," *Playboy* (October 1975): 51.

90. "Motels with X-Rated Films Thrive on Coast," *New York Times,*
February 17, 1975, 22.

91. AutoLodge Motel advertisement, *Los Angeles Times,* August 20, 1972,
CAL_44.

92. Quoted in Stephen J. Sansweet, "Playing to Fantasies: Some Motels
Thrive on Adult Patronage," *Wall Street Journal,* March 2, 1977, 1, 83.

93. Experience Motel, advertisement, *Los Angeles Times,* April 22, 1973,
22.

94. Western and Crest advertisement, *Los Angeles Times,* February 9, 1973,
22.

95. "L.A.'S X-Rated Motels: Pornopix & Water Beds," *Variety,* March 7,
1973, 1, 79.

96. David Shaw, "The 'X-Rated' Motels: It's Usually SRO," *Los Angeles
Times,* June 16, 1973, 1, 22–23.

97. Jim Stingley, "Squares amid the Alien Porn," *Los Angeles Times,*
February 5, 1975, 1. Later, various municipalities tried more elaborate legal
mechanisms to prevent adult motels from opening. For example, in June 1977,
the city of San Clemente, California, passed an ordinance requiring motel operators to obtain a permit to show adult films, modeled on the same statute that
had effectively prevented adult bookstores from opening in the city. The city
also regulated parking, traffic, architecture, and location—all with the intended
purpose of making it difficult for businesses to operate. "Use Permit Required
for Adult Motel Operators," *Los Angeles Times,* June 6, 1977, OC3.

98. Nicola Simpson, "Coming Attractions: A Comparative History of the Hollywood Studio System and the Porn Business," *Historical Journal of Film, Radio, and Television* 24, no. 4 (2004): 642.

99. Richard Smith, *Getting into Deep Throat* (Chicago: Playboy Press, 1973), 46.

100. "Motels with X-Rated Films Thrive on Coast," 22.

101. B.C. Kaye, "X-Rated Motels for Adventurous Couples," *Sexology* (September 1975): 11–15.

102. Needless to say, prostitution was a steady and profitable economy in and around adult motels, despite the owners' protestations. By 1982, the city of Hollywood had cracked down on eight adult motels, forcing them to close until they had instituted new policies that included requiring identification, names, addresses, and twenty-four-hour minimum room rentals. Myrna Oliver, "City Closes 2 Motels Used by Prostitutes," *Los Angeles Times,* December 15, 1982, E3.

103. Eithne Johnson circles similar questions about a slightly earlier era in "The 'Colonoscopic' Film and the 'Beaver' Film: Scientific and Pornographic Scenes of Female Sexual Responsiveness," in *Swinging Single: Representing Sexuality in the 1960s,* eds. Hilary Radner and Moya Luckett (Minneapolis: University of Minnesota Press, 1999), 301–24. She also details the representations and constructions of women's pleasure in terms of adult film *content,* a topic in critical need of more work. "Excess and Ecstasy: Constructing Female Pleasure in Porn Movies," *Velvet Light Trap* 32 (Fall 1993): 30–49.

104. Quoted in Shaw, "The 'X-Rated' Motels," 1. Antiquo would go on to found Video Innovation, a company that specialized in installing closed-circuit systems in adult motels. Michael Price, "A Coward's Guide to X-Rated Motels," *Oui* (February 1978): 121.

105. Jim Stingley, "Middle Class Tunes In, Turns On," *Los Angeles Times,* February 4, 1975, 1, 6–7; Price, "A Coward's Guide to X-Rated Motels," 121.

106. Shearlean Duke, "A Nice Place for a Family Affair," *Los Angeles Times,* July 27, 1980, OCA1, 4–6.

107. *Miller v. California,* 413 U.S. 15, Supreme Court of the United States, June 21, 1973, LexisNexis (accessed January 29, 2013).

108. Quoted in Sansweet, "Playing to Fantasies," 1.

109. In August 1973, the owner of Sir Waight's Court, an adult motel in Kansas City, made a similar argument, publicly challenging the *Miller* decision by suggesting that motels afford the same right to privacy as the home, clearly marking the temporary space as one that comes with protection from legal interference. The pronouncement was not made in relation to an obscenity prosecution or even arrest; instead, it seems to have been more of a preemptive strategy designed to alleviate community concerns in Kansas City that the motel was violating the law—or even to attract customers with a promise of protection. "Motels 'Privacy' Shield on Porn?" *Variety,* August 22, 1973, 11.

110. Stingley, "Middle Class Tunes In, Turns On," 1.

111. 1st Run Theater advertisement, *Los Angeles Times,* April 20, 1973, I14; 1st Run Theater advertisement, *Los Angeles Times,* June 1, 1973, H23; 1st Run Theater advertisement, *Los Angeles Times,* June 20, 1973, I14.

112. Quoted in Stingley, "Squares amid the Alien Porn," 14.

113. "Leon Film Enterprises," *Independent Film Journal,* March 30, 1972, 4.

114. "Holders Get Report From Intl. Film Org.; 4 Un-Tradescreened," *Variety,* December 31, 1969, 4.

115. "Hollywood," *Variety,* February 8, 1967, 61; "Sidney Pink's Westside International Productions, Madrid, Spain," *Back Stage* 7, no. 14 (April 8, 1966): 14.

116. Quoted in Sansweet, "Playing to Fantasies," 83.

117. For a first-hand account of the mechanics of film piracy during this period, see Bob Navins and Howard Polskin, "'I Knew It Was the Feds the Moment I Drove Up to My Office,'" *Panorama* (August 1980): 39–42.

118. Robert McG. Thomas Jr., "Suspect in Piracy of Films Seized," *New York Times,* February 20, 1975, 1, 38; "Raid on Print Pirate; Title Range Shock," *Variety,* February 26, 1975, 28.

119. Kerry Segrave, *Piracy in the Motion Picture Industry* (New York: McFarland, 2003).

120. James Monaco, "Stealing the Show: The Piracy Problem," *American Film* 3, no. 9 (July 1, 1978): 57–67; Decherney, *Hollywood's Copyright Wars,* 155–69; Adrian Johns, *Piracy: The Intellectual Property Wars from Gutenberg to Gates* (Chicago: University of Chicago Press, 2009), 448–60; Prince, *A New Pot of Gold,* 98–99.

121. Quoted in "Motels with X-Rated Films Thrive on Coast," 22.

122. For example, in 1978, Norm Arno changed the name of his S&L Distributors to VCX, creating one of the first major adult video companies. His initial stock was made up of pirated tapes originally produced by rival TVX. David Jennings, *Skinflicks: The Inside Story of the X-Rated Video Industry* (Bloomington, IN: 1st Books, 2000), 70–71.

123. Even after the adult film industry began moving toward legitimacy, piracy continued, in part because the underground legacy of the industry continued to linger. In 1986, for example, *Videography* magazine openly accused Show/Tapes, a small distributor in Miami, Florida, of bootlegging adult material, including *Deep Throat.* Show/Tapes claimed to have purchased that film's rights from Sal Esposito of Scorpio Films in Reseda, California—but they were actually owned by Plymouth Distributors of Brooklyn, New York, making the bootlegging a multitiered effort. "Show/Tapes," *Videography* (June 1978): 26; "Star Wars Story," *Videography* (June 1978): 65.

Such tensions continue to haunt the industry, particularly concerning films from the era in which the industry was not concerned with protecting its investment, but which continue to hold tremendous monetary value. More recently, VCX and Arrow Productions submitted a stipulation, approved by a judge, that would prevent VCX from distributing *Deep Throat* (which Arrow believed it owned) and Arrow from distributing *Debbie Does Dallas* (which VCX believed it owned), despite the possibility that both films were technically in the public domain, thus demonstrating the complicated landscape upon which adult films continue to reside. Eriq Gardner, "How a Nasty Legal Fight over 'Deep Throat,' 'Debbie Does Dallas' Was Settled," *Hollywood Reporter,* October 26, 2011, www.hollywoodreporter.com/thr-esq/how-a-nasty-legal-fight-252525 (accessed February 26, 2013).

124. For a thorough and thoughtful examination of copyright in the context of home video, see Lucas Hilderbrand, *Inherent Vice: Bootleg Histories of Videotape and Copyright* (Durham, NC: Duke University Press, 2009), 77–114.

For a legal analysis of the issues of adult film, obscenity, and copyright, see Nicole Chaney, "Cybersex: Protecting Sexual Content in the Digital Age," *John Marshall Review of Intellectual Property Law* 11 (Spring 2012): 815–40.

125. In that case, the court ruled that a theater owner who had played a bootleg version of *Behind the Green Door* (1972) could not claim as a defense that the film was obscene and therefore not entitled to copyright protection. *Mitchell Brothers Film Group v. Cinema Adult Theater,* 604 F.2d 852, United States Court of Appeals for the Fifth Circuit, October 16, 1979, LexisNexis (accessed February 26, 2013).

126. Quoted in Shaw, "The 'X-Rated' Motels," 23. For more on the "medicalization" involved in mixing pornography and education, and the subsequent simultaneous encouragement and containment of pleasure, see Robert Eberwein, *Sex Ed: Film, Video, and the Framework of Desire* (New Brunswick, NJ: Rutgers University Press, 1999).

127. While details on whether other motel owners were involved in production are scarce, one other, disturbing detail does recur in the discourse. According to police reports, at least one motel used a two-way mirror in one room to capture patrons' sexual activity on camera, which later would be played back to other patrons. In addition to providing the titillation of illicit, unpredictable sexual behavior, such accounts serve two purposes: first, they prop up a cultural belief that the police were "protecting" the public from perverted motel owners; and, second, they circulate a belief that adult motels (and pornography) were dangerous, unpredictable places that could only get patrons into "trouble." It is not surprising that another common discourse at the time, also circulated by police, was that the motels were running an elaborate extortion ring, in which patrons who checked in with a "girlfriend" were subjected to blackmail plots. Both the two-way mirror and extortion discourses (which border on urban legends) ultimately serve as containment strategies on pleasure, seeking to keep "innocent" members of the public from going too far in pursuit of sexual satisfaction. Shaw, "The 'X-Rated' Motels," 22; Stingley, "Middle Class Tunes In, Turns On," 7.

128. Bayot, "George Atkinson Dies at 69," A23; McLellan, "George Atkinson," B17.

129. Greg Hernandez, "Prerecorded Visionary Creator of Videos for Rent Living Simple Life 25 Years after Concept Changed U.S.," *Daily News,* December 13, 2002, B1.

130. Lardner, "How Hollywood Learned to Stop Worrying and Love the VCR," N14.

131. Alfred W. Lees, "Sit Back and Enjoy Yourself: New Projectors Put on the Whole Show," *Popular Science* (March 1962): 73–74.

132. Lardner, "How Hollywood Learned to Stop Worrying and Love the VCR," N14; Lardner, *Fast Forward,* 170; "Conversation with George Atkinson," *Videography* (June 1982): 51.

133. Lardner, *Fast Forward,* 170; "Conversations with George Atkinson," 51.

134. "Conversations with George Atkinson," 51. Atkinson purchased the tapes from Greatest Fights of the Century and Big Fights Inc., boxing video companies founded by collectors Jimmy Jacobs and Bill Clayton in 1959. Robert H. Boyle, "Really the Greatest," *Sports Illustrated,* March 7, 1966, www.si.com /vault/1966/03/07/607662/really-the-greatest (accessed March 2, 2013).

135. For a firsthand account of this era, see Samuel K. Rubin, *Moving Pictures and Classic Images: Memories of Forty Years in the Vintage Film Hobby* (Jefferson, NC: McFarland, 2004).

136. Nicholas Jarecki, *Breaking In: How 20 Film Directors Got Their Start* (New York: Broadway Books, 2001), 190–201; Waleed Ali, "Home Video's Pioneers: In Their Own Words," *TWICE: This Week in Consumer Electronics,* August 17–21, 1987, 32–33.

137. Vernon Scott, "Pirates of the Film Kingdom," *Los Angeles Times,* April 23, 1976, E22; Joe McBride, "28-Yr. Renewal Failure Throws Films into Public Doman, and onto Ex-Pirate's Lawful List," *Variety,* August 28, 1974, 5, 28; William K. Knoedelseder Jr., "Confessions of a Hollywood Film Pirate," *Los Angeles Times,* July 22, 1977, G1; David Pierce, "Forgotten Faces: Why Some of Our Cinema Heritage Is Part of the Public Domain," *Film History* 19, no. 2 (2007): 125–43.

138. Home Theater Systems advertisement, *Los Angeles Times,* June 8, 1975, CAL_48.

139. Home Theater Systems advertisement, *Los Angeles Times,* August 24, 1975, P46.

140. Home Theater Systems advertisement, *Los Angeles Times,* September 7, 1975, R44; Home Theater Systems advertisement, *Los Angeles Times,* September 18, 1975, G16.

141. For an overview of the creation and introduction of the Sony Betamax, see Marlow and Secunda, *Shifting Time and Space,* 118–21.

142. Kalton C. Lahue, "Get Ready for X-Rated TV!" *Velvet* (December 1978): 90.

143. Quoted in Anna Quindlen, "The Times Will Curb Ads for Pornographic Films," *New York Times,* June 21, 1977, 46.

144. Otis Chandler, "Times Rejects Porno Ads," *Los Angeles Times,* August 23, 1977, G1.

145. Dennis McDougal, *Privileged Son: Otis Chandler and the Rise and Fall of the L.A. Times Dynasty* (Cambridge, MA: Perseus Publishing, 2001), 317; Marshall Berges, *The Life and Times of Los Angeles: A Newspaper, a Family, and a City* (New York: Atheneum, 1984), 208–09.

The Pussycat Theater chain, desperate to find a new advertising space, briefly ran television commercials in Southern California after the *LA*

Times ban. "Take Hardcore Ads into Homes Via TV," *Variety*, January 11, 1978, 1, 82.

146. Home Theater Systems advertisement, *Los Angeles Times*, August 17, 1977, F16.

147. Video Visions advertisement, *Los Angeles Times*, January 20, 1977, SE2; Classified advertisement, *Los Angeles Times*, May 15, 1977, A23.

148. For more on Blay's crucial role in home video history, see Andre A. Blay, *Pre-Recorded History: Memoirs of an Entertainment Entrepreneur* (Centennial, CO: Deer Track, 2010); Radcliffe Joe, "Magnetic Video Enters CTV Software as Triple-Front Producer," *Billboard*, April 3, 1971, 35; Lardner, *Fast Forward*, 163–70; McDonald, *Video and DVD Industries*, 113; Ali, "Home Video's Pioneers," 36–37; Hernandez, "Prerecorded Visionary Creator of Videos for Rent Living Simple Life 25 Years after Concept Changed U.S.," B1.

149. Video Club of America advertisement, *TV Guide*, November 26–December 2, 1977, 48–49.

150. Lardner, *Fast Forward*, 168.

151. Ibid., 171; Hernandez, "Prerecorded Visionary Creator of Videos for Rent Living Simple Life 25 Years after Concept Changed U.S.," B1.

152. Atkinson initiated his rental concept even before thinking through the legality of such a model. A month after opening his store, he approached Blay at the January 1978 Consumer Electronics Show in Las Vegas and asked him if he could rent the Magnetic Video tapes to customers—a question that Blay could not answer. Atkinson then contacted Steve Roberts, president of telecommunications at 20th Century Fox, who (incorrectly) assumed royalties would be involved. Eventually, Fox consultant Robert Townsend warned Atkinson that the rental strategy constituted copyright infringement. It was at this point that Atkinson's attorney argued that the "First Sale" doctrine of the Copyright Act of 1976 (in which the copyright owner loses control of the copy after the first sale, permitting the new owner to dispose of the item as she sees fit—including renting it to others), allowed Atkinson's business model to stay intact. As long as he did not make unauthorized copies or publicly exhibit the films, Atkinson could rent the tapes without royalty payments. Atkinson would go on, particularly as the president of the Video Software Dealers Association, to be a relentless champion of the First Sale doctrine. The accompanying struggles between early retailers and studios, in many ways, define the home video industry in the 1980s. George Rush, "Home Video Wars," *American Film* 10, no. 6 (April 1, 1985): 61–62; Lardner, *Fast Forward*, 173–74.

153. At least one adult bookstore, Party Time in San Jose, California, was renting celluloid adult films as early as February 1977. Party Time advertisement, *Berkeley Barb*, February 25–March 3, 1977, A12.

154. For more on the history of selling home video, as well as the early tensions between Hollywood and the rental industry, see McDonald, *Video and DVD Industries*, 114–27.

155. Jacobson contemplated adding hardcore to his Home Cinema Services catalogue numerous times in the 1970s, but he wanted to avoid legal trouble. In the 1980s, he opened five successful mainstream video stores in Hartford,

Connecticut, and served on the board of directors of the Connecticut Video Software Dealers Association. The arrival of Blockbuster Video eventually shuttered all his stores—leading him to open an adult video–only store to stay in business. Eventually, Jacobson moved to an online-only adult video operation. Joel Jacobson, telephone interview with author, June 18, 2012; Joel Jacobson, email to author, July 2, 2012; Howard Polskin, "Pornography Unleashed," *Panorama* (July 1980): 35–39; Mike Boone, "Business in Erotic Videotapes Booming," *Montreal Gazette*, October 2, 1981, 1, 12.

156. Jacobson also eventually signed a deal with Al Goldstein, publisher of *Screw* magazine, to distribute "best of" compilations of Goldstein's public-access television show *Midnight Blue*. Polskin, "Pornography Unleashed," 35–39.

157. Cinema Concepts advertisement, *Videography* (October 1976): 55.

158. Polskin, "Pornography Unleashed," 37–38.

159. "Tube Job!" *Playboy* (December 1976): 268.

160. Valentine Products advertisement, *Oui* (July 1977): 134. Valentine Productions was headed by a friend of Jacobson's who primarily distributed magazines in the United States and England and had favorable advertising deals in publications such as *Oui*. Jacobson gave him a 50 percent split to advertise and distribute Home Cinema Service tapes using these deals. Joel Jacobson, telephone interview with author, June 18, 2012.

161. Entertainment Video Releasing advertisement, *New York Times*, October 12, 1975, 224. It is important to note that Slade was interested in video *discs*, which, in the early years of home video, were a technology in the running to take over the consumer market. While many systems went into prototype stages, and a few even made it to store shelves (MCA's DiscoVision, most notably), none were ultimately succesful. For more, see McDonald, *Video and DVD Industries*, 42–50.

162. Polskin, "Pornography Unleashed," 37.

163. "Erotic Entertainment," *Videography* (March 1977): 63.

164. "Porn Again," *Videography* (March 1978): 85; "National Video Marketing," *Videography* (June 1978): 25; "International Video Movie Club," *Village Voice*, August 28, 1978, 65; "X Marks the Spot," *Videography* (June 1977): 25.

165. Polskin, "Pornography Unleashed," 37; Magnetic Communications advertisement, *Videography* (June 1977): 62.

166. Astronics Tele-Cine advertisement, *Videography* (December 1977): 51; Astronics Tele-Cine advertisement, *Penthouse* (December 1978): 207; Astronics Tele-Cine advertisement, *Billboard*, November 17, 1979, HV-10.

167. "X Marks the Spot," 25.

168. International Home Video advertisement, *Variety*, May 5, 1979, 247.

169. Mitchell Bros. advertisement, *Videography* (June 1978): 70; Mitchell Bros. advertisement, *Penthouse* (November 1978): 202; Mitchell Bros. advertisement, *Home Video* (March 1981): 64.

170. "Video Porn," *Velvet Talks!* 5 (1979): 25; "Mitchell Bros.," *Videography* (July 1978): 65.

171. "Freeway Video Enterprises," *Videography* (March 1979): 100.

172. See *Videography* magazine between January 1978 and June 1979.

173. "Tuning into the Video-Tape Scene," *Playboy* (April 1979): 203.

174. "Video Tapes & Cable Add Up to Increased Profits for Mature Films," *Film Journal*, May 4, 1981, 20; James Cook, "The X-Rated Economy," *Forbes*, September 18, 1978, 81–92; Lahue, "Get Ready for X-Rated TV!" 29, 89–91; Polskin, "Pornography Unleashed," 35–39; "Small Screen Porno," *NBC Evening News*, New York, aired February 15, 1979.

175. Tony Schwartz, "The TV Pornography Boom," *New York Times*, September 13, 1981, 44, 120, 122, 127, 132, 136.

176. Quality X advertisement, *Screw*, October 10, 1977, 29.

177. David Chute, "Wages of Sin, II," *Film Comment* 22, no. 5 (September 1986): 60; TVX advertisement, *Videography* (June 1979): 40; "TVX Distributors," *Videography* (June 1979): 46; TVX advertisement, *Billboard*, April 14, 1979, 60. For more on Friedman's immense importance to adult film history as an exploitation filmmaker, see Schaefer, *Bold! Daring! Shocking! True!;* and David Chute, "The Wages of Sin," *Film Comment* 22, no. 4 (July 1986): 32–48.

178. TVX Distributors, *TVX Video Cassettes: X-Rated Motion Pictures on Video Tape, 1979 Catalog* (author's collection).

179. Schwartz, "The TV Pornography Boom," 44. Friedman, in late summer 1979, also convinced Lou Sher, owner of Sherpix and the twenty-eight-location Art Theatre Guild adult movie house chain, to sell adult videos in his theater lobbies. By early 1981, more than seventy-five adult theaters sold videotapes in their lobbies, carrying mainstream titles alongside the adult offerings, with the mainstream fare selling at twice the rate of adult. Friedman and Morowitz spoke on the subject at the 1981 Show-West convention in Reno, Nevada, urging theater owners to adopt the model—or, as Morowitz had done, to lease property nearby and set up dedicated video stores. Will Tusher, "Sexplicit Sites Turn Lobbies into Porn Vidcassette Marts; Also Find Non-Erotica Sells," *Variety*, February 4, 1981, 5, 30.

While the video store/movie theater concept never really took off, some smaller chains and independent theater owners did occasionally try the strategy in the mid-1980s after the idea resurfaced at the 1984 ShoWest convention in Las Vegas. With larger, established chains uninterested in having competition directly inside their primary businesses, however, the trend quietly disappeared. Alan Karp, "Selling Video in the Theatre," *Box Office* (June 1984): 9–10, 16–19; Randy Lewis, "Movies: Popcorn and Videos," *Los Angeles Times*, August 30, 1984, 1, 4; Dick Polman, "Pornography Is Moving from the Big Screen to the Living Room," *Philadelphia Inquirer*, August 28, 1985, D1.

180. Quoted in P. D. Rastee, "Video Porn: The Retail Lowdown from Video Shack's Arthur Morowitz," *Film Journal*, March 4, 1983, 41, 49.

181. Sweetheart's Home Video Center advertisement, *Videography* (October 1978): 97.

182. "Conversation with Al Goldstein," *Videography* (January 1979): 44–49.

183. Video Shack advertisement, *Videography* (June 1979): 47; "Videotape Libraries: Pre-Recorded Tape," *Billboard*, May 12, 1979, TAV-16, 17.

184. Tom Cech, "Retail/Distrib Network Shaping," *Billboard*, November 17, 1979, 62, 66; Joel A. Samberg, "The Video Shack: Spotlight on Success," *Video Programs Retailer* (January 1981): 42–45.

185. All these early figures had organized crime associations—another legacy that the industry would have to dissociate itself from in order to move toward capitalist legitimacy. For more, see U.S. Attorney General's Commission on Pornography, *Attorney General's Commission on Pornography: Final Report*, 1037–1212.

186. Tim Connelly, "It's Now Official: Hustler Acquires VCA; Deal Comes a Year after Vivid Pact," *AVN*, May 22, 2003, http://business.avn.com/articles /video/It-s-Now-Official-Hustler-Acquires-VCA-Deal-Comes-a-Year-After-Vivid-Pact-Cementing-Hustler-As-31858.html (accessed March 17, 2013).

187. William M. Alpert, "What's Wrong with This Picture?" *Barron's*, September 21, 1987, 8–9, 46–48.

188. The adult video industry's history with conventions, expos, and trade shows has long been contentious. At the Video Expo at Madison Square Garden in October 1978, for example, multiple adult video distributors purchased floor space to show off their wares—but were exiled by the organizers to "software Siberia," an area in the rear of the hall, where they were not allowed to show any of the material. Describing the incident, *Variety* wrote: "It's understood that some equipment manufacturers complained that the presence of porn distributors lowered the status of the whole exhibit." "Home Video Market Puts Accent on Porn," *Variety*, November 1, 1978, 2.

By January 1980, the Consumer Electronics Show (CES), sponsored by the National Association of Recording Merchandisers and the Electronics Industries Association/Consumer Electronics Group, enforced a strict "no viewing" policy at the annual Las Vegas event. Adult distributors were again segregated from other parts of the convention. Such policies continued through the 1980s, and the adult portion of CES was eventually moved: to the basement of the convention hall in Las Vegas, and to a tent in the parking lot in Chicago. In 1999, *Adult Video News* created the AVN Expo, a separate convention for the adult entertainment industry held annually in Las Vegas at the same time as CES. In 2012, the AVN Expo was moved, for the first time, to a different set of dates, breaking what had been a decades-long association between the two conventions. "Video Expo Draws Video Community to New York; Software Presence Grows," *Videography* (November 1978): 11; Stephen Traiman, "Winter CES Is SRO; Video, 'Super-Fi' Grow," *Billboard*, September 1, 1979, 49–50; Brian Caulfield, "Sex and CES," *Forbes*, January 7, 2009, www.forbes.com/2009/01/07/ces-sex-adult-tech-personal-cx_bc_0107sex.html (accessed March 31, 2013); Amanda Finnegan, "Gadgets and Garters: CES, Porn Convention Sharing Annual Space," *Las Vegas Sun*, January 7, 2010, http://lasvegassun.com/news/2010 /jan/07/gadgets-and-garters/ (accessed March 31, 2013); Nick Wingfield, "Silicon and Silicone Split, as C.E.S. And Adult Entertainment Expo Part Ways," *New York Times*, January 9, 2012, http://gadgetwise.blogs.nytimes

.com/2012/01/09/silicon-and-silicone-split-as-c-e-s-and-porn-show-part-ways/?_r=0 (accessed March 31, 2013).

189. David Rensin, "Tuning in to Channel Sex," *Playboy* (November 1981): 220–21.

190. Quoted in Jennings, *Skinflicks,* 157.

191. "Piracy and Porno," *Videography* (April 1979): 77.

192. Quoted in David Chute, "Tumescent Market for One-Armed Videophiles," *Film Comment* 17, no. 5 (September–October 1981): 66.

193. Ibid.

194. Connelly, "It's Now Official"; Rensin, "Tuning in to Channel Sex," 224; Gregg Kilday, "Inside Marilyn Chambers," *Home Video* 2, no. 1 (January 1981): 24–27; Frank Segers, "Porno Pushers' Big Promotion at Chi Show," *Variety,* June 10, 1981, 1, 84.

195. Jennings, who uses a pseudonym, is a 1970 UCLA film school graduate who recorded his experiences working in the adult film industry on audiotape, planning from the beginning to write a book on the topic (Jennings, *Skinflicks*). David Jennings, email to author, February 10, 2012.

196. Love TV advertisement, *Videography* (March 1979): 101; "Hustling Home Video," *Videography* (March 1979): 99.

197. Love TV advertisement, *Videography* (March 1979): 101.

198. Kalton C. Lahue, "Video Porn," *Velvet Talks!* 6 (1979): 12–13.

199. Bill Margold, telephone interview with author, March 30, 2013. For more on Margold, former director of the Free Speech Coalition, cofounder of Fans of X-Rated Entertainment (FOXE) and Protecting Adult Welfare (PAW), and elder statesman of the adult film industry, see Ian Jane, "God Created Man, William Margold Created Himself: An Interview with the Renaissance Man of Porn," April 25, 2011, www.rockshockpop.com/forums/content.php?1382-God-Created-Man-William-Margold-Created-Himself (accessed March 1, 2016); Robert J. Stoller, *Porn: Myths for the Twentieth Century* (New Haven, CT: Yale University Press, 1991); and Robert J. Stoller and I.S. Levine, *Coming Attractions: The Making of an X-Rated Video* (New Haven, CT: Yale University Press, 2003).

200. Seka (born Dorothea Hundley) became arguably the first adult video star. After starting as a clerk in an adult video store in Virginia, she met Bill Margold at the Sunset International modeling agency in Los Angeles in May 1978, where, according to Margold, "she dared me to make her famous" (Margold, telephone interview with author, March 30, 2013). After receiving top billing in her first film, *Dracula Sucks* (1978, dir. Phil Marshak, screenplay by Margold), she appeared regularly in Caballero's *Swedish Erotica* loop series, eventually starred in hundreds of loops and features, and appeared often in adult magazines. She was also the subject of the documentary *Desperately Seeking Seka* (2002, dirs. Christian Hallman and Magnus Paulsson) and in 2013 released an autobiography. Margold, telephone interview with author, March 30, 2013; "Seka," *Video X* (August 1980): 12–13; "Daughter of the Video Revolution," *Playboy* (October 1984): 49; "Seka, Raising Penises for Three Generations," *Vice* (July 2012), www.vice.com/read/seka-raising-penises-for-

three-generations (accessed March 18, 2013); Michelle Craven, "Seka: Hollywood's Hottest New Sex Star Sells Passion—with Pride," *Cheri* (March 1980): 57–64; Jill C. Nelson, *Golden Goddesses: 25 Legendary Women of Classic Erotic Cinema, 1968–1985* (Duncan, OK: BearManor Media, 2012), 534–63; Seka, with Kerry Zukus, *Inside Seka: The Platinum Princess of Porn* (Duncan, OK: BearManor Media, 2013).

201. Preston Johns, "Inside 'Inside Hollywood,'" *Adam* (September 1980): 22, 84.

202. Jared Rutter, "Video Interview: Alan Colberg," *Adam* (September 1980): 24.

203. Colberg also shot *Nanci Blue* and *Bad Girl* directly on video in 1979. These are frequently credited as Scorpio productions, but Margold confirmed to me they were not. Margold, telephone interview with author, March 30, 2013.

204. "Home Video Market Puts Accent on Porn," 2.

205. Quoted in "Electronics Show Gives Glimpse of Show Biz Technology of Future," *Variety*, January 10, 1979, 116.

206. Chute, "Tumescent Market for One-Armed Videophiles," 68.

207. Quoted in Dick Polman, "Store Owners Divided on Adult Tapes," *Philadelphia Inquirer*, September 7, 1986, J1.

208. John Johnson, "Sex-Film Maker Pleads Guilty to Tax Evasion," *Los Angeles Times*, August 23, 1991, 3.

209. John Johnson, "Adult Movies Filmed at the YWCA Building," *Los Angeles Times*, December 23, 1989, 3.

210. Quoted in Ben Pesta, "X-Rated Video: Will It Make Adult Theaters and Men's Magazines Obsolete?" *Hustler* (October 1984): 38.

211. Quoted in Chute, "Tumescent Market for One-Armed Videophiles," 68.

2. ADULT VIDEO NEWS

1. *Video-X* (May 1983): 68–77.

2. For more on the history and importance of *Playboy*, see Elizabeth Fraterrigo, *Playboy and the Making of the Good Life in Modern America* (New York: Oxford University Press, 2011); and Russell Miller, *Bunny: The Real Story of Playboy* (New York: Henry Holt, 1985).

3. Rick Altman, *Silent Film Sound* (New York: Columbia University Press, 2004), 17.

4. Andrew Ross, *No Respect: Intellectuals & Popular Culture* (New York: Routledge, 1989), 173.

5. Information taken from the AVN Media Network website, avn.com (accessed March 24, 2013).

6. Pierre Bourdieu, *Distinction: A Social Critique of the Judgment of Taste*, trans. Richard Nice (1979; Cambridge, MA: Harvard University Press, 1984), 466.

7. Ibid., 7.

8. Henry Schipper, "Filthy Lucre: A Tour of America's Most Profitable Frontier," *Mother Jones* (April 1980): 32.

9. Joshua M. Greenberg, *From Betamax to Blockbuster: Video Stores and the Invention of Movies on Video* (Cambridge, MA: MIT Press, 2008), 23–40.

10. TVX advertisement, *Video Swapper* (January 1982): 59.

11. TGA Video advertisement, *Video Swapper* (January 1982): back cover.

12. Adult video distributors in the early days advertised wherever they thought home video consumers might look, as Joel Jacobson (whose history is detailed in chapter 1) told me, noting that *Popular Science, Popular Photography,* and *Popular Mechanics* were among the most common early venues for ads. VCX, another early adult video distributor, placed its first advertisements in spring 1978 in magazines such as *Merchandiser, Dealerscope,* and *Electronics Wholesaler. Videography* magazine, a technical journal devoted mostly to the technical side of the burgeoning video production industry, was also a fixture, as is discussed in this chapter. Joel Jacobson, telephone interview with author, June 18, 2012; David Jennings, *Skinflicks: The Inside Story of the X-Rated Video Industry* (Bloomington, IN: 1st Books, 2000), 79.

13. Ricky Jones, "Interview with . . . Vanessa Del Rio," *Adult Video Swapper* (December 1983): 6–7.

14. Baker Video advertisement, *Adult Video Swapper* (December 1983): 17.

15. When *Adult Video Swapper* folded in February 1984, publisher Gary Mancuso gave his eleven hundred subscribers to *AVN*, which promptly extended them all one-year subscriptions. *AVN*, always quick to spot an opportunity, was eager for the subscribers' list—invaluable data in the early days of adult video, when tracking such specifics was difficult. See Paul Fishbein, "Editorial for Our Readers," *AVN* (February–March 1984): 12.

16. *Adam Film World* (July 1980): 4.

17. Ibid.

18. *Adam Film World* (July 1980): 52.

19. "Rising Stars," *Cinema-X* (February 1980): 69.

20. "Open Call," *Cinema-X* (February 1980): 55.

21. "Out of the Can: *Intimate Desires,*" *Cinema-X* (February 1980): 82.

22. "Private Stock," *Cinema-X* (February 1980): 38.

23. Cinema Tech advertisement, *Cinema-X* (February 1980): 18–19. While this is called the Lesllie Bovee collection, Bovee typically spelled her first name Leslee.

24. "Video Corner," *Cinema-X* (February 1980): 28.

25. "The Source!" *Video X* (March 1980): 5.

26. *Velvet's Erotic Film Guide* (January 1983): 6–7.

27. Ibid., 7.

28. Ibid., 91–95.

29. *Adult Cinema Review* (October 1983). For an inside perspective on the process of creating adult magazine letters and responses, see Robert Rosen, *Beaver Street: A History of Modern Pornography* (London: Headpress, 2010), 49.

30. *Adult Cinema Review* (October 1983): 44.

31. Lou Meyers, "Foreplay," *Video-X* (May 1983): 26.

32. "The Softer Side of Ambrosia," *Video-X* (May 1983): 45.

33. Quoted in Lawrence Cohn, "Pornmakers Surface in the Mainstream," *Variety*, March 9, 1988, 26.

34. Greenberg, *From Betamax to Blockbuster*, 6.

35. "King Smut," *Philadelphia Magazine* (November 2004), www.phillymag .com/articles/king-smut (accessed November 6, 2012).

36. Paul Cahill, "The United States and Canada," in *Video World-Wide: An International Study*, ed. Manuel Alvarado (Paris: UNESCO, 1988), 127–28.

37. Ibid., 132.

38. Chuck Kleinhans, "The Change from Film to Video Pornography: Implications for Analysis," in *Pornography: Film and Culture*, ed. Peter Lehman (New Brunswick, NJ: Rutgers University Press, 2006), 154–67.

39. Jonathan Coopersmith, "Pornography, Videotape, and the Internet," *IEEE Technology and Society Magazine* (Spring 2000): 27.

40. Cited in Howard Polskin, "Pornography Unleashed," *Panorama* (July 1980): 35.

41. Keith Justice, *Adult Video Index '84* (Jefferson, NC: McFarland, 1984), 1; Bob Rimmer, *Bob Rimmer's Continuously Up-Dated Adult Video Tape Guide* (Quincy, MA: Challenge Press, 1986), 1.

42. Kleinhans, "The Change from Film to Video Pornography," 154–67.

43. Paul Fishbein, "The Five-Year Roller Coaster," *AVN* (February 1988): 5.

44. Paul Fishbein, transcript of telephone interview with Josh Greenberg, April 15, 2003.

45. Anthony Layser, "Porn Supremacy," *Philadelphia Weekly*, January 9, 2008, www.philadelphiaweekly.com/arts-and-culture/porn_supremacy -38463929.html (accessed November 7, 2012).

46. Fishbein, interview with Greenberg, April 15, 2003; "King Smut."

47. Clyde DeWitt, "Adult Video Newsmaker," *AVN* 28, no. 3 (March 2012): 38–39.

48. Gene Ross, "Adult Video News: The First Five Years," *AVN* (February 1988): 46.

49. Paul Fishbein and I. L. Slifkin, "I Want One with a Story!" *AVN* (March 1983): 5.

50. Begelman quoted in Justin Wyatt, "The Stigma of X: Adult Cinema and the Institution of the MPAA Ratings System," in *Controlling Hollywood: Censorship and Regulation in the Studio Era*, ed. Matthew Bernstein (Piscataway, NJ: Rutgers University Press, 1999), 238–63, quote 257.

51. R. Smith, "Bad Boxes," *AVN* (March 1985): 3.

52. Jack Bailey, "Store Help," *AVN* (March 1985): 3.

53. Altman, *Silent Film Sound*, 18.

54. Mark Kernes, "Shot-on-Video: The Future Is Now," *AVN* (June 1986): 16.

55. Quoted in "Femme-X Picks Films for Stores," *Adult Video News Confidential* (September 1985): 2.

56. Alex Thomas, "The Marketing of Three Major Titles," *Adult Video News Confidential* (June 1985): 18.

57. Darla Hewitt, "Darla's Eye View," *AVN* (November 1984): 23.

58. Fishbein, interview with Greenberg, April 15, 2003.

59. Quoted in *"Angel Cash* to Retail for $39.95," *AVN* (March 1983): 6.

60. *The Erotic World of Angel Cash* advertisement, *AVN* (July 1983): 5.

61. Cabarello Video advertisement, *AVN* (February–March 1984).

62. VCA Pictures advertisement, *AVN* (January 1985): 5; Jim Holliday, "The Changing Face of Adult Video," *AVN* (March 1987): 88.

63. Starlet Video advertisement, *AVN* (January 1985): 8.

64. Fishbein, "Editorial for Our Readers," *AVN* (February–March 1984): 4.

65. Cahill, "The United States and Canada," 128.

66. Quoted in Ben Pesta, "X Rated Video: Will It Make Adult Theaters and Men's Magazines Obsolete?" *Hustler* (October 1984): 52.

67. Nicholas D. Kristof, "X-Rated Industry in a Slump," *New York Times*, October 5, 1986, 6.

68. Pesta, "X Rated Video," 54.

69. "Disco Sex Action," *Velvet Talks!* 4 (1979): centerfold.

70. "The Partner Television Show," *Partner* (June 1979): 79.

71. "I Fucked Five Men! An Uninspiring Sexual History," *Partner* (June 1979): 80–81; "New York Couple Advertises: 'We Want a Girl with Big Boobs to Swing with Us,'" *Partner* (June 1979): 82, 94, 96; "The Mad Professor & His Loco-Dildo: Turning a Blueprint into a Blue Reality," *Partner* (June 1979): 83, 94; "Squashed Tits & Stinky Pits: Amateur Grappling Comes of Age in Connecticut," *Partner* (June 1979): 84–85, 94.

72. *The Partner Television Show* advertisement, *Partner* (June 1981): 82.

73. Stuart Karl, after realizing there might be a market for home videos other than Hollywood films in the early 1980s, began producing home-and-self-improvement tapes under the Karl Home Video banner, as well as creating *Video Store* magazine. After seeing the success of *Jane Fonda's Workout Book,* which went to number 1 on the *New York Times* bestseller list in 1981, he approached Fonda to shoot what became its wildly successful companion video. Karl also tried (unsuccessfully) to partner with David Jennings to market and distribute the Love TV tapes, described in chapter 1, in the pages of *Video Store.* Jane Fonda, *Jane Fonda's Workout Book* (New York: Simon & Schuster, 1981); *Jane Fonda's Workout* (1981, dir. Sid Galanty, RCA Video Productions, VHS); Jane Fonda, "30th Anniversary of My First Workout Video," April 24, 2012, www.janefonda.com/30th-anniversary-of-my-first-workout-video/ (accessed March 26, 2013); Marc Mancini, "Video S.I.P.," *Film Comment* 23, no. 1 (January 1987): 44–49; Richard W. Stevenson, "From Fonda and Hart to Flops and Hot Water," *New York Times*, February 7, 1988, F11; Jennings, *Skinflicks*, 130–38.

74. *New Look: The First Video Cassette Magazine for Men* (1981, International Videopresse, VHS); "Blay Back with Spicy Vidcassette 'Magazine,'" *Billboard,* January 23, 1982, 45; "'Big Time' Lures Blay," *Dealerscope II* (July 1982): 37.

75. *Men's Video Magazine* (1984, VCX, VHS).

76. *Adult Video News Video Magazine: Volume 1* (1986, Adult Video News, Betamax); *Adult Video News Video Magazine* advertisement, *Adult Video News Confidential* (July 1986): 17.

77. Jim Holliday, "Truths, Misconceptions, and Observations," *AVN* (October 1986): 4, 50.

78. "King Smut."

79. Ibid.

80. *Adult Video News Confidential* advertisement, *AVN* (February 1985): 38.

81. "How to Make Your Adult Customers Comfortable," *Adult Video News Confidential* (May 1986): 10.

82. In his wide-ranging tour of remaining video rental stores, Dan Herbert frequently encountered just such indifference, in which owners carried adult titles as a business decision rather than as a political statement or because of a personal investment (or interest) in pornography. *Videoland: Movie Culture at the American Video Store* (Berkeley: University of California Press, 2014), 121–52.

83. Michael Matza, "The Black and White of Paul Fishbein," *Philadelphia Inquirer*, September 27, 1989, F1, http://articles.philly.com/1989–09–27/news /26104499_1_adult-magazines-adult-tapes-obscene-video (accessed March 14, 2016).

84. Clay Calvert and Robert Richards, "Law and Economics of the Adult Entertainment Industry: An Inside View from the Industry's Leading Trade Publisher," *University of Denver Sports & Entertainment Law Journal* 4 (Spring 2008): 39.

85. Rod Hopkins, "Industrial-Strength Jenna," *Sexposé* (December 1996): 30–37.

86. "Going Undercover: Lethal Affairs with Chasey Lain and Janine," *Sexposé* (December 1996): 67–73.

87. Calvert and Richards, "Law and Economics of the Adult Entertainment Industry," 51.

88. *Video View* (June 1993): 20–21, 60–61.

89. Red Light District advertisement, *AVN* (September 2009): 226.

90. Kernes, "Shot-on-Video," 16.

91. "King Smut."

92. Ibid.

93. Ibid.; DeWitt, "Adult Video Newsmaker"; "Paul Fishbein Announces Full-Time Departure from AVN," June 1, 2011, https://xxxwasteland.wordpress .com/2011/06/21/paul-fishbein-announces-full-time-departure-from-avn / (accessed November 21, 2012).

94. "New Television Network Launched to Provide Consumer News, Entertainment, Documentaries & Talk Shows about the Adult Industry," March 20, 2013, www.prweb.com/releases/2013/3/prweb10543949.htm (accessed July 19, 2014).

95. Paul Fishbein and Barry R. Rosenblatt, "Editorial to Our Readers," *AVN* (February 1986): 3.

96. Quoted in "King Smut."

97. The Adult Film Association of America (AFAA) started handing out its Erotic Film Awards in 1977, and the Critics Adult Film Association (CAFA)

followed suit in 1981. Both (along with many other organizations) served pre-dictable legitimizing and celebratory functions for the industry. Film festivals have also served this function, with particular political and culture importance in the early 1970s, when pornography was a lightning rod, as Elena Gorfinkel has shown. "Wet Dreams: Erotic Film Festivals of the Early 1970s and the Utopian Sexual Public Sphere," in *Sex Scenes: Media and the Sexual Revolution,* ed. Eric Schaefer (Durham, NC: Duke University Press, 2014), 126–50.

3. THE MEANS OF PRODUCTION

1. "Charting the Adult Video Market," *AVN* (August–September 1986): 7.

2. Jean Callahan, "Women and Pornography: Combat in the Video Zone," *American Film* 7, no. 5 (March 1982): 63. Such arguments are often even fur-ther complicated by the fact that female directors were often (1) mere fronts for the men behind the scenes; (2) pseudonyms for male directors (as was the case in a handful of Candida Royalle's films in which she appears as a per-former); or (3) given such positions simply to sell the public on the idea of "female sensibility."

The most obvious example of a front was Gail Palmer, who was credited as the director on numerous films, including *The Erotic Adventures of Candy* (1979), but was long suspected of (and later admitted to) being a director in name only; the actual director was notorious Michigan strip club owner, adult theater operator, and loop kingpin Harry Mohney. Palmer, who was often included in lists of "women behind the camera" and cited as a feminist success story, is an ideal example of the ways in which the adult film industry, fre-quently seeking to garner larger and more diverse audiences, will market wom-en's roles in ways not matching the lived realities. Such tactics also further obscure the key roles many women did play during this time. See "Girls of the Big 10," *Playboy* (September 1977): 146–47; "Gail Palmer," *Playboy* (November 1978): 46; Peter Sagal, *The Book of Vice: Very Naughty Things (and How to Do Them)* (New York: HarperCollins, 2007), 185–246; Gail Palmer's Pleasure Products advertisement, *Penthouse* (September 1979): 275; "Porn Producer Projects a Girl-Next-Door Image," *Miami News,* December 14, 1976, 1; "X-Rated Director Gail Palmer Shows Us Her Cinema X," *Cheri* (January 1979): 8–9; Gail Palmer, "Gail Palmer: X-Rated Film Director," *Cheri* (January 1979): 30, 98; and Jill C. Nelson, *Golden Goddesses: 25 Legendary Women of Classic Erotic Cinema, 1968–1985* (Duncan, OK: BearManor Media, 2012), 925–27.

3. Quoted in Jeffrey Wells, "Sex in the Home (Where It Belongs)," *Film Journal* 85, no. 15 (June 28, 1982): 22.

4. Ginger Lynn did not respond to my interview requests, and representa-tives of Vivid Video did not authorize the use of images associated with her or the company in this book. Candida Royalle declined to participate, citing ill health from her long struggle with ovarian cancer. She died as this chapter was in its final revisions. See Sam Roberts, "Candida Royalle, Who Made Erotic

Films for Women, Dies at 64," *New York Times*, September 10, 2015, www
.nytimes.com/2015/09/11/movies/candida-royalle-maker-of-x-rated-films-
dies-at-64.html?_r=0 (accessed September 10, 2015).

5. Candida Royalle, *How to Tell a Naked Man What to Do: Sex Advice from
a Woman Who Knows* (New York: Fireside, 2004), xiii.

6. "Love 'Em & Shoot 'Em," *Playboy* (April 1987): 136.

7. Allen Salkin, "The XXX Men," *Details* (June 2001): 113–14.

8. Ralph Frammolino and P. J. Huffstutter, "The Actress, the Producer, and
Their Porn Revolution," *Los Angeles Times Magazine*, January 6, 2002, 10.

9. Salkin, "The XXX Men," 113.

10. AVC catalogue, 1980 (author's collection).

11. This strategy carried on the tradition of similar practices stretching
back to the pre-hardcore era of exploitation films that traveled an exhibition
circuit around the United States, relying heavily upon salacious (and false)
advertising and myriad ballyhoo tactics to lure in unsuspecting rubes. For a
comprehensive history, see Eric Schaefer, *Bold! Daring! Shocking! True!
A History of Exploitation Films, 1919–1959* (Durham, NC: Duke University
Press, 1999).

12. Frammolino and Huffstutter, "The Actress, the Producer, and Their Porn
Revolution," 10.

13. Jared Rutter, "The Man Who Changed Adult," *AVN* (September 2009):
78.

14. Twenty years older than Hirsch, the soft-spoken and rarely interviewed
James bears a biography worthy of fiction. The son of a coal miner and nurse
from Blaengarw, Wales, James quit school at fifteen and followed his father
(who would die of black lung disease) into the mines. At seventeen, he joined
the British army, where he spent most of the next fourteen years as part of an
antiterrorism unit. In 1979, he landed (as an illegal alien) in Los Angeles, working in the underground economy until eventually finding a job selling tickets
at an adult movie theater. Salkin, "The XXX Men," 114.

15. Paul Karon, "Vivid Aims Its Appeal at John Q. Public," *Variety*, March
9, 1998, 1; Salkin, "The XXX Men," 114.

16. Frammolino and Huffstutter, "The Actress, the Producer, and Their Porn
Revolution," 10.

17. Rutter, "The Man Who Changed Adult," 78.

18. Vivid Video would have failed had it chosen Traci Lords, given the company's gamble to build the entire company's foundation on a single performer.
In a massive understatement, Hirsch later noted as much: "Fortunately, we
chose the right one" (quoted in ibid.).

In 1984, at age fifteen, Lords (who was born Nora Kuzma) used a stolen
birth certificate (with the name Kristie Nussman) to obtain an official California
identification card and U.S. passport, and she convinced agent Jim South (along
with the many producers and magazine publishers she later worked for) that
she was of legal age. In May 1986, federal authorities were notified that she was
underage and arrested her. Also arrested were South and producers Ronald
Kantor and Rupert Macnee, who had made *Those Young Girls* (1984, dir. Miles

Kidder) with Lords. South eventually pleaded guilty to one count of sexual exploitation of a minor. Kantor's and Macnee's indictments were dismissed when they were able to convince the court that Lords's identification documents "proved" (albeit falsely) that she was of legal age to work. Lords was not charged, and Los Angeles District Attorney Ira Reiner said, "The thrust of the investigation is directed toward the pornographic film industry that exploited her." Ronald Soble, "Sex Film Star Not Facing Charges, Reiner Says," *Los Angeles Times,* July 19, 1986, 1; "Man Pleads Guilty in Traci Lords Porn Case," *Los Angeles Times,* April 1, 1987, 26; Kim Murphy, "Porno Case Is Dismissed," *Los Angeles Times,* May 4, 1989, 1.

After Lords's arrest, an overnight purge of her films took place in video stores across the country, a significant undertaking given that she had appeared in more than one hundred films. Some (such as *New Wave Hookers*) were reedited by producers to remove her scenes, while others (such as *Talk Dirty to Me III*) were reshot with other actresses. Lords sold the video rights to *Traci I Love You* (1987, dir. Jean Charles) to Caballero; made after her eighteenth birthday, shortly after her arrest, it remains her only title legally available in the United States. The rest of her films are classified as child pornography. Dave Palermo, "Sex Films Pulled; Star Allegedly Too Young," *Los Angeles* Times, July 18, 1986, 1; Terry Atkinson, "Mixed News in Adult Video Market," *Los Angeles Times,* June 26, 1987, 20.

These events caused major turmoil in the adult industry, and many performers, producers, crew, and industry veterans continue to blame Lords for causing the scandal, suggesting that she was working with the authorities to engineer the arrests to create publicity for the mainstream career she was hoping to obtain. Lords has denied those allegations. For more, see John Paone, "The Traci Lords Saga: Still Not Many Answers," *AVN* (September 1986): 18, 20, 51. Lords herself writes (very briefly) on the subject in her autobiography, *Underneath It All* (New York: Harper, 2004).

19. For more on Lynn's early life, see Nelson, *Golden Goddesses,* 698–742.

20. Legs McNeil, Jennifer Osborne, and Peter Pavia, *The Other Hollywood: The Uncensored Oral History of the Porn Film Industry* (New York: Regan Books, 2005), 350–51; Suze Randall, "Queens of the X-Rated Cinema: Ginger," *Penthouse* (March 1985): 125–33.

21. McNeil, Osborne, and Pavia, *The Other Hollywood,* 365–66.

22. Lynn shot at least six loops in November 1983. Four were for director Michael Carpenter: *Hot Box,* with Greg Derek (Golden Girls 172); *Peach Pie,* with Ron Jeremy (Golden Girls 174); *She Can't Help It,* with Greg Rome (Golden Girls 179); and *It Isn't the Money,* with Marc Wallice (Golden Girls 192). She also shot one loop for Noel Bloom's Caballero Control Corporation, *She's Been a Bad Girl* (Swedish Erotica 0545). Details of the sixth loop remain a mystery, although both Lynn and performer Tom Byron have described its production. McNeil, Osborne, and Pavia, *The Other Hollywood,* 366–67; Ginger Lynn, "Headitorial," *For Adults Only* (July 1984): 3; Frammolino and Huffstutter, "The Actress, the Producer, and Their Porn Revolution," 10.

23. Frammolino and Huffstutter, "The Actress, the Producer, and Their Porn Revolution," 10; Sheila Johnston, "Sleeping Your Way to the Top," *The Independent*, December 3, 1993, 27.

24. Fishbein, "Interview: Ginger Lynn," *AVN* (February 1985): 30, 34, 36; Gene Ross, "Ginger: I Resent Being Called a Vivid Girl," October 20, 2004, www.adultfyi.com/read.aspx?ID=6499 (accessed October 8, 2012). Lynn talks at some length about her career and life in an 2014 episode of *The Rialto Report* podcast: "Ginger Lynn: The Girl Next Door," November 2, 2014, www.therial-toreport.com/2014/11/02/ginger-lynn-the-girl-next-door-podcast-43 / (accessed January 5, 2014).

25. Richard Dyer, *Heavenly Bodies: Film Stars and Society* (New York: St. Martin's Press, 1986), 5.

26. Carrie Pitzulo, *Bachelors and Bunnies: The Sexual Politics of Playboy* (Chicago: University of Chicago Press, 2011), 40–41.

27. Dyer, *Heavenly Bodies*, 19–66.

28. Fishbein, "Interview: Ginger Lynn," 30, 34.

29. Frammolino and Huffstutter, "The Actress, the Producer, and Their Porn Revolution," 10.

30. Nicola Simpson, "Coming Attractions: A Comparative History of the Hollywood Studio System and the Porn Business," *Historical Journal of Film, Radio, and Television* 24, no. 4 (2004): 646.

31. Salkin, "The XXX Men," 114.

32. Penny Antine, interview with author, April 11, 2014; Nelson, *Golden Goddesses*, 830–61; "Penny Antine: The Accidental Pornographer," *Alicubi* (November 2000), www.alicubi.com/articles/penny_01.html (accessed February 10, 2012).

33. "Penny Antine."

34. Antine, interview with author, April 11, 2014. Later Lynn acknowledged the impact her films had had on female viewers: "Video made it so anyone could watch a movie. I get so many letters from women." Quoted in John Paone, "Ginger," *AVN* (April 1987): 17.

35. Frammolino and Huffstutter, "The Actress, the Producer, and Their Porn Revolution," 10.

36. Quoted in Rutter, "The Man Who Changed Adult," 79.

37. For example, *AVN*'s review of *Ginger* called it a "run-of-the-mill sexvid recommended only for those not burned out on Lynn's sexual antics." Alvin Zbryski, "Ginger," *AVN* (February 1985): 27.

38. Vivid did little to emphasize that Antine wrote the Ginger productions, which could have been an effective marketing strategy. However, as was (and is) typical of the adult film industry, writers rarely received much attention or publicity and were certainly not part of marketing strategies.

39. Jared Rutter, "A Day with Ginger," *Adam* (September 1986): 26–31.

40. Rutter, "The Man Who Changed Adult," 78.

41. Ibid., 89–90; Paul Keegan, "Prime-Time Porn Borrowing Tactics from the Old Hollywood Studios," June 1, 2003, http://money.cnn.com/magazines/business2/business2_archive/2003/06/01/343376/ (accessed March 10, 2013).

42. The strategy worked: Vivid, Hirsch, and the performers were featured in *Details, Los Angeles Magazine, Time, Variety, Bikini, Forbes,* the *Wall Street Journal,* the *Economist, Vanity Fair,* and other places. See Salkin, "The XXX Men," 110–17; Steve Appleford, "The Money Shot," *Bikini* (April 1999): 86–91; Karon, "Vivid Aims Its Appeal at John Q. Public," 1; Joel Stein, "Porn Goes Mainstream," *Time,* June 24, 2001, http://content.time.com/time/magazine /article/0,9171,139893,00.html (accessed March 13, 2012); Brett Pulley, "The Porn King," *Forbes,* March 7, 2005, www.forbes.com/2005/03/07/cz _bp_0307vivid.html (accessed March 10, 2013); "The Actresses," *Vanity Fair* (April 2003): 394–95; "Branded Flesh," *Economist,* August 14, 1999, www .economist.com/node/232069; "Vivid Imagination," *Economist,* November 19, 1998, www.economist.com/node/17667 (accessed March 30, 2013); and Dave Gardetta, "The Lust Tycoons," *Los Angeles Magazine* (December 1998): 140–45, 184–85.

The Vivid Girls have also become brand accessories: the company cross-markets them in various campaigns featuring FreshJive Clothing, Control Skateboards, Pony Shoes, and Sims Snowboards, among other products. See FreshJive advertisement, *Spy* (June 1997): 4–5; "Control Skateboards' Vivid Series," October 15, 2008, www.tackyworld.com/skateboard/article/?id=101370 (accessed March 30, 2013); T.L. Stanley, "'Surreal Life': Porn Crosses over to Media Mainstream," *Advertising Age,* January 26, 2004, http://adage.com /article/news/surreal-life-porn-crosses-media-mainstream/97495/ (accessed January 12, 2014); and "Vivid Girls on Snowboard, Jenna Hosts Party," January 29, 2003, www.ainews.com/Archives/Story4411.phtml (accessed March 30, 2013).

43. Quoted in Rutter, "The Man Who Changed Adult," 90; see also Colin Rowntree, "Penetrating into the Mainstream," March 21, 2013, www.xbiz.com /articles/160764 xbiz.com (accessed March 30, 2013).

44. "The Actresses," 394–95.

45. Keegan, "Prime-Time Porn"; Pulley, "The Porn King."

46. "Steve Hirsch to Receive First Visionary Award at AVN Awards," November 10, 2011, http://business.avn.com/articles/video/Steve-Hirsch-to-Receive-First-Visionary-Award-at-AVN-Awards-454298.html (accessed March 20, 2013).

47. P.J. Huffstutter, "U.S. Indicts Porn Sellers, Vowing Extensive Attack," *Los Angeles Times,* August 8, 2003, A1.

48. Paone, "Ginger," 16.

49. In 1991, the IRS charged Lynn, along with other adult performers including her frequent costar Tom Byron, with tax evasion. She has long maintained that the IRS investigation was retribution for her refusal to testify for the government in the Traci Lords investigation. In May 1991, Lynn was convicted of one count of tax evasion and sentenced to probation; in early 1992, she failed a drug test, violating the terms of her probation, and was incarcerated on the original charge. Alan Mercer, "The Colorful Story of Ginger Lynn," May 9, 2009, http://amprofile.blogspot.com/2009/05/colorful-story-of-ginger-lynn .html (accessed March 8, 2016); Scott Collins, "Ginger Lynn Shares Her Past

with Charlie Sheen," March 8, 2011, http://articles.latimes.com/2011/mar/08/entertainment/la-et-ginger-lynn-auction-20110308 (accessed March 8, 2016).

50. *AVN*, for example, listed Lynn at number 7 in its "Top 50 Porn Stars" issue, describing her as the "one star" who stood out from the video era and the "quintessential 'girl next door,' a beauty whose sexuality smoldered just below the surface until it exploded on screen." "Impact: The 50 Top Porn Stars of All Time," *AVN* (January 2002): 48, 50.

51. Paone, "Ginger," 16.

52. Quoted in Ross, "Ginger: I Resent Being Called a Vivid Girl."

53. For a more complete history of San Francisco's importance to pornography history, see Herbert Asbury, *The Barbary Coast: An Informal History of the San Francisco Underworld* (New York: Alfred A. Knopf, 1933); Arthur Berger, "Varieties of Topless Experience," *Journal of Popular Culture* 4, no. 2 (Fall 1970): 419–24; Andrew Blake, *Topless* (New York: Belmont, 1969); Alan Levy, "A Morality Play in Three Acts," *Life*, March 11, 1966, 79–87; Bob Ellison, "Topless Craze in S.F—It's a Jungle of Sweaty Gyrations," *Los Angeles Times*, September 8, 1965, C11; Daryl E. Lembke, "Nudity, Noise Pay Off in Bay Area Night Clubs," *Los Angeles Times*, February 14, 1965, G5; Eric Schaefer and Eithne Johnson, "Open Your Golden Gates: Sexually Oriented Film and Video," in *Radical Light: Alternative Film and Video in the San Francisco Bay Area, 1945–2000*, eds. Steven Anker, Kathy Geritz, and Steve Seid, 191–93 (Berkeley: University of California Press, 2010); and John Bryan, "Gold in the Hills, Sex in the Streets: A 125 Year Romp through San Francisco's Bawdy Past," *Berkeley Barb*, February 4–18, 1977, 6–7.

54. Kevin Heffernan, "Seen as a Business: Adult Film's Historical Framework and Foundations," in *New Views on Pornography: Sexuality, Politics, and the Law*, eds. Lynn Comella and Shira Tarrant, 37–56 (Santa Barbara, CA: Prager, 2015).

Like many adult performers, Royalle did not use her birth surname (which is occasionally spelled "Vitala") during her performance career. She addressed this topic in the context of her identity at various times. For example, she noted that she "never dated men who were looking to date Candida Royalle" and spoke about the duality related to adult film work. "Before I enter a social situation, I ask myself: am I Candida or Candice? I make up my mind. If I decide I'm Candice, which is usually [at] private parties and intimate gatherings, don't you dare start asking me about my career! I spend about a quarter of my professional life giving interviews, so I need to protect my private time." Candida Royalle, "The Early Days . . . How Did a Nice Girl Like You . . . ?" n.d., http://candidaroyalle.com/blog/faqs/candidaroyalle.com (accessed September 7, 2012); see also Jill Nagle, "First Ladies of Feminist Porn: A Conversation with Candida Royalle and Debi Sundahl," in *Whores and Other Feminists*, ed. Jill Nagle, 158 (New York: Routledge, 1997).

55. Royalle, *How to Tell a Naked Man What to Do*, ix; "Sexy Spreads: Candida Royalle," August 6, 2003, www.eros-guide.com/articles/2003-08-26/candida (accessed September 1, 2008); "3 Naked Ladies with Candida Royalle: Plan B," December 9, 2009, http://onlythejodi.com/2014/08/3nl-candida-

royalle/ (accessed September 3, 2012); "Cumming of Age," *High Society* (May 1980): 35.

56. Erik Hedegaard, "Sexual Healing," *Details* (September 1991): 140.

57. Quoted in Olivia de Court, "Candida Royalle," n.d., www.girlphoria.com /wie/candida.html (accessed August 1, 2012).

58. Royalle, *How to Tell a Naked Man What to Do*, x.

59. J.D. Bauchery, "20 Questions with Candida Royalle," August 10, 2009, www.hotmoviesforher.com/sex-blog/lesbian-blog/20-questions-with-candida-royalle-part-1/ (accessed September 3, 2012). Isley, who performed under a variety of pseudonyms, including Danny Spats, Fred James, Spender Travis, and Spencer Davis, appeared with Royalle in *Hot & Saucy Pizza Girls* (1977, dir. Bob Chinn). Marianne Macy, *Working Sex: An Odyssey into Our Cultural Underworld* (New York: Carroll & Graf, 1996), 51; Nelson, *Golden Goddesses*, 236, 254.

60. Royalle, *How to Tell a Naked Man What to Do*, x.

61. Ibid., xi.

62. Candida Royalle, "Vertical Smiles and Cum-Soaked Aisles: Confessions of a Porn Queen," *High Times* (July 1982): 40–41. Royalle appeared in the loops *School's Out* (Showgirl 205), *Game of Lust* (Debauchery Films 2), *Through the Looking Glass* (Swedish Erotica 182), *The Handyman* (Swedish Erotica 184), *Bikini Ball* (Pleasure Productions 2077), *Bathroom Strip* (Pleasure Productions 2072), *Lesbian Party* (Pleasure Productions 2079), *Cock Teasing Anal* (Showgirl Superstars S-101), *The Royal Treatment* (Limited Edition 24), *Pajama Party* (Limited Edition 29), and a different *Lesbian Party* (Cover Girl 21).

63. In addition to producing and directing adult films (usually under pseudonyms that included Gerald Greystone, Gerald Graystone, Susan Martin, Zachary Youngblood, and Zachary Strong), Abrams was the founder of Jerry Abrams Head Lights, a performance-art group that provided light shows for 1960s psychedelic rock groups in San Francisco. He also made avant-garde films. *Eyetoon* (1968) illustrates Abrams's competing interests, combining a collage of images, lights, and sounds with softcore sex scenes, and *Sub Rosa Rising* (1971) was a feature-length documentary on the San Francisco sex culture. He was an early beaver film producer, and his hardcore loops of the 1970s further cement the link between the San Francisco youth culture scene and the adult film industry. Schaefer and Johnson, "Open Your Golden Gates," 192.

64. Linda Williams writes at length about the "money shot," calling it both the "ultimate confessional moment of 'truth'" in adult films and the "very limit of the visual representation of sexual pleasure." *Hard Core: Power, Pleasure, and the "Frenzy of the Visible"* (Berkeley: University of California Press, 1989), 101.

Steven Ziplow, in a 1977 adult filmmakers' handbook, writes, "There are those who believe that the come shot, or, as some refer to it, 'the money shot,' is the most important element in the movie and that everthing else (if necessary) should be sacrificed at its expence [*sic*]. One thing is for sure: if you don't have come shots, you don't have a porno picture." *The Film Maker's Guide to Pornography* (New York: Drake, 1977), 34.

65. Royalle, asked years later about *The Analyst,* expressed her distaste for the film, shattering the very mythology presented in the film's narrative:

> I really don't like to talk about my first film, because, in some ways, the memory is painful. While I'm not an anti-porn zealot, I feel that I was exploited in some ways. The director and producer of my first film—he was a sleazeball, not one of the big names—was very unkind. During an anal scene—which I had never done—I was in pain, and the director didn't ask the cameras to stop until the actor saw how I felt and asked. ("Interview: Candida Royalle," *Fox* [March 1986]: 20)

66. Williams describes the meat shot as the "quintessential stag film shot: a close-up of penetration that shows the hard-core sexual activity is taking place" and also notes that "most current feature-length pornos would not be complete without a great many meat shots in any given sex sequence." *Hard Core,* 72.

67. Netta Gilboa, "Heart to Heart with Candida Royalle," spring 1993, www.grayarea.com/candida.htm (accessed June 21, 2007).

68. Bill Margold, legendary producer-director-actor-agent, went as far as to say that "oral sex . . . is the backbone of our business," while Jim Holliday, noted industry historian, repeatedly claimed that the blowjob was the foundation of the industry. He once suggested that if he wrote a book, it would be titled *What Is Porn All About: Blow-Jobs and Losers.* Robert J. Stoller and I.S. Levine, *Coming Attractions: The Making of an X-Rated Video* (New Haven, CT: Yale University Press, 2003), 29; Robert J. Stoller, *Porn: Myths for the Twentieth Century* (New Haven, CT: Yale University Press, 1991), 167.

Royalle, too, acknowledged the power of these mythologies. "The idea when we were making these older films was that wives wouldn't do oral sex, so you have all these blow job scenes. When I started [Femme,] the theory was that now the wives wouldn't do anal sex." Quoted in Macy, *Working Sex,* 48.

Later, with Femme, Royalle encountered similar obstacles when trying to find an established company willing to distribute her films. Even VCA, which eventually did agree to serve as Femme's distributor, initially resisted because of Royalle's refusal to include anal sex in early Femme films. "I know who watches these films. It's the husbands who buy these movies, to show their wives what they want them to do," a VCA representative told Royalle, evoking *The Analyst* scenes in which Anita is "taught" to appreciate anal sex. Candida Royalle, "Porn in the USA," *Social Text* 37 (Winter 1993): 30.

69. Ten of Royalle's appearances were in nonsex roles, and eleven were in short loop films, leaving thirty unique appearances with sexual performances in feature-length adult films. She also sang the title song in *One Way at a Time* (1979, dir. Alan Colberg). She appeared under twelve different names in her fifty-one films: Candida Royalle, Candida Royale, Candice Ball, Mary Pearson, Candice Chambers, Bettina Mia, Candice Royalle, Sharon Lucas, Candice, Candida Royal, Candita Royalle, and Jeanne Toller. Often erroneously attributed to her is the name Cyntnia Pleschette.

70. The experience of working on *Femmes de Sade* for De Renzy was not a positive one for Royalle, but it did provide another opportunity for her bur-

geoning feminist activism. In one of the script's key scenes, a group of female characters urinate on a character played by actor Ken Turner. Before shooting, Royalle refused, claiming she had not agreed to do the scene, and she convinced several other performers to refuse as well. An angry De Renzy informed Royalle that she would never work for him again—which turned out to be correct. Nelson, *Golden Goddesses*, 238.

71. "Interview: Candida Royalle," 20.

72. Macy, *Working Sex*, 53–54.

73. Ibid., 53.

74. "Cumming of Age," 95.

75. Mitchell Lawrence, "Candida Goes Candid," *Adam Film World* (September 1980): 17.

76. Royalle, *How to Tell a Naked Man What to Do*, xii.

77. Much of this history of the Sjöstedt family's dealings with the American adult film industry is drawn from my correspondence with Larry Revene: email with the author, December 26, 2012. Sjöstedt had served as producer and investor for American director Joe Sarno on such Swedish films as the "Girl Meets Girl" trilogy, starring Marie Forså, all in 1974, and *Fäbodjäntan* (Come Blow the Horn!) in 1978, perhaps the most famous adult film in Sweden's history. Through Sarno, Sjöstedt maintained connections to the adult filmmaking network in New York, particularly with Sam Lake at Mature Pictures, where Sarno had made many of his early sexploitation films. Per became assistant producer and production manager for Lake alongside producer Robert Sumner. Lake's connections in the industry were deep, with links to Howard Farber and Arthur Morowitz's Distribpix, among the most important sexploitation film producers in the United States. As explored in chapter 1, Sumner also founded Quality-X Video, while Morowitz founded the Video Shack chain of rental video stores, making their connection to Sjöstedt—which eventually led to the formation of Femme—part of a much larger trajectory in adult film history.

78. Royalle, "Vertical Smiles and Cum-Soaked Aisles," 87.

79. Given her stance on the topic, it would be tempting to ascribe the avoidance of money and meat shots in *Blue Magic* to Royalle; Revene, however, was responsible for the decision. In his 2012 autobiography, Revene writes: "The custom of a guy withdrawing and ejaculating on a woman's face did not fit any of my own fantasies or probably too many women's. In fact it made me a little uncomfortable. I did not then and still do not understand this phenomenon. Objectification is an attitude that regards a person as a commodity, an object for use without regard for the individual. I have always tried to be respectful of women and find the practice demeaning." Revene, *Wham Bam $$ Ba Da Boom! Mob Wars, Porn Battles, and a View from the Trenches* (New York: Hudson Delta Books, 2012), 766.

When I asked him about the specific lack of the trope in *Blue Magic*, he noted: "Because of my gender . . . I was expected to subscribe to the normal male approach to making sex films. Cumming on a woman's face, then as now, does not seem in the realm of eroticism to me, but more in the arena of humiliation." Revene, email with the author, December 26, 2012.

80. Gilboa, "Heart to Heart with Candida Royalle"; Royalle, *How to Tell a Naked Man What to Do*, xii.

81. Gilboa, "Heart to Heart with Candida Royalle."

82. Nagle, "First Ladies of Feminist Porn," 165.

83. Candida Royalle, "Off Camera," *High Society* (February 1982): 21.

84. Ibid.; Candida Royalle, "The Royalle Treatment," *Cinema-X* (April 1981): 20–21, 55.

85. Robert Rosen, who worked on a variety of Drake's adult magazines, provides an invaluable history of the company in *Beaver Street: A History of Modern Pornography* (London: Headpress, 2010), 67–84, 177–78. Also see Bruce Jay Friedman, *Even the Rhinos Were Nymphos* (Chicago: University of Chicago Press, 2000), 15–26.

86. Candida Royalle, "High Society Gets the Stock Market Up!" *High Society* (September 1981): 16–19.

87. Robin Perez, "Behind the Scenes with Candida Royalle," n.d., www .sexherald.com/interview-sex-professionals/behind_the_scenes_with_candida _royalle__author,_lect.html (accessed August 10, 2012). Rosen, *Beaver Street*, 11–16, offers a pertinent history of phone sex, given the connections between Drake Publishing and that industry: the first phone sex lines were initiated by *High Society* magazine in mid-1982.

88. Royalle, "The Royalle Treatment," 18.

89. Despite her reinvention with Femme in 1984, Royalle continued to work for various adult publications as a gossip columnist, freelance writer, and critic, often uncredited or under pseudonyms. For example, she was still listed as a contributing writer for *Cheri* magazine in July 1987, and a February 1988 profile in the *San Francisco Chronicle* notes that she was still working for that publication as a sex columnist. Masthead, *Cheri* (July 1987): 2; John Stanley, "Film Maker Gives Erotica a Woman's Point of View," *San Francisco Chronicle*, February 21, 1988, 55.

90. Royalle, "Vertical Smiles and Cum-Soaked Aisles," 38–41, 67, 85–87.

91. "Porn Star of the Month: Candida Royalle," *High Society* (October 1982): 61.

92. Candida Royalle, "Untitled," *Blue Movie Expose!* (September 1983): 11.

93. Laura Fraser, "Nasty Girls," *Mother Jones* (March 1990): 50; McNeil, Osborne, and Pavia, *The Other Hollywood*, 371–76.

94. Arlene Raven, "Looking beneath the Surface: Deep inside Porn Stars," *High Performance* 7, no. 28 (1984): 26.

95. C. Carr, "The Fiery Furnace: Performance in the '80s, War in the '90s," *TDR* 49, no. 1 (Spring 2005): 22.

96. McNeil, Osborne, and Pavia, *The Other Hollywood*, quote 374–75; Annette Fuentes and Margaret Schrage, "Deep inside Porn Stars," *Jump Cut: A Review of Contemporary Media* 32 (April 1987): 41–43.

97. Carr, "The Fiery Furnace," 22.

98. The title of the show was a play on the *Inside* series of adult films from Evart Films, particularly *Deep inside Annie Sprinkle* (1981, dir. Sprinkle, with help from Joe Sarno), which was a watershed moment in feminist pornography

history. The previous *Inside* films (*Inside Jennifer Welles* in 1977, *Inside Gloria Leonard* in 1978, and *Inside Seka* in 1981) had purported to show the "real lives" of the performers but were in actuality merely more of the same typical adult film tropes and fantasies. *Deep inside Annie Sprinkle* expands and explores these notions, offering an examination of Sprinkle's struggles over the constructed nature of identity (and making plain the simultaneous difficulties of being both Ellen Steinberg—her birth name—and Annie Sprinkle the performer) as well as presenting her trademark anything-goes sexual appetites and desires, including orgies, "golden shower" sequences, and other boundary-pushing moments. The film, in addition to being a groundbreaking work of feminist pornography, was a smash hit and remains popular with fans and critics. Linda Williams, "A Provoking Agent: The Pornography and Performance Art of Annie Sprinkle," *Social Text* 37 (Winter 1993): 117–33.

99. McNeil, Osborne, and Pavia, *The Other Hollywood*, 375; Williams, *Hard Core*, 330; Toni Sant, *Franklin Furnace and the Spirit of the Avant-Garde: A History of the Future* (New York: Intellect Ltd., 2011), 52–53; Sally Everett, ed., *Art Theory and Criticism: An Anthology of Formalist, Avant-Garde, Contextualist, and Post Modernist Thought* (New York: McFarland, 1995), 206.

100. Shannon Bell, *Reading, Writing, and Rewriting the Prostitute Body* (Bloomington: Indiana University Press, 1994), 146.

101. Quoted in Macy, *Working Sex*, 63.

102. Quoted in Rebecca Schneider, *The Explicit Body in Performance* (New York: Routledge, 1997), 13.

103. McNeil, Osborne, and Pavia, *The Other Hollywood*, 376. Franklin Furnace was reprimanded by the National Endowment for the Arts and dropped by several corporate sponsors for hosting the event, further illustrating the tensions surrounding feminist pornography in the mid-1980s. Timothy J. Haskell, "The Legendary Franklin Furnace Presents a Retrospective: The History of the Future: A Franklin Furnace View of Performance Art, One Night Only—April 27th, 2007," March 9, 2007, http://franklinfurnace.org/research/projects/thotf_performance/press_release.html (accessed October 3, 2012).

104. While the show was mostly a public success, conservative groups (predictably) decried it. The Morality Action Committee picketed, and religious groups across the country, upon hearing about the show, sent angry letters to Congress and the many corporate funders of Franklin Furnace, resulting in Exxon and Woolworth pulling their support; some blocks of federal funding were also lost. Carr, "The Fiery Furnace," 22.

105. Quoted in Fuentes and Schrage, "Deep inside Porn Stars," 42. Not all feminists supported or appreciated the project. For example, antiporn activist Susan Griffin, upon viewing the performance, argued that the Club 90 members were only pretending to be honest—a common critique in the antiporn movement, which did not distinguish between adult films made with feminist intentions and those made without them, arguing that pornography was harmful to women no matter its context. Raven, "Looking beneath the Surface," 27.

106. Gilboa, "Heart to Heart with Candida Royalle."

107. Niemi was clearly disinterested in publicity and, to my knowledge, never spoke publicly about Femme during or after her time in the adult film industry. In one of her final interviews, Royalle said, "I credit her with equal responsibility for the initial launch of Femme Productions." Quoted in Nelson, *Golden Goddesses*, 248.

108. Gilboa, "Heart to Heart with Candida Royalle."

109. Quoted in Court, "Candida Royalle."

110. Quoted in Nagle, "First Ladies of Feminist Porn," 165.

111. Gilboa, "Heart to Heart with Candida Royalle." Depending on the context, these details of Royalle's biography are often left out, glossed over, or carefully managed. For example, Marianne Macy, in her overview of Femme's history, describes Sture Sjöstedt as being "involved with Scandinavia's largest video production and distribution company" without acknowledging his connection to adult film history (Macy, *Working Sex*, 64). Royalle's *New York Times* obituary notes: "Members of [the Sjöstedt] family, who were film distributors in Europe, helped finance Femme Productions" (Roberts, "Candida Royalle, Who Made Erotic Films for Women, Dies at 64"). In 2012, Royalle described Sture Sjöstedt as "a successful producer and distributor in Europe who had invested in several big-budget American erotic features" and said that he "had mentioned a few times that he thought I would make a good director, so upon hearing our concept he offered to finance it" (Candida Royalle, "What's a Nice Girl Like You . . . ," in *The Feminist Porn Book*, eds. Tristan Taormino et al., 58–70 [New York: Feminist Press at the City University of New York, 2012]).

112. Quoted in Nagle, "First Ladies of Feminist Porn," 163.

113. Lenny Wide, "Review: *Urban Heat*," *Video-X*, 6, no. 10 (1984): 32.

114. "Three Daughters," *Gent* (November 1987): 20.

115. Sean Greaney, "Selling Sex," *Marketing* (June 2010): 23.

116. Marcia Pally, "Getting Down with Candida Royalle," *Forum* (April 1986): 45.

117. Susan Squire, "How Women Are Changing Porn Films," *Glamour* (November 1985): 282.

118. Ibid., 322.

119. Greaney, "Selling Sex," 24.

120. Pally, "Getting Down with Candida Royalle," 45.

121. John Leo, "Romantic Porn in the Boudoir," *Time*, March 30, 1987, 64.

122. Quoted in Jodie Gould, "Debbie Directs Dallas: Video Erotica Made by Women for Women," *Elle* (April 1992): 144.

123. Nagle, "First Ladies of Feminist Porn," 163.

124. Natalie Martin, "Candida Royalle, Ceo, Femme Productions," June 1, 2007, http://business.avn.com/executive-suite/Candida-Royalle-CEO-Femme-Productions-66429.html (accessed January 7, 2013).

125. natural-contours.com, n.d. (accessed March 24, 2013).

126. "Interview: Candida Royalle," 22.

127. Macy, *Working Sex*, 89.

128. Lee Irving, "The Women behind the Scenes," *AVN* (May 1986): 46.

129. Carl Esser, "Intro," *Adam Film World and Adult Video Guide* (November 1986): 5.

130. Desiree Valentine, "Does It Take a Woman to Make a Good Couples Film?" *Adam Film World and Adult Video Guide* (November 1986): 59.

131. Ibid., 60.

132. "Dreamland Gets Romantic," *Adult Video News Confidential* (May 1986): 4.

133. These educational videos, as Kevin Heffernan describes them, were heavily stylized and mixed entertainment with pedagogy: "[The tapes] were originally distributed on videotape, and were the approximate length of a pornographic feature film, suitable for viewing in a single sitting, and like the feature, they contain non-diegetic music that often underscores heavily edited, stylized arias of transcendent sexual bliss that reach a climax in a final production number where the tips and techniques offered by Nina in the first sections have reached an unselfconscious virtuosity." Heffernan, "From 'It Could Happen to Someone You Love' to 'Do You Speak Ass?': Women and Discourses of Sex Education in Erotic Film and Video," in *The Feminist Porn Book*, eds. Taormino et al., 237–54.

Robert Eberwein, in *Sex Ed: Film, Video, and the Framework of Desire* (New Brunswick, NJ: Rutgers University Press, 1999), 181–213, traces the long history of "sex education" films, including the rise of such material on video. The genre goes back, Eberwein writes, to at least *Damaged Goods* (1914), which emphasized venereal disease as a social problem. As Linda Williams notes (*Hard Core*, 97), a clear turning point occurred after the Supreme Court ruled in *Memoirs v. Massachusetts* (1966) that a work was not obscene if it had "redeeming social importance," leading to films such as *Pornography in Denmark: A New Approach* and *A History of the Blue Movie* (both 1970, dir. Alex de Renzy), both of which purported to be "educational" documentaries and histories while nevertheless providing viewers with depictions of sexual pleasure. After the adult film industry transitioned to video, educational material (such as Hartley's tapes) became standard product.

134. An outspoken feminist, Hartley frequently appears (much as Royalle did) at academic conferences, workshops, and in the media to present a sex-positive message. She has appeared in nearly one thousand adult films, including two for Royalle with Femme: *Rites of Passage* (1987) and *Bridal Shower* (1997). She authored a sex advice book in 2006, has been the subject of scores of interviews and academic analyses, and writes feminist essays on adult films and sex work. She also appeared in Paul Thomas Anderson's mainstream film *Boogie Nights* (1997). For a few examples, see Nina Hartley, *Nina Hartley's Guide to Total Sex* (New York: Avery, 2006); Sheldon Ranz, "Interview: Nina Hartley," *Shmate: A Magazine of Progressive Jewish Thought* 22 (Spring 1989): 15–29; Nina Hartley, "Reflections of a Feminist Porn Star," *Gauntlet* 5 (1993): 62–68; Nina Hartley, "Porn: An Effective Vehicle for Sexual Role Modeling and Education," in *The Feminist Porn Book*, eds. Taormino et al., 228–36; and Nelson, *Golden Goddesses*, 862–907.

135. Hartley, "Reflections of a Feminist Porn Star," 62.

136. Taormino and Lust, in particular, have inherited Royalle's mantle. Erika Lust, *Good Porn: A Woman's Guide* (Berkeley, CA: Seal Press, 2010); Tristan Taormino, *Down and Dirty Sex Secrets: The New and Naughty Guide to Being Great in Bed* (New York: William Morrow, 2003); Tristan Taormino, "Calling the Shots: Feminist Porn in Theory and Practice," in *The Feminist Porn Book*, eds. Taormino et al., 255–64.

The other significant inheritor of Royalle's rhetoric has been Cindy Gallop, an advertising executive who, after her much-discussed TED Talk on pornography in 2009 (and her subsequent TED book), created makelovenotporn.tv, a website dedicated to user-submitted "real world" hardcore video clips, which she claims is "not porn." The site insists that videos have be "contextualized" and that they "show and tell a backstory," furthering many arguments in this book.

137. Anne G. Sabo, *After Pornified: How Women Are Transforming Pornography & Why It Really Matters* (New York: John Hunt, 2012), 53.

138. Ibid., 54.

139. Quoted in Jesse Sposato, "Hot and Saucy: Candida Royalle's Top That," *Sadie Magazine* (Summer 2012), www.sadiemagazine.com/past-issues/issue-no-8/top-that/hot-and-saucy-candida-royalle-s-top-that (accessed January 3, 2013).

140. Royalle, "What's a Nice Girl Like You . . . ," 68.

141. Susan Walker, "Men's Porn Is Not Women's Erotica," *Toronto Star*, August 27, 1994, H1.

142. Since Royalle created Femme, the debate over the validity and availability of pornography for women has never ceased, and every new newspaper article, magazine essay, television talk show, or blog post asks and answers the same questions as if for the first time. The trend shows no signs of stopping. Some notable examples over the years include Dennis Hunt, "'Feminine' Porn Finds a Niche in the Marketplace," *Los Angeles Times*, May 18, 1990, 17; Wendy Melillo, "Visualizing Erotica," *Washington Post*, July 21, 1992, Z13; Gerald Nachman, "Women Get a Turn at Erotica," *Washington Post*, January 25, 1993, D1; Mireya Navarro, "Women Tailor Sex Industry to Their Eyes," *New York Times*, February 20, 2004, A1, A22; and Susan Abram, "Porn, for Women, by Women," *Daily News*, June 8, 2007, N12.

143. For one of many examples, see Rhiannon Lucy Cosslett, "Can Porn Empower Women?" *Guardian*, March 2, 2015, www.theguardian.com/lifeand-style/2015/mar/02/pornography-might-suit-some-women-but-not-all-women (accessed April 20, 2015).

144. Williams, *Hard Core*, 246.

145. Quoted in Jim Holliday, "Directors of the Decade," *AVN* (April 1999): 25.

146. Quoted in Melillo, "Visualizing Erotica," Z13.

147. Gayle Rubin, "Thinking Sex: Notes for a Radical Theory of the Politics of Sexuality," in *Pleasure and Danger: Exploring Female Sexuality*, ed. Carole S. Vance (London: Pandora Press, 1984), 283.

4. SAVING THE FAMILY

1. Maricopa County Attorney's Office, "About Us," n.d., www.maricopa-countyattorney.org/about-us/ (accessed April 4, 2013).

2. U.S. Bureau of the Census, "Intercensal Estimates of the Resident Population of States and Counties 1980–1989," March 1992, www.census.gov /popest/data/counties/totals/1980s/tables/e8089co.txt (accessed April 4, 2013).

3. Citizens for Decency through Law was founded in the mid-1950s in Cincinnati by Charles H. Keating Jr. It was first called Citizens for Decent Literature, and it advocated the eradication of "smut." Later renamed, CDL eventually boasted three hundred national chapters and more than one hundred thousand members, making it the largest antipornography organization in the United States. In the 1980s, it served as a clearinghouse for antipornography groups, assisted in local obscenity cases, and generally put pressure on the government to eradicate pornography. Whitney Strub traces the long history of CDL, as well as the role of grassroots antipornography organizations in general, in his comprehensive book *Perversion for Profit: The Politics of Pornography and the Rise of the New Right* (New York: Columbia University Press, 2011).

4. Paul Rubin, "Desperado, Esq.," *Phoenix New Times,* August 21, 1997, www.phoenixnewtimes.com/news/desperado-esq-6422858 (accessed April 4, 2013).

5. Michael Cieply, "Risque Business: Video Outlets Face Mounting Pressure to Stop Carrying X-Rated Cassettes," *Wall Street Journal,* April 21, 1986, 1.

6. "Porn Suit Subject Sues Prosecutors," *Mohave Daily Miner,* May 28, 1986, 3.

7. Natasha Zaretsky, *No Direction Home: The American Family and the Fear of National Decline, 1968–1980* (Chapel Hill: University of North Carolina Press, 2007), 10.

8. Quoted in Robert Lindsey, "Outlets That Offer Explicit Sex Tapes Facing Prosecution," *New York Times,* June 3, 1985, A1.

9. Quoted in Dick Polman, "Store Owners Divided on Adult Tapes," *Philadelphia Inquirer,* September 7, 1986, J1.

10. Cieply, "Risque Business," 1.

11. Bob Davis, "X-Rated Video Losing Share of Tape Sales," *Wall Street Journal,* January 19, 1984, 1; Randi Henderson, "Pornography Moves from Seedy Theaters into Living Rooms," *Evening Tribune,* October 11, 1985, C2.

12. *Roth v. United States,* 354 U.S. 476, Supreme Court of the United States, June 24, 1957, LexisNexis (accessed April 21, 2013).

13. Thomas C. Mackey, *Pornography on Trial: A Handbook with Cases, Laws, and Documents* (Santa Barbara, CA: ABC-CLIO, 2002), 52–55.

14. *Miller v. California,* 413 U.S. 15, Supreme Court of the United States, June 21, 1973, LexisNexis (accessed February 10, 2012).

15. A complete review and analysis of the long, complicated, and contentious history of obscenity law is far outside the bounds of this book, but I have drawn on several invaluable resources: Mackey, *Pornography on Trial;* Edward

De Grazia, *Girls Lean Back Everywhere: The Law of Obscenity and the Assault on Genius* (New York: Vintage, 1993); Christopher Nowlin, *Judging Obscenity: A Critical History of Expert Evidence* (Montreal: McGill–Queen's University Press, 2003); and Leon Friedman, ed., *Obscenity: The Complete Oral Arguments before the Supreme Court in the Major Obscenity Cases* (New York: Chelsea House, 1980).

16. The five tapes: *Pumpkin Farm* (1983, dir. D.R. Williams), *Desire for Men* (1981, dir. Carol Connors), *Divine Atrocities* (1983, dir. Kim Christy), *Taboo 2* (1982, dir. Kirdy Stevens), and *800 Fantasy Lane* (1979, dir. Svetlana). General Video of America, *White Paper* (General Video of America, 1985), L-13.

17. Alongside Gibson, Collins and Wakefield also targeted another store, Arizona Video Cassettes, leading to indictments on similar charges. "Porn Suit Subject Sues Prosecutors," 3; Lindsey, "Outlets That Offer Explicit Sex Tapes Facing Prosecution," A1.

18. John Sippel, "VSDA Given X-Vid Update," *Billboard*, January 25, 1986, 74.

19. General Video of America, *White Paper*, L-13.

20. "First Video Trial Set to Begin," *Prescott Courier*, October 14, 1985, 1B; "Defendant Says Others Do Same," *Prescott Courier*, October 29, 1985, 6A.

21. "Porn Suit Subject Sues Prosecutors," 3. Collins and Wakefield also initiated raids on and indictments of other video stores in spring 1986. In June 1987, Bill Bavaro of K&K Video was acquitted by a jury, ending Collins and Wakefield's efforts to convict mainstream video store owners on obscenity charges. "AZ Video Store Operator Indicted for Obscenity," *Adult Video News Confidential* (February 1987): 5; "Arizona Jury Acquits Video Store on Obscenity Charges," *Adult Video News Confidential* (September 1987): 26.

22. Sippel, "VSDA Given X-Vid Update," 74. Gibson's trial ended up becoming a minor farce for Maricopa County. In late May 1986, long after his trials had ended, Gibson sued Collins, Wakefield, and the county for misconduct and slander, alleging that Wakefield's promise not to prosecute storeowners who had removed adult inventory had been violated (the same conclusion that Judge Kamin had reached in Gibson's second trial). Gibson also alleged that Wakefield had slandered him during a public speech by suggesting a link among Gibson, Arizona Home Video, and organized crime—a statement that Collins later defended. During the ensuing investigation, grand jury member Charles Scott, a customer at Arizona Home Video, was indicted for leaking information to Gibson before the original indictment. Gibson was given immunity to testify against Scott, and the lawsuit against Collins was eventually dismissed because of Scott's actions. "Porn Suit Subject Sues Prosecutors," 3; "Lawyer Opposes Grand Jury Probe," *Mohave Daily Miner*, July 22, 1986, A3; "Limited Immunity Offered," *Mohave Daily Miner*, July 30, 1986, 2; "Grand Juror Indicted in Information Leak," *Prescott Courier*, November 16, 1986: 13A.

23. Quoted in Lindsey, "Outlets That Offer Explicit Sex Tapes Facing Prosecution," B14.

24. Quoted in Cieply, "Risque Business," 1.

25. Tony Schwartz, "The TV Pornography Boom," *New York Times,* September 13, 1981, 44.

26. Quoted in Lindsey, "Outlets That Offer Explicit Sex Tapes Facing Prosecution," B14.

27. Gayle Rubin, "Thinking Sex: Notes for a Radical Theory of the Politics of Sexuality," in *Pleasure and Danger: Exploring Female Sexuality,* ed. Carole S. Vance (London: Pandora Press, 1992), 267.

28. Quoted in Joe Swickard, "Pickets Vow to Shut New Adult Bookstore," *Detroit Free Press,* February 29, 1980, n.p.

29. "They Won the Battle," *Detroit Free Press,* April 9, 1980, n.p.

30. Cincinnati's first efforts to regulate pornography occurred as early as 1956, and county prosecutor Simon Leis effectively eliminated the sale of pornography there between 1971 and 1983. As described above (see note 3), Keating founded CDL in the city in the mid-1950s, and Jerry Kirk's National Coalition against Pornography formed there in 1983. Both Reuben Sturman, whose pornography empire was based out of Cleveland, and Larry Flynt, who opened his first strip club in Dayton before opening franchises all over the state (and creating *Hustler* magazine), faced numerous prosecutions in Ohio. Michael Burns, "Cincinnati: Anti-Porn Capital," *United Press International,* October 19, 1986.

31. Earl Paige and Edward Morris, "Obscenity Trials: Messer in Clear, Emerson on Hold," *Billboard,* April 12, 1986, 84; Polman, "Store Owners Divided on Adult Tapes," J1.

32. Quoted in Marc Berman, "Jack Messer of the Video Store: First Amendment Advocate, First-Rate Retailer," *Video Business* (January 1986): 124.

33. The five titles: *Doing It* (1982, dir. Sven Conrad), *Tapestry of Passion* (1976, dir. Alan Colberg), *Swedish Erotica 33* (1981, dir. unknown), *Penetration* (1984, dir. unknown), and *French Classmates* (1978, dir. unknown). General Video of America, *White Paper,* L-12.

34. Michael Matza, "A Question of Privacy: Anyone Who Rents Videotapes Is at Risk of Having the List Made Public," *Philadelphia Daily News,* October 21, 1987, http://articles.philly.com/1987-10-21/news/26215608_1_judge-robert-h-bork-rental-records-privacy (accessed April 10, 2013); Berman, "Jack Messer of the Video Store," 123.

35. Quoted in Polman, "Store Owners Divided on Adult Tapes," J1.

36. "Ohio's Messer Cleared of Obscenity Charges," *Adult Video News Confidential* (May 1986): 1.

37. Whitman quoted in Polman, "Store Owners Divided on Adult Tapes," J1; Paige and Morris, "Obscenity Trials," 84.

38. Polman, "Store Owners Divided on Adult Tapes," J1. As with Gibson, some of these legal bills were paid by adult video distributors. Select Essex, Caballero Control Corporation, Cal Vista, Holiday Video, VCA, and GVA all paid into the defense fund, as did the Cincinnati Dealer's Coalition. General Video of America, *White Paper,* L-12.

39. Howard Polskin, "Pornography Unleashed," *Panorama* (July 1980): 36.

40. Joan Sweeney, "Sex-Oriented Videotapes Seized after Two-Month 'Sting' Operation in L.A.," *Los Angeles Times*, March 15, 1980, A16; "Coast Raid Set to Shut Nine Pornography Mills," *New York Times*, March 16, 1980, 18. The raided companies were TVX, Wonderful World of Video, Arrow Films, S&L Distributors, Four Star Video, Video Home Library, V.T.S. Enterprises, Cal Vista Video, and JA-RAE Productions.

41. Polskin, "Pornography Unleashed," 36.

42. Ibid.

43. "U.S. Indicts 45 on Smut, Film Piracy Charges," *Los Angeles Times*, February 14, 1980, A3.

44. Quoted in Allan J. Mayer and Ron LaBrecque, "Crackdown on Porn," *Newsweek*, February 25, 1980, 37.

45. The MIPORN investigation ultimately became an embarrassment for the FBI when Livingston could not disengage from his undercover persona. He left his wife and children, was arrested for shoplifting in Lexington, Kentucky, on November 10, 1981, used his undercover identity during the arrest, and generally exhibited psychologically unstable behavior. Deemed an unreliable witness, he was dropped by MIPORN prosecutors, who were forced to reindict or drop many of the cases. Ron LaBrecque, "An Agent Whose Role Got the Best of Him," *Newsweek*, December 20, 1982, 41; Legs McNeil, Jennifer Osborne, and Peter Pavia, *The Other Hollywood: The Uncensored Oral History of the Porn Film Industry* (New York: Regan Books, 2005), 244–62, 309–14, 326–31; Ron LaBrecque, *Lost Undercover: An FBI Agent's True Story* (New York: Dell, 1987).

46. Quoted in "Child Pornography Law Enacted," *New York Times*, May 22, 1984, A20.

47. For more on the conservative movement during (as well as before) the Reagan era, see Allan J. Lichtman, *White Protestant Nation: The Rise of the American Conservative Movement* (New York: Grove Press, 2008).

48. Leslie Bennetts, "Conservatives Join on Social Concerns," *New York Times*, July 30, 1980, A1, B6; Kenneth A. Briggs, "Evangelicals Debate Their Role in Battling Secularism," *New York Times*, January 27, 1981, A12.

49. Morality in Media was originally founded by an interfaith clergy group in New York in 1962. Father Morton Hill, Rabbi Julius Neumann, and Reverend Robert Wittenburg created a group named Operation Yorkville to combat pornography in local neighborhoods. They were later joined by Reverend Constantine Volaitis and renamed the group in 1968. Like CDL, Morality in Media became a vocal supporter of grassroots protests and assisted local prosecutors in obscenity cases. Donald J. Farole, *Interest Groups and Judicial Federalism* (New York: Praeger, 1998), 135–36.

50. Quoted in Don Irwin, "President Tells Morality Group He May Appoint a 'Smut Czar,'" *Los Angeles Times*, March 29, 1983, A10.

51. Charles Austin, "Bishops in Plea against Smut," *New York Times*, May 25, 1983, A19.

52. A notorious illustration of Meese's view on crime and punishment occurred when he was asked, in 1985, by *U.S. News & World Report* to explain his criticisms of the Supreme Court's *Miranda* ruling (1966), which requires

police to read suspects their constitutional rights and inform them of their right to have a lawyer present before answering any questions. Meese responded: "Suspects who are innocent of a crime should [have those rights]. But the thing is, you don't have many suspects who are innocent of a crime. That's contradictory. If a person is innocent of a crime, then he is not a suspect." Quoted in "Justice under Reagan: Reagan Seeks Judges with 'Traditional Approach,'" *U.S. News & World Report*, October 14, 1985, 67.

53. President's Commission on Obscenity and Pornography, *The Report of the Commission on Obscenity and Pornography* (New York: Random House, 1970), 51.

54. Ibid., 26.

55. Strub, *Perversion for Profit*, 142.

56. For a more detailed history of tension surrounding the suburban home, see Matthew D. Lassiter, *The Silent Majority: Suburban Politics in the Sunbelt South* (Princeton, NJ: Princeton University Press, 2006).

57. Quoted in Warren Weaver, "Nixon Repudiates Obscenity Report as Morally Void," *New York Times*, October 25, 1970, 1.

58. Quoted in "Senate Votes, 60–5, to Reject and Censure Obscenity Report," *New York Times*, October 14, 1970, 30.

59. Charles H. Keating, "Statement of Charles H. Keating, Jr.," in *The Report of the Commission on Obscenity and Pornography*, ed. Commission on Obscenity and Pornography (New York: Random House, 1970), 511–49, quote 548.

60. "Court Enjoins Publication of Obscenity Report," *Publishers Weekly*, September 21, 1970, 37.

61. President's Commission on Obscenity and Pornography, *The Report of the Commission on Obscenity and Pornography*, 523–27.

62. See, e.g., Charles H. Keating, "The Report That Shocked the Nation," *Reader's Digest* (January 1971): 37–41.

63. Whitney Strub, "Perversion for Profit: Citizens for Decent Literature and the Arousal of an Antiporn Public in the 1960s," *Journal of the History of Sexuality* 15, no. 2 (May 2006): 260.

64. Keating was later convicted in both state and federal courts of fraud, racketeering, and conspiracy, and he served more than four years in prison, in addition to paying massive fines, due to his role in the savings and loan crisis of the 1980s. Michael Binstein, *Trust Me: Charles Keating and the Missing Billions* (New York: Random House, 1993).

65. Ronald Reagan, "Remarks on Signing the Child Protection Act of 1984," American Presidency Project, May 21, 1984, www.presidency.ucsb.edu/ws /?pid=39953 (accessed April 13, 2013).

66. Quoted in "Q&A: Is New Action Needed on Pornography?" *New York Times*, June 23, 1985, E24.

67. *Attorney General's Commission on Pornography: Final Report*, 2 vols. (Washington, DC: U.S. Government Printing Office, 1986), 1:215.

68. Philip Shenon, "Meese Names Panel to Study How to Control Pornography," *New York Times*, May 21, 1985, A21.

69. Stephen Vaughn, *Freedom and Entertainment: Rating the Movies in an Age of New Media* (London: Cambridge University Press, 2005), 126.

70. Quoted in "Q&A: Is New Action Needed on Pornography?" E24.

71. Hudson was perhaps an ideal fit for the position, given Meese's law-and-order emphasis. In 1980, freshly elected as Arlington County's prosecutor, he told a reporter that "I live to put people in jail" and that he got "a great deal of satisfaction from removing people from our community who prey on others." Quoted in Sandra G. Boodman, "'I Live to Put People in Jail'; Henry Hudson: Chief Prosecutor Making a Name," *Washington Post*, July 30, 1980, B1.

72. Quoted in "Q&A: Is New Action Needed on Pornography?" E24.

73. Quoted in "The Lawyer behind the Government's Pornography Report," *Barrister* 13 (1986): 39.

74. Quoted in Shenon, "Meese Names Panel to Study How to Control Pornography," A21.

75. Attorney General's Commission on Pornography, *Final Report of the Attorney General's Commission on Pornography* (Nashville, TN: Rutledge Hill Press, 1986), 480.

76. Ibid., 479–80.

77. Ibid., 478, 486–87.

78. Quoted in Matthew Scully, "'Dark Side' Still a Threat 2 Years Later," *Prescott Courier*, March 23, 1988, 1B.

79. Attorney General's Commission on Pornography, *Final Report of the Attorney General's Commission on Pornography*, 481; Hendrik Hertzberg, "Big Boobs: Ed Meese and His Pornography Commission," *New Republic*, July 14–July 21, 1986, 21.

80. Attorney General's Commission on Pornography, *Final Report of the Attorney General's Commission on Pornography*, 478; Vaughn, *Freedom and Entertainment*, 128.

81. Attorney General's Commission on Pornography, *Final Report of the Attorney General's Commission on Pornography*, 479–80.

82. Ibid., 477, 480–81.

83. This workshop, attended by none of the commission members except Hudson, took place from June 22 to 24, 1986, at a hotel in Arlington, Virginia. Since the commission had designated no funding for any research, Koop convinced the Department of Justice to allocate $50,000 for the workshop, which was designed to produce an addendum to the commission's final report. Nineteen participants, mostly social scientists, attended, and five papers were presented, all on the social effects of pornography. Koop delivered the findings to Hudson on August 1, 1986—nearly a month after the commission had released its final report, making the entire event all but pointless. C. Everett Koop, "Report of the Surgeon General's Workshop on Pornography and Public Health," *American Psychologist* 42, no. 10 (October 1987): 944–45; Edward P. Mulvey and Jeffrey J. Haugaard, *Report of the Surgeon General's Workshop on Pornography and Public Health* (Washington, DC: U.S. Department of Health and Human Services, Office of the Surgeon General, August 4, 1986).

84. Attorney General's Commission on Pornography, *Final Report of the Attorney General's Commission on Pornography*, 465–70. Philip Nobile and Eric Nadler, editors of *Forum* magazine (a subsidiary of *Penthouse*), documented the proceedings in *The United States of America vs. Sex: How the Meese Commission Lied about Pornography* (New York: Minotaur Press, 1986). See also Edwin McDowell, "Some Say Meese Report Rates an X," *New York Times*, October 21, 1986, 13.

85. Hertzberg, "Big Boobs," 23.

86. *Attorney General's Commission on Pornography: Final Report*, 1:129.

87. Robert Pear, "Panel Calls on Citizens to Wage National Assault on Pornography," *New York Times*, July 10, 1986, A1, B7. The Government Printing Office issued the *Report* in two volumes after its release, pricing it at $35, but sold few copies. Anyone could reprint the *Report*, which was public domain, but every major publishing house declined to do so. Given that the *Report's* recommendations included making it easier to prosecute those who disseminated adult material and that the *Report* itself was filled with descriptions of such material, no one was willing to gamble on a potential obscenity trial. Finally, in September 1986, Rutledge Hill Press of Nashville, which specialized in books about Tennessee and the Southeast, reprinted the report in a single volume, with edited sections and none of the images, shrink-wrapped and with a warning label (see Attorney General's Commission on Pornography, *Final Report of the Attorney General's Commission on Pornography*). Antipornography groups were by far the largest purchaser of Rutledge's edition, buying more than thirty thousand copies, with an additional seven thousand copies going to bookstores. Religiously conservative bookstores hesitated to carry the book, however, with one dealer noting: "I agree with the commission's findings, but there are many things objectionable in the book." Quoted in McDowell, "Some Say Meese Report Rates an X," 13. See also Terry Teachout, "The Pornography Report That Never Was," *Commentary* 84, no. 2 (1986): 51–57.

Publishers had reason to worry. In late 1971, a jury had convicted William Hamling, longtime publisher of adult books via his Greenleaf Classics company, and two of his employees on obscenity charges related to their printing and distribution of the 1970 *Report*. Hamling had included more than five hundred images with the book and sent out more than fifty thousand advertisements and pamphlets. Unable to decide whether the publication itself was obscene (particularly as the images' framing text was a government document), the jury instead convicted the three for the related advertising and pamphlets. "Illustrated Version of Obscenity Study Brings Indictments," *New York Times*, March 6, 1971, 24; Murray Schumach, "Obscene Photos Pornographic Regardless of Text, Court Says," *New York Times*, August 5, 1971, 30; Everett R. Holles, "4 Are Convicted in Smut Mailings," *New York Times*, December 25, 1971, 22.

88. "Briefing," *New York Times*, July 11, 1986, A12. In 2002, Attorney General John Ashcroft covered the statue—and its male counterpart—with curtains, which were removed by his successor, Alberto Gonzalez, in 2005. Dan

Eggen, "Sculpted Bodies and a Strip Act at Justice Dept.," *Washington Post*, July 25, 2005, A2.

89. *Attorney General's Commission on Pornography: Final Report*, 1:260. The first draft of the *Report*, written by nine staff members under the guidance of Executive Director Sears, tallied twelve hundred pages, including two hundred pages of testimony. Commission member Frederick Schauer objected, calling many parts of the draft one-sided and simplistic, and wrote a new draft himself, which became the basis of what was eventually released. Hertzberg, "Big Boobs," 22.

90. Attorney General's Commission on Pornography, *Final Report of the Attorney General's Commission on Pornography*, 461.

91. William E. Brigman, "Politics and the Pornography Wars," *Wide Angle* 19, no. 3 (1997): 159.

92. *Attorney General's Commission on Pornography: Final Report*, 1:363–64.

93. Congress enacted RICO in 1970 as Title IX of the Organized Crime Control Act in order to limit the influence of organized crime on legitimate businesses and unions. In addition to enhanced fines, prison terms, and other penalties, RICO made it possible for courts to seize property and profits involved in and derived from criminal activity—even property and profits from otherwise legitimate activities. In order for a prosecution to invoke RICO, what the legislation deemed "predicate acts," or previous and related criminal actions, had to be present, thus establishing a pattern. It was not necessary to have a legal record of these predicate acts; in fact, no prior prosecution was necessary, and even acquitted charges could be used as the basis for prosecution under RICO.

Originally, Congress did not consider obscenity violations to be predicate acts, but, on the last day of the 1984 Congressional session, Republican Senator Jesse Helms of North Carolina buried an amendment that included them in an extensive rewriting of the federal criminal code (which was itself buried in a continuing resolution intended to keep the government functioning). Helms's amendment received no debate, no press coverage, and no dissent. Matthew D. Bunker, Paul H. Gates, and Sigman L. Splichal, "RICO and Obscenity Prosecutions: Racketeering Laws Threaten Free Expression," *Journalism Quarterly* 70, no. 3 (Autumn 1993): 692–99.

94. Attorney General's Commission on Pornography, *Final Report of the Attorney General's Commission on Pornography*, 86.

95. Ibid., 104–06.

96. While there had been numerous prostitution and pandering arrests throughout the adult film industry's history, the issue escalated to a serious degree in the early 1980s when police crackdowns on adult film production led to most producers leaving Los Angeles to shoot outside city limits or in San Francisco. In 1982, the passage of a California law requiring a mandatory three-year prison sentence for anyone convicted of hiring people to perform sex acts made the situation even more dire. Harold Freeman, veteran adult filmmaker, was arrested in October 1983 on five counts of pandering related to the produc-

tion of *Caught from Behind II* (1983). The five counts were for hiring female performers for the film, and did not include the male performers. Freeman was convicted in May 1985, lost on appeal to the California Court of Appeals, and finally had his conviction overturned by the California Supreme Court, which ruled on February 1, 1989, that pandering would apply to an adult film production only if the performers were paid for the sexual gratification of the producers or the actors, rather than merely for their performance. This groundbreaking decision makes adult film production possible in California and highlights the performance-based nature of pornography, regardless of its basis in sexual activity. Stephen G. Bloom, "Judge Refuses to Give Mandatory 3 Years to Maker of Porn Films," *Los Angeles Times*, July 16, 1985, V_A6; *California v. Harold Freeman*, 488 U.S. 1311, California Supreme Court, February 1, 1989, *Open Jurist* (accessed April 20, 2013); McNeil, Osborne, and Pavia, *The Other Hollywood*, 402–14.

97. Attorney General's Commission on Pornography, *Final Report of the Attorney General's Commission on Pornography*, 100.

98. Ibid., 72.

99. John Herbers, "Grass-Roots Groups Go National," *New York Times*, September 4, 1983, SM22.

100. Quoted in Dennis Hunt, "Home Video Industry Voices Concern over Attorney General's Pornography Report," *Los Angeles Times*, July 11, 1986, H19.

101. Attorney General's Commission on Pornography, *Final Report of the Attorney General's Commission on Pornography*, 82–83.

102. Carole S. Vance, "Negotiating Sex and Gender in the Attorney General's Commission on Pornography," in *Uncertain Terms: Negotiating Gender in American Culture*, eds. Faye Ginsberg and Anna Lowenhaupt Tsing (Boston: Beacon Press, 1990), 118–34.

103. Vance notes that Hudson acknowledged the lack of testimony on the possibility of pleasure and that he was fond of asking journalists if they knew anyone who could relate positive experiences. He even said the staff had been unable to find such people, further illustrating how panic discourses created deep divides between "decent" and "contaminated" people. Ibid., 130.

104. For a detailed history of the ways such "straying" beyond boundaries resulted in regulatory responses, see George Chauncey, *Gay New York: Gender, Urban Culture, and the Making of the Gay Male World, 1890–1940* (New York: Basic Books, 1995).

105. Attorney General's Commission on Pornography, *Final Report of the Attorney General's Commission on Pornography*, 478–79, 491–92.

106. Ibid., 507–09.

107. Ibid., 512. Ritter grew Covenant House into the largest shelter network for homeless teenagers in the United States, with sites in fifteen cities and more than $90 million in annual funding. In 1990, he was forced to resign after allegations of sexual misconduct with young people under his care, as well as financial mismanagement. He was never charged with a crime, although the statute of limitations had expired for his accusers. He died in seclusion on

October 7, 1999. Tina Kelley, "In Quiet Fields, Father Ritter Found His Exile," *New York Times*, October 22, 1999, B1; Kathleen Hendrix, "Bruce Ritter: A Puzzle for His Friends," *Los Angeles Times*, April 19, 1990, 1.

108. Attorney General's Commission on Pornography, *Final Report of the Attorney General's Commission on Pornography*, 540.

109. Vance, "Negotiating Sex and Gender in the Attorney General's Commission on Pornography," 121.

110. Nan D. Hunter, "Contextualizing the Sexuality Debates: A Chronology," in *Sex Wars: Sexual Dissent and Political Culture*, eds. Lisa Duggan and Nan D. Hunter (New York: Routledge, 1995), 16.

111. My very brief examination of the antipornography feminist movement hardly does justice to what is an extraordinary period in American history. Carolyn Bronstein masterfully details the intricate and detailed histories of these three groups in *Battling Pornography: The American Feminist Anti-Pornography Movement, 1976–1986* (New York: Cambridge University Press, 2011). Also see Laura Lederer, ed., *Take Back the Night: Women on Pornography* (New York: William Morrow, 1980).

112. Quoted in Judy Klemesrud, "Women, Pornography, Free Speech: A Fierce Debate at N.Y.U.," *New York Times*, December 4, 1978, D10.

113. Andrea Dworkin, *Pornography: Men Possessing Women* (New York: Perigree, 1979).

114. Georgia Dullea, "In Feminists' Antipornography Drive, 42d Street Is the Target," *New York Times*, July 6, 1979, A12. John D'Emilio, in his account of the WAP slideshow and tour in 1980, notes the ways in which the event was framed to discourage debate or disagreement and argues that it reached simplistic conclusions, blurred distinctions, ignored any concept of fantasy, and assumed causal connections where there were none, all in an effort to create absolutist links between pornography and violence. "Women against Pornography: Feminist Frontier of Social Purity Crusade?" in *Making Trouble: Essays on Gay History, Politics, and the University* (New York: Routledge, 1992), 202–15.

115. "Samois," in *Encyclopedia of Lesbian, Gay, Bisexual, and Transgender History in America*, ed. Marc Stein (New York: Thomson Gale, 2004), 67–69.

116. Samois, ed., *Coming to Power: Writing and Graphics on Lesbian S/M* (San Francisco: Alyson Books, 1981); Robin Ruth Linden et al., eds., *Against Sadomasochism: A Radical Feminist Analysis* (Palo Alto, CA: Frog in the Well Press, 1982).

117. The "sex wars" erupted most visibly at the "Toward a Politics of Sexuality" conference at Barnard College in April 1982, at which antipornography feminist groups protested and disrupted the proceedings, leading administrators to pull the conference program from distribution. This watershed event and the chaos it produced were a historical turning point, pushing both sides of the issue into increased public action. The events at Barnard are detailed in an anthology of works presented at the conference, and the conference program was also eventually published. Carole S. Vance, ed., *Pleasure and Danger: Exploring Female Sexuality* (London: Pandora Press, 1992); Carole S. Vance,

ed., *Diary of a Conference on Sexuality* (New York: Faculty Press, 1983); Elizabeth Wilson, "The Context of 'Between Pleasure and Danger': The Barnard Conference on Sexuality," *Feminist Review* 13 (Spring 1983): 35–41.

Also see Duggan and Hunter, *Sex Wars;* Ann Snitow, Christine Stansell, and Sharon Thompson, eds., *Powers of Desire: The Politics of Sexuality* (New York: Monthly Review Press, 1983); and Alison Assiter and Avedon Carol, eds., *Bad Girls and Dirty Pictures: The Challenge to Reclaim Feminism* (Boulder, CO: Pluto Press, 1993).

118. Gayle Rubin, "Misguided, Dangerous, and Wrong: An Analysis of Anti-Pornography Politics," in *Bad Girls and Dirty Pictures,* eds. Assiter and Carol, 20, 25.

119. The model ordinance is included in Franklin Mark Osanka and Sara Lee Johann, *Sourcebook on Pornography* (Lexington, MA: 1989), 519–21, quote 520.

120. Catharine MacKinnon and Andrea Dworkin, eds., *In Harm's Way: The Pornography Civil Rights Hearings* (Cambridge, MA: Harvard University Press, 1997).

121. *American Booksellers Assocation. v. Hudnut,* 475 U.S. 1001, 7th Circuit Court of Appeals, 1986, LexisNexis (accessed April 13, 2013).

122. MacKinnon and Dworkin, eds., *In Harm's Way.* In response to the censorship efforts proposed by MacKinnon and Dworkin in the civil rights ordinances, pro-sex feminists and other free speech advocates formed the Feminist Anti-Censorship Taskforce (FACT), with groups in New York; Madison, Wisconsin; San Francisco; Los Angeles; and Cambridge, Massachusetts. Their responses are collected in Caught Looking Inc., ed., *Caught Looking: Feminism, Pornography & Censorship,* 2nd ed. (East Haven, CT: LongRiver Books, 1992).

123. Attorney General's Commission on Pornography, *Final Report of the Attorney General's Commission on Pornography,* 198–99.

124. Vance, "Negotiating Sex and Gender in the Attorney General's Commission on Pornography," 121–22.

125. Ibid., 123.

126. Ibid., 125.

127. Quoted in ibid., 124. See also David Firestone, "Battle Joined by Reluctant Allies," *Newsday,* July 10, 1986, 5.

128. "Chill Factor," *Time,* June 23, 1986, 46. Attached to the letter was a copy of Wildmon's testimony, though it was not labeled as such. In part, it read: "Few people realize that 7-Eleven convenience stores are the leading retailers of porn magazines in America." Hertzberg, "Big Boobs," 24.

129. That pressure also included direct action. In September 1985, well before Sears's letter, Jerry Falwell led five thousand marchers past 7-Eleven's corporate headquarters in Dallas as part of an antipornography rally. "Falwell Rally Protested," *Washington Post,* September 3, 1985, A12.

130. Quoted in "No More Adults: 7-Eleven Bans Skin Mags," *Time,* April 21, 1986, http://content.time.com/time/magazine/article/0,9171,961154,00 .html (accessed April 14, 2013).

131. Quoted in Paul Richter, "Thrifty Drug to Quit Selling Adult Magazines," *New York Times*, May 2, 1986, 1.

132. Quoted in ibid., 12.

133. Donald Wildmon, *The Home Invaders* (Wheaton, IL: Victor Books, 1985); Donald Wildmon, *The Case against Pornography* (Wheaton, IL: Victor Books, 1986), 34–35, 179, 187.

134. "Chill Factor," 46; Lillienstein quoted in Philip Shenon, "Playboy and Booksellers Suing Pornography Panel," *New York Times*, May 20, 1986, A24.

135. Shenon, "Playboy and Booksellers Suing Pornography Panel," A24.

136. Penn quoted in Philip Shenon, "Pornography Panel Barred from Publicizing Retailers," *New York Times*, July 4, 1986, A6; "Court Bars Porn Panel from Listing Retailers in Report," *Publishers Weekly*, July 18, 1986, 16.

137. Quoted in "The Lawyer behind the Government's Pornography Report," 15.

138. Thomas B. Rosenstiel, "Sex Losing Its Appeal for Playboy," *Los Angeles Times*, August 25, 1986, 17.

139. Ben Pesta, "X-Rated Video: Will It Make Adult Theaters and Men's Magazines Obsolete?" *Hustler* (October 1984): 54.

140. Vance, "Negotiating Sex and Gender in the Attorney General's Commission on Pornography," 119.

141. Quoted in Philip Shenon, "Meese, in a Move on Pornography, Creates Special Prosecution Team," *New York Times*, October 23, 1986, A21. Meese's action was welcomed by conservatives, particularly since the first major political test of the reaction to the *Report* had resoundingly failed: on June 11, 1986, Maine voters overwhelmingly voted against legislation that would have made it a crime to sell or promote obscenity, as defined by the community-standards test established by *Miller*. It was the first such statewide measure proposed in the country. In some senses, the measure itself was meaningless, since obscenity was not constitutionally protected anyway; the measure, then, can be seen as indicative of the larger panic gripping the nation in the mid-1980s that drove some to legislate reassurance. Its defeat was among the few bright spots for those seeking to stem the relentless containment and eradication of pornography. Matthew L. Wald, "Obscenity Debate Focuses Attention on Maine, Where Voters Weigh Issue," *New York Times*, June 10, 1986, A18; Matthew L. Wald, "Maine Anti-Obscenity Plan Soundly Defeated," *New York Times*, June 12, 1986, A27.

142. Kent Jenkins Jr., "3 in Fairfax Indicted in Pornography Case; Charges Brought under Racketeering Law," *Washington Post*, August 15, 1987, G1.

143. Caryle Murphy, "Federal Grand Jury Probe Launched; U.S. Grand Jury in Alexandria Subpoenas Records of 11 Firms," *Washington Post*, November 29, 1986, B1.

144. In 2002, President George W. Bush nominated Hudson to be a federal judge in the U.S. District Court for the Eastern District of Virginia. Linda Greenhouse, "Prosecutor in Pentagon Case: Quiet 'Bulldog' and Moralist," *New York Times*, June 28, 1988, A20; "Biographical Directory of Federal Judges:

Hudson, Henry E," Federal Judicial Center, n.d., www.fjc.gov/servlet/nGetInfo ?jid=2954&cid=999&ctype=na&instate=na (accessed April 13, 2013).

145. "Racketeering Law Used for First Time on Obscenity Case," *New York Times*, August 16, 1987, 29.

146. Caryle Murphy, "Tape Seizures Part of Wider Investigation; Area Obscenity Probe Linked to N.Y., Ohio," *Washington Post*, October 16, 1986, A37; Caryle Murphy and Kent Jenkins, "Obscenity Case Battlefield Shifts; Meese's Pornography Crusade Hinges on Forfeiture," *Washington Post*, November 12, 1987, C1; Caryle Murphy, "Va. Pornography Dealers Guilty of Racketeering," *Washington Post*, November 11, 1987, A1; Robert F. Howe, "Panel Upholds Racketeering Conviction in Va. Pornography Case," *Washington Post*, April 11, 1990, B4.

The four adult videos were *She-Male Encounters 9: She-Male Confidential* (1984, dir. Kim Christy), *Wet Shots* (1981, dir. unknown), *The Girls of the A-Team* (1985, dir. Jerome Tanner), and *The Punishment of Anne* (1975, dir. Radley Metzger). The nine magazines were *Torment, She . . . Who Must Be Obeyed, Bottoms Up, Slave Training, Tied Up, Super Bitch, Tender Shavers, Crotches*, and *Poppin' Mamas. United States of America v. Dennis Pryba*, 900 F.2d 748, United States Court of Appeals for the Fourth Circuit, April 9, 1990, LexisNexis (accessed April 13, 2013).

147. James Lardner, "A Pornographer's Rise, Fall; the Rise and Fall of City's First King of Pornography," *Washington Post*, January 12, 1978, A1. Womack fought against obscenity prosecutions of gay publications, created a chain of adult bookstores and cinemas for gay men, established Guild Press to print and distribute gay books and magazines, supported the Mattachine Society (among the earliest homophile organizations in the United States, founded in 1950) by printing its publications at his print shop, and published the national newspaper *Gay Forum*, among other activities. He died in 1985. Rainbow History Project, "Dr. Herman Lynn Womack," Rainbow History Project, n.d., https://rainbowhistory.omeka.net/exhibits/show/womack/pioneer/womack_intro (accessed April 13, 2013).

148. "P.G. Shop Owner Found Guilty in Porno Case," *Washington Post*, May 4, 1977, B8.

149. Michael McQueen, "Portable Porn; Porno Migration; Suburbanites Fear Influx of Sex-Oriented Businesses," *Washington Post*, March 5, 1981, MD1.

150. Quoted in McQueen, "Portable Porn," MD1.

151. Murphy, "Federal Grand Jury Probe Launched," B1; Jenkins, "3 in Fairfax Indicted in Pornography Case," G1.

152. Murphy, "Va. Pornography Dealers Guilty of Racketeering," A1.

153. Ibid.

154. The federal government could not sell the inventory of pornographic material. It was placed into storage, as perhaps the ultimate (to use Walter Kendrick's term) "secret museum." Caryle Murphy, "Adult Book Store Owner Sentenced to Three Years," *Washington Post*, December 19, 1987, F3.

155. Ibid.

156. Ruth Marcus, "Racketeering Test Upheld in Va. Obscenity Case," *Washington Post*, October 16, 1990, B5.

157. Murphy, "Adult Book Store Owner Sentenced to Three Years," F3.

158. *Barbara A. Pryba, Dennis E. Pryba, Educational Books, Inc. and Jennifer G. Williams v. United States*, 498 U.S. 924, Supreme Court of the United States, October 15, 1990, LexisNexis (accessed April 13, 2013).

159. *United States of America v. Dennis Pryba.*

160. Ronald Selinger, owner of Transworld Video Sales, a wholesaling operation in Florida, was another victim of RICO prosecutions in the mid-1980s. Prosecuted twice, Selinger was the focus of two sting operations in which authorities created phony operational video stores to ensnare him and his employees on obscenity and racketeering charges. Paul Blythe, "Dealer Charged: Boca Police Arrest Film Wholesaler," *Palm Beach Post*, June 14, 1985, B1; Earl Paige, "Racket Busts Hit Fla. Sellers of Adult Video," *Billboard*, July 13, 1985, 1, 74; Lisa Getter, "15 Arrested in Probe of Pornography." *Miami Herald*, September 26, 1986, 1PB.

RICO proscecutions were upheld as a valid legal strategy by the United States Supreme Court in *Alexander v. United States* in 1992, in which the court ruled that property forfeiture under RICO as punishment for the distribution of obscene materials did not constitute "prior restraint" on speech in violation of the First Amendment. See Bruno C. Bier, "RICO and the First Amendment," *Fordham Intellectual Property, Media, and Entertainment Law Journal* 6, no. 1 (1995): 369–425; *Alexander v. United States*, 509 U.S. 544, Supreme Court of the United States, *Justia*, June 28, 1993, https://supreme.justia.com/cases/federal/us/509/544/case.html (accessed September 25, 2015).

161. Philip Shenon, "Justice Dept. Plans Anti-Racketeering Drive against Pornographers," *New York Times*, January 12, 1988, A16.

162. "Five Video Stores Busted for Obscenity in St. Louis," *Adult Video News Confidential* (February 1987): 4.

163. "X-Rated Film Shown as Evidence in Obscenity Trial," *Los Angeles Times*, March 1, 1986, SD_A3.

164. Jan Klunder, "Porn Suspect Allegedly in Organized Crime," *Los Angeles Times*, February 15, 1986, V_A10; John H. Weston, "It's the Law? Obscenity Laws and the Effects on Video Retailers," *Adult Video News Confidential* (September 1987): 12; John H. Weston, "Nine Misdemeanor Obscenity Cases Filed against Video Wholesalers," *Adult Video News Confidential* (May 1986): 8.

165. Quoted in "20 Charged in L.A. Obscenity 'Sting,'" *Los Angeles Times*, February 14, 1986, V_A3.

166. The eight films: *Sex Busters* (1984, dir. Adam), *Night of the Spanish Fly* (1976, dir. Bob Mason), *Fast Cars Fast Women* (1981, dir. Scott McHaley), *Seduction of Lana Shore* (1984, dir. Kaye Vie), *Ass Busters* (year, dir. unknown), *Blazing Zippers* (1976, dir. Boots McCoy), *Up 'n Coming* (1982, dir. Godfrey Daniels), and *Bodacious TA-TA's* (1985, dir. Paul Vatelli). "Michigan Prosecuting Attorneys Crack Down on Obscenity," *Adult Video News Confidential* (June 1986): 6.

167. Michael Silverman, "X-Rated HV Suppliers Stay Blue, but over Competition, Not Meese," *Variety*, September 3, 1986, 117; *Strong Kids, Safe Kids* (1984, dir. Rick Hauser, VHS).

168. Bloom's was one of the cases dropped in the MIPORN investigation due to Livingston's shoplifting arrest (see note 46).

169. Quoted in Thomas Omestad, "Alarm Sounds in Thousand Oaks over Sex Video Supplier," *Los Angeles Times*, April 20, 1986, V_A4.

170. Seth S. King, "Foes of Pornography Winning a Few Skirmishes, but Not the Major Battles," *New York Times*, November 28, 1975, 52.

171. John Kifner, "Boston 'Combat Zone' Becomes Target of Police Crackdown," *New York Times*, December 4, 1976, 10.

172. "Americana: Taming the Combat Zone," *Time*, September 19, 1977, http://content.time.com/time/magazine/article/0,9171,915473,00.html (accessed March 12, 2013); "Quarantined! A Case Study of Boston's Combat Zone," in *Hop on Pop: The Politics and Pleasures of Popular Culture*, eds. Henry Jenkins, Tara McPherson, and Jane Shattuc (Durham, NC: Duke University Press, 2002), 430–53.

173. "The Porno Plague," *Time*, April 5, 1976, 58–63.

174. *Mayor of Detroit Young, et al. v. American Mini Theatres, Inc., et al.*, 427 U.S. 50. Supreme Court of the United States, June 24, 1976, LexisNexis (accessed April 13, 2013).

175. *City of Renton, Inc. et al. v. Playtime Theatres, et al.*, 475 U.S. 41. Supreme Court of the United States, February 25, 1986, LexisNexis (accessed April 13, 2013).

176. For more on the nuances of zoning laws and pornography regulation, see Mackey, *Pornography on Trial;* and Sam R. Collins, "Adults Only! Can We Zone Away the Evils of Adult Businesses?" *Journal of Natural Resources and Environmental Law* 13, no. 1 (1997–98): 177–98.

177. Daniel Linz and his research partners have done invaluable analysis of the efficacy of the "secondary effects" principles that continue to serve as justification for the draconian zoning laws that control pornography enterprises in the United States. Daniel Linz, B. Paul, and M.Z. Yao, "Peep Show Establishments, Police Activity, Public Place and Time: A Study of Secondary Effects in San Diego, California," *Journal of Sex Research* 43, no. 2 (2006): 182–93; Daniel Linz et al., "An Examination of the Assumption That Adult Businesses Are Associated with Crime in Surrounding Areas: A Secondary Effects Study in Charlotte, North Carolina," *Law and Society Review* 38, no. 1 (2004): 69–101.

178. Such concerns led to the brief moment in which the VSDA and the Motion Picture Association of America (MPAA), bitter historical enemies due to battles over the "first sale" legal doctrine, which guaranteed the right to resell and/or rent video tapes after purchase without paying royalties, nearly formed a coalition against censorship, fearing that community groups might begin pressuring prosecutors to go after "obscene" content in Hollywood films. Nothing came of the idea. Earl Paige, "VSDA & MPAA May Team to Battle Porno Legislation," *Billboard*, March 22, 1986, 86. For more on the first sale

doctrine, see Peter Decherney, *Hollywood's Copyright Wars: From Edison to the Internet* (New York: Columbia University Press, 2012), 177–81.

179. Quoted in Chris Morris, "Fighting the Climate of Censorship," *Billboard*, August 30, 1986, 13.

180. Quoted in Tony Seideman, "Video Dealers Are Tense over Anti-Porn Drive," *Billboard*, August 30, 1986, 88.

181. Hunt, "Home Video Industry Voices Concern," H1, H19.

182. In 1985, a Los Angeles company marketed a set of books and labels to keep behind video store rental counters, suggesting they would "allow dealers to protect their family image." "The Adult Blue Book," *Billboard*, May 18, 1985, 28.

183. Dan Herbert describes the structure of the back room and the generic categories used to organize tapes in *Videoland: Movie Culture at the American Video Store* (Berkeley: University of California Press, 2014), 62–63. J. Steven Witkowski analyzes the layout of adult video in a group of video stores in "Mapping Hardcore Space," *Media Fields* 1 (2010), www.mediafieldsjournal.org/mapping-hardcore-space/ (accessed September 9, 2015).

184. Jonathan Coopersmith, "Pornography, Technology and Progress," *Icon* 4 (1998): 94–125, quote 117.

185. Sheila M. Poole, "Video Rental Company Saw More Than a Fad," *Atlanta Journal and Constitution*, June 16, 1995, 1G.

186. Seth Lubove, "Porn Gallery," *Forbes*, February 28, 2005, www.forbes.com/forbes/2005/0228/042a.html (accessed April 12, 2013). Movie Gallery's policy came under fire in 2001 when the American Family Association (AFA) formed a coalition of conservative groups, including the Christian Coalition, Family Policy Network, Kids Hurt Too, and the Florida Family Association to protest. AFA Special Projects Director Randy Sharp had multiple meetings with Movie Gallery executives, but the company steadfastly refused to change its policy. "Movie Gallery's position is and will remain that we can't allow any organization, or person, or handful of people, to censor the product lines that we carry," said a company spokesperson during the protests. It was a remarkable— and exceedingly rare—moment in video rental history that a major chain stood up to protest groups in defense of pornography. Quoted in "Movie Gallery Refuses to Remove Porn," American Family Association, January 2001, www.afajournal.org/2001/january/porna.asp (accessed April 12, 2013).

Movie Gallery's longstanding corporate policy met criticism again in 2005 when the company acquired Hollywood Video, then the second-largest chain in the United States, taking Movie Gallery's total number of stores to nearly five thousand. The AFA, fearing that Movie Gallery would permit adult video in former Hollywood Video locations, initiated a massive publicity campaign. Supporters sent thirty-four thousand emails to Mark Wattles, the devoutly Mormon founder of Hollywood Video, urging him to stop the merger, but Wattles was powerless given his 10 percent overall ownership of the company. He ultimately quit rather than work for Movie Gallery—which, ultimately, never placed adult movies into the old Hollywood Video locations. Lubove, "Porn Gallery."

187. Douglas Gomery, *Shared Pleasures: A History of Movie Presentation in the United States* (Madison: University of Wisconsin Press, 1992), 281–83.

188. Quoted in Luis Aguilar, "Erol's Video: Rental King Made the 'American Dream' His Own," *Washington Post,* July 1, 1984, 5.

189. David Meine, "The X-Rated Image," *Video Store* (August 1986): 12.

190. Quoted in Polman, "Store Owners Divided on Adult Tapes," J1.

191. Ibid.

192. "Adventureland Video Buys Video Biz and . . . Raps R-Rated Pix," *Video Business* (September 1986): 16; Earl Paige, "Adventureland Video Maps Growth," *Billboard,* March 16, 1985, 4.

193. Quoted in "National Bans X-Rated from New Franchises," *Video Business* (August 1986): 16.

194. Quoted in "Major Video Chain Bans Adult Videos," *Adult Video News Confidential* (July 1986): 3.

195. Quoted in "Commtron Drops All Adult Videos," *Billboard,* February 15, 1986, 78.

196. Quoted in "National Bans X-Rated from New Franchises," 16.

197. "Viewpoint," *Adult Video News Confidential* (July 1986): 3.

198. William M. Alpert, "What's Wrong with This Picture?" *Barron's,* September 21, 1987, 8–9, 46–48; John Sippel, "National's Major Chain Puts Emphasis on Superstores," *Billboard,* May 3, 1986, 42, 45; Homer Brickey, "Entrepreneur Tries Franchising New Type of Motorized Game," *Toledo Blade,* October 23, 1983, C6; Dave Gardetta, "The Lust Tycoons," *Los Angeles Magazine* (December 1998): 141–45, 184–85.

199. Alan Abelson, "Up & Down Wall Street," *Barron's,* September 1, 1986, 45; Alpert, "What's Wrong with This Picture?" 8–9, 46–48.

200. Quoted in Gail DeGeorge, *The Making of a Blockbuster* (New York: Wiley, 1996), 95–98.

201. Alpert, "What's Wrong with This Picture?" 98–99.

202. Richard Sandomir, "Wayne Huizenga's Growth Complex," *New York Times Magazine,* June 9, 1991, 25; David Altaner, "Fort Lauderdale Investors Close Deal on Video Stock," *Sun Sentinel,* February 14, 1987, http://articles.sun-sentinel.com/1987–02–14/business/8701100526_1_video-stores-huizenga-blockbuster (accessed October 24, 2012).

203. Sandomir, "Wayne Huizenga's Growth Complex," 24; DeGeorge, *The Making of a Blockbuster,* 28–91.

204. Sandomir, "Wayne Huizenga's Growth Complex," 24.

205. DeGeorge, *The Making of a Blockbuster,* 125–26; Geraldine Fabrikant, "Viacom Announces Merger and Raises Bid for Paramount," *New York Times,* January 8, 1994, 51.

206. Sandomir, "Wayne Huizenga's Growth Complex," 25.

207. DeGeorge, *The Making of a Blockbuster,* 126–27.

208. Greg Clarkin, "Fast Forward," *Marketing and Media Decisions* (March 1990): 57.

209. Quoted in Sandomir, "Wayne Huizenga's Growth Complex," 24. See also DeGeorge, *The Making of a Blockbuster,* 127. Major Video was acquired by

Blockbuster in a highly contentious deal in 1989, and National Video's acquisition followed a year later (DeGeorge, *The Making of a Blockbuster*, 143–44, 151–56). Sounds Easy was acquired by Home-Vision in 1994, which was itself later swallowed by Movie Gallery. "Sounds Easy, Home-Vision to Join Forces," *Sun Journal*, August 11, 1994, 3. Adventureland Video was sold to RKO-Warner Video in 1989. See Roger Pusey, "Placing Ads on Sides of Semitrailers Puts Utah Firm in Fast Lane," *Deseret News*, September 2, 1990, 4.

210. Chuck Kleinhans and Julia Lesage, "The Politics of Sexual Representation," *Jump Cut* (March 1985), www.ejumpcut.org/archive/onlinessays/JC3ofolder/PoliticsSexRep.html (accessed January 10, 2010).

211. According to a Department of Justice summary in 1995, the Child Exploitation and Obscenity Unit (CEOS), which grew out of Meese's National Obscenity Enforcement Unit, had garnered more than more 126 obscenity convictions involving more than $24 million in fines and forfeitures since its inception in 1987. Among those convicted were many early pioneers in adult video, including Anthony, Louis, and Joseph Peraino of Arrow Video; Charles Brickman of Cinderella Distributors; Russ Hampshire of VCA; Reuben Sturman of GVA; Rubin Gottesman and Steven Orenstein of Excitement Video; and Andre D'Apice of VHL. While I have detailed the beginnings of the adult video industry's history, further work on the topic would undoubtedly trace these cases. See U.S. Department of Justice, Criminal Division, Child Exploitation and Obscenity Section, *Summary of Activity of the Child Exploitation and Obscenity Section*, October 16, 1995, 11–15.

212. Robert P. Hey, "Uncle Sam and Private Citizens Go after Child Pornography," *Christian Science Monitor*, September 28, 1987, www.csmonitor.com/1987/0928/aporn.html (accessed April 13, 2013). In 1985, Kirk published an action plan for local communities seeking to stamp out pornography that included many of the strategies outlined in this chapter. See Jerry Kirk, *The Mind Polluters* (New York: Thomas Nelson, 1985).

213. Shenon, "Justice Dept. Plans Anti-Racketeering Drive against Pornographers," A16.

214. "Project Postporn," *Playboy* (September 1990): 49–50.

215. ACLU Arts Project, *Above the Law: The Justice Department's War against the First Amendment* (Medford, NY: American Civil Liberties Union, 1991), 5–7.

216. Quoted in Eileen Putnam, "Pornography Outlets Charged in Obscene Mailings," Associated Press, www.apnewsarchive.com/1988/Pornography-Outlets-Charged-In-Obscene-Mailings/id-ef34940485644cdf3d-53309bad270432, July 1, 1988 (accessed January 15, 2013).

217. One of the companies targeted by Project: Postporn was PHE, Inc., a major adult video distributor through its Adam & Eve line (which distributed Candida Royalle's Femme films, as described in chapter 3). PHE's founder and president, Philip Harvey, decided to fight what ended up being an astounding set of repeated efforts to shutter his business—eventually resulting in multiple and simultaneous indictments in various locations around the United States in an effort to drive him to bankruptcy. Harvey eventually pleaded guilty to lesser

charges but won resounding victories on the majority of the charges. "Project Postporn," 49–50; Philip D. Harvey, *The Government vs. Erotica: The Siege of Adam & Eve* (Amherst, NY: Prometheus Books, 2001).

218. For more on the culture wars and their legacy, see B.J. Bullert, *Public Television: Politics and the Battle over Documentary Film* (New Brunswick, NJ: Rutgers University Press, 1997); Richard Jensen, "The Culture Wars, 1965–1995: A Historian's Map," *Journal of Social History* 29 (Midwinter 1995): 17–37; Duggan and Hunter, eds., *Sex Wars;* and Brian Wallis, Marianne Weems, and Philip Yenawine, eds., *Art Matters: How the Culture Wars Changed America* (New York: New York University Press, 1999).

219. Recent models in this regard are Mireille Miller-Young, *A Taste for Brown Sugar: Black Women in Pornography* (Durham, NC: Duke University Press, 2014); and Jennifer C. Nash, *The Black Body in Ecstasy: Reading Race, Reading Pornography* (Durham, NC: Duke University Press, 2014), which expertly combine textual and contextual analysis to reconsider crucial intersectional questions.

220. John H. Weston, "How Many Stars in the Sky?" *Adult Video News Confidential* (September 1987): 6.

221. Susan Squire makes the same argument in an insightful *Playboy* essay, published after the release of the *Meese Report,* in which she follows a single video store in Bellwood, Illinois, for one weekend in 1986. Her portrait captures a landscape in which adult videos were being rented consistently, continually, and quite happily by "ordinary, decent" Middle Americans. Susan Squire, "Ordinary People," *Playboy* (November 1986): 113–14, 159–61.

222. Ian Jane, "God Created Man, William Margold Created Himself: An Interview with the Renaissance Man of Porn," *Rock Shock Pop,* April 25, 2011, www.rockshockpop.com/forums/content.php?1382-God-Created-Man-William-Margold-Created-Himself (accessed March 14, 2016).

223. Kleinhans and Lesage, "The Politics of Sexual Representation."

224. Quoted in Polman, "Store Owners Divided on Adult Tapes," J1.

225. Al Goldstein, "Pay Dirt, as It Were," *New York Times,* July 23, 1986, A23.

226. Michel Foucault, *The History of Sexuality: An Introduction* (New York: Random House, 1990), 35.

227. Ibid., 48.

228. Quoted in Marc Berman, "See No Evil," *Video Business* (November 1984): 26.

EPILOGUE. LIMOUSINES AND LEGACIES

1. Mark Rabinowitz, "An Interview with Paul Thomas Anderson, Director of *Boogie Nights,*" indiewire.com, October 31, 1997 (accessed May 17, 2015).

2. Gillis was not a fan of the *On the Lookout* sequence in *Boogie Nights.* "I was horrified," he said later, "because for me the experience was a wonderful event. I loved doing it, it was a great adventure. But what happened in *Boogie Nights* was they took it and made it into a very depressing and kind of ugly

thing." Quoted in Jared Rutter, "From the Annals: Jamie Gillis Sets the Record Straight," avn.com, February 20, 2010 (accessed May 1, 2014).

3. These are precisely the qualities that characterize the majority of the clips available on online streaming video sites (called tube sites), even those that are edited out of longer, feature-length films. These clips are radically decontextualized, sorted into categories by content (and spectatorial desire), and often devoid of everything but the sex—maximum gonzo, as it were, and absolutely the offspring of the much-longer trajectory from stag films to loops to Gillis's excursion into the San Francisco night. For more, see Susanna Paasonen, *Carnal Resonance: Affect and Online Pornography* (Cambridge, MA: MIT Press, 2011), esp. 31–70.

4. Linda Williams, *Hard Core: Power, Pleasure, and the "Frenzy of the Visible"* (Berkeley: University of California Press, 1989), 49.

5. Jamie Gillis and Peter Sotos, *Pure Filth* (Port Townsend, WA: Feral House, 2012), 42.

6. Ibid.

7. For example, Jim Holliday argues that *The Opening of Misty Beethoven* "stands head and shoulders" above the other roughly 10,500 adult feature-length films that had been made before it: "Lavishly produced, superbly scored and edited . . . solid plot, outstanding acting, dialogue so clever that it ranks among the most sophisticated ever written for the adult genre, and the sex scenes are simply sensational." Jim Holliday, *Only the Best* (Van Nuys, CA: Cal Vista Direct, 1986), 45.

8. As Will Sloan points out, this unpredictability goes hand in hand with the film's lack of conventional eroticism. In the case of the film's first two pickups, Carl (who cannot maintain an erection) and Shawn (who must remove his condom to have sex with Morgan—a startling moment in a film produced in San Francisco during the AIDS epidemic), that unpredictability becomes part of the action. "At first they can't believe their luck, but then they realize they have to perform with a porn star, while being judged by a porn star, in a way that appeals to porn viewers. When Renee tells them, 'I'm very professional at what I do,' it calls attention to how acutely unprofessional they are." Will Sloan, "The Godfather of Gonzo Porn," http://hazlitt.net/longreads/godfather-gonzo-porn hazlitt.com, November 21, 2013 (accessed May 17, 2015).

9. Rich Moreland, "Recognition of the Cameraman," http://3hattergrindhouse .com/2012/03/22/recognition-of-the-cameraman-6/, March 22, 2012 (accessed August 23, 2012).

10. Enrico Biasin and Federico Zecca, "Contemporary Audiovisual Pornography: Branding Strategy and Gonzo Film Style," *Cinéma & Cie* 9, no. 12 (Spring 2009): 134.

11. I agree with Chauntelle Anne Tibbals, who writes: "Gonzo . . . is not a genre—it is a filmmaking form. Consequently, it is possible for any and all adult content to include moments of gonzo." Tibbals, "Gonzo, Trannys, and Teens—Current Trends in US Adult Content Production, Distribution, and Consumption," *Porn Studies* 1, nos. 1–2 (2014): 127–135, quote 129.

12. Jay Kent Lorenz, "Going Gonzo! The American Flaneur, the Eastern European On/Scene, and the Pleasures of Implausibility," in *Porn 101: Eroticism, Pornography, and the First Amendment*, eds. James Elias et al. (New York: Prometheus Books, 1999), 353.

While Gillis, Powers, and Stagliano found success with gonzo techniques (and paved the way for many others, such as Rodney Moore, Adam Glasser, and Bob East), they were not the first to come up with the idea of first-person videography of sexual encounters. George Urban roamed the streets of Manhattan in the 1970s and 1980s with a video camera strapped to his back, wearing a silver jumpsuit, talking women into exposing their breasts and occasionally having sex with him on camera. The footage was aired on public-access television in New York as part of *The Ugly George Hour of Truth, Sex, and Violence*, which ran from 1976 to 1991 and was the target of numerous censorship efforts. Moore later cited Urban as an influence for his own productions. Alex Mindlin, "The Hunt for Beauties: Ugly George Roams Again," *New York Times*, July 10, 2005, CY5; Acme Anderson, "The Genesis of Gonzo," *XBIZ*, August 8, 2007, www.xbiz.com/articles/82784 (accessed August 23, 2012); D. Keith Mano, "The Cheap Agony of Ugly George," *Playboy* (November 1982): 146–50, 194–200; D. Keith Mano, "Ugly George Talks about TV," *National Review*, October 14, 1988, 57–59.

13. David James, *Allegories of Cinema* (Princeton, NJ: Princeton University Press, 1989), 12.

14. Peter Lehman, "*Boogie Nights:* Will the Real Dirk Diggler Please Stand Up?" *Jump Cut* 42 (December 1998): 38.

15. Whose pleasures, exactly, are depicted and how are a different matter; that question, however, is neither a new one nor limited to gonzo.

16. *Skin Game* (1985, dir. Carriere as Marc Curtis) offers a prototypical Carriere plotline. A group of men and women gather by a pool and have, as Buffy (Mindy Rae) puts it in the film's opening moments, "a lot of wild partying and a lot of wild sex." Some of them seem to know one another, but any context is minimal, brief, and irrelevant. After five pairings, some in an unclear interior location, some in or around the pool (including the requisite "lesbian" number), the film concludes with an orgy set to a rock song replete with lyrics about "playing that skin game." Films such as these all but anticipated gonzo in that they were barely holding on to narrative at all.

17. Biasin and Zecca, "Contemporary Audiovisual Pornography," 143–44.

18. Eugenie Brinkema, "Rough Sex," in *Porn Archives*, eds. Tim Dean, Steven Ruszczycky, and David Squires (Durham, NC: Duke University Press, 2014), 263.

19. Biasin and Zecca, "Contemporary Audiovisual Pornography," 143. Emphasis original.

20. Gail Dines, "The White Man's Burden: Gonzo Pornography and the Construction of Black Masculinity," *Yale Journal of Law and Feminism* 18, no. 1 (2006): 286.

21. Gillis and Sotos, *Pure Filth*, 42.

22. Michael Warner, *The Trouble with Normal: Sex, Politics, and the Ethics of Queer Life* (Cambridge, MA: Harvard University Press, 1999), 1. Emphasis original.

23. Pornography's subsequent great transition—from home video to online spaces—must remain the subject of other work. For some of the critically important research done in in this area, see Lewis Purdue, "EroticaBiz: How Sex Shaped the Internet," in *Net.SeXXX*, ed. Dennis D. Waskul (New York: Peter Lang, 2004), 259–94; Frederick S. Lane III, *Obscene Profits: The Entrepreneurs of Pornography in the Cyber Age* (New York: Routledge, 2001); Katrien Jacobs, *Netporn: DIY Web Culture and Sexual Politics* (New York: Rowman & Littlefield, 2007); Paasonen, *Carnal Resonance*; and Jonathan Coopersmith, "Pornography, Videotape, and the Internet," *IEEE Technology and Society Magazine* (Spring 2000): 27–34.

Selected Bibliography

This book draws from hundreds of articles and advertisements from newspapers, trade journals, and magazines, as well as interviews, popular press books, websites, press releases, and other ephemera. These sources are all catalogued in the notes. This bibliography includes scholarly publications and a select group of other material deemed especially crucial.

Aaron, Chloe. "The Alternate Media Guerrillas." *New York,* October 19, 1970, 50–53.

ACLU Arts Project. *Above the Law: The Justice Department's War against the First Amendment.* Medford, NY: American Civil Liberties Union, 1991.

Ali, Waleed. "Home Video's Pioneers: In Their Own Words." *TWICE: This Week in Consumer Electronics,* August 17–21, 1987, 32–33.

Alilunas, Peter. "The Necessary Future of Adult Media Industry Studies." *Creative Industries Journal* 7, no. 1 (2014): 393–403.

Allen, Robert C. *Horrible Prettiness: Burlesque and American Culture.* Chapel Hill: University of North Carolina Press, 1992.

Altman, Rick. *Silent Film Sound.* New York: Columbia University Press, 2004.

Alvarado, Manuel, ed. *Video World-Wide: An International Study.* Paris: UNESCO, 1988.

Anderson, Acme. "The Genesis of Gonzo." *XBIZ,* August 8, 2007. www.xbiz .com/articles/82784.

Appleford, Steve. "The Money Shot." *Bikini* (April 1999): 88–91.

Arcand, Bernard. *The Jaguar and the Anteater: Pornography Degree Zero.* Trans. Wayne Grady. London: Verso Books, 1993.

Armes, Roy. *On Video.* New York: Routledge, 1988.

Asbury, Herbert. *The Barbary Coast: An Informal History of the San Francisco Underworld.* New York: Alfred A. Knopf, 1933.

Assiter, Alison, and Avedon Carol, eds. *Bad Girls and Dirty Pictures: The Challenge to Reclaim Feminism.* Boulder, CO: Pluto Press, 1993.

Attorney General's Commission on Pornography: Final Report. 2 vols. Washington, DC: U.S. Government Printing Office, 1986.

Attorney General's Commission on Pornography. *Final Report of the Attorney General's Commission on Pornography.* Nashville, TN: Rutledge Hill Press, 1986.

Bahktin, Mikhail. *Rabelais and His World.* Bloomington: University of Indiana Press, 1984.

Balio, Tino. *The American Film Industry.* Madison: University of Wisconsin Press, 1985.

————, ed. *Grand Design: Hollywood as a Modern Business Enterprise.* History of the American Cinema. Berkeley: University of California Press, 1993.

Bell, Shannon. *Reading, Writing, and Rewriting the Prostitute Body.* Bloomington: Indiana University Press, 1994.

Benson-Allott, Caetlin. *Killer Tapes and Shattered Screens: Video Spectatorship from VHS to File Sharing.* Berkeley: University of California Press, 2013.

Berger, Arthur. "Varieties of Topless Experience." *Journal of Popular Culture* 4, no. 2 (Fall 1970): 419–24.

Berges, Marshall. *The Life and Times of Los Angeles: A Newspaper, a Family, and a City.* New York: Atheneum, 1984.

Berlant, Lauren, and Michael Warner. "Sex in Public." *Critical Inquiry* 24, no. 2 (Winter 1998): 547–66.

Bianco, Anthony. *Ghosts of 42nd Street: A History of America's Most Infamous Block.* New York: HarperCollins, 2004.

Biasin, Enrico, and Federico Zecca. "Contemporary Audiovisual Pornography: Branding Strategy and Gonzo Film Style." *Cinéma & Cie* 9, no. 12 (Spring 2009): 133–50.

Bier, Bruno C. "RICO and the First Amendment." *Fordham Intellectual Property, Media, and Entertainment Law Journal* 6, no. 1 (1995): 369–425.

Blake, Andrew. *Topless.* New York: Belmont, 1969.

Blay, Andre A. "Home Video's Pioneers: In Their Own Words." *TWICE: This Week in Consumer Electronics,* August 17–21, 1987, 32–33.

————. *Pre-Recorded History: Memoirs of an Entertainment Entrepreneur.* Centennial, CO: Deer Track, 2010.

Blumenthal, Ralph. "Porno Chic: 'Hard-Core' Grows Fashionable—and Very Profitable." *New York Times Magazine,* January 21, 1973, 28, 30, 32–34.

Bordwell, David. *The Way Hollywood Tells It: Story and Style in Modern Movies.* Berkeley: University of California Press, 2006.

Bourdieu, Pierre. *Distinction: A Social Critique of the Judgment of Taste.* Trans. Richard Nice. 1979; Cambridge, MA: Harvard University Press, 1984.

Boyle, Deirdre. "From PortaPak to Camcorder: A Brief History of Guerrilla Television." *Journal of Film and Video* 44, nos. 1–2 (Spring–Summer 1992): 67–79.

"Branded Flesh." *Economist,* August 12, 1999, www.economist.com/node /232069.

Brennan, Peter. "The Lick, Lick Show." *Screw,* May 24, 1971, 23.

Brigman, William E. "Politics and the Pornography Wars." *Wide Angle* 19, no. 3 (1997): 149–70.

Brinkema, Eugenie. "Rough Sex." In *Porn Archives,* eds. Tim Dean, Steven Ruszczycky, and David Squires, 262–83. Durham, NC: Duke University Press, 2014.

Bronstein, Carolyn. *Battling Pornography: The American Feminist Anti-Pornography Movement, 1976–1986.* New York: Cambridge University Press, 2011.

Bryan, John. "Gold in the Hills, Sex in the Streets: A 125 Year Romp through San Francisco's Bawdy Past." *Berkeley Barb,* February 4–18, 1977, 6–7.

Bunker, Matthew D., Paul H. Gates, and Sigman L. Splichal. "RICO and Obscenity Prosecutions: Racketeering Laws Threaten Free Expression." *Journalism Quarterly* 70, no. 3 (Autumn 1993): 692–99.

Burger, John Robert. *One-Handed Histories: The Eroto-Politics of Gay Male Video Pornography.* Philadelphia: Haworth Press, 1995.

Butler, Heather. "What Do You Call a Lesbian with Long Fingers? The Development of Lesbian and Dyke Pornography," in *Porn Studies,* ed. Linda Williams, 167–97. Durham, NC: Duke University Press, 2004.

Butsch, Richard. "Bowery B'hoys and Matinee Ladies: The Re-Gendering of Nineteenth-Century America." *American Quarterly* 46, no. 3 (September 1994): 374–405.

Cahill, Paul. "The United States and Canada." In *Video World-Wide: An International Study,* ed. Manuel Alvarado, 127–28. Paris: UNESCO, 1988.

Caldwell, John. *Production Culture: Industrial Reflexivity and Critical Practice in Film and Television.* Durham, NC: Duke University Press, 2008.

Callahan, Jean. "Women and Pornography: Combat in the Video Zone." *American Film* 7, no. 5 (March 1982): 62–63.

Calvert, Clay, and Robert Richards. "Law and Economics of the Adult Entertainment Industry: An Inside View from the Industry's Leading Trade Publisher." *University of Denver Sports & Entertainment Law Journal* 4 (Spring 2008): 2–69.

Cante, Rich, and Angelo Restivo. "The Cultural-Aesthetic Specificities of All-Male Moving-Image Pornography." In *Porn Studies,* ed. Linda Williams, 142–66. Durham, NC: Duke University Press, 2004.

Capino, José. "Homologies of Space: Text and Spectatorship in All-Male Adult Theaters." *Cinema Journal* 45, no. 1 (Autumn 2005): 50–65.

Carr, C. "The Fiery Furnace: Performance in the '80s, War in the '90s." *TDR* 49, no. 1 (Spring 2005): 19–28.

Caught Looking Inc., ed. *Caught Looking: Feminism, Pornography & Censorship.* 2nd ed. East Haven, CT: LongRiver Books, 1992.

Champagne, John. "'Stop Reading Films!' Film Studies, Close Analysis, and Gay Pornography." *Cinema Journal* 36, no. 4 (Summer 1997): 76–97.

Chaney, Nicole. "Cybersex: Protecting Sexual Content in the Digital Age." *John Marshall Review of Intellectual Property Law* 11 (Spring 2012): 815–40.

Chaplin, Sarah. *Japanese Love Hotels: A Cultural History*. New York: Routledge, 2007.

Church, David. "'This Thing of Ours': Heterosexuality, Recreational Sex, and the Survival of Adult Movie Theaters." *Media Fields Journal* 8 (May 9, 2014). www.mediafieldsjournal.org/this-thing-of-ours/.

Chute, David. "Tumescent Market for One-Armed Videophiles." *Film Comment* 17, no. 5 (September–October 1981): 66, 68.

———. "The Wages of Sin." *Film Comment* 22, no. 4 (July 1986): 32–48.

———. "The Wages of Sin, II." *Film Comment* 22, no. 5 (September 1986): 56–61.

Cohen, Stanley. *Folk Devils and Moral Panics: The Creation of the Mods and Rockers*. London: MacGibbon and Kee, 1972.

Collins, Sam R. "Adults Only! Can We Zone Away the Evils of Adult Businesses?" *Journal of Natural Resources and Environmental Law* 13, no. 1 (1997–98): 177–98.

"Conversation with George Atkinson." *Videography* (June 1982): 50–52, 54, 56–59.

Cook, James. "The X-Rated Economy." *Forbes*, September 18, 1978, 81–92.

Coopersmith, Jonathan. "Pornography, Technology and Progress." *Icon* 4 (1998): 94–125.

———. "Pornography, Videotape, and the Internet." *IEEE Technology and Society Magazine* (Spring 2000): 27–34.

Crafton, Donald. *The Talkies: American Cinema's Transition to Sound, 1926–1931*. Berkeley: University of California Press, 1994.

Cubitt, Sean. *Timeshift: On Video Culture*. New York: Routledge, 1991.

Dawson, Max. "Home Video and the 'TV Problem': Cultural Critics and Technological Change." *Technology and Culture* 48, no. 3 (July 2007): 524–49.

Decherney, Peter. *Hollywood's Copyright Wars: From Edison to the Internet*. New York: Columbia University Press, 2012.

DeGeorge, Gail. *The Making of a Blockbuster*. New York: Wiley, 1996.

De Grazia, Edward. *Girls Lean Back Everywhere: The Law of Obscenity and the Assault on Genius*. New York: Vintage, 1993.

Delany, Samuel R. *Times Square Red, Times Square Blue*. New York: New York University Press, 1999.

D'Emilio, John. *Making Trouble: Essays on Gay History, Politics, and the University*. New York: Routledge, 1992.

DiCaprio, Lisa. "*Not a Love Story*: The Film and the Debate." *Jump Cut* 30 (March 1985): 39–42.

Di Lauro, Al, and Gerald Rabkin. *Dirty Movies: An Illustrated History of the Stag Film: 1915–1970*. New York: Chelsea House, 1988.

Dines, Gail. "The White Man's Burden: Gonzo Pornography and the Construction of Black Masculinity." *Yale Journal of Law and Feminism* 18, no. 1 (2006): 283–97.

Dobrow, Julia, ed. *Social and Cultural Aspects of VCR Use*. Hillsdale, NJ: Lawrence Erlbaum, 1990.

Doherty, Thomas. *Pre-Code Hollywood: Sex, Immorality, and Insurrection in American Cinema, 1930–1934.* New York: Columbia University Press, 1999.

Douglas, George H. *All Aboard! The Railroad in American Life.* New York: Paragon House, 1992.

Duggan, Lisa, and Nan D. Hunter, eds. *Sex Wars: Sexual Dissent and Political Culture.* New York: Routledge, 1995.

Duke, Shearlean. "A Nice Place for a Family Affair." *Los Angeles Times,* July 27, 1980, OCA1, 4–6.

Duong, Joseph Lam. "San Francisco and the Politics of Hardcore." In *Sex Scene: Media and the Sexual Revolution,* ed. Eric Schaefer, 297–318. Durham, NC: Duke University Press, 2014.

Dworkin, Andrea. *Pornography: Men Possessing Women.* New York: Perigree, 1979.

Dyer, Richard. "Gay Male Pornography: Coming to Terms." *Jump Cut* 30 (March 1985): 27–29.

Dyer, Richard. *Heavenly Bodies: Film Stars and Society.* New York: St. Martin's Press, 1986.

Eberwein, Robert. *Sex Ed: Film, Video, and the Framework of Desire.* New Brunswick, NJ: Rutgers University Press, 1999.

Egan, Timothy. "Erotic Inc: Technology Sent Wall Street into Market for Pornography." *New York Times,* October 23, 2000. www.nytimes.com /2000/10/23/us/erotica-special-report-technology-sent-wall-street-into-market-for-pornography.html.

Eisenstein, Elizabeth L. *The Printing Revolution in Early Modern Europe.* Cambridge: Cambridge University Press, 1983.

Elias, James, et al., eds. *Porn 101: Eroticism, Pornography, and the First Amendment.* Amherst, NY: Prometheus Books, 1999.

Elias, Norbert. *A History of Manners.* New York: Pantheon, 1978.

Erdman, Dan. "Let's Go Stag! How to Study and Preserve Dirty Films with a Clean Conscience." Presentation, "Sex, Media, Reception: New Approaches Conference," Ann Arbor, MI, February 15, 2014.

Escoffier, Jeffrey. *Bigger Than Life: The History of Gay Porn Cinema from Beefcake to Hardcore.* Philadelphia: Running Press, 2009.

Everett, Sally, ed. *Art Theory and Criticism: An Anthology of Formalist, Avant-Garde, Contextualist, and Post Modernist Thought.* New York: McFarland, 1995.

"Fanfare: Glad There's Code; Sees Cassettes 'Next Porn Boom.'" *Variety,* March 31, 1971, 7.

Farole, Donald J. *Interest Groups and Judicial Federalism.* New York: Praeger, 1998.

"First Home V'cassettes on View." *Variety,* June 14, 1972, 42.

Fishbein, Paul, and I. L. Slifkin. "I Want One with a Story!" *Adult Video News* (March 1983): 5.

Ford, Luke. *A History of X: 100 Years of Sex in Film.* Amherst, NY: Prometheus Books, 1999.

Frammolino, Ralph, and P. J. Huffstutter. "The Actress, the Producer, and Their Porn Revolution." *Los Angeles Times Magazine*, January 6, 2002, 10.

Fraser, Laura. "Nasty Girls." *Mother Jones* (March 1990): 50.

Frasier, David K. *Russ Meyer: The Life and Films*. New York: McFarland, 1997.

Fraterrigo, Elizabeth. *Playboy and the Making of the Good Life in Modern America*. New York: Oxford University Press, 2011.

Friedman, Bruce Jay. *Even the Rhinos Were Nymphos*. Chicago: University of Chicago Press, 2000.

Friedman, Josh Alan. *Tales of Times Square*. New York: Delacorte, 1986.

Friedman, Leon, ed. *Obscenity: The Complete Oral Arguments before the Supreme Court in the Major Obscenity Cases*. New York: Chelsea House, 1980.

Fuentes, Annette, and Margaret Schrage. "Deep inside Porn Stars." *Jump Cut: A Review of Contemporary Media* 32 (April 1987): 41–43.

Fung, Richard. "Looking for My Penis: The Eroticized Asian in Gay Video Porn," in *How Do I Look? Queer Film and Video*, ed. Bad Object-Choices, 145–68. Seattle: Bay Press, 1991.

Ganley, Gladys, and Oswald Ganley. *Global Political Fallout: The First Decade of the VCR 1976–1985*. Cambridge, MA: Harvard University Press, 1987.

Gardetta, Dave. "The Lust Tycoons." *Los Angeles Magazine* (December 1998): 140–45, 184–85.

Gilfoyle, Timothy J. "From Soubrette Row to Show World: The Contested Sexualities of Times Square, 1880–1995." In *Policing Public Sex: Queer Politics and the Future of AIDS Activism*, eds. Ephen Glenn Colter et al., 263–93. Boston: South End Press, 1996.

Gillis, Jamie, and Peter Sotos. *Pure Filth*. Port Townsend, WA: Feral House, 2012.

"Ginger Lynn: The Girl Next Door." *Rialto Report*, November 2, 2014. www .therialtoreport.com/2014/11/02/ginger-lynn-the-girl-next-door-podcast-43/.

Ginzburg, Carlo. "Morelli, Freud and Sherlock Holmes: Clues and Scientific Method." *History Workshop Journal* 9, no. 1 (1980): 5–36.

Goldstein, Al. "Pay Dirt, as It Were." *New York Times*, July 23, 1986, A23.

Gomery, Douglas. "The Coming of Television and the 'Lost' Motion Picture Audience." *Journal of Film and Video* 37, no. 3 (Summer 1985): 5–11.

———. "Theatre Television: The 'Missing Link' of Technical Change in the US Motion Picture Industry." *Velvet Light Trap* 21 (Summer 1985): 54–61.

Goode, Erich, and Nachman Ben-Yehuda. *Moral Panics: The Social Construction of Deviance*. Oxford: Blackwell, 1994.

Goodman, Paul. "Pornography, Art & Censorship." *Commentary* 31, no. 3 (March 1961): 209.

Gorfinkel, Elena. "Wet Dreams: Erotic Film Festivals of the Early 1970s and the Utopian Sexual Public Sphere." In *Sex Scenes: Media and the Sexual Revolution*, ed. Eric Schaefer, 126–50. Durham, NC: Duke University Press, 2014.

Gould, Jodie. "Debbie Directs Dallas: Video Erotica Made by Women for Women." *Elle* (April 1992): 144.

Gray, Ann. *Video Playtime: The Gendering of a Leisure Technology.* London: Routledge, 1992.

Grazia, Edward De. *Girls Lean Back Everywhere: The Law of Obscenity and the Assault on Genius.* New York: Vintage, 1993.

Green, Harvey. *The Light of the Home: An Intimate View of the Lives of Women in Victorian America.* New York: Pantheon Books, 1983.

Greenberg, Joshua M. *From Betamax to Blockbuster: Video Stores and the Invention of Movies on Video.* Cambridge, MA: MIT Press, 2008.

Grieveson, Lee. *Policing Cinema: Movies and Censorship in Early-Twentieth-Century America.* Berkeley: University of California Press, 2004.

Grundberg, Andy. "I Lost It at the Commodore." *New York Magazine,* July 3, 1972, 56.

Gunning, Tom. "Film History and Film Analysis: The Individual Film in the Course of Time." *Wide Angle* 12, no. 3 (July 1990): 4–19.

Hall, Stuart, et al. *Policing the Crisis: Mugging, the State, and Law and Order.* New York: Holmes & Meier, 1978.

Harberski, Raymond J. Jr. "Critics and the Sex Scene." In *Sex Scene: Media and the Sexual Revolution,* ed. Eric Schaefer, 383–406. Durham, NC: Duke University Press, 2014.

Hartley, Nina. "Reflections of a Feminist Porn Star." *Gauntlet* 5 (1993): 62–68.

———. "Porn: An Effective Vehicle for Sexual Role Modeling and Education." In *The Feminist Porn Book,* eds. Tristan Taormino et al., 228–36. New York: Feminist Press at the City University of New York, 2012.

Harvey, Philip D. *The Government vs. Erotica: The Siege of Adam & Eve.* Amherst, NY: Prometheus Books, 2001.

Haskell, Timothy J. "The Legendary Franklin Furnace Presents a Retrospective: The History of the Future: A Franklin Furnace View of Performance Art, One Night Only—April 27th, 2007." March 9, 2007. http://franklinfurnace .org/research/projects/thotf_performance/press_release.html.

Hayes, Arthur S. "First Amendment Lawyers Are Upbeat over Chances to Win Obscenity Cases." *Wall Street Journal,* February 12, 1991, B8.

Hebditch, David, and Nick Anning. *Porn Gold: Inside the Pornography Business.* London: Faber and Faber, 1989.

Hedegaard, Erik. "Sexual Healing." *Details* (September 1991): 140.

Heffernan, Kevin. "From 'It Could Happen to Someone You Love' to 'Do You Speak Ass?': Women and Discourses of Sex Education in Erotic Film and Video." In *The Feminist Porn Book,* eds. Tristan Taormino et al., 237–54. New York: Feminist Press at the City University of New York, 2012.

———. "Seen as a Business: Adult Film's Historical Framework and Foundations." In *New Views on Pornography: Sexuality, Politics, and the Law,* eds. Lynn Comella and Shira Tarrant, 37–56. Santa Barbara, CA: Prager, 2015.

Herdt, Gilbert. "Introduction: Moral Panics, Sexual Rights, and Cultural Anger." In *Moral Panics, Sex Panics: Fear the Fight over Sexual Rights*. Ed. Gilbert Herdt, 1–46. New York: New York University Press, 2009.

Hertzberg, Hendrik. "Big Boobs: Ed Meese and His Pornography Commission." *New Republic*, July 14–21, 1986, 21–24.

Herzog, Amy. "Illustrating Music: The Impossible Embodiments of the Jukebox Film." In *Medium Cool: Music Videos from Soundies to Cellphones*, eds. Roger Beebe and Jason Middleton, 30–58. Durham, NC: Duke University Press, 2007.

———. "In the Flesh: Space and Embodiment in the Pornographic Peep Show Arcade." *Velvet Light Trap* 62 (Fall 2008): 29–43.

———. "Fetish Machines: Peep Shows, Co-Optation, and Technological Adaptation." In *Adaptation Theories*, ed. Jillian St Jacques, 47–89. Maastricht, Netherlands: Jan Van Eyck Academie Press, 2011.

Hier, Sean P. "Conceptualizing Moral Panic through a Moral Economy of Harm." *Critical Sociology* 28, no. 3 (2002): 311–34.

Hilderbrand, Lucas. *Inherent Vice: Bootleg Histories of Videotape and Copyright*. Durham, NC: Duke University Press, 2009.

Holliday, Jim. *Only the Best*. Van Nuys, CA: Cal Vista Direct, 1986.

———. "A History of Modern Pornographic Film and Video." In *Porn 101: Eroticism, Pornography, and the First Amendment*, eds. James Elias et al., 341–51. Amherst, NY: Prometheus Books, 1999.

"Home Video Market Puts Accent on Porn." *Variety*, November 1, 1978, 2.

Hose, Wally. *Soundies*. St. Louis, MO: Wally's Multimedia, 2007.

Hunt, Lynn. "Introduction: Obscenity and the Origins of Modernity, 1500–1800." In *The Invention of Pornography: Obscenity and the Origins of Modernity, 1500–1800*, ed. Lynn Hunt, 9–45. New York: Zone Books, 1993.

Lynn Hunt, ed. *The Invention of Pornography: Obscenity and the Origins of Modernity, 1500–1800*. New York: Zone Books, 1993.

Hunter, Nan D. "Contextualizing the Sexuality Debates: A Chronology." In *Sex Wars: Sexual Dissent and Political Culture*, eds. Lisa Duggan and Nan D. Hunter, 16–29. New York: Routledge, 1995.

Hyde, H. Montgomery. *A History of Pornography*. New York: Dell, 1964.

Irvine, Janice M. "Transient Feelings: Sex Panics and the Politics of Emotion." *GLQ* 14, no. 1 (2008): 1–40.

Jacobs, Katrien. *Netporn: DIY Web Culture and Sexual Politics*. New York: Rowman & Littlefield, 2007.

James, David. *Allegories of Cinema*. Princeton, NJ: Princeton University Press, 1989.

Jennings, David. *Skinflicks: The Inside Story of the X-Rated Video Industry*. Bloomington, IN: 1st Books, 2000.

Johns, Adrian. *Piracy: The Intellectual Property Wars from Gutenberg to Gates*. Chicago: University of Chicago Press, 2009.

Johnson, Eithne. "Excess and Ecstasy: Constructing Female Pleasure in Porn Movies." *Velvet Light Trap* 32 (Fall 1993): 30–49.

———. "The 'Colonoscopic' Film and the 'Beaver' Film: Scientific and Pornographic Scenes of Female Sexual Responsiveness." In *Swinging Single: Representing Sexuality in the 1960s*, eds. Hilary Radner and Moya Luckett, 301–24. Minneapolis: University of Minnesota Press, 1999.

Juffer, Jane. *At Home with Pornography: Women, Sex, and Everyday Life.* New York: New York University Press, 1998.

Karon, Paul. "Vivid Aims Its Appeal at John Q. Public." *Variety,* March 9, 1998, 1.

Katzman, Lisa. "The Women of Porn: They're Not in It for the Money Shot." *Village Voice,* August 24, 1993, 31–33.

Kaye, B.C. "X-Rated Motels for Adventurous Couples." *Sexology* (September 1975): 11–15.

Keating Jr., Charles H. "Statement of Charles H. Keating, Jr." In *The Report of the Commission on Obscenity and Pornography*, ed. Commission on Obscenity and Pornography, 511–49. New York: Random House, 1970.

———. "The Report That Shocked the Nation." *Reader's Digest* (January 1971): 37–41.

Keen, Ben. "'Play It Again, Sony': The Double Life of Home Video Technology." *Science as Culture* 1, no. 1 (1987): 7–42.

Kelley, Andrea. "'A Revolution in the Atmosphere': The Dynamics of Site and Screen in 1940s Soundies." *Cinema Journal* 54, no. 2 (Winter 2015): 72–93.

Kendrick, Walter. *The Secret Museum: Pornography in Modern Culture.* Berkeley: University of California Press, 1987.

"King Smut." *Philadelphia Magazine* (November 2004). phillymag.com /articles/king-smut/.

Kipnis, Laura. "(Male) Desire, (Female) Disgust: Reading *Hustler*." In *Cultural Studies*, eds. Lawrence Grossberg, Cary Nelson, and Paula A. Treicher, 373–92. New York: Routledge, 1992.

———. *Bound and Gagged: Pornography and the Politics of Fantasy in America.* Durham, NC: Duke University Press, 1996.

Kirk, Jerry. *The Mind Polluters.* New York: Thomas Nelson, 1985.

Kleinhans, Chuck. "The Change from Film to Video Pornography: Implications for Analysis." In *Pornography: Film and Culture*, ed. Peter Lehman, 154–67. New Brunswick, NJ: Rutgers University Press, 2006.

Kleinhans, Chuck, and Julia Lesage. "The Politics of Sexual Representation." *Jump Cut* (March 1985). www.ejumpcut.org/archive/onlinessays/JC30folder /PoliticsSexRep.html.

Klinger, Barbara. *Beyond the Multiplex: Cinema, New Technologies, and the Home.* Berkeley: University of California Press, 2006.

Knight, Arthur, and Hollis Alpert. "The History of Sex in Cinema: Part Seventeen: The Stag Film." *Playboy* (November 1967): 154–58.

Koop, C. Everett. "Report of the Surgeon General's Workshop on Pornography and Public Health." *American Psychologist* 42, no. 10 (October 1987): 944–45.

Kuhn, Annette. "Lawless Seeing." In idem., *The Power of the Image: Essays on Representation and Sexuality.* Boston: Routledge & Kegan Paul, 1985, 19–47.

Lahue, Kalton C. "Get Ready for X-Rated TV!" *Velvet* (December 1978): 90.

———. "Video Porn." *Velvet Talks!* 6 (1979): 12–13.

Lancaster, Roger N. *Sex Panic and the Punitive State.* Berkeley: University of California Press, 2011.

Lane, Frederick S. III. *Obscene Profits: The Entrepreneurs of Pornography in the Cyber Age.* New York: Routledge, 2001.

Lardner, James. "How Hollywood Learned to Stop Worrying and Love the VCR: Home Video Has Diminished the Power of the Studios—but Not Their Profits." *Los Angeles Times,* April 19, 1987, 12–19.

———. *Fast Forward: Hollywood, the Japanese, and the Onslaught of the VCR.* New York: W.W. Norton, 1987.

Lassiter, Matthew D. *The Silent Majority: Suburban Politics in the Sunbelt South.* Princeton, NJ: Princeton University Press, 2006.

"L.A.'s X-Rated Motels: Pornopix & Water Beds." *Variety,* March 7, 1973, 79.

Lawrence, Mitchell. "Candida Goes Candid." *Adam Film World* (September 1980): 17.

Layser, Anthony. "Porn Supremacy." *Philadelphia Weekly,* January 9, 2008. www.philadelphiaweekly.com/arts-and-culture/porn_supremacy-38463929.html.

Lederer, Laura, ed. *Take Back the Night: Women on Pornography.* New York: William Morrow, 1980.

Lees, Alfred W. "Sit Back and Enjoy Yourself: New Projectors Put on the Whole Show." *Popular Science* (March 1962): 73–74.

Lehman, Peter. "*Boogie Nights:* Will the Real Dirk Diggler Please Stand Up?" *Jump Cut* 42 (December 1998): 32–38.

———, ed. *Pornography: Film and Culture.* New Brunswick, NJ: Rutgers University Press, 2006.

———. "Revelations about Pornography." In *Pornography: Film and Culture,* ed. Peter Lehman, 87–98. New Brunswick, NJ: Rutgers University Press, 2006.

Leo, John. "Romantic Porn in the Boudoir." *Time,* March 30, 1987, 64.

Levy, Alan. "A Morality Play in Three Acts." *Life,* March 11, 1966, 79–87.

Levy, Mark, ed. *The VCR Age: Home Video and Mass Communication.* London: Sage, 1989.

Lewis, Jon. *Hollywood v. Hard Core: How the Struggle over Censorship Created the Modern Film Industry.* New York: New York University Press, 2002.

Lichtman, Allan J. *White Protestant Nation: The Rise of the American Conservative Movement.* New York: Grove Press, 2008.

Linden, Robin Ruth, et al., eds. *Against Sadomasochism: A Radical Feminist Analysis.* Palo Alto, CA: Frog in the Well Press, 1982.

Linz, Daniel, et al. "An Examination of the Assumption That Adult Businesses Are Associated with Crime in Surrounding Areas: A Secondary Effects Study in Charlotte, North Carolina." *Law and Society Review* 38, no. 1 (2004): 69–101.

Linz, Daniel, B. Paul, and M.Z. Yao. "Peep Show Establishments, Police Activity, Public Place and Time: A Study of Secondary Effects in San Diego, California." *Journal of Sex Research* 43, no. 2 (2006): 182–93.

Lorenz, Jay Kent. "Going Gonzo! The American Flaneur, the Eastern European On/Scene, and the Pleasures of Implausibility." In *Porn 101: Eroticism, Pornography, and the First Amendment*, eds. James Elias et al., 352–58. New York: Prometheus Books, 1999.

"Love 'Em & Shoot 'Em." *Playboy* (April 1987): 136.

Lubove, Seth. "Porn Gallery." *Forbes*, February 28, 2005. www.forbes.com /forbes/2005/0228/042a.html.

Lukow, Gregory. "The Archaeology of Music Video: Soundies, Snader Telescriptions, and Scopitones." In *1986 National Video Festival Program*, ed. National Video Festival, 36–39. Los Angeles: American Film Institute, 1986.

———. "The Antecedents of MTV: Soundies, Scopitones and Snaders, and the History of an Ahistorical Form." In *Art of Music Video: Ten Years After*, ed. Long Beach Museum of Art, 6–9. Long Beach, CA: Long Beach Museum of Art, 1991.

Lust, Erika. *Good Porn: A Woman's Guide.* Berkeley, CA: Seal Press, 2010.

MacGillivray, Scott, and Ted Okuda. *The Soundies Book: A Revised and Expanded Guide.* New York: IUniverse, 2007.

Mackey, Thomas C. *Pornography on Trial: A Handbook with Cases, Laws, and Documents.* Santa Barbara, CA: ABC-CLIO, 2002.

MacKinnon, Catharine, and Andrea Dworkin, eds. *In Harm's Way: The Pornography Civil Rights Hearings.* Cambridge, MA: Harvard University Press, 1997.

Macy, Marianne. *Working Sex: An Odyssey into Our Cultural Underworld.* New York: Carroll & Graf, 1996.

Maltby, Richard. "The Production Code and the Hays Office." In *Grand Design: Hollywood as a Modern Business Enterprise*, ed. Tino Balio, 37–72. History of the American Cinema. Berkeley: University of California Press, 1993.

Mancini, Marc. "Video S.I.P." *Film Comment* 23, no. 1 (January 1987): 44–49.

Marchand, Henry L. *The French Pornographers, Including a History of French Erotic Literature.* 1933; New York: Book Awards, 1965.

Marlow, Eugene, and Eugene Secunda. *Shifting Time and Space: The Story of Videotape.* New York: Praeger, 1991.

Marwick, Alice E. "To Catch a Predator? The MySpace Moral Panic." *First Monday*, June 2, 2008. http://firstmonday.org/article/view/2152/1966.

Matza, Michael. "A Question of Privacy: Anyone Who Rents Videotapes Is at Risk of Having the List Made Public." *Philadelphia Daily News*, October 21, 1987. http://articles.philly.com/1987-10-21/news/26215608_1_judge-robert-h-bork-rental-records-privacy.

———. "The Black and White of Paul Fishbein." *Philadelphia Inquirer*, September 27, 1989, http://articles.philly.com/1989-09-27/news/26104499_1_adult-magazines-adult-tapes-obscene-video (accessed March 14, 2016).

McDonald, Paul. *Video and DVD Industries.* London: British Film Institute, 2008.

McDonough, Jimmy. *Big Bosoms and Square Jaws: The Biography of Russ Meyer, King of the Sex Film.* New York: Random House, 2005.

McDougal, Dennis. *Privileged Son: Otis Chandler and the Rise and Fall of the L.A. Times Dynasty.* Cambridge, MA: Perseus Publishing, 2001.

McNeil, Legs, Jennifer Osborne, and Peter Pavia. *The Other Hollywood: The Uncensored Oral History of the Porn Film Industry.* New York: Regan Books, 2005.

Meine, David. "The X-Rated Image." *Video Store* (August 1986): 12.

Miller, Russell. *Bunny: The Real Story of Playboy.* New York: Henry Holt, 1985.

Miller-Young, Mireille. *A Taste for Brown Sugar: Black Women in Pornography.* Durham, NC: Duke University Press, 2014.

"Modern Living: Sinema in Osaka." *Time,* March 22, 1971, 62.

Monaco, James. "Stealing the Show: The Piracy Problem." *American Film* 3, no. 9 (July 1, 1978): 57–67.

Moran, James. *There's No Place Like Home Video.* Minneapolis: University of Minnesota Press, 2002.

"Motels with X-Rated Films Thrive on Coast." *New York Times,* February 17, 1975, 22.

Mulvey, Edward P., and Jeffrey J. Haugaard. *Report of the Surgeon General's Workshop on Pornography and Public Health.* Washington, DC: U.S. Department of Health and Human Services, Office of the Surgeon General, August 4, 1986.

Nagle, Jill. "First Ladies of Feminist Porn: A Conversation with Candida Royalle and Debi Sundahl." In *Whores and Other Feminists,* ed. Jill Nagle, 156–66. New York: Routledge, 1997.

Nash, Jennifer C. *The Black Body in Ecstasy: Reading Race, Reading Pornography.* Durham, NC: Duke University Press, 2014.

Nelson, Jill C. *Golden Goddesses: 25 Legendary Women of Classic Erotic Cinema, 1968–1985.* Duncan, OK: BearManor Media, 2012.

Newman, Michael Z. *Video Revolutions: On the History of a Medium.* New York: Columbia University Press, 2014.

Newman, Michael Z., and Elena Levine. *Legitimating Television: Media Convergence and Cultural Status.* New York: Routledge, 2012.

Nobile, Philip, and Eric Nadler. *The United States of America vs. Sex: How the Meese Commission Lied about Pornography.* New York: Minotaur Press, 1986.

Nornes, Abé Markus, ed. *The Pink Book: The Japanese Eroduction and Its Contexts.* Ann Arbor, MI: Kinema Club, 2014.

Nowlin, Christopher. *Judging Obscenity: A Critical History of Expert Evidence.* Montreal: McGill–Queen's University Press, 2003.

O'Toole, Lawrence. *Pornocopia.* London: Serpent's Tail, 1998.

Paasonen, Susanna. *Carnal Resonance: Affect and Online Pornography.* Cambridge, MA: MIT Press, 2011.

Pally, Marcia. "Getting Down with Candida Royalle." *Forum* (April 1986): 45.

Penley, Constance. "A Feminist Teaching Pornography? That's Like Scopes Teaching Evolution!" In *The Feminist Porn Book,* eds. Tristan Taormino et al., 179–99. New York: Feminist Press at the City University of New York, 2012.

"Penny Antine: The Accidental Pornographer." *Alicubi,* November 2000. www .alicubi.com/articles/penny_01.html.

Pesta, Ben. "X-Rated Video: Will It Make Adult Theaters and Men's Magazines Obsolete?" *Hustler* (October 1984): 36–40, 42, 52, 54.

Pierce, David. "Forgotten Faces: Why Some of Our Cinema Heritage Is Part of the Public Domain." *Film History* 19, no. 2 (2007): 125–43.

"Piracy and Porno." *Videography* (April 1979): 77.

Pitzulo, Carrie. *Bachelors and Bunnies: The Sexual Politics of Playboy.* Chicago: University of Chicago Press, 2011.

Polskin, Howard. "Pornography Unleashed." *Panorama* (July 1980): 35–39.

"Pornography Goes Public." *Newsweek,* December 21, 1970, 26–32.

"The Porno Plague." *Time,* April 5, 1976, 58–63.

President's Commission on Obscenity and Pornography. *The Report of the Commission on Obscenity and Pornography.* New York: Random House, 1970.

Price, Michael. "A Coward's Guide to X-Rated Motels." *Oui* (February 1978): 121.

Prince, Stephen. *A New Pot of Gold: Hollywood under the Electronic Rainbow, 1980–1989.* New York: Charles Scribner's Sons, 2000.

"Project Postporn." *Playboy* (September 1990): 49–50.

Pulley, Brett. "The Porn King." *Forbes,* March 7, 2005. www.forbes.com/2005 /03/07/cz_bp_0307vivid.html.

Purdue, Lewis. "EroticaBiz: How Sex Shaped the Internet." In *Net.SeXXX,* ed. Dennis D. Waskul, 259–94. New York: Peter Lang, 2004.

Ranz, Sheldon. "Interview: Nina Hartley." *Shmate: A Magazine of Progressive Jewish Thought* 22 (Spring 1989): 15–29.

Rastee, P.D. "Video Porn: The Retail Lowdown from Video Shack's Arthur Morowitz." *Film Journal,* March 4, 1983, 41, 49.

Rausch, Andrew J., and Chris Watson. *Dirty Talk: Conversations with Pornstars.* Albany, GA: BearManor Media, 2012.

Raven, Arlene. "Looking beneath the Surface: Deep inside Porn Stars." *High Performance* 7, no. 28 (1984): 24–27, 90.

Rensin, David. "Tuning in to Channel Sex." *Playboy* (November 1981): 220–21.

Reveaux, Anthony. "New Technologies for the Demystification of Cinema." *Film Quarterly* 27, no. 1 (Autumn 1973): 42–51.

Revene, Larry. *Wham Bam $$ Ba Da Boom! Mob Wars, Porn Battles, and a View from the Trenches.* New York: Hudson Delta Books, 2012.

Rimmer, Bob. *The X-Rated Videotape Guide.* New York: Arlington House, 1984.

———. *Bob Rimmer's Continuously Up-Dated Adult Video Tape Guide.* Quincy, MA: Challenge Press, 1986.

Roberts, Edwin A. *The Smut Rakers.* Silver Spring, MD: National Observer, 1966.

Roosevelt, James. *My Parents: A Differing View.* Chicago: Playboy Press, 1976.

Rosen, Robert. *Beaver Street: A History of Modern Pornography*. London: Headpress, 2010.

Ross, Andrew. *No Respect: Intellectuals & Popular Culture*. New York: Routledge, 1989.

Ross, Gene. "Adult Video News: The First Five Years." *Adult Video News* (February 1988): 46.

Rotsler, William. *Contemporary Erotic Cinema*. New York: Penthouse/Ballantine, 1973.

Royalle, Candida. "Vertical Smiles and Cum-Soaked Aisles: Confessions of a Porn Queen." *High Times* (July 1982): 40–41.

———. "Porn in the USA." *Social Text* 37 (Winter 1993): 23–32.

———. *How to Tell a Naked Man What to Do: Sex Advice from a Woman Who Knows*. New York: Fireside, 2004.

———. "'What's a Nice Girl Like You. . . .'" In *The Feminist Porn Book*, eds. Tristan Taormino et al., 58–70. New York: Feminist Press at the City University of New York, 2012.

Rubin, Gayle. "Thinking Sex: Notes for a Radical Theory of the Politics of Sexuality." In *Pleasure and Danger: Exploring Female Sexuality*, ed. Carole S. Vance, 267–319. London: Pandora Press, 1984.

———. "Misguided, Dangerous, and Wrong: An Analysis of Anti-Pornography Politics." In *Bad Girls and Dirty Pictures: The Challenge to Reclaim Feminism*, eds. Alison Assiter and Avedon Carol, 18–40. Boulder, CO: Pluto Press, 1993.

Rubin, Samuel K. *Moving Pictures and Classic Images: Memories of Forty Years in the Vintage Film Hobby*. Jefferson, NC: McFarland, 2004.

Rush, George. "Home Video Wars." *American Film* 10, no. 6 (1 April 1, 1985): 61–63.

Rutter, Jared. "The Man Who Changed Adult." *Adult Video News* (September 2009): 76–80, 84, 86, 90, 92, 113.

Sabo, Anne G. *After Pornified: How Women Are Transforming Pornography & Why It Really Matters*. New York: John Hunt, 2012.

Sagal, Peter. *The Book of Vice: Very Naughty Things (and How to Do Them)*. New York: HarperCollins, 2007.

Salkin, Allen. "The XXX Men." *Details* (June 2001): 110–17.

Samberg, Joel A. "The Video Shack: Spotlight on Success." *Video Programs Retailer* (January 1981): 42–45.

Samois, ed. *Coming to Power: Writing and Graphics on Lesbian S/M*. San Francisco: Alyson Books, 1981.

Sandler, Kevin S. *The Naked Truth: Why Hollywood Doesn't Make X-Rated Movies*. Newark, NJ: Rutgers University Press, 2007.

Sandomir, Richard. "Wayne Huizenga's Growth Complex." *New York Times Magazine*, June 9, 1991, 25.

Sanson, Dwight. "Home Viewing: Pornography and Amateur Film Collections, a Case Study." *Moving Image* 5, no. 2 (Fall 2005): 136–40.

Sant, Toni. *Franklin Furnace and the Spirit of the Avant-Garde: A History of the Future*. New York: Intellect Ltd., 2011.

Satchell, Michael. "The Big Business of Selling Smut." *Parade,* August 19, 1979, 4–5.

Schaefer, Eric. "The Obscene Seen: Spectacle and Transgression in Postwar Burlesque Films." *Cinema Journal* 36, no. 2 (Winter 1997): 41–66.

———. *Bold! Daring! Shocking! True!: A History of Exploitation Films, 1919–1959.* Durham, NC: Duke University Press, 1999.

———. "Gauging a Revolution: 16mm Film and the Rise of the Pornographic Feature." *Cinema Journal* 41, no. 3 (Spring 2002): 3–26.

———. "Dirty Little Secrets: Scholars, Archivists, and Dirty Movies." *Moving Image* 5, no. 2 (Fall 2005): 79–105.

———. "Plain Brown Wrapper: Adult Films for the Home Market." In *Looking Past the Screen,* eds. Jon Lewis and Eric Smoodin, 201–26. Durham, NC: Duke University Press, 2007.

———. "The Problem with Sexploitation Movies." *Iluminace* 3 (2012): 148–52.

———. "Pornography Is Geography: Porn, Place, and the Historiography of Early Theatrical Hardcore." Presentation, "Society for Cinema and Media Studies Annual Conference," Seattle, WA, March 20, 2014.

———, ed. *Sex Scene: Media and the Sexual Revolution.* Durham, NC: Duke University Press, 2014.

Schaefer, Eric, and Eithne Johnson. "Quarantined! A Case Study of Boston's Combat Zone." In *Hop on Pop: The Politics and Pleasures of Popular Culture,* eds. Henry Jenkins, Tara McPherson, and Jane Shattuc, 430–53. Durham, NC: Duke University Press, 2002.

———. "Open Your Golden Gates: Sexually Oriented Film and Video." In *Radical Light: Alternative Film and Video in the San Francisco Bay Area, 1945–2000,* eds. Steven Anker, Kathy Geritz, and Steve Seid, 191–93. Berkeley: University of California Press, 2010.

Schipper, Henry. "Filthy Lucre: A Tour of America's Most Profitable Frontier." *Mother Jones* (April 1980): 31–33, 60–62.

Schlosser, Eric. *Reefer Madness and Other Tales from the American Underground.* New York: Penguin Books, 2003.

Schneider, Rebecca. *The Explicit Body in Performance.* New York: Routledge, 1997.

Schwartz, Adolph A., and Russ Meyer. *A Clean Breast: The Life and Loves of Russ Meyer.* 3 vols. Los Angeles: Hauck Publishing, 2000.

Schwartz, Tony. "The TV Pornography Boom." *New York Times,* September 13, 1981, 44, 120, 122, 127, 132, 136.

See, Carolyn. *Blue Money: Pornography and the Pornographers.* New York: David McKay, 1974.

Segrave, Kerry. *Piracy in the Motion Picture Industry.* New York: McFarland, 2003.

———. *Movies at Home: How Hollywood Came to Television.* New York: McFarland, 2009.

Shamberg, Michael, and Raindance Corporation. *Guerrilla Television.* New York: Henry Holt, 1971.

Shanley, Caitlin. "Clandestine Catalogs: A Bibliography of Porn Research Collections." In *Porn Archives*, eds. Tim Dean, Steven Ruszczycky, and David Squires, 441–55. Durham, NC: Duke University Press, 2014.

Sharp, Jasper. *Behind the Pink Curtain: The Complete History of Japanese Sex Cinema*. London: FAB Press, 2008.

Shaw, David. "The 'X-Rated' Motels: It's Usually SRO." *Los Angeles Times*, June 16, 1973, 1, 22–23.

Sherman, William. *Times Square*. New York: Bantam Books, 1980.

"Sherpix: The Unusual Company with an Unusual Future." *Independent Film Journal*, April 27, 1972, 20–21.

Simpson, Nicola. "Coming Attractions: A Comparative History of the Hollywood Studio System and the Porn Business." *Historical Journal of Film, Radio, and Television* 24, no. 4 (2004): 635–52.

Sklar, Robert. *Movie-Made America*. New York: Random House, 1975.

Slade, Joseph W. "Pornographic Theaters off Times Square." *Transaction* (November–December 1971): 37.

———. "Inventing a Sexual Discourse: A Rhetorical Analysis of Adult Video Box Covers." In *Sexual Rhetoric: Media Perspectives on Sexuality, Gender, and Identity*, eds. Meta G. Carstarphen and Susan C. Zavoina, 239–54. Westport, CT: Greenwood Press, 1999.

———. *Pornography in America: A Reference Handbook*. Santa Barbara, CA: ABC-CLIO, 2000.

Sloan, Will. "The Godfather of Gonzo Porn." November 21, 2013. http://hazlitt .net/longreads/godfather-gonzo-porn.

Snitow, Ann, Christine Stansell, and Sharon Thompson, eds. *Powers of Desire: The Politics of Sexuality*. New York: Monthly Review Press, 1983.

Sontag, Susan. "The Pornographic Imagination." *Partisan Review* 34 (Spring 1967): 181–212.

Spielmann, Yvonne. *Video: The Reflexive Medium*. Cambridge, MA: MIT Press, 2008.

Spigel, Lynn. "Installing the Television Set: Popular Discourses on Television and the Domestic Space, 1948–1955." In *Private Screenings: Television and the Female Consumer*, eds. Lynn Spigel and Denise Mann, 3–40. Minneapolis: University of Minnesota Press, 1992.

———. *Welcome to the Dreamhouse: Popular Media and Postwar Suburbs*. Durham, NC: Duke University Press, 2001.

Squire, Susan. "How Women Are Changing Porn Films." *Glamour* (November 1985): 282.

———. "Ordinary People." *Playboy* (November 1986): 113–14, 159–61.

Staiger, Janet. *Bad Women: Regulating Sexuality in Early American Cinema*. Minneapolis: University of Minnesota Press, 1995.

Standage, Tom. *The Victorian Internet: The Remarkable Story of the Telegraph and the Nineteenth Century's On-Line Pioneers*. New York: Walker and Co., 1998.

Stanley, John. "Film Maker Gives Erotica a Woman's Point of View." *San Francisco Chronicle*, February 21, 1988, 55.

Stecklow, Steve. "Adult Video News Rates Tapes That Are XXX'd Out By Other Reviews." *Chicago Tribune*, April 5, 1985.

Stein, Joel. "Porn Goes Mainstream." *Time*, June 24, 2001. http://content.time .com/time/magazine/article/0,9171,139893,00.html.

Steinem, Gloria. "Erotica and Pornography: A Clear and Present Difference." *Ms.* (November 1978), repr. in Laura Lederer, ed. *Take Back the Night: Women on Pornography* (New York: William Morrow, 1980), 35–39.

Stingley, Jim. "Middle Class Tunes In, Turns On." *Los Angeles Times*, February 4, 1975, 1, 6–7.

———. "Squares amid the Alien Porn." *Los Angeles Times*, February 5, 1975, 1.

Stoller, Robert J. *Porn: Myths for the Twentieth Century.* New Haven, CT: Yale University Press, 1991.

Stoller, Robert J., and I. S. Levine. *Coming Attractions: The Making of an X-Rated Video.* New Haven, CT: Yale University Press, 2003.

Strager, Stephen. "What Men Watch When They Watch Pornography." *Sexuality and Culture* 7, no. 1 (Winter 2003): 50–61.

Strub, Whitney. "Perversion for Profit: Citizens for Decent Literature and the Arousal of an Antiporn Public in the 1960s." *Journal of the History of Sexuality* 15, no. 2 (May 2006): 258–91.

———. *Perversion for Profit: The Politics of Pornography and the Rise of the New Right.* New York: Columbia University Press, 2011.

———. *Obscenity Rules: Roth v. United States and the Long Struggle over Sexual Expression.* Lawrence: University of Kansas Press, 2013.

Taormino, Tristan. *Down and Dirty Sex Secrets: The New and Naughty Guide to Being Great in Bed.* New York: William Morrow, 2003.

———. "Calling the Shots: Feminist Porn in Theory and Practice." In *The Feminist Porn Book*, eds. Tristan Taormino et al., 255–64. New York: Feminist Press at the City University of New York, 2012.

Taormino, Tristan, et al. *The Feminist Porn Book: The Politics of Producing Pleasure.* New York: Feminist Press at the City University of New York, 2012.

Teachout, Terry. "The Pornography Report That Never Was." *Commentary* 84, no. 2 (1986): 51–57.

Terenzio, Maurice, Scott MacGillivray, and Ted Okuda. *The Soundies Distributing Corporation of America: A History and Filmography of Their "Jukebox" Musical Films of the 1940s.* New York: McFarland, 1991.

Thompson, Dave. *Black and White and Blue: Adult Cinema from the Victorian Age to the VCR.* Toronto: ECW Press, 2007.

"Tube Job!" *Playboy* (December 1976): 268.

"Tuning into the Video-Tape Scene." *Playboy* (April 1979): 203.

Turan, Kenneth. "Sex Films in San Francisco Reach Plateau of Legitimacy." *Los Angeles Times*, October 30, 1970, 20.

Turan, Kenneth, and Stephen F. Zito. *Sinema.* New York: Praeger, 1974.

Usai, Paolo Cherchi. "Pornography." In *The Encyclopedia of Early Cinema*, ed. Richard Abel, 525. New York: Routledge, 2005.

Valentine, Desiree. "Does It Take a Woman to Make a Good Couples Film?" *Adam Film World and Adult Video Guide* (November 1986): 59.

Vance, Carole S. *Diary of a Conference on Sexuality.* New York: Faculty Press, 1983.

———. "Negotiating Sex and Gender in the Attorney General's Commission on Pornography." In *Uncertain Terms: Negotiating Gender in American Culture,* eds. Faye Ginsberg and Anna Lowenhaupt Tsing, 118–34. Boston: Beacon Press, 1990.

———, ed. *Pleasure and Danger: Exploring Female Sexuality.* London: Pandora Press, 1992.

Vaughn, Stephen. *Freedom and Entertainment: Rating the Movies in an Age of New Media.* London: Cambridge University Press, 2005.

Verrill, Addison. "TV Cassettes Bid for Sex Pix." *Variety,* January 27, 1971, 1, 54.

"Video Cartridges: A Promise of Future Shock." *Time,* August 10, 1970. http://content.time.com/time/magazine/article/0,9171,876748,00.html.

"Video Porn." *Velvet Talks!* 5 (1979): 25.

Video Shack advertisement. *Videography* (June 1979): 47.

"Video Tapes & Cable Add Up to Increased Profits for Mature Films." *Film Journal,* May 4, 1981, 20.

"Vivid Imagination." *Economist,* November 19, 1998. www.economist.com/node/176678.

Walter, Barbara. "The Cult of True Womanhood: 1820–1860." *American Quarterly* 18, no. 2 (Summer 1966): 151–74.

Warner, Michael. *The Trouble with Normal: Sex, Politics, and the Ethics of Queer Life.* Cambridge, MA: Harvard University Press, 1999.

Wasko, Janet. *How Hollywood Works.* Los Angeles: Sage, 2003.

Wasser, Frederick. *Veni, Vidi, Video: The Hollywood Empire and the VCR.* Austin: University of Texas Press, 2001.

Waugh, Thomas. *Hard to Imagine: Gay Male Eroticism in Photography and Film from Their Beginnings to Stonewall.* New York: Columbia University Press, 1996.

Waugh, Thomas. "Homosociality in the Classical American Stag Film," in *Porn Studies,* ed. Linda Williams, 127–41. Durham, NC: Duke University Press, 2004.

Wells, Jeffrey. "Sex in the Home (Where It Belongs)." *Film Journal* 85, no. 15 (June 28, 1982): 22.

West, Ashley. "Martin Hodas, King of the Peeps." *Rialto Report,* June 29, 2014. www.therialtoreport.com/2014/06/29/marty-hodas-king-of-the-peeps-podcast-38/.

Weston, John H. "It's the Law? Obscenity Laws and the Effects on Video Retailers." *Adult Video News Confidential* (September 1987): 12.

"Who's Who of Victorian Cinema: Léar (Albert Kirchner)." British Film Institute, n.d. www.victorian-cinema.net/lear.php.

Wiener, Leonard. "Video Tape Promises TV of Your Choice—Someday." *Chicago Tribune,* April 15, 1974, C9.

Wildmon, Donald E. *The Home Invaders*. Wheaton, IL: Victor Books, 1985.

———. *The Case against Pornography*. Wheaton, IL: Victor Books, 1986.

Williams, Linda. "Film Body: An Implantation of Perversions." In *Narrative, Apparatus, Ideology*, ed. Philip Rosen, 507–34. New York: Columbia University Press, 1986.

———. *Hard Core: Power, Pleasure, and the "Frenzy of the Visible."* Berkeley: University of California Press, 1989.

———. "A Provoking Agent: The Pornography and Performance Art of Annie Sprinkle." *Social Text* 37 (Winter 1993): 117–33.

———, ed. *Porn Studies*. Durham, NC: Duke University Press, 2004.

———. "Pornography, Porno, Porn: Thoughts on a Weedy Field." *Porn Studies* 1, nos. 1–2 (March 2014): 24–40.

Willis, Ellen. "Feminism, Morality, and Pornography." In *Powers of Desire: The Politics of Sexuality*, eds. Ann Snitow, Christine Stansell, and Sharon Thompson, 460–67. New York: Monthly Review, 1983.

Wilson, Elizabeth. "The Context of 'Between Pleasure and Danger': The Barnard Conference on Sexuality." *Feminist Review* 13 (Spring 1983): 35–41.

Witkowski, J. Steven. "Mapping Hardcore Space." *Media Fields* 1 (2010). www.mediafieldsjournal.org/mapping-hardcore-space/.

Wyatt, Justin. "The Stigma of X: Adult Cinema and the Institution of the MPAA Ratings System." In *Controlling Hollywood: Censorship and Regulation in the Studio Era*, ed. Matthew Bernstein, 238–63. Piscataway, NJ: Rutgers University Press, 1999.

Zaretsky, Natasha. *No Direction Home: The American Family and the Fear of National Decline, 1968–1980*. Chapel Hill: University of North Carolina Press, 2007.

Ziplow, Steven. *The Film Maker's Guide to Pornography*. New York: Drake, 1977.

Index

Page numbers in italics denote illustrations.

adult film industry *(continued)*
199–200; "porno plague" discourse
of 1970s, 21, *22;* professionalization
of, and cultural panic, 32, 162;
publicness of, 21, 23, 159; video as
saving, 21–23. *See also* adult content;
adult video; piracy
Adult Loop Database (adult-loopdb.
nl), 217n98
adult magazines. *See* magazines, adult
video industry; magazines, adult
adult motels: adult content, supply
of, 63–66, 70; advertising and
marketing of, 57, *58,* 59–62, 66;
development of, 56–57, 59,
232nn87,89; "love" hotels (Japan),
56, 57, 232n87; numbers of, 59; and
obscenity prosecutions, 59, 63; and
privacy, 50–51, 59, 60, 62, 233n109;
prostitution and "by-the-hour"
trysts, 51, 59, 60, 61, 233n102; as
public/private space, 50–51, 61, 63;
as re-creating patriarchal control,
61–62; regulatory strategies and,
51, 59, 61, 62–63, 232n97, 233n102,
233n109; and respectability,
discourse chosen to favor, 59–62;
technology and, 56–57, 61, 233n104;
two-way mirror and extortion
discourses and, 235n127; women as
customers of, 60–62
adult-only video stores: Arizona
prosecutions of, 158–159;
community protests of, 163–164,
164; and pushing of pornography
back into the shadows, 193, 196;
Virginia prosecutions of (Pryba
case), 183–186, 273nn146,154. *See
also* mainstream video rental stores
carrying adult video
adult theaters. *See* theatrical
exhibition of adult films
"adult T.V.," 7
adult video: accessibility of,
antipornography protests and, 24,
159–160, 161–163, *164;* and
adoption of home video in general,

2; adult film industry saved by,
21–23; and family and nation, fear
of transformation of, 158–159;
history, absence of study of, 8,
27–30, 217–218nn97–99,101–103;
number of companies specializing
in, 159; number of titles available,
97–98, 159; as "Silver Age," 210–
211n18; underground economy and,
41–42. *See also* adult content; adult-
only video stores; adult video rental
industry; antipornography as
movement; privacy; quality;
respectability; video sales
Adult Video Corporation (AVC), 77,
119–120
Adult Video Index, 97–98
Adult Video News (AVN), 83; and
Adult Video Swapper subscribers,
243n15; and advertising, end of
sampling form of, 86, 93, 96, 107,
112, 114; advertising in, 106–108,
107, 114, 115; advertising in,
removal of narrative from, 114;
AVN Awards, 116; AVN Expo, 240–
241n188; AVN Media Network, 86;
blurring of lines with adult video
industry, 115; and capitalist
legitimization of pornography,
96–97, 115–116; circulation of, 86,
108; couples genre tracked by, 150;
establishment and development of
company, 86, 93, 96–100, 111–113,
115; as industry trade journal,
36–37, 105–108; as legal advisor
(unofficial), 109, 111, 112; and
Ginger Lynn, 252n50; mediation
role of, 97, 99–103, 106, 107, 113;
narrative as locus of quality in quest
for female audience, 100–101, 103–
105; nudity and explicit language
excluded from, 99–100; poll on
gender of rental customers, 25, 117–
118, 215n78; quality as focus of, 37,
100, 101–103, 114–115; and social-
difference legitimization, 87–88; as
tastemaker, 87–88, 105; video

obscenity *(continued)*
   Meese advisors as National Obscenity
   Enforcement Unit (NOEU), 197–
   198, 278–279nn211,217; Meese
   Commission threats to retailers
   and removal of adult magazines
   from shelves, 180–183, 271nn128–
   129; message sent by, danger of
   pornography, 167; national task
   force (Meese Commission
   recommendation), 175, 183; in Ohio,
   164–166, 263n30, 263n38; and
   Panoram, 46; phony front businesses
   used by authorities, 166, 186, 264n40,
   274n160; pornographic empires
   and, 49; post–Meese Commission
   environment and, 183–187, 272n144,
   273nn146–147,154, 274n160,
   275nn168; for printing the 1970
   Report, 267n87; publicity and, 46;
   RICO Act and, 174, 183–186, 197,
   268n93, 273nn146,154, 274n160;
   Candida Royalle and avoidance of,
   149–150; Reuben Sturman and, 119,
   228n47, 263n30; Vivid Video and,
   129. *See also* community standards;
   prosecutions for tax and other
   problems
Ohio, regulation of pornography in,
   164–166, 263n30, 263n38
Onaran, Erol, 191
On Command (hotel pay-per-view), 55
On the Lookout (sequence in *Boogie
   Nights*), 201, 202, 279–280nn2–3
On the Prowl (dir. Jamie Gillis), 202–
   205, *203–204*, 207, 208, 280nn3,8
The Opening of Misty Beethoven
   (1976, dir. Radley Metzger), 204,
   280n7
Operation Yorkville, 264n49
Optronics Libraries, 54, 231n77
oral and anal sex, assumed by industry
   to be preferred by male audience,
   135, 254n68
Orenstein, Steven, 278n211
organized crime: Martin Hodas and,
   227n43; insinuations of, and

obscenity prosecutions, 262n22;
   pornographic empires and, 49;
   Reuben Sturman and, 228n47; and
   video sales industry, 240n185
Organized Crime Control Act. *See*
   RICO
Osco, Bill, 53–54
O'Toole, Lawrence, 5, 39

Pachard, Henri (pseud. of Ron
   Sullivan), 103, 117, 127, 131
Palmer, Gail, 118, 150, 247n2
Panasonic: half-inch player, 51; video
   players, 222–223n3
panic. *See* moral panic
Panoram: in adult bookstores, 47–49,
   226–227nn35,38,43; and display of
   female nudity vs. sexual behavior,
   46, 47; financial figures, 48;
   homoeroticism and, 44, 224n16;
   independently produced content for,
   45, 46, 226nn28–29; other failed
   technologies, 223n11; police raids
   on, 46; and privacy, 43–44, 45, 46,
   47, 49; solo use conversion units for,
   43–45, *44*, 224–225n16; Soundies
   corporation and, 42–43, 45–46,
   224n12. *See also* adult motels;
   home; peep shows
Paramount Home Video, 186; *Star
   Trek II* sell-through price lowered
   by, 106–107
Paramount Pictures, 230n61
Park-Miller theater (Times Square), 6
Parrish, H. Harrison, 191
Partner magazine, 108–109
The Partner Television Show, 108–109
Party Time (San Jose), 237n153
patriarchal control: adult-motel
   discourse reinforcing, 61–62. *See
   also* containment
Pederson, Peer, 194
peep shows: booths, 49–50, 175–176,
   228–229nn46–47,50; financial
   figures, 48, 228n46; glory holes,
   228–229n50; homoeroticism and,
   175, 176, 228–229n50; instruction

video run in, 49; masturbation and, 49; Meese Commission recommendations to regulate, 175–176; regulation via behavioral supervision, 50, 228–229n50; women as spectators at, 60. *See also* Panoram

Penley, Constance, 222n140

Penn, John Garret, 182

Penthouse magazine: circulation lost to adult video, 182; and Meese Commission, 181, 182; microfilm archive of, 29; video versions of, 109

Peoples Drug, 181

Peraino, Anthony, 278n211

Peraino, Joseph, 278n211

Peraino, Louis, 77, 278n211

The Perfect Gift (1978, dir. David Jennings), 79

performers: frozen-in-time aspect for retired performers, 131, 140; of Golden Age moving into video age, 9, 11; lack of power of, 130–131, 144, 157; nonprofessional, amateur adult video and, 25; as preferred term, 209n2; pseudonym use by, 252n54; San Francisco as site of entry into adult film, 131–132

Perry, Ann, 136, 150

PHE, Inc. (distributor), 278–279n217

phone sex, 33, 141, 220–221n121

Phonovision video disc system, 7

photography technology, 33–34

Pickett, Lowell, 132

pink films, 56

Pink, Sidney, 64

piracy: and adult motel content, 63, 64–65, 70; and closed-circuit channels in bars, 70; and early adult video rentals, 70; legitimizing of industry and prevention of, 75; proprietary prevention systems, 74; public-domain film distribution and, 67, 70; transfers of celluloid to video, 64–65. *See also* copyright issues

Pirou Eugène, 34

Pitzulo, Carrie, 123

Placido, Nick, 164

Playboy magazine: *Adam* magazine as competition with, 89; on adult video sales, 74; advertising in, 90, 108; and Cinema Concepts, 72; circulation lost to adult video, 182; community protests of, 1–2; and "girl next door" trope, 123; and legitimization of pornography, 90; on Ginger Lynn, 118; and Meese Commission, 181, 182–183, 279n221; microfilm archive of, 29; and powerlessness of the "girls next door," 157; representation of sex and, 84; Spice channel, 128; video versions of, 109; and VSDA convention (1986), 189

Playgirl magazine, 181

Playmate (producer-distributor), 49

PlayTape/Avco Cartrivision, 53, 54–55

pleasure, bodily: anxiety about, advances in privacy and regulatory reaction to, 45, 50; *AVN*'s legacy and continued suspicion and anxiety about, 116; consensual, conservatives and antipornography feminists and denial of, 177, 178; disregarded by court in community standards decision, 160; erotica as removed from, 18–19, 82, 212n51; gonzo style and, 206, 207, 281n15; the home as legally protected site for, 50, 63, 68, 81, 176, 233n109; for its own sake, 20; Meese Commission and discourses of shame about, 175–177, 180, 269n103; obscenity law as devaluing, 160, 212–213n53; perpetual machine of regulation and, 200; "something more" requirement and essentialization of women, 19, 103–105, 150–151; zoning strategies as devaluing, 188. *See also* containment of pleasure, especially women's pleasure; "something more"

Pleasure Productions, 92

Plymouth Distributors, 234–235n123

Sony Corp. of America v. Universal
City Studios, Inc. (1984), 229n58
Sony U-Matic: adult films and
manufacturer of, 53; in adult motels,
56–57, 61; in bars, 67, 68; as
Betamax precursor, 61; and early
video rental club, 222–223n3; in
hotel pay-per-view systems, 51; lack
of success in consumer market, 8;
release of (1971), 8; and shot-on-
video productions, 78; and television
news industry, 8; video sales in
format of, 72, 73
Soundies Distribution Corporation,
42–43, 224n12
Sound Recording Amendment (1971),
65
Sounds Easy (video rental chain), 192,
277–278n209
South America, early adult film
industry in, 34
South, Jim, 121–122, 248–249n18
Southland Corporation (7-Eleven
stores), 181, 196, 271nn128–9
Sovereign News Corp., 119
Span, Anna, 153
spectatorship of pornography: female,
60, 131, 224–225n16; gonzo style
and, 205; male, 60, 224–225n16
Spectradyne, 55
Spice Hot (hardcore satellite channel),
128
Spigel, Lynn, 218n102
Spinelli, Anthony (pseud. of Sam
Weston), 77, 103, 132–133, 135
The Spirit of Justice (statue, Justice
Department), 172, 173, 267–268n88
Sprinkle, Annie, 142, 143, 149, 256–
257n98
Squire, Susan, 279n221
stag films, 51, 63, 64, 70
Stagliano, John, 205, 281n12
Staiger, Janet, 34
Standage, Tom, 33
Standard Pictures Corporation, 46
Stanley v. Georgia (1969), 23, 50, 63
Starlet Video, 108

Stars of Sex (producer-distributor), 49
Star Trek II (1982, dir. Nicholas
Meyer), sell-through price lowered,
106–107
Steinberg, Ellen. See Sprinkle, Annie
Steinem, Gloria, 19, 213n56
Steinman, Jeff, 82
Steinman, Joe and Jeff, 77
Stevens, Kirdy, 46, 226n28
Stimmler, Irving, 54, 231n77
Stoller, Robert J., 1
Strager, Stephen, 224–225n16
Strong Kids, Safe Kids, 186–187
Strong, Zachary. See Abrams, Jerry
Strub, Whitney, 168, 261n3
Sturman, Reuben, 49, 77, 119, 189,
228n47, 263n30, 278n211
Sub Rosa Rising (1971, dir. Jerry
Abrams), 253n63
suburban areas, accessibility of home
video and, 24
Sullivan, Ron (pseud. Henri Pachard),
103, 117, 127, 131
Sulzberger, Arthur, 70
Summers, David (pseud. of Daniel
Symms), 80
Summers, Jamie, 113, 128
Sumner, Robert, 74, 77, 255n77
Sunrise Films, 119
Super-Ware Party (1979, dir. Bill
Margold), 80
Sutter Cinema (San Francisco), 20
Svetlana, 150
Swedish Erotica (distributor), 77
Sweetheart's Home Video Center
(New York), 75, 76
Swindell, William, 162
Symms, Daniel (pseud. David
Summers), 80

Taormino, Tristan, 153, 260n136
Taylor, Bruce, 165
Technicolor Instant Movie Projector,
66–67, 68–69
technology, 36; Ampex 7500 one-inch
system, 51; Ampex Quadruplex, 7;
Ampex videotape playback prototype

trace historiography, 30, 218n102

Trans America Films, 231n77

transgression: as objective of pornography, 16–18, 19, 213n58; prostitution and, 17; women's struggle against containment viewed as, 214n66

Trans-World Productions, 52–53, 56

Transworld Video Sales, 274n160

Trego, Lisa (pseud. Lisa DeLeeuw), 49, 84, 94, 95, 123

Trouble, Courtney, 153

TVX (distributor), 75, 88, 234n122, 264n40

2 Live Crew, 198

The Ugly Goerge Hour of Truth, Sex, and Violence (George Urban footage), 281n12

Ulcigan, George, 45

underground economy: and adult-motel content, 63–64; capitalist disregard of, 41–42; distribution as mired in, 120; and invention of adult video rentals, 41–42; and Panoram, 45; and piracy, 234–235nn122–123; and private labs for duplication, 67–68; public-domain industry as, 67; and publicity of police raids, 46. *See also* piracy

underground video movement, 219n108

Unique Video Specialties (phony distribution front), 166

United States v. 12 200-ft. Reels of Super 8mm. Film (1973), 23, 50

Urban, George, 281n12

Urban Heat (1984, Femme), 146, 150

Urban Industries (Louisville KY), 48

Usai, Paolo Cherchi, 33

U.S. Post Office: as censor, 33; mailed advertisements as obscenity, 21, 23, 197–198, 278–279nn211,217

U.S. Supreme Court: *Alexander v. United States* (1992), 274n160; *American Booksellers Association v. Hudnut* (1986), 179; *City of Renton, Inc. et al. v. Playtime Theatres, et al.*

(1986), 188; and Dial-a-Porn laws, 220–221n121; *Ginzberg v. United States* (1966), 21, 22; *Mayor of Detroit Young, et al. v. American Mini Theatres, Inc., et al.* (1976), 188; *Memoirs v. Massachusetts* (1966), 259n133; *Miller v. California* (1973), 62–63, 65, 70, 160, 165, 171, 212–213n53, 233n109, 272n141; *Miranda* ruling (1966), 264–265n52; and Pryba case (1990), 185; *Sable Communications of California v. Federal Communications Commission* (1989), 220–221n121; *Sony Corp. of America v. Universal City Studios, Inc.* (1984), 229n58; *Stanley v. Georgia* (1969), 23, 50, 63; *United States v. 12 200-ft. Reels of Super 8mm. Film* (1973), 23, 50

Vadala, Candice. *See* Royalle, Candida

Valenti, Jack, 52

Valentine, Desiree, 151–152

Valentine Productions, 72, 238n160

Vance, Carole S., 35, 175–176, 180, 183, 269n103

Vanity Films, 46

Variety, Top 50 box office list of, 53–54

VCA Pictures (Video Company of America), 77, 78, 108, 145, 148–149, 218n104, 254n68, 263n38

VCRs: and peep-show feeds, 49; sales of, 97, 159; and *Sony Corp. of America v. Universal City Studios, Inc.* (1984), 229n58; and spectator as editors of their own programming, 25–26, 215n81

VCX, 77–78, 98, 109, 234–235nn122–123, 243n12

Velvet's Erotic Film Guide magazine, 88, 93–95

Velvet Talks!, 108

Vera, Veronica, 142, 149

Verrill, Addison, 9, 54

VHL (Video Home Library), 274n40, 278n211

VHS: George Atkinson's home video rental service offering, 71;

Lightning Source UK Ltd.
Milton Keynes UK
UKHW010142110223
416836UK00006B/221